What's in a
NAME?

Reflections of an Irrepressible Name Collector

Other Books on Language
by Paul Dickson

Toasts

Words

Family Words

The Dickson Baseball Dictionary

What Do You Call a Person From...?

Slang!

Dickson's Joke Treasury

The Congress Dictionary (with Paul Clancy)

War Slang

What's in a NAME?

Reflections of an Irrepressible Name Collector

ADELINE DINGLEDINE

NELIOUS KEE

OTIS PEBBLES MOTLEY

OPAL LIVELY ZICKAFOOSE

MEBA ULCH

Paul Dickson

Merriam-Webster, Incorporated
Springfield, Massachusetts

A GENUINE MERRIAM-WEBSTER

The name *Webster* alone is no guarantee of excellence. It is used by a number of publishers and may serve mainly to mislead an unwary buyer.

Merriam-Webster™ is the name you should look for when you consider the purchase of dictionaries or other fine reference books. It carries the reputation of a company that has been publishing since 1831 and is your assurance of quality and authority.

To the onomastiphiles who for more than a decade have helped with the collections presented herewith, including members of my own family who have, among other things, squinted long and hard to help spot quirky boat names. A full list of those who have "named names" appears at the back of the book—a supporting cast of hundreds.

CONTENTS

With knowledge of the name comes a distincter recognition and knowledge of the thing.

—HENRY DAVID THOREAU

Introduction

As a person who would rather spend a spare hour poring over a Seattle phone book or a road map of Oklahoma than the latest best-selling novel, I confess to a near fetishistic fascination with what persons, places, and things are called. This odd predilection has turned me into a collector of names who has attracted other collectors.

Ten years ago an earlier version of this book, entitled *Names*, was published and instead of getting it all out of my system, it has intensified the fascination.

In addition, the earlier book attracted the interest of hundreds of name collectors and devotees who have not only added to my original collections but flooded me with collections, large and small, of their own.

An Ohio man shared his collection of golf courses and clubs including such wonderful Scottish venues as Leighton Buzzard, Liphook, Muckhart, St. Bees, Looe Bin Down, Magpie Hall Lane, Ffesiniog, and Whipsnade. His American prizes include Lilac Brothers, Wiffletree Hill, West's Mogadore, and Elks 797. He, like I, would like to play these courses not only because we love golf but also because we love names.

A gent from Iowa, Dan Crawford, wrote with many bits of name lore as well as a description of his own collection: "I collect names of superheroes in the comic books, myself. World War II was the best era, the years that produced Red Rover, the Crimson Crimebuster, and Flexo, the Rubber Robot. Nowadays one doesn't get names like Starr Flagg, Undercover Girl, or Nadir, Master of Magic. Writers prefer single-word concepts like Halo, Raven, Jade, Firefly, and Nightcrawler. Names like Hip Knox, Super Hypnotist or Dr. Voltz, the Human Generator would go nowhere. The Silver Surfer and the Martian Manhunter were probably the last of the era that produced Miss Arrowette, the Green Turtle, the Purple Tigress, the Blazing Scarab, and the Red Bee.

"There is also worthwhile hunting among theme names. Besides the Phantom, comic books featured Bob Phantom, the Blonde Phantom, the Fantom of the Fair, the Phantom Sphinx, and X–The Phantom Fed. There was the Green Mask, the Blue Mask, the Purple Mask, the Gray Mask, the Red Mask, the Black Mask, the Fiery Mask, Ms. Masque, and, of course, the Mask, not to be confused with the current merchandise line of MASK heroes. I have found 58 Captains so far, from Captain Action to Captain Wonder, including Captain Nice, Captain Milksop, Captain Pureheart, and Captain Tootsie. But most of the good names today are in parodies, where one can still find superheroes with names like Normalman, Cutey Bunny, or Bob Violence."

Others have written to confess their addiction to names. "My dad tied trout flies," writes Sally Pecor of Washington, D.C., "and I'd ask him what they were just to hear the name. I traveled back and forth to college on 'The Adirondack' (a train, of course). I had a childhood friend named Donna Salmon, whose mother's maiden name was Pike."

A few wrote to tell of bad name experiences. One woman [name withheld for obvious reasons] wrote to tell what it is like to live with a last name that is a slang synonym for *death*. Long-time correspondent Joseph E. Badger wrote recently with a special request: "If you do happen to mention my name in print again, please, say I live in Bloomington, Indiana, not Santa Claus, Indiana. I moved from there for more than one reason, and one of those reasons was to avoid the ribbing and having to explain that yes, Virginia, there *is* a Santa Claus, Indiana. Though I'm retired from the Indiana State

Police, I work occasionally as a consultant to attorneys and insurance companies regarding traffic accident reconstruction. This means I must testify now and then and it seems like every time a lawyer asked, 'Mr. Badger, where do you live?' and I answered by saying 'Santa Claus, Indiana,' many on the jury giggled."

Others have written to share an assortment of New Age, psychic, and numerological theories of naming including one from a practitioner who drew a picture of me in the womb based solely on my name. (I was, it seems, a cone. And who's to argue? I do love ice cream so much that I once wrote a book on the topic.)

This larger, revised edition reflects the distillation of the many letters and newspaper clippings which have landed on my desk in the last ten years in addition to new discoveries of my own.

Names! I have been known to drive miles out of my way to go through an oddly named place; dreamed about stopping in Truth or Consequences, New Mexico; taken particular pleasure in driving over a bridge in Harpswell, Maine, because it goes over a channel called Will's Gut; and always taken special pleasure in being in Chicago because I know it's the only place in the world with that name. Pee Dee, North Carolina, beckons because it is my initials.

Names! I have bought things not because of what *Consumer Reports* says about them but because of how they are named, and when I was a kid I would choose things like a Shakespeare fishing reel, a Hawkeye camera, and a Rollfast bike because each was, to me at least, well-named. As an adult I went out to buy a new bike and fell in love with a model named the Mount St. Helen's in part because of the appealing incongruity of the name.

Names! I am fascinated with the variety of names that can be given to the same thing. Cape shark, a true shark, but far from the great white size and ferocity of *Jaws* fame, is sold under a raft of names, such as *spiny dogfish, spurdog, picked dogfish, greyfish, steakfish, rock salmon,* and *flake.* Black tautog finds itself marketed under such names as *black bass* and *Boston bass,* while Pacific rockfish, for sales appeal, is distributed as *Pacific Red Snapper* and *Pacific Snapper.*

Not long ago I ate a Goonburger for the simple reason that it was a Goonburger and that I could add it to my collection of "Named Burgers, Eaten" along with such specimens as a Northburger, Southburger, Searsburger, Barnburger, Murphyburger (once served at G. C. Murphy Company lunchcounters), and a Wimpyburger. I am starting to draw lines in this particular pursuit because I cannot possibly keep up with the national mania for naming and re-naming burgers. As the late Erma Bombeck once asked, "Can you remember when you last saw a menu with the plain word hamburger on it?"

In the name of names, I react differently. If I find myself lucky enough to be in Coronado Beach or Boothbay Harbor, my eyes are not drawn to the yachts but the names on them. Sighting a vessel named *Sea Duction* is as much a thrill as another collector might get from finding a rare stamp. As part of this odyssey, I have attended a robotics convention just to see how robots are named, spent hours in the morgue of the *Detroit Free Press* to find leads on car names, and have—in the name of onomastics—watched many undulating fannies to spot designer-jean names. Fascination with course titles has led me to compulsive scanning of open university catalogs for gems like

"Lover Shopping at Bloomingdale's," "Bunnetics," and "You, Yourself Unlimited."

I have tracked down private citizens who collect colorful names and begged from them some of their favorite examples. I spent more than a few hours tracking down Margaret Whitesides, formerly of the *Chicago Daily News*, to get her pet names from years of collecting at that newspaper's copy desk. The hunt was clearly worth it because on July 14, 1984 I finally heard from Ms. Whitesides, who told me that her all-time favorites were Magdalena Babblejack and Eloise Tittlekitty.

Over time I have deputized friends and associates to help me satisfy my lust for names. When, for instance, in 1984 I decided that I needed to collect Valentine's Day classified ads from newspapers to extract "love" names, I set up an international task force of people who, at the appointed hour, grabbed that section from the paper and passed it along. The Valentine sections keep rolling in, and I now have them up through February 14, 1996.

And the proliferation of vanity license plates has amounted to a major cultural advance on the order of the advent of retail establishments named for their pun value. These punstores have, by the way, driven me to delighted distraction as I now maintain long lists of them including what may be an ever-growing museum-quality collection of beauty parlor names which are puns or plays on words. More of these later, but a few here to whet your appetite: Hair at Last, O'Hair (Chicago), The Hair Raid, Hank of Hair, The House of Correction, Best Little Hair House, Sweeney Todd's, and Cutting Corners.

All of this has led me to an increasingly strong set of name opinions. I have, in fact, become so opinionated that I am convinced that the 1930s was the best decade in this century for first names, that no object has ever been as lyrically or diversely named as the apple in all of its many varieties, and that there are more odd names on the map of North Carolina than any other American state (although Arkansas and Kentucky come in as close seconds). This opinion was an abstract one until a trip to the state when in a matter of minutes I was able to savor a spin through Barco, Coinjock, and Moyock.

I am also taken with the lists of last names that stress American diversity…the kind that showed up in World War II movies and speeches of the era. My favorite? FDR's last campaign speech on November 4, 1944, in Boston's Fenway Park. His words summed up a belief that seemed to democratize and unite America for a period in a way the nation has not been since: "Today, in this war, our fine boys are fighting magnificently all over the world and among those boys are the Murphys and the Kellys, the Smiths and the Joneses, the Cohens, the Carusos, the Kowalskis, the Schultzes, the Olsens, the Swobodas, and—right in with all the rest of them—the Cabots and the Lowells."

It has also occurred to me that some things are rendered much more fascinating because of the names themselves. Value is added. For this reason I think that the basic allure of American quilts is design which is significantly enhanced when the design is given a name like Aunt Eliza's Star, World Without End, Churn Dasher, Shoo Fly, and Bear Paw. Part of our fascination with magicians may be the bold single names that they go by— Houdini, Kellar, and the like—and the fact that all of their tricks are titled—the Chinese Compass, the Jacoby Tie, and the Chain Gang Escape to name a few.

I also think that trout flies and roller coasters are well-named, passenger trains used to be, and candy bars have always been. Conversely, fishing lures, merry-go-rounds, airline routes, and cookies are poorly named. Compare, for instance, great train names like the Twentieth Century Limited, the Corn King, the Egyptian Zipper, the Yankee Clipper, the Mercury, and the Superchief to Flight 465.

It is also my belief that names are not quite what they used to be and a central premise of this book is that they require more than passing attention.

If there is a clear and present danger it is the dark force of digitalization. It is a powerful force which has already killed off telephone exchange names. John O'Hara's *BUtterfield 8* is now 288 and fine old Manhattan exchange names like MUrray Hill, CHelsea, HAmilton, AUdubon, CAthedral, BOwling green, COurtland, GReely, and TRafalgar live only in the pages of old detective novels.

London lost its hundreds of three-letter exchanges in 1966, and in one moment there was no more calling such evocative places as MINcing Lane, SWIss Cottage, UPPer Clapton, BELgravia, FOOts Cray, DREadnought, HIGate Wood, VIGilant, FLOral, BLUbell, DICkens, RAVensbourne, or PEKham Rye. A few months before this book went to press P. D. Sterling of Dallas sent me a total collection of all London exchanges in use between 1927 and 1966. On several occasions, I have read these names aloud for the sheer pleasure of hearing them.

This same force has, to cite one more of many available examples, turned the modern camera shop into a confusing maze of numbers and letters which sit on shelves where proud Hawkeyes, Premos, and Ponies once sat.

Ultimately, one fears that the codes will become more important than the names themselves. It bothers me that Tombstone, Arizona, is now better known as 85638 to many postal workers while Dogpatch, Arkansas, is 72648 and Eighty Eight, Kentucky, is 42130. The zip for Zap (North Dakota) is 58580. Great Britain and Canada have mixed numbers and letters producing such respective monstrosities as W1P 6JD and M5W 1E6 (neighborhoods in London and Toronto, respectively). These are better than all-number U.S. zip codes because one has a better chance of remembering them. The Canadian Post Office even urged householders to make up a sentence to recall their codes—R6B 4B0 could be "Remember Sixpence Buys Four Big Oranges."

The number-namers not only rob us of real names, but like to change numbers once we get used to them. For years I lived in the heart of zip code 20766, but then on one fateful day in June of 1982, the Postal Service announced that I was now in 20896 and that 20766 was being shipped off to another county. By 1996 I had finally used up all of the 20766 stationery in the house, but still get an occasional letter with the old zip.

In some fields, names have become so digitized that a real name has become a rarity. When Apple brought out its new Macintosh at the beginning of 1984, part of the attention paid to it had to do with the fact that it was not given a model number (usually a combination of initials and numbers) but, as *Popular Science* termed it, "a funny name." The Macintosh became the Mac to many which begat the Power Mac. Apple now has a Performa line to match up with IBM's Aptiva and Micron has a Millennia line, all echoing the automobile industry's fascination for names ending in -*a* that have no meaning (Altima, Accura, Supra, Maxima, Miata, etc.). As if this weren't enough, a second threat has developed in the form of dreaded name compression.

Lest there be any question, the author loves long, textured names, a prejudice dating back many years. When I was a kid, my parents used to take us to a family resort in Sherman, Connecticut. There was a nearby tributary of the Housatonic River called the Naromiyocknowhusunkatankshunk Brook. I never really got over the fact that (a) I could say it (*narrow-my-ock-now-who-sanka-tank-shunk*) and (b) I took inordinate pleasure in saying it.

Today long names seem to be a burden to society. This is what happens when it is decided that a name which extends beyond a certain number of letters cannot be digested by a machine or that it sounds old-fashioned to have a name that actually means something. Not long ago the *New Yorker* reported that one state's motor vehicle director had warned that anyone with a first name with more than nine letters and a last name with more than thirteen letters would find the offending letters chopped off by the state's computer. Corporations in particular have become possessed of an odd affliction that has compelled them to create names which sound more like a symptom of intestinal distress than something that could be written on a letterhead. The Government Employee's Insurance Company officially became Geico; Swift and Co. turned itself into Esmark; Republic Aviation is now the RAC Corp.; and Hart Schaffner and Marx has become Hartmarx Corp. It has been argued that one of the worst byproducts of the phone company breakup was the creation of an entity with the cacophonous and totally nonsensical name of *Nynex*.

One of the largest employers in the Washington, D.C., area is called M/A COM Inc. Writing in the *Washington Post,* Jerry Knight has termed it the worst-named company in the area and asked readers to "...try to find it in the phone book, or pronounce it, let alone figure out what it is."

Others have decided that spaces and hyphens are counter-compressive, so we now have entities with names like *HarperCollins.*

❊ ❊ ❊

In the face of these threatening forces, what follows is intended as a counterforce— a big, new and improved rich, textured dose of names and nicknames for people, places, and things. Trains, apes, boats, houses, extraterrestrials, actors, teams, games, food, towns, pool hustlers, gangsters, baseball players, nuclear power plants, hurricanes, streets, and more. You name it, it's probably here.

❊ ❊ ❊

The most important names in this book, of course, are those of the individuals who helped make it a reality. A small army of helpers and fellow name collectors are thanked at the end of the book. Meanwhile, thanks to Kara L. Noble, who managed to convert the files from my ancient word processor into something usable by the rest of the world; Mary W. Cornog and Thomas F. Pitoniak, who read my entire manuscript in search of errors typographical, factual, or otherwise; and Lynn Stowe Tomb, who designed and produced the pages of this book. Finally, thanks also to John M. Morse and Frederick C. Mish for their support of this project.

What's in a NAME?

Reflections of an Irrepressible Name Collector

Anagrams

Flipped and Scrambled People, Places, and Things

L ITERALLY, AN ANAGRAM MEANS A WORD BACKWARDS, BUT IT HAS COME TO REFER TO ALL sorts of scrambled combinations and the anagram is the basis for numerous games. Many have played with names in the manner of the following which I have collected from friends and associates (my friends and associates find things like this important):

Florence Nightingale = Flit on, cheering angel.
HMS Pinafore = Name for ship.
Disraeli = Sir, I lead.
The Leaning Tower of Pisa = What a foreign stone pile.
Beverly Sills = Silvery Bells.
The Mona Lisa = No hat, a smile.
William Shakespeare = We all make his praise. (Or, if you prefer: I ask me, has Will a peer?)

Ralph Waldo Emerson = Person who all read.
Clint Eastwood = Old west action.
Cinerama = American.
Xerxes = Sex rex.
Republican = Incurable.
Democratic = Rated comic.
Liberace = Lice bear.
Father Christmas = Er… Mr Fat hits cash.
Michael Jordan = Land heroic jam.
Geraldine Ferraro = Gerri, deal Ron fear.

The last item in the list is from Walt Gianchini, who once used Ronald Wilson Reagan to come up with "No girls and no ERA law" and "Now Nader Rolls Again." A. Ross Eckler of *Word Ways* magazine feels that Reagan has been a boon to anagrammatists and can rattle off a number of RWR anagrams including: "Age, war, and sin roll on," "A Dollar Grown Insane," "Insane Anglo war lord," and "Nan, all are Dior gowns." Eckler discovered that Richard Milhous Nixon was not the only president whose name contained the letters of the word *criminal* but that it could be used to create the following anagram: "Hush—Nix Criminal Odor."

The names of more recent presidents have also generated some apt anagrams. George Bush, for instance, gives us "He bugs Gore" and "Hugs Gorbee."

In 1993, the Sunday contest section of the *Washington Post* ran an anagram contest in which the winner saw the following anagrammatic possibility in the name William Jefferson Clinton: "Slim-n-fit. Join Now. Call Free!"

Incidentally, some of the contest participants took aim at the name of the contest, Style Invitational, with stunning results, such as "A vinyl toilet stain" and "Total evil insanity."

Some have put great stock in anagrams. Louis XIII retained an anagrammist named Thomas Billon whose job was to scramble and rescramble the letters in people's names to discover their true nature. Queen Elizabeth took comfort when one of her subjects discovered that "Elizabeth Regina Anglorum" could be made into *Gloria regni salvi manebit* ("the glory of the kingdom shall remain intact"), and Marie Touchet, the mistress of Charles IX, granted a pension to a writer who deduced from her name *Je charme tout* ("I charm all"—an anagram which was made possible because *i*'s and *j*'s used to be interchangeable.)

Lewis Carroll showed his dislike for William Ewart Gladstone in two anagrams: "Wild agitator! Means well," and "Wilt tear down all images." In his book *Our Secret Names*, Leslie Alan Dunkling points to a particularly chilling example. Frère Jacques Clément, the assassin of Henry III, works out as *c'est l'enfer m'a cree*: "It was hell which created me."

For what it's worth, the author has worked unsuccessfully on an anagram of his own name for years. Recently, however, a friend came up with the disarming solution, "A clod is punk."

While most of the above examples are used in games, there are real examples of anagrams having been purposely created as an anagram and applied to a real person, place, or thing. They are hard to find. What follows is a collection of anagrams, backward names, palindromes, name mysteries, and other assorted bits of name trickery which more than twenty people helped put together.

A

AC/DC. A popular rumor has it that this provocative rock group's name means "Anti-Christ/Devil's Child." Group member Angus Young says that the name came from the back of his sister's sewing machine and refers to power.

A Toyota. A perfect product palindrome. Other product names which unintentionally spell something different when reversed include Seiko and Strohs. Akron, Ohio, once had its own soft drink bottled under the name Norka. Tulsa distinguishes itself among cities for those who read backwards.

ACEEEFFGHHILLMMNNOORRSSSTUV. Pseudonym of German novelist Christoffel Von Grrimmelshausen, a rare alphabetical anagram.

Adanac. *Canada* spelled backwards. It has been used many times as a commercial or product name in Canada, but its strangest application has been its use as the name of the military cemetery at Miraumont, France. It was opened in 1916 for Canadian soldiers killed in the First World War. There is a town in Saskatchewan named Adanac and one in Nevada named Adaven. Aksala and Adavan are names which have been used for businesses in Alaska and Nevada respectively.

Agoom Agooc. The name of a record company set up by Pat Boone in the late 1950s which was the name of another one of his companies, Cooga Mooga Inc., spelled backwards.

Ak-sar-ben. A Nebraska race track which is the state's name in reverse. *Ak-Sar-Ben* was also the name of a Chicago Burlington & Quincy train which ran from Chicago to Lincoln. It has a wonderful ring to it, as does *Yenrougis Park,* which is the name of a park in Sigourney, Iowa.

Alcofribas Nasier. A pseudonym for French writer François Rabelais which is an anagram of his name.

Arnold Scassi. Name of a fashion designer whose real name is Issacs, which spelled backwards is *Scassi.*

C

Cilohocla. Name of a dog who began winning big in 1975 at Florida's Derby Lane greyhound track. According to *Sports Illustrated* there was all sorts of speculation about the source of the name (Hispanic? Gallic?) until someone spelled it backwards.

D

Darnoc. Brand of house gin found on a room service menu in a Hilton Hotel which presumably was named in honor of Conrad Hilton.

Drew Dogyear. One of many anagrams of his own name which have been used in the works of Edward Gorey. Others:

Dogear Wryde	Grey Redwoad
Wardore Edgy	Dedge Yarrow
Dreary Wodge	Orde Graydew
Regera Dowdy	Waredo Dyrge
G. E. Deadworry	Deary Rewdgo
D. Awdrey-Gore	Dewda Yorger
Roger Addyew	Addee Gorrwy

This list was provided to the author some years ago by Cornelius Van S. Roosevelt, who could think of no other writer who has used so many anagrams. Roosevelt added at the time that Gorey hadn't used one other possibility: Codder Weary.

Dyju Langard. Name used by actress Liza Minnelli when she appeared on the *Tonight Show* when it was hosted by Jack Paar. It is an anagram for Judy Garland, her mother.

E

Eando Binder. Pen name for science fiction writer brothers Earl and Otto Binder.

Ear Mit. Tim Rae's name spelled backwards. The Baltimore man had a moment of fame in 1991 when a man named Dan Bloom of Juneau, Alaska, set up his National Registry of Backward Names. More than 500 people had sent their names to Nad Moolb, as he preferred to be called in his role as Registrar of Backward Names, when the Associated Press circulated a story about the Registry. Ed Clayfoot of Dallas, De Toofyalc in the registry, sent in 27 Toofyalc names including the family dog Leber.

Ecidujerp. This word used to run in public service ads in the New York City subways. Sponsored by the Commission on Intergroup Relations, the ad said, "ECIDUJERP spelled backwards is prejudice. Either way it doesn't make sense."

Edwin. A brand of designer jeans which was created by scrambling the word "denim" and then turning the *m* upside down.

Emanon. Street in Rochester, New York, which, according to the *Rochester Democrat & Chronicle*, was created by Morley B. Turpin of the city engineer's office when the residents of the street could not decide on a name.

Enidras. Roger Enidras made news in the late 1950s when he decided he wanted to change his name back to the original Roger Sardine.

G

Georgina Spelvin. Name of pornographic movie actress which is an adaptation of George Spelvin, which is a name often used by an actor who takes two parts in the same play. Traditionally, the actor lists his real name for the larger part but Spelvin for the smaller part.

Glenelg. A palindromic town on the west coast of Scotland which gave its name to a village in Nova Scotia, a suburb of Adelaide, Australia, and a village in Maryland.

H

H. A. Largelamb. An anagram of Alexander Graham Bell, who wrote a number of articles for the *National Geographic* under this name. He felt that the magazine was taking articles because of his fame and wanted to sell them on their own merit.

Harpo. Oprah Winfrey's television production company.

Hidell. Alek J. Hidell was the pseudonym Lee Harvey Oswald gave himself. According to a November 1, 1964, article in the *New York Times*, psychologists have suggested that the name was a play on Robert Louis Stevenson's Dr. Jekyll and Mr. Hyde. It was also suggested that this was Oswald's conscious or unconscious way of telling the world of his split personality.

I

Idol Theatre. Located in—where else?—Lodi, Ohio.

Initram. Street name given by a developer in Santa Ana, California. It caused a furor, and the people living there petitioned to have it changed.

K

Kenova. A West Virginia town which is on the Kentucky and Ohio borders and compresses the names of the three states into one name. Texarkana—in Texas and Arkansas—is the largest boundary name jurisdiction, but there are many more. California alone has five of them: Calneva and Calada, on the Nevada border; Calor facing Oregon; Calzona, which looks into Arizona; and Calexico, which is across the border from Mexicali, itself a boundary name. The Canalaska Mountain shows that Canadians go for these blends as well. The Pennsylvania-Maryland line has a Pen Mar and a Sylmar, while Kentucky has Kenvir and Kensee, which front on Virginia and Tennessee. Virgilina (where Virginia and North Carolina meet) has a certain charm, as do Moark, Illmo, Arkla, Texhoma, Florala, Idavada, Kanorado, Tennga, Monida, Mexhoma, and Delmar, which are all real places.

Kinnikinnik St. Street in Milwaukee which has the longest palindromic street name that could be found. According to *Webster's Third New International Dictionary*, it is an Indian smoking mixture made of bark and leaves but no tobacco. At nine letters Kinnikinnik, Alberta, is among the rarest of palindromic towns along with Kanakanak, Alaska.

L

Leuname Notsgnivil. A letter from this person says in part, "In public school we always turned people's names backwards. I generally go by my nickname, 'Bud,' but my real name is Emanuel, which turns me into 'Leuname Notsgnivil' when spelled backwards. To this day one of my friends

from the paleozoic era calls me 'Leu.' One of the better backwards names appeared on my bowling team. George Carpenter became 'Egroeg Retneprac.' "A similar letter from Nerraw Nosinbor Notsnhoj has the correct form of that name mirror-written—in longhand—with the comment, "*Strong* righthanders (who tend to be very black-and-white people temperamentally) just can't do it; it takes us ambiguity-ridden, indecision-prone (but all-shades-of-gray-comprehending) ambidextrous types to do it at all easily."

Levander. Harold Levander, former Minnesota governor, had every kid in the state spelling his last name backwards.

Llareggub. The name of the Welsh village in Dylan Thomas's *Under Milk Wood* which, according to Ray Leedy who pointed this out, when "reversed, isn't very nice at all." According to Ross Reader, in early British published editions the name was changed to *Llareggyb*, but modern editions have gone back to the original.

M

Melusa Moolson. Pseudonym for writer Samuel Solomon, according to the *Dictionary of Literary Pseudonyms*. Note that the first and second names are separately anagrammatized.

N

Naeb Llahsram. When Marshall Bean got deeply in debt, he began to spell his name backwards as a means of dodging bill collectors. A veteran, he was drafted under the new name but was able to get an honorable discharge in 1968 when he convinced the Army he was in for the second time. A story on this in one newspaper carried the headline, SSEM A TAHW.

NAGIRROC YAWGNORW OT LIAH. Newspaper headline of July 17, 1938, celebrating the flight of Douglas "Wrong Way" Corrigan to Ireland.

Navillus Road. According to Stephen V. Masse of Amherst, Massachusetts, this is a street name in North Reading, so called to avoid confusion with Mr. Sullivan's other namesake: Sullivan Road.

Nessiteras rhombopteryx. The scientific name given to the Loch Ness Monster by Sir Peter Scott and Alan Wilkens. Soon after Scott and Dr. Robert Rines introduced the name in *Nature* magazine, Nicholas Fairbairn, a Scottish member of Parliament, figured out that the name was an anagram for "Monster Hoax by Sir Peter S." The namers were stunned by the coincidence.

Neuquen. The capital of the Argentinian province of Neuquen which is on the Neuquen River. It is, as far as can be told, the only palindromic place name with a *q* in the middle.

Nevele. The name of a resort in the Catskill Mountains which is eleven spelled backwards.

Nikep. Town in Maryland which has two names: *Pekin* and *Nikep*, which is *Pekin* spelled backwards. The official state map calls it "Pekin (Nikep)," the postal service calls it Nikep, but longtime residents call it Pekin. Some years ago the postmaster

George Budries explained what happened to a reporter: "It used to be just Pekin. Then 30 or 40 or 50 years ago it got a post office. Now there was another town in Indiana named Pekin. And when you write 'Md' and 'Ind' in script, they look almost the same. So the towns kept getting each others' mail. Postal workers noticed this, and declared that hereafter this place would be called Nikep."

Nitram Rendrag. A rare palindromic pseudonym which was used by Martin Gardner as the byline on a ballad about the son of Casey which appears in his *Annotated Casey at the Bat.*

Nome. Not an anagram, but the name of this city in western Alaska has an unusual history. The discovery of gold at nearby Anvil Creek led to a minor gold rush and the creation of a mining camp called Anvil City. By 1900 Anvil City had a population of 20,000; however, by 1903 the population had decreased, and by the time of the 1920 census it had declined to 852. The town was then renamed for nearby Cape Nome. The name of that cape first appears on an 1849 map and is believed to be a British naval draftsman's misinterpretation of the query "?Name."

O

O. B. Enebo. One of a number of real life people with palindromic names. Others who have been noted: Bob Laval, Mark Kram, Lon Nol, Revilo Oliver, and any number of people whose first name is Ava, Anna, Otto, or Hannah. A particularly odd case of palindromania was reported in 1972 when the UPI discovered a Vinton, Ohio, couple who gave each of their eleven children a middle name which was the reversed spelling of the first name. They included: Noel Leon, Lledo Odell, Laur Rual, Loneva Avenol, Lebanna Annabel, and Leah Hael.

P

Paul Dickson. The author's given name and one that was attacked by anagrammatists who wrote to me as Mr. Olin Ducksap and worse after the first edition of *Names* appeared. The most determined was Scott L. Vannater of Beech Grove, Indiana, who came up with 179 words from those eleven letters, and if you include plurals using the *s* in *Dickson*, the total becomes 256 words. The longest word that has been created so far is *duckpins.* Just as it was somehow reassuring to find that my name contained the makings of words like *lucid, icon, idol, pen, pun, placid, solid,* and *social,* it was also unnerving to find words like *panic, anus, suck, sulk, clod,* and *pus* on the list.

Professor Osseforp. In the March 1972, issue of the *Harvard Bulletin* there is an interview with Osseforp who has been appointed to the Emor D. Nilap Chair in Palindromology at Harvard. In the interview, written by Solomon W. Golomb, the Professor answers all sorts of questions palindromically. He is, for instance, asked the name of the annual Ivy League track meet and answers, "Yale Relay."

R

Rednaxela Terrace. A road in Hong Kong is supposedly a Chinese rendering of Alexander, Chinese sometimes being written from right to left.

Reflipe W. Thanuz. Back in the days when the New York newspapers were at war, William Randolph Hearst's *Journal* ran a bulletin on the death of this man which was reprinted by *The News* in its next edition. The *Journal* jubilantly announced that "Reflipe W." was "we pilfer" spelled backwards and that "Thanuz" was "the news" spelled phonetically. Later *The News* planted the name Lister A. Itaah in an article and, after the *Journal* lifted it, pointed out that the name was an anagram for "Hearst is a liar."

Retlaw Hotel. A hotel in Fond du Lac, Wisconsin, owned by Walter Schroder. This must have had a remarkable impact on people, since so many have brought it to my attention. *Retlaw* is also the name of a Walt Disney family corporation.

Rockcor. A corporation whose stock price used to be shown in the over-the-counter listings, but which has been acquired by the Olin Corporation.

Rolyat. A town in Texas which is *Taylor* spelled backwards. Texas may lead in this area as it also boasts Maharg, which is *Graham* spelled backwards, along with Reklaw, Sacul, Notla, and Tesnus. There are a number of states with at least one town with a backward name including Enola, Arkansas; Etlah, Missouri; Remlik, Virginia; Retsof, New York; Lebam, Washington; and Egnar, Colorado.

S

Salvador Dali. Writer Martin Gardner reports that this name yields the anagram Avida Dollars—*avida* is Spanish for greedy or covetous of—which is said to have been made up by Dali's friend Andre Breton.

Seroco. Town in North Dakota which is an acronym for Sears, Roebuck & Co. which did a lot of business there. Another rare acronym town is Atco, Georgia, coined from the name of the Atlantic Transportation Co. Atco was named in 1866 and the rarity of such abbreviations at the time, as George R. Stewart points out in his *Names on the Land*, "was shown by the later attempt of a historian to prove its Indian origin." Later the *-co* suffix on a town name was a clear giveaway that it was a company town (Weslaco = W. E. Steward Land Company, or Gamerco = Gallup American Coal Company).

Serutan. Madison Avenue's most famous contribution to backward naming, a remedy which boasted it was *natures* spelled backwards. Another backward trade name is that of Trebor, the British candy company, which began in a place called "Trebor Villas," a development named for a Robert who turned his name around.

Silopanna. The name of a street in downtown Annapolis, Maryland.

Silogram. Oil additive produced in Boston and named after its inventor Ed Margolis.

SOS. Hit song by the Swedish group ABBA making it, according to Will Schortz of *Games* magazine, one of the few, if not the only, top ten hits with a palindromic title by a palindromic group. The files of Martin Gardner contain a note suggesting that *Ole ELO* (by the Electric Light Orchestra) may be the first palindromic album title.

Svengali. Anagrammatic title of a 1988 album by jazzman Gil Evans.

T

Ted Morgan. Formerly Sanche de Gramont, he recounts in a chapter on name changing in his book *On Becoming American* that he submitted his old name to a whiz at anagrams who came up with Ted Morgan as well as Monte Drag, Grand Tome, Madge Torn, Tom Danger, O. D. Garment, R. D. Megaton, and Mo Dragnet.

Tensed. The name of a town in Idaho which is a true rarity in that it is an anagrammatic error. It was originally called Desmet for the name of the Jesuit missionary Pierre De Smet, but there was another Desmet in Idaho, so it was rejected by the postal service. The people of the town spelled it backwards and resubmitted it, but a typographical error crept in at some point and the name was accepted as *Tensed*, not *Temsed*.

Teragram. Perhaps the most famous ship with a backward name, it was donated to the Coast Guard Academy as a training vessel by a man who had named it for his wife. If *Teragram* is the most famous backward name afloat, *Topknits* (noted in a 1962 *Newsweek* article on boat names) may be the oddest, but there are many more including *Ygrella* on a doctor's boat.

Theda Bara. An anagram for Arab Death. Her original name was Theodosia Goodman, and she was the daughter of a Cincinnati tailor.

Therbligs. Name for the eighteen patterns of kinetic energy discovered by engineer Frank Gilbreth (1868-1924), who used them to establish principles of "motion economy" in the workplace. *Therblig* is *Gilbreth* spelled backwards with the *h* and *t* transposed.

Tnemec. Name of a California company that produces cement.

Tunlaw Road. Both Baltimore and Washington, D.C., have these which were, according to local legend, created because each city already had a Walnut.

V

Voltaire. His real name was François-Marie Arouet, and his pseudonym was supposedly an anagram of *Arouet l[e] j[eune]*. (The anagram only works if you treat *i* and *j* and *u* and *v* as interchangeable.)

W

Wassamassaw. Palindromic swamp in South Carolina.

Wordbrad Darbrow. A real person's name collected by the late Barbara Fletcher. Such constructions are rare. Another is Emorb Brome, which is the name given to the son of a Somerset squire according to John Newton Friend in *Words: Tricks and Traditions*.

X

Xenejenex. One of a number of palindromic business names, but the only one to come to light that begins and ends in *x*. Dan Tilque of Hood River, Oregon, found the Boston-based Xenejenex along with the likes of Maxaxam of Ann Arbor, Michigan, and Enidine of Orchard Park, New York.

Y

Yma Sumac. Many noted that the name of this popular singer of the mid-1950s could be spelled backwards easily and the story grew that was it Amy Camus from Brooklyn taking on Peruvian airs. Not so. Her real name was Emperatriz Chavarri, and she was born in Peru in 1927.

Yreka Bakery. When Jack Smith of the *Los Angeles Times* was asked if there really was such a bakery in Yreka, California, he answered, "Once there was, but it is now the Yrella Gallery."

Animal Names

Quick! What Did J. Edgar Hoover Call His Dog?

The ends to which people will go to come up with a proper name for an animal is nowhere better demonstrated than in Jean E. Taggart's book *Pet Names*. Among other things, she comes up with 30 appropriate names for pet spiders and four for pet rats. Should you be in the market for a good rat name, Taggart suggests Grandpa, Susie, Ta Ka (an Indian name for rat), and Whiskers. To these you could, of course, add Ben, the name of the movie rat who appeared in the film which trivia lovers recall had a title song which was Michael Jackson's first hit without his brothers.

When it comes to dog and cat names, Taggart lists hundreds, as do others. In *The Cat Doctor's Book of Cat Names*, Susan McDonough, D.V. M., explores every conceivable category including counterculture cat names such as Rasta, Astral Pussy, Mescaline, Kilo, Wow, Fuzz, and Manson (!).

Not only are there people to help us name pets, but others who theorize about why we choose the names we do. Here are just two of the many theories which have been advanced:

• That a person who gives a pet a familiar name like Peter or George feels a much greater attachment to the animal than one who gives it a generic name like Spot or Tabby. This was originally advanced by a Chicago vet named Lloyd Prasuhn who noted this in his practice.

• That the name you choose reflects "many things about your character and personality that you are not aware of yourself." This from Jacob Antelyes, D.V. M., in an essay on cat names in *The Cat Catalog*. For this reason, a family of low social status may choose a regal name like Prince or Queen for a household animal.

Clearly, this is fertile ground for the name collector because animal names come from so many sources. The results of a 1994 national survey of 1,049 pet owners conducted by the American Animal Hospital Association (AAHA) indicated that 28 percent of dogs and 19 percent of cats have typical pet names. Forty-six percent of dogs and 55 percent of cats have human names. Twenty-six percent of dogs and 26 percent of cats have names that are neither typical of pet or human names. Pet names come from a variety of sources. According to the same survey, 20 percent were the result of suggestions by family and friends, 25 percent were named because of appearance or a physical attribute, 23 percent were made-up names, 11 percent were named because of registry requirements, 2 percent reflect ethnic or area themes, and 14 percent were named after someone or something. In addition, 56 percent of our pets have nicknames in addition to their proper names.

Here then is a collection which not only includes canine and feline names but good equine, lupine, cervine, ovine, bovine, porcine, leporine, otarine, elapine, elephantine, ranine, ursine, piscine, and corvine names. (Should you want to have these fine -*ine* words decoded, you'll have to wait to the end of the chapter. Meanwhile see how many of them you can figure out.)

A

Able and Miss Baker. The first primates (spider monkeys) who went into space and returned to earth, an event which took place on May 28, 1959, aboard a Jupiter rocket. Miss Baker lived until 1984 when she was buried ceremonially at the entrance to the Alabama Space and Rocket Center in Huntsville. Later Sam, Miss Sam, and Ham followed.

Aethenoth. Lady Godiva's horse. Other notable names: El Cid's Babieca, Thomas Paine's Button, Napoleon's Marengo, General Custer's Vic, Alexander the Great's Bucephalus, Paul Revere's Brown Beauty, and the name of the elephant that Hannibal personally rode across the Alps.

Andy. Top pet bird name, for no apparent reason, according to a 1990 survey.

Assault. Until 1946, when this horse won the Kentucky Derby, the Brown Hotel in Louisville used to name a room in the inn for the winner.

B

Black Diamond. The name of the bison on the buffalo nickel.

Buff Orpington. Chickens are seldom individually named, but they make up for it in breed names like this one and the Penciled Wyandotte. Pigeon breeds include Birmingham Roller, Chinese Owl, English Pouter, Giant Runt, and Ice.

What's in a Neigh...m

Bates Motel. A highly touted colt of the early 1980s named, oddly, for the hotel in *Psycho* where Norman Bates behaved badly. One can name a horse anything one wants. However, the rules are quite stringent when it comes to Thoroughbreds who are registered with the Jockey Club in New York for entry in the *American Stud Book*. The name cannot be longer than 18 letters and must comply with the rules which mainly tell which names are not eligible:

1. Those of horses currently racing. A full 15 years must elapse before a name can be used again, and some names (Citation, War Admiral, Kelso, Native Dancer, etc.) have been permanently retired.
2. Names of living persons cannot be used without their written permission. So if you spot Willard Scott or Chris Evert on your race card (both real horses), it's because the permission of those celebrities was obtained. The names of infamous people like Hitler are not allowed.
3. No trade names—although they goofed in allowing Cook's Tour, Go Big Mac, Flick and Bick (sic) and others—and no initials. Names of songs and books cannot be used either.
4. Tasteless names are banned although a number of borderline cases have slipped by, including Up Your Assets and Bodacious Tatas. Little Lass looked fine on paper but not when announced on the track PA system. Also, names which make the horse seem undignified are vetoed. For such reasons, all foreign and "coined" names submitted must be translated. Some that have gotten through are J. Strap and Poopit.
5. In addition, a name cannot include the words *filly* or *colt*, the name of a racetrack or stake, 2nd's, 3rd's, and other numerical designations.

There are also informal customs, including the one which says that you don't name a horse negatively. As Ernest Hemingway once noted, no horse named Morbid ever won a race.

Given all these rules and the fact that so many names are taken it's clear why there are a lot of odd names on the order of Bates Motel, Disco Inferno, English Muffin, Leo Pity Me, Cold Shower, T.V. Doubletalk, Ranikaboo, Holy Cats, Hadn't Orter, Honeybunny Boo, Strong Strong, and Race Horse, who raced in the early 1970s. According to the *New York Times* a horse who raced in the late 1960s was called You Name It because so many names had been rejected by the Jockey Club that the horse's owner finally scrawled "you name it!" across the application.

One of the better horse namers was Alfred Vanderbilt, who gave his horses outlandish names like Social Climber, Crashing Bore, Social Outcast, Loser Weeper, and Cold Shoulder (out of Glacier). His superhorse was Native Dancer.

It has been argued that the greatest horses, like Native Dancer, somehow have names that help maintain their legendary reputations: Citation, Secretariat, Man o' War, Whirlaway, War Admiral, Seattle Slew, and Affirmed. Scott Regan, a Maryland trainer, told the *Washington Post* in 1992 that you never really see a real good horse with a stupid name. Regan had watched a horse he had named Nyuk, Nyuk, Nyuk, a Curleyism from the Three Stooges, go nowhere.

C

Cat. Name of Holly Golightly's cat in the movie *Breakfast at Tiffany's*. Dog was the name of the basset belonging to Inspector Columbo in the eponymous TV series.

Chicadee. One of a handful of bird names which are echoic in that they sound like the bird's call. Others: the cuckoo, bob-white, whippoorwill, curlew, and chacha-laca.

E

Elsie. The most famous cow name ever. Elsie was born in 1932 with the name You'll Do Lobelia. Her bull was Elmer (of Elmer's Glue) and their calves were Beauregard and Elmo.

Other trade animals: Tige, who lived in the shoe with Buster Brown; Lawrence, who is the Hartford Insurance Company's elk; and Chauncey, the star cougar of the Mercury Cougar ads who died in 1975.

Elysabeth Dalrymple. The name of the elephant which crossed the Alps in the 1930s in Richard Haliburton's *Seven League Boots*. Other elephant names from the archives: Oodles, Thonglow, Belle, Pet, Rosy, Mtoto, Jumbo, and Mona.

G

G-Boy. The name of J. Edgar Hoover's dog. Other celebrity dogs include Flush (Elizabeth Barrett Browning's spaniel), Fuzzy (one of Ronald Reagan's dogs), Brumus (Robert Kennedy's dog, the name is a Newfoundlandism for "midnight snack"), Ginger (Hubert H. Humphrey's dog), Blondi (Hitler's), Bowser (Mr. Magoo's), Davie (President Wilson's Airedale), Pete (Our Gang's), Heidi (Ike's weimaraner), and Him and Her (LBJ's beagles).

Godiper. Name of a cat which belonged to Joann Lee of Berkeley, California, which was based on her original reaction of "You've got a purr." "Godiper," she points out, "like T. S. Eliot's Bombalurina, Mun-kustrap, Coricopat, and Jellylorum, is a name 'that never belong(s) to more than one cat.' "

H

Hector. The name of President Grover Cleveland's pet bulldog which inspired the naming of Hector, Arkansas.

Heinz. A mongrel of "57 varieties."

Holy Bull. Horse running in top form in the mid-1990s owned by the Vatican and personally named by Pope John Paul II. There was a rumor, however, that this Kentucky Derby horse was owned by a Phil Rizzuto fan who discovered that the name Holy Cow was already taken.

J

John Beresford Tipton. What else could you call a salmon with a million dollar price on it? The fish, released for a Puget Sound salmon derby, was named after the television character of the 1950s who gave money away a million dollars at a clip. The fish got away so nobody claimed the million.

L

Llulu. A llama, of course. It was one of several winning entries in a contest to name zoo llamas held in 1950. Llama Turner and Llama Bean also made the final cut.

M

Martha. The name of the last passenger pigeon who died in the Cincinnati Zoo in 1913.

Muffie/Muffin. Top dog name in 1990 according to one survey; Cocoa and its variations came in second, and Lady, Lucky, and Ginger tied for third. A 1989 study concluded that these were the top ten names in descending order: Lady, Max, Brandy, Duke, Rocky, Princess, Ginger, Pepper, Blacky, and Lucky. A 1985 survey put Duke at the top followed by Brandy, Max, Sam, and Shadow.

N

Nibbles. Beloved of trivia experts, Nibbles was Elizabeth Taylor's pet chipmunk when she was a girl. Her book on the subject: *Nibbles and Me.*

O

Onan. Dorothy Parker's pet canary, so called because he spilled his seed.

P

Punxsutawney Phil. The Pennsylvania groundhog that allows the wire service each Groundhog's Day to predict whether the rest of the winter will be cold or not.

In recent years Phil has been joined by other well-named woodchucks including Octorara Orphy of Quarryville, Pennsylvania; Atlanta's General Lee and Scarlett; and Dunkirk Dave, of Dunkirk, New York.

Pyewacket. Cat in the play and movie, *Bell, Book and Candle,* a name that has been popular ever since.

R

Reincarnation. W. R. Anderson of Chiago had a kitten named Carnation which "lost a race with a truck." When his family found a carbon-copy kitten they felt compelled to name it Reincarnation.

Rover. The origin of the name Rover as a dog's name is not clear, but one fascinating theory appears at the beginning of Abraham Katsh's *The Biblical Heritage of American Democracy.* He tells of a 17th-century churchgoer who named his dog Moreover after the passage from the book of Judges: "moreover, the dog came and lapped up the water." He suggests it was a short leap from Moreover to Rover. It is the most popular dog name in the United States according to a 1984 survey by Kal Kan, the dog food manufacturer.

S

Sam Dash. Walt Gianchini of San Francisco named his cat Sam Dash during the Watergate hearings. Dash, the cat, asked Gianchini to drop a note to Dash, the special prosecutor, to tell him of the naming, and Dash wrote back telling Gianchini to "give the cat a stroke for him." Gianchini says a friend named a goat Earl Butz.

Sam Spade. A kitten, as was Cornelius McGillikitty. Laurie Taylor of Minneapolis presented a collection of cat names including Oedipus (because he Oedipus supper) and Buttons (poorly housebroken and in need of more buttons on his fly).

Secretariat. Name of the Triple Crown winner from 1973 whose owner Penny Chenery had tried to name it Scepter. Other names rejected by the Jockey Club for one of the greatest horses of all times: Royal Line, Something Special, Games of Chance, and Deo Volente.

Shall and Will. The names of Christopher Morley's cats "because no one can tell them apart."

Siegel. Harpo Marx's pet seagull.

T

Tomoka. An ape in the National Zoo in Washington which was named by public contest in 1961. After zoo officials checked all the major African languages to make sure the name meant nothing, it was found that Tomoka was the name of a legendary Indian chief of the Timucuan tribe of Florida. There is an Interstate Highway sign in northern Florida for Tamoka Creek.

Other gorilla names: Audi (a gorilla born at the Audubon Zoo in New Orleans), Colo (the first gorilla born in captivity so named because he was born in the Columbus, Ohio, Zoo), Massa (until his death in late 1984, the oldest gorilla in captivity), and Paul (the gorilla on *Electric Company*).

W

Waterhole Ike. One of a select group of animals with a Social Security number—530-80-4623. Ike is a pig who drinks beer, and when a group of bar patrons decided to promote the pig for commercial purposes, a bank account was started in his name.

Whiz Taylor. Great horse pedigree name from two horses named Taylor's Special and Whiz Along.

X

Xoloitzquintli. A rare breed of dog which brings up the whole issue of breed names for domestic animals. Many are directly traceable to the geographical locations such as the Boston (Massachusetts) Terrier, Manx (for the Isle of Man), Skye (the Hebrides) Terrier, and the Dalmatian (region in the former Yugoslavia). Others are named for what they do—pointer, setter, and the bulldog which was originally used to bait bulls—and a few can be traced to breeders like Louis Doberman's terrier (*pinscher* is German for "terrier").

One, the Dandie Dinmont Terrier, was named for a character in a novel. The dog was discovered by Sir Walter Scott in the Teviotdale Hills of Scotland. In the 1815 novel *Guy Mannering*, he described a farmer named Dandie Dinmont who had six of these terriers. Henceforth, the breed had its name.

Y

Ytu brutus. A puckish taxonomic name for a beetle, attributed to Smithsonian entomologist Paul Spanger in Phillip Kopper's book *National Museum of Natural History*. Kopper also tells of the crab which was named *Enchantor modestus* which is Latin for "modest flasher." It was named by curator Raymond B. Manning because the crab constantly exposed its copulatory organ. Such names are a vast improvement in a field where an amphipod can be labeled *Siemienkiewicziechinogammarussiemin-kiewicz*, a name which makes us pity the poor crustacean.

In his book *Composition of Scientific Words*, paleontologist Roland Brown crusaded against both the unspeakably complex and the boringly redundant. After bringing up such real prime subspecies as *Bison bison bison*, *Cardinalis cardinalis cardinalis*, and *Rattus rattus rattus*, he concluded, "Nomenclature need not compete with the Hallelujah Chorus."

The Testudine & the Leporine

The *-ine* words were given to the author by Warren E. Steffen of Nice, California, and Joseph E. Badger of Bloomington, Indiana, who collect them. They are as follows:

bees = apian
bear = ursine
birds with feet for perching = passerine
bulls = taurine
calf or veal = vituline
cat = feline
civets = viverine
cow = bovine
crow = corvine
deer = cervine
dog = canine
elephant = elephantine
fish = piscine
foxes = vulpine

frog = ranine
goat = caprine
goose = anserine
gull = larine
hare = leporine
horse = equine
peacocks = pavonine
pig = porcine
rats and mice, eyes (sorry) = murine
sable = zibeline
seal = otarine, (phocine)
sheep = ovine
snake = elapine, (anguine, colubrine)
songbirds = oscine
toilets (sorry) = latrine
tortoise = testudine
wasps = vespine
weasel, badger = musteline
wolf = lupine

Apples

Beyond the Red Delicious 3

KING LUSCIOUS winter Queen

Red Baron

Densmore
wealthy

CENTER:
REINE DES
POMMES

Bleinheim
Orange

Lord
Lambourne SIR PRISE PRINCE DUCHESS OF DUKE OF
         GEORGES OLDENBURG DEVONSHIRE

The Royal Family of Apples

A s a collector of such things, I think the finest names ever assigned to animal, vegetable or mineral were given to apples. I'm not just talking about the half-dozen or so apples which you find in the modern American supermarket, but the hundreds and hundreds of varieties which exist—or existed—somewhere in the apple-loving universe. For reasons unclear, apples seem to get crisp, sweet names which are most appropriate. After asking himself why the apple got all the good names, food writer Robert Farrar Capon commented, "It is almost as if the apple, having been associated with the failure in Eden, has spent the rest of history as a name-dropping overachiever."

Some years ago I began collecting apple names with a passion and even got the Department of Agriculture and the New York State Agricultural Experiment Station involved, hitting paydirt when I got a computer printout listing the 1,500 apple varieties growing at the the New York State Agricultural Experiment Station in Geneva, New York. I dug through the files of the *Bangor Daily News,* which once actually ran a column on bygone Maine varieties called "Apple Memories," and I enlisted the aid of my friend Howard Channing, who ran around his state of Washington hunting down names. Channing's greatest find came when he discovered the original records of the late W. H. Mitchell in an agricultural extension service library. Mitchell was one of a small group of orchardists preserving some of the old varieties. From this I located other small operators, including Southmeadow Fruit Gardens of Lakeside, Michigan, and the Sonoma Antique Apple Nursery of Healdsburg, California, which cater both to apple connoisseurs and home gardeners by growing and selling rootstock of hundreds of older varieties. Catalogs from these nurseries proved to be invaluable. The Southmeadow catalog, boasting 281 apple varieties in its Spring 1996 catalog, is pure poetry. Describing a new variety in 1995, the Hidden Rose, which was discovered in an abandoned Oregon farmyard, the catalog says that it has "hard, crisp, breaking, juicy, sweet, fine-flavored, rose-red flesh under a green skin (hence the name Hidden Rose) and a long keeper."

Meanwhile the apple world has begun to stir. In Britain where the apple is king—writing in 1718 Richard Bradley said of the fruit "I hold it almost impossible for the English to live without it"—there are "apple namers," professionals who can taste an apple and declare it "an Ellison's Orange." Biochemist Joan Morgan, according to an article in the *Weekend Telegraph* of October 14, 1995, has tasted more than 2,000 varieties. That same article reported: "Apple naming is a booming business in Britain, and dozens of old varieties are being rescued and replanted." At Brogdale Farm in Kent 2,500 varieties grow on 30 acres shielded from the wind by high cedar hedges.

The urge to preserve and savor has gotten to the point where even the British supermarkets have gone way beyond supermarket apples. The English Safeway, according to a recent article in the *Times* of London, carries no less than 50 British varieties. One can walk into a market in Great Britain and find James Grieves, Handsome Normans, Lord Derbies, and Ingrid Maries.

With all of this help, I've collected over two thousand apple names, which is a relatively modest list. According to the estimate of Elizabeth Hellfman in her book *Apples, Apples, Apples*, there are as many as 8,000 apple names past and present.

Here are 365 plus—an apple a day with a few extra thrown in for leap year—which I plucked from my orchard of names. I intended this to be a pure, poetic list but a few apples required a few words of comment. After all, these are not just names but, to quote Southmeadow's now retired founder Robert A. Nitschke, symbols of the fact that "no other food or drink provides the fascinating diversity of flavors, textures, colors, shapes as does the apple."

There are other well named fruits, but nothing to compare with the infinite vari-

text continued on page 24

An Apple a Day

A

Abbondanza
Acme
Adams Pearmain
Alamanka
Aldenhamensis
Alexander ("Almost as large as a saucer," is how a woman described this apple in a letter to the *Bangor Daily News.* "We always saved them for March and April as they kept well and were wonderful for spring eating or for baking in pies.")
Alexstone
Alice
All-Over-Red
Alton
Amellia
American Beauty
Anna
Annie Elizabeth
Anoka
Arctic Autumn
Arkansas Black
Armentrout's Appeaser
Arnoldiana
Arrow
Ashmead's Kernel
Ashworth Old McIntosh
Astrosanguina
Atlas
Aunt Lucy
Aurora
Australian Gravenstein

B

Baccata Costata
Baldwin (Like most popular apples, the Baldwin has more than one name. It has also been called the Woodpecker, the Pecker, and Steele's Red Winter.)

Barbara Ann
Bascombe Mystery
Baxter's Black
Beacon
Beating Hammer
Beautiful Arcade
Bedfordshire Foundling
Belle of Boskoop
Bellfleur Record

Ben Davis (For those who think there is a halo around all the old apples, consider the Ben Davis, which by many accounts tasted like sawdust, but looked good and stored well. Prof. F. A. Waugh of the University of Vermont said of it in 1902, "When a buyer has no more discrimination than to buy Ben Davis, he knows [or cares] nothing for quality. Ben Davis is sold on its looks, not on its flavor." Others disagree holding that they can be quite good when grown in certain parts of the South. The Southmeadow catalog says, "Controversy still rages over this apple.")

Ben Hur
Benoui
Better Than Good
Beverly Hills
Bingo
Bisbee Winesap
Black Gilliflower
Black Mac
Black Mickey
Blanch Ames
Blaze
Blenheim Orange
Blue Pearmain (According to the *Bangor Daily News* this apple was known as the Blue Pear Maine north of Boston.)
Blushing Gold

Bob White
Bramley's Seedling
Brigg's Auburn
Buckingham
Buckley Giant
Burgundy

C

California Sweet
Calville Blanc
Canada Red
Cap of Liberty

Caravel (One of three new varieties introduced by the Canadian Department of Agriculture in 1964. The other two: the Ranger and the Quinte.)

Cardinal
Carla
Charlamoff
Chautauqua
Cheal's Golden Gem
Chehalis
Chenango Strawberry
Chieftain
Chinese Golden Early
Clear Gold
Cleopatra
Cole's Quince
Converse Red June
Coombs Wealthy

Cornish Gilliflower (A fragrant apple about which John Lindley in his 1841 *Pomologia Britannica* said, "This is the best apple that is known, if high flavor combined with a very rich sub-acid saccharine juice we most desire.")

Cornwall Greening
Cox's Orange Pippin
Crimson Superb
Criterion

D

Dabinett
Dakota
Daniel's Red Streak
Danver's Winter Sweet
Deacon Jones
Delawine
Densmore Wealthy
Derman Paragon
Derman Triple Red
    Delicious
Devonshire Quarrendon
Discovery
Dobson
Dochdiany
Dorsett Golden
Duchess of Oldenburg
Dukat
Duke of Devonshire
Dulsis

E

Early Harvest
Early Joe
Eastman Sweet
Ebenezer Lambkin
Echo
Egremont Russet
Empire (Named in 1966, this was developed at Cornell University and is a cross between a McIntosh and a Red Delicious.)
English Redstream
Epicurian
Etter's Gold
Excells Delicious

F

Falconer
Fallawater
Fameuse (or Snow Apple)
Father Abraham
Feuillard

Fireside
Flame
Flower of Kent
Fourth of July
Foxwhelp (Described in the 1982-1983 Southmeadow catalog, cider category, as "a bright red apple with sharp golden juice of high specific gravity, produces one of the finest of all ciders, keeping for many years, even decades.")
Freeborn Jonared
Freyberg
Frostproof
Fuji
Full Red Jack Delicious

G

Gala
Genesee Chief
Ginnygold
Gloria Mundi
Golden Noble
Goldspur
Goolsbey
Granny Smith
Greene Spy
Grimes Golden
Grove

H

Hall Keeper
Happy Birthday
Hawkeye (Discovered and named by farmer Hesse Hiatt of Iowa, the rights to it were bought out in 1895 by a commercial nursery which renamed it "Delicious." Now the most popular apple in America, Hiatt twice tried to destroy the original— because of its irregular growth—but it kept growing back.)

Herb's Delicious
Hereford Redstreak
Hilltop Red Cortland
Holdfast
Holiday
Hollow Log
Holly (A cross between a Jonathan and a Delicious.)
Honey Gold
Honora
Hoople's Antique Gold (A Golden Delicious mutation brought into the apple world by an Ohio orchardist.)
Hubbardston Nonesuch
Hudson Golden Gem
Huntsman Favorite

I

Idared (Initially developed in Idaho.)
Imperial Stayman
Irish Peach

J

James Grieve
Jay Darling
Jerseymac
John Standish
Jonalicious
Jonathan (Discovered in 1826 in Woodstock, New York.)
Jonwin
Joyce (From Mitchell's notes: "It is more striped than McIntosh . . . and earlier in season. It is about the heaviest bearing apple. The branches hang down as if loaded with stones, very good flavor.")
Juicy Bite
June Wealthy

K

Keepsake
Kentucky Long Stem
Kerry Pippin
Keswick Codlin
Kibbe Spy
Kidd's Orange Red
King David
King Luscious
King's Acre Pippin
King Tonkin
Knobbed Russet
Kokko
Kyokko

L

Large Early Bough
Large Yellow Siberian
Late Sweet McIntosh
Lawyer Nutmeg
Laxton's Fortune
Lemoine
Levering Limbertwig
Linda
Liveland Raspberry
Loachapoka
Lodi
Loop Russet Baldwin
Lord Lambourne
Lyman Prolific

M

Macoun
Magnolia Gold
Maiden Blush
Maidstone Favorite
Maigold
Malinda
Manchurian
Manitoba
Margaret Anderson
Martha Stripe
Mayqueen
McClintock Grimes

McIntosh (Named for Ontario farmer John McIntosh who first cultivated it in 1796.)
McNicholas Greening
Megumi
Melrouge
Melt-in-the-Mouth
Merton Knave
Miami Stark
Michael Henry Pippin
Mindon Sweet
Minkler
Minnehaha
Missing Link
Morse Beauty
Mother (Not to be confused with the Mother-in-Law, a New Zealand apple developed and announced in 1965 and described as "rosy-cheeked, . . . but very sour." The term mother-in-law has a nice sound to it and is appropriate to an apple.)

N

Nelson's Victory
Nero Rome
Nestor
Newell
Newtown Pippin ("This is in most of its varieties the finest apple of our country, and probably of the world," wrote William Coxe in one of the first books on apples published in the United States in 1817. Today the Southmeadow catalog calls it, "...THE classic American apple" and notes that it was George Washington's favorite.)
Niagara
Nickajack (Named for a stream near which it was discovered in North Carolina.)

Nine Partners
Niobe
Nittany
Nodhead
Northern Spy (Writing about her childhood in Vermont, Dorothy Canfield Fisher said of this variety, "Their presence would go far beyond the dining room and pervade the house with an aroma which...became the characteristic odor of home, bringing back childhood with [an] actual... presence." The name is something of a mystery. It first grew in East Bloomfield, New York, which was an active point in the Underground Railroad, and some believe it had something to do with the name. In a recent Southmeadow Fruit Gardens catalog Robert A. Nitschke speculates it is a corruption of what was originally, and prosaically, the Northern Pie Apple.)
Nubeena
Nugget

O

Ohio Nonpareil
Okanoma Delicious
Old Nonpareil (Quoting the Southmeadow catalog, "An ancient English apple of surpassing excellence possibly dating back to Queen Elizabeth's time and first described by 17th-century French writers.")
Onondaga
Ontario
Opalescent
Oratia Beauty
Oregon Spur
Oriole
Ozark Gold

P

Pacific Pride
Paducah
Palmer Greening
Palouse
Pandora
Paradise Sweet
Paradisiana
Pasley Grant
Paulared
Pawpaw
Peace Garden
Peck Pleasant
Penrome
Perfect
Pewaukee
Piervomaiskoie
Pink Pearl
Pink Satin
Pocomoke
Polly Eades
Pomme Pierre
Porter (Named for a Rev. Samuel Porter who discovered it in 1840. A 19th-century writer gave it this review: "An apple for the connoisseur, who will delight in its crisp, tender, juicy, perfumed flesh, richly flavored and sufficiently aciduous to make it one of the most refreshing of all apples.")
Potomac
Pound Sweet
Prairie Rose
Prince Georges
Pumpkin Sweet
Purple Wave

Q

Quaker Beauty
Quebec Belle
Quindell

R

Radiance
Rambo (A Pennsylvania apple which was the favorite of Johnny Appleseed.)
Ranger
Raritan
Razabols
Real McCoy Delicious
Red Astrachan (An editor-ialist in a Maine newspaper in bemoaning the fact that this apple was no longer being cultivated wrote pas-sionately, "The delicate red-dish tinge in red astrachan applesauce is the touchstone of the superlative, and it can only be enjoyed by those who have red astrachans.... You can have a thousand advantages in this world, and own a degree from a university, but you can't have red astrachan apple-sauce unless you have some red astrachan apples.")
Red Baron
Red Delicious (The world's leading apple.)
Red Hook
Red Ingrid Marie
Red Seek-No-Further
Red Sport of Sharon
Redsumbo
Regal Red
Reine des Pommes
Reineta Encarnada
Rhode Island Greening
Ribston Pippin
Rings Wealthy
Roanoke
Robusta
Rocket
Roman Stem
Rosalie
Rose Bud

Rosilda
Rosthern
Roxbury Russet (This, according to Peter Wynn in his *Apples: History, Folklore, Horticulture and Gastronomy,* "may be the oldest named variety in America." The variety was discovered in Roxbury, Massachusetts, in the early 17th century. Rare today, its undoing may have been its rough, tough skin which earned it the nick-name "Leathercoat.")
Royal Jubilee
Runkel
Rush's Favorite
Rustycoat

S

Saint Cecilia
Saint Edmonds Pippin
Salome
Sam Young
Saugahatchee
Scarlet Crofton
Schoharie Spy
Scotia
Secando
Seek-No-Further
Sentinel
Sergeant McIntosh
Sharon
Shawnee
Shenandoah
Shin-Indo
Shiwassee
Signe Tillisch
Simpson Starking
Sir Prise
Skyline Supreme
Smokehouse
Snowdrift
Somerset of Maine
Sops of Wine

Sparkler Crab
Sparta
Spectabilis
Spokane Beauty
Squirrel Tail
Stark Earliblaze
Stark Splendor
State Fair
Stevenson Wealthy
Stone Ridge Golden
    Delicious
Strawberry St. Lawrence
Sturmer Pippin
Sugar Loaf
Summerlong
Sungift
Sutton's Beauty
Swaar
Swayzie
Sweet and Sour
(An old catalog refers to its "sections of sweet and sour alternating; grown chiefly as a curiosity.")
Sweetbough
Sweet Copin
Sweet Sixteen
Sylvestris

T

Talman's Sweet
Tangier
Tasty
Taunton Cross
Timiskaming
Tioga
Tohoku
Tolman Sweet
Tom McClean
Transparent (Janet Kleckner of Portland, Oregon, has written to nominate this apple to the list, which she describes as "light yellow, crisp-meated.")
Tremlett's Bitter
Tumanga
Turley's Winesap
Twenty Ounce
Tyker

U

Utter

Pignose Apple

V

Van Buren Duchess
Vanderpool Red
Vandevere
Verired
Victory
Viking
Vista Bella

W

Washington Strawberry

Wayne Spur Delicious
Wealthy
Weatherly Early Spy
Webster
Westfield Seek-No-Further
Westland
White Angel
Whittier Sweet
Wickson
William's Favorite
Willie Sharp
Willis Williams
Willow Twig
Wilson Juicy
Winter Banana
Winter Queen
Wismer's Dessert (A Canadian apple which when first reported on in 1897 was said to be of "such fine grain and buttery flavor that one might easily take it for a pear.")
Wolf River
Worcester Cross

X

Xanthocarpa

Y

Yarlington Mill
Yellow Bellflower
York-a-Red
Young America

Z

Zabaoani
Zalesak
Zeeland Spur
Zorza

ety of crunchy, delicious apple names. The only examples of less than pretty apple names I've been able to find are Pignose, Esopus Spitzenberg, and Nipissing. On the other hand there are plums with names like Elephant Heart, Yellow Egg, Hand, Quackenboss, Milton, Cluck, German Prune, and Gueii. Peaches tend to punky names like Slappey, Grosse Mignonne, and Stump-the-World, and pear names tend to sound like the names of skin diseases: Bosc, Magness, Michelmas Nelis, Passe Crassane, Seckel, Rostiezer, Shinseiki, Boussock, Koonce, Hoosic, Rutter, and Lady Clapp. One pear is actually named Souvenir Du Congress. Strawberries sound like they were named by an editor at *Penthouse* or a condom manufacturer: Beaver, Climax, Rough Rider.

Collecting apple names has an interesting side effect: the desire to hold and taste them. In many cases, it is too late. Some were killed by disease and others were abandoned because of natural spots or colors which did not sell well. James Trager in his *Foodbook* points out, "Some trees were cut down by temperance workers fighting the evils of cider and applejack. Quite a few were felled during the 1930s Depression when it was thought they harbored insects and diseases that menaced commercial orchards." In Britain some orchards were "grubbed up" during World War II to make room for other crops, and there was not a new orchard planted in Great Britain until 1950.

The German Prune

Some losses would seem to be greater than others:

A legend has grown up around an apple called the Wild Rose Sweeting which was discovered growing wild in the woods near Norway, Maine, in the last century. It was a natural fruit from one tree discovered and named by a boy named Willis Murch. Like the Baldwin, a natural found growing in Massachusetts, the Wild Rose Sweeting could have been propagated, but Murch made the mistake of selling apples from the tree and soon encountered resentment from other boys. The spiteful boys found the tree which bore fruit that "melted on the palate like a spoonful of ice cream" and destroyed it.

Years later, essayist Arthur G. Staples of the *Lewiston Journal Press* wrote of the Wild Rose Sweeting as "an apple that was lost, an apple that perhaps surpassed in flavor any other apple that ever grew, an apple that was a gift of Nature to a wicked world, that rejected it, a loss greater, perhaps, than all the gold mines or the diamond mines that are 'lost' in the tales of treasure hunters."

The good news is that apple enthusiasts and evangelists are at work hunting down old varieties and finding new ones created by design or mutation. The religious zeal which the apple lovers have mustered is not inappropriate. To the early European Protestants the apple was God's own fruit, a treasure that has escaped from Eden and whose cultivation brought the orchardist closer to the Holy State.

Aptronyms

Names That Fit Real Good

4

A *ptronym* is a word coined by Franklin P. Adams for a name that is aptly suited to its owner. I have been collecting them since getting a letter some years ago from a distinguished professor at Brown University. Quoting that letter:

I might also mention that I have a very large collection of instances where persons' names and either their occupations or preoccupations are in synchrony. This is an area…which has not been sufficiently or seriously organized. I knew that there was orderliness here when I noted that on the Brown University campus a Mrs. Record was in charge of alumni files, Mr. Banks was the Controller, and Mr. Price was in charge of purchasing. Looking a bit beyond my own campus, I found that Dr. Fish was indeed the head of the University of Rhode Island Oceanographic Institute, and he had hired one staff member named Saila and another named Seaman. I won't belabor the situation further, beyond mentioning simply that my own research area is that of sucking behavior in infants.

Sincerely Yours,
Lewis P. Lipsitt
Professor of Psychology and Medical Science;
Director, Child Study Center

Lipsitt began his collection as a way of showing his students what appeared to be a cause-and-effect relationship but was not. He picked on what had been termed "the compulsion of the name," which has been discussed for years. Carl Jung, among others, addressed the issue but, like Lipsitt, missed the cause-and-effect relationship. Jung was nonetheless impressed by the aptness of his own name and that of his colleagues. As he noted in his *Synchronicity: An Acausal Connecting Principle*, "Herr Freud (joy) champions the pleasure principle, Herr Adler (eagle) the will-to-power, Herr Jung (young) the idea of rebirth, and so on."

Jung gave many other examples which demonstrate that once you get hooked hunting for aptronyms it is hard to stop. I have put together a good representative collection, borrowing heavily from others including Dr. Lipsitt and relying on the sharp eyes of friends who spot them for me. The vast majority come from newspapers and telephone books.

It is generally good fun but gets a bit unnerving when you run into those which are horrifyingly apt: Will Drop, a Montreal window cleaner who died in a fall; Dr. Deadman, the city pathologist for Hamilton, Ontario, in the 1930s; and Willburn and Frizzel, who on the grim morning of October 6, 1941, went to the electric chair at the Florida State Prison. Dr. Robert Fry was the physician appointed to make sure that Linwood Briley was dead after his 1984 electrocution at the Virginia State Penitentiary.

Here are selected items from the collection which grows all the time and is fed by a dozen or so helpers who scan newspapers and phone books throughout the English-speaking world looking for examples. I have held with *aptronyms* as the name for this phenomenon rather than *aptonyms*, which is favored by a number of newspaper columnists who collect them. Bob Levey, who pens fairly regular *Washington Post* columns on the phenomenon, calls them PFLNs, or Perfect Fit Last Names.

These are some of the museum quality examples:

Individuals

Identified by positions which they hold now or once held (as these were collected over a long period of time).

A

Fred Allspaugh, animal trainer.

The Reverend Jack Aman.

J. H. Argue, attorney-at-law, Oliver, British Columbia.

Sheila Askew, image consultant.

B

J. T. Ball and N. C. Ball, coauthors of *Joy in Human Sexuality.*

Floyd Baskette and Jack Scissors, coauthors of *The Art of Editing.*

Matt Batts, former major league catcher.

Donald Beavers, star running back for the Oregon State Beavers football team.

I. Bidwell, contractor.

Hiram R. Bird, head of the Poultry Sciences Department at the University of Wisconsin.

Jeffrey Bland, author of *The Junk-Food Syndrome.*

Daniel Boone teaches forest ecology at Johns Hopkins' School of Continuing Studies.

Mary Breasted, author of *Oh! Sex Education.*

John Buckmaster, bank manager, Maryland.

James Bugg, exterminator, not to be confused with **Bob Bugg,** who is an entomologist at the University of California at Davis.

Joe Bunt, baseball coach at Duchess Community College.

B. U. Bury, mortician.

C

James Cabbage, Indiana grocer.

Henry Calamity, an inaptronym, as this man was named the Santa Fe Railroad's "safety man of the month" for March 1969.

Walter Candy, wholesale confectioner.

Edmund Careful, Army driver cited for safety record.

Robert C. Cashmore, investment advisor.

Louis Chase, Oklahoma highway patrolman.

The Cheatham family, midwestern group of seven related individuals arraigned in St. Louis for bank, mail, and bankruptcy fraud.

Philander Claxton, who once ran the State Department's population affairs bureau.

Edward H. Clinkscale, coeditor of *A Musical Offering.*

Thomas Coffey, author of *The Long Thirst.*

Howard Countryman, investigator of passport fraud for the State Department.

George W. Coupe, founder of the Coupe Chevrolet Agency.

Forrest Crabtree, Jr., manager of the Wood Products group, International Paper Co.

Bernard D. Crook, Montgomery County, Maryland, police chief.

Dick Curd, spokesman for the Carnation Milk Company (labeled as one of the greatest aptronyms of all time in the Winter 1989 issue of the *Bulletin of the North Central Name Society*).

Lt. D. C. Current, member of the electrical sciences department at the U.S. Naval Academy. Father's name: A.C.

D

Alan DeFend, Air Force colonel.

George Devine, once chairman of the Religious Studies Department at Seton Hall University.

Art DeWire, electrical contractor, Milford, New Jersey.

Marvin Dime, stamp and coin dealer.

Bill Dollar, accountant.

Elwood "Woody" Driver, former vice chairman of the National Transportation Safety Board.

Hugo W. Druehl, president of a bottled water company.

Dan Druff, Billings, Montana, barber.

Carbon Petroleum Dubbs, perfected oil cracking process.

E

Mr. and Mrs. Easterday, who had a baby on Easter Sunday.

W. L. Edge, author of *The Theory of Ruled Surfaces.*

Oscar Egg, inventor of an oval bicycle frame.

F

Frank Fee, clerk of the Vermont court.

Rollie Fingers, major league pitcher.

Charles J. Fish, professor of marine biology.

Paul Flacks, in charge of public affairs for the Zionist Organization of America.

Priscilla Flattery, EPA publicist.

Seville Flowers, University of Utah botanist.

Hugh Foot, editor of *Pedestrian Accidents.*

Charles R. Forgetsnothing, an unfortunate citizen who was sentenced to six months in jail for forgetting to appear in court, according to a wire service story from 1972.

Robert Furlong, Massachusetts racing commissioner.

G

Richard Gayer, chief legal counsel for a San Francisco gay rights group.

P. J. Gillette, author of the book, *Vasectomy: The Male Sterilization Process.*

Rev. James R. God, minister of the Baptist Church in Congress, South Carolina.

Robert Goodland, the World Bank's environmental chief for South America.

Brick Grunt, rower on the crew of the University of California, Berkeley team.

H

Glenn Hausfater, one of the editors of the book *Infanticide: Comparative and Evolutionary Perspectives.*

Price Hay, Lexington, Kentucky, horse trainer.

Bill Headline, Washington Bureau Chief for Cable News Network.

Julia Heiman, author of the article "The Physiology of Erotica: Women's Sexual Arousal."

Alex Hogg, officer of the American Association of Swine Practitioners.

Roy Holler, Wisconsin auctioneer.

Pat Hunt and Lois Peck, secretaries to the Palmdale, California, city manager.

J

Viking Jerk, Swede who worked for the Nazis.

William Justice, federal judge.

K

T. N. Koffey, a coffee and tea merchant from Brooklyn in business since 1910.

L

Forrest Land, Kentucky real estate salesman.

Keith Level, teacher of surveying and other engineering courses at Santa Barbara City College.

L. Lines, author of *Solid Geometry.*

R. R. Lines, employee of the Union Pacific railroad.

Bob Lucid, chair of the English Department at University of Pennsylvania.

M

Minnie Magazine, for years chief of *Time* magazine's cable desk.

Pave Maginot, contractor and builder.

Bill Mailer, California collector of overdue accounts.

C. Sharpe Minor, an organist.

Marion Gaddis Moon, maiden name of the mother of Colonel Buzz Aldren, the second man on the moon.

J. W. G. Musty, with the British Inspectorate of Ancient Monuments.

N

U. S. Navey, member of the U.S. Marine Corps. His father C.B. Navey had been a member of the Seabees.

Penny Nichols, from Money, Mississippi.

Sam Nikum, barber of Custer, Montana.

P

Soon B. Park, Washington cab driver.

Jerry Penn, stationery store operator.

Rev. Wendell Pew, pastor.

Tom Pipecarver, Princeton, New Jersey, tobacconist.

Rodney Pitchfork, winner of a British hay-tossing competition.

Crymes Pittman, Mississippi attorney.

Frank Plank, Philadelphia coffin maker of yore.

Gary Player, professional golfer.

Royal O. Plenty, financial editor at the *Philadelphia Inquirer* during the 1960s.

Dean Plowman, administrator of the Agricultural Research Service.

Jay A. Posthumas, funeral director.

Money Price, man acquitted of tax evasion charges in 1955.

Dan Printup, Memphis photographer.

Dorothy Projector, formerly in charge of long-range forecasting at the Social Security Administration.

R

John Razor, Covington, Kentucky, barber nicknamed "Safety."

Claire Annette Reed, daughter of a college professor of music.

Dorothy Reading, once an Illinois librarian.

Sally Ride, astronaut. (Lipsitt comments, "She's a two-way winner, because of the Sally forth possibility.")

Earl Risky, Chicago stockbroker.

Ray Roach, office manager of the Ballantyne Pest Control Co. in Chicago.

Louise Rumpp, manager of a diet center.

S

John Scattergood, head of the Pittsburgh Red Cross.

Tony Schinto (pronounced "toe knee shin toe"), soccer coach at New Trier High School in Illinois.

Stanford Schwimmer, Stanford University swimmer.

Elizabeth Shelver of the Minneapolis Public Library.

Violet Silk, seamstress from Houston.

Richard Sincere of the Ethics and Public Policy Center in Washington, D.C.

Paul Sinn, a congregational minister.

Rev. Richard Sinner of Fargo, North Dakota.

Dick Sinnot, former Boston city censor.

Bill Slick, on the board of Exxon.

I. Q. Smart, a resident of Braintree, Massachusetts.

Clinton Smoke, editor of *Fire Command* magazine.

Lt. Col. Will B. Snow, head of the Pentagon's Northern Warfare Training.

R. J. Sparkes, noted volcanologist.

Larry Speakes, spokesman for President Ronald Reagan.

Lake Speed, race car driver.

Tom Stamper, president of the Miami branch of the National Association of Letter Carriers.

T. Steel, New England ironmaster.

Eugene Sunshine, once acting director of the New York State Energy Office's division of conservation.

T

F. G. Tellwright, public relations man.

Lionel Tiger and Robin Fox, authors of *The Imperial Animal.*

Neil Title, Arlington, Virginia, attorney specializing in real estate work.

Rev. J. J. Toogood, rector of Kirkby Overblow, Yorkshire.

Linda Toote, flautist in an orchestra in Florida.

Dick Tracy, once police chief in Corning, California.

Juan Trippe, former head of Pan American Airlines.

Tommy Trotter, once secretary to the New York Racing Association.

Ralph True, lie-detector expert.

M. Turnipseed, assistant at Cornell University's Department of Vegetable Crops.

Valerie Turtle, director of aquatic sports at the University of Massachusetts.

Bernard Twigg, horticulture professor at the University of Maryland.

U

Jerry Usheroff, sergeant-at-arms in a B'nai B'rith chapter.

V

P. J. Vile, in the rubbish removal business.

Richard P. Vine, winemaker for Warner Vineyards in Michigan.

W

Scott Waffle, spokesman for the Internal Revenue Service.

Apt Medical Directory
Novelist Anthony Trollope named a fictional physician Abel Fillgrave, M.D., but that name has nothing on some of the real names, present and past, in the medical community.

A

H. A. Achen, M.D.

Francious Alouf, a psychiatrist.

Fern Asthma, M.D.

B

Joseph Badger, D.V.M.

Mike Basset, D.V.M.

Paul H. Biever, a gynecologist.

M. D. Bonebreak, M.D.

G. E. Bonecutter, M.D.

Sir Ronald Brain, British neuro-physiologist.

C

Leona Couch, a psychiatrist.

Pauline Cutting, British surgeon.

D

William C. Dement, professor of psychiatry.

I(van) Doctor, M.D., optometrist of Ferndale, Michigan.

F

Cutting B. Favour, M.D., specializing in vasectomies in Oakdale, California.

Barry Filler, London dentist with a nurse named Jane Pullam.

Frederick J. Fillmore, D.D.S., from Indiana.

Sherwood B. Fein, M.D., Seattle.

C. B. Footlick, a podiatrist.

Akin Frame, a chiropractor.

O. O. Fuzzy, optometrist.

G

Stephen Glasser, optometrist.

Blayne A. Gumm, D.D.S.

Bedrettin Y. Gunc, M.D.

Herbert K. W. Gutz, M.D.

H

William Hartwell, a cardiologist.

Alex Hogg, D.V.M.

K

O. C. Keener, an optometrist.

William Kinder, M.D., pediatrician, Natick, Massachusetts.

L. Allen Korn, a podiatrist, Bethesda, Maryland.

L

William Lady, a gynecologist.

Coy Lay, M.D., former president of the American Fertility Society.

Ann Looney, a psychologist.

M

Dr. Nancy Mello, specialist in drugs and drug therapy.

Floyd Miracle, M.D., Santa Ana, California.

N

S. W. Needleman, hematologist.

M. D. Nudelman, M.D.

Dr. Edward J. Neveril, M.D., an eye, ear, and throat man.

O

O. O. Oops, M.D., surgeon.

Ralph Organ, M.D.

Zoltan Ovary, gynecologist.

P

Carl J. Paternita, obstetrician.

William G. Payne, M.D.

P. P. Peters, urologist.

Les Plack, a dentist, and the author's candidate for the most apt of all.

Donald Posthumus, a doctor, according to Herb Caen, who is at the same California hospital as Dr. Donald Stiff and Dr. Michael Butcher.

Joseph E. Pulley, D.D.S., along with several Pullens.

R

Frank Redo, M.D., plastic surgeon.

Dan Roach, D.V.M., Edmond, Oklahoma.

Noel Root, a dentist.

S

Charles Shuffle, a podiatrist.

Louis Skinner, a dermatologist.

Robert Skullman, a psychiatrist.

William Slaughter, plastic surgeon.

Harry Smiley, orthodontist.

Louis A. Sorto, was the medical director for the Race America footrace in Chicago in 1984.

Mark Spitz, Olympic medalist and dental student.

Robert Strange, director of the Northern Virginia Mental Health Institute.

Arnold Surgeon, a surgeon.

T

M. A. Tartar, a dentist.

William Toothaker, D.D.S., Pomona, California.

Lacy Leon Toothman, a dentist. (Also, Ronald Toothman.)

Wonderful A. Trembly, a psychologist.

Jeffrey Treadwell, a podiatrist.

W

M. Worms, Ph.D., author of the article "The Needs of a Parasitologist."

This is just a start. In 1981, *Medical Economics* reported that the American Medical Association Directory contained Arms, Bones, Blood, Colon, an Eye, a Finger, a Knee, one Lung, an Ovary, and a Tongue. It also found doctors named Pill, Dose, Gauze, Ill, Heal, Cure, Fees, and Bills. Ten years earlier Richard Armour was able to find Billers, Butchers, Akers, among many others, and a medical book salesman kept a list between 1915-1920 which included an Ill, a Mesick, a Pillmore, an Ayling, and a Bledso. The last list, which appeared in the *Bulletin of the American Name Society*, contained what must be the most unfortunate medical name of all: Inquest Coffin, M.D.

Partnerships and Firms

B

Block and Cleaver, butchers in Kingston, Ontario.

Buckett and Son, Ltd., Southampton plumbers.

Burnham and Overbake, bakers from Newark, New Jersey.

Bury Funeral Home, Buffalo, New York.

C

Coffin and Coffin, landscape architects for Arlington National Cemetery.

Crook Advertising, Dallas.

Crumbie Pipe Tongs, Dallas, an oil well supply company.

D

Diggs and Hurtz, a dental partnership in Columbia, Missouri, in the 1930s.

Drinkard's Water Service, Jefferson City, Missouri.

E

Earthman's, Houston funeral home.

F

Flood Plumbers, whose sign is prominent on the Whitehurst Freeway in Washington, D.C.

G

Goforth and Ketchum, Long Beach, California, patrol car team in the 1950s.

Gummy and Wrecks, a real estate firm advertised on a Point Pleasant, New Jersey, billboard.

H

Drs. Holleran and Yellen, family practice in California's Imperial Valley in the 1930s and 1940s.

House and Son, Estate Agents, Bournemouth, England.

K

Knell Mortuary, Joplin, Missouri.

L

Look and Look, Honolulu optometrists.

M

McNutt, Hurt and Blue, Indianapolis law firm.

Mush and Sons, fruits and vegetables, Dayton, Ohio.

O

O'Neill and Pray, manufacturers of church equipment, Chicago.

P

Poor and Swanke, New York architectural partnership.

S

Schilling and Chilling, Inc., air conditioning and engineering, Indianapolis.

W

Weads Lawn Service, Toledo, Ohio.

Will Crumble and Sons, Memphis plasterers.

There are unlimited opportunities for the collector of aptronyms. James O. Stevenson of Bethesda, Maryland, suggests scanning membership directories for material. Looking at the rolls of the American Fisheries Society he has found two Bass, a Chubb, two Rays, and a Roe, while that of the American Ornithologist's Union contained Birds, Byrds, a Crane, a Finch, six Martins, a Partridge, a flock of Robbins, a Teal, and a Gosling (from Canada). Another variant is to look through law books for gems like *Bologna vs. Weiner* which you will find on page 610, Volume 9, *New York Supplementary Law Reports*.

Also, there are apt meetings and matings which are mostly found in the papers. I have clippings recording the marriage of James Bass and Marie Fish, a Stone-Wacker engagement notice, and a report on an automobile collision between a Dear and a Darling. Herbert H. Paper, who was on the faculty of the University of Michigan in 1953-1957 with Herbert Penzl (pronounced pencil), has written to the author, reporting that he once suggested that they work on a paper together just so the footnotes would read Penzl and Paper, but nothing ever came of it. On the other hand, Austin Tack Wilkie of Charlottesville, Virginia, reports that back in the days

when young women sought Mr. Right, the daughter of Canadian Prime Minister George MacKinnon Wrong (1860-1948) actually married a Mr. Wright.

Perhaps the most fertile area of all has been explored in two papers by Hank Davis of the psychology department at the University of Guelph in Guelph, Ontario. Published in the now-defunct *Worm Runner's Digest*, Davis explored the names of animal behaviorists and concluded, "People who study animal behavior tend to have animal surnames." A few examples from Davis' work: R.C. Albino, A.D. Bass, C. Bird, J. Crane, T.J. Crow, D. Dove, S.W. Duck, N.B. Eales, G. Finch, D.R. Griffin, W.T. Heron, M.S. Katz, R.C. Martin, J. Peacock, P. Rabbitt, H.C. Raven, A.G. Snapper, J.G. Swann, O.L. Tinklepaugh, and T.N. Wiesel.

Dan Druff

Astro-Nomics

Craters, Crannies, and Craft in Space

5

As more and more has been learned about the moon, planets, and other celestial bodies, a name gap has emerged. Craters, mountains, and chasms are being discovered at a faster rate than they can be named. When, for instance, the Soviet *Zond 3* spacecraft first photographed the back of the moon, some 3,500 unnamed features were discovered, and when the American *Pioneer* spacecraft first began mapping Venus, a host of new features emerged. During its 1.8 billion-mile journey, *Voyager 2* discovered 26 previously unknown moons orbiting various planets, including ten circling Uranus—all needing new names.

The group which must deal with this gap is the International Astronomical Union, which meets once every three years or so to give names that are internationally acceptable. Gradually a system has emerged. The outer solar system has retained names from ancient mythology, while large lunar and Martian craters are named for "world famous deceased scientists," and Mercury is reserved for nonscientists, which is why Johann Sebastian Bach and Homer are now the names of craters. Lunar craters are now being named for astronauts and other prominent individuals. In 1988 seven craters were named for the astronauts on the ill-fated *Challenger* shuttle which exploded in 1986. On Mars small craters are named for villages and small towns on earth, which explains why there is a Wahoo crater (named for Wahoo, Nebraska) on the Red Planet. Venus is reserved for female names as well as those of radio and radar scientists and engineers. Asteroids were first named for goddesses, but as more were discovered, all sorts of women's names have been used. A comet, on the other hand, is named for the person who discovers it, whether it be Halley, Kohoutek, or Wilson's for Christine Wilson, a graduate student at California Institute of Technology, who discovered her own comet in 1986.

So much for generalizations. Here are some specific names in space along with the stories behind them:

A

Adonis. One of the many suggested name changes sent in by the public to NASA. The Adonis suggestion occasioned this dry official response: "Thank you for your thoughtful letter…suggesting a change in the name of the earth to Adonis.… We doubt at this late date, the nations of the Earth could ever agree to renaming any of the planets in our solar system."

NASA's files also contain a number of suggestions from VIPs including one from Robert S. McNamara asking that a spot on the moon be named for President John F. Kennedy. Another from a Congressman suggested that the *Apollo 11* spacecraft be named after Kennedy. Not only had the lunar lander already been named "Eagle," but a NASA official pointed out, "We, of course, feel very confident of the success of our mission; however, should anything take place to mar its success, it would fail to enhance the memory of President Kennedy."

Apollo. To date the most famous name in space exploration, it was created by Abe Silverstein, who headed NASA's Space Flight Development Program. According to the official *Origins of NASA Names*, it was proposed because Apollo was a god with "attractive connotations," and it fit the precedent of naming manned spacecraft for mythological gods, which had been set with Project Mercury, which was also named by Silverstein. In a 1969 interview with the *Cleveland Plain Dealer* Silverstein said, "I thought the image of the god Apollo riding his chariot across the sun gave the best representation of the proposed program. So I chose it."

Armstrong Crater. A small lunar crater near the Sea of Tranquility, it is one of the very few officially sanctioned names of a living person. Named for astronaut Neil Armstrong, it was one of a dozen astronaut and cosmonaut names bestowed by the ISU in 1970. The first living woman to have a site named after her was Valentina Nikolayevna-Tereshkova, also the first woman in space.

Aurora 7. One of the original Mercury capsules, it was named by astronaut Scott Carpenter. In the official NASA history of the project, Carpenter says he picked it "because I think of Project Mercury and the open manner in which we are conducting it for the benefit of all as a light in the sky. Aurora also means dawn—in this case the dawn of a new age. The 7, of course, stands for the original seven astronauts." The report adds, "Coincidentally, the astronaut as a boy had lived at the corner of Aurora and Seventh Avenues in Boulder, Colorado."

All of the six Mercury missions were named with the number 7, beginning with *Freedom 7*, which was named by Commander Alan Shepard following the old tradition of pilots naming their aircraft. In addition there were *Liberty Bell 7* (because of the shape of the capsule), *Friendship 7*,

Sigma 7, and *Faith 7*. There was some worry in the space agency that if the last capsule was lost it would set off a spate of "America loses Faith" headlines.

C

Cytherean. The adjective now generally used to describe Venus. It came into play when the first probes were made of Venus in the late 1960s, and astronomers shied away from the logical choice of *venereal* which was too closely associated with human passion. The next logical choice was the Greek *aphrodesian* which had the same sexual overtones. The final choice of *cytherean* came from the island of Cythera from which Aphrodite emerged. Similarly, Carl Sagan pointed out in an article in the *New York Times* that it had been suggested that a Martian volcano be named *Mons Veneris* until he pointed out that it "had been preempted by quite a different field of human activity."

D

The Dogs of Summer. This is the name the astronauts of the 1992 *Endeavour* mission gave themselves, each one taking a dog nickname. *Endeavour* Commander David "Red Dog" Walker showed off a bag of dog food in a news conference 213 miles above earth.

E

Eric Clapton. Name of an asteroid approved by the International Astronomical Union. He is not the only rock 'n' roller in space. In 1990 four asteroids were named for the Beatles. Brian Skiff and Dr. Edward Bowell, Beatles fans, spotted the

EROS

The name given by the Department of the Interior to its Earth Resources Observation Satellites, which, in 1966, it announced it would soon begin launching. It was a mammoth hoax because the Department of the Interior had no way to start its own space program. EROS was meant to embarrass NASA, which then Interior Secretary Stewart Udall thought was dragging its feet in starting a program to observe the earth from space. Even the lusty EROS acronym was clearly meant to provoke NASA, which has always been prudish about names. When NASA finally decided to launch such a satellite in 1970 it gave it the un-erotic name of *ERTS* (for Earth Resources Technology Satellite).

Ironically, the press was taken in by the EROS announcement with, for instance, the *Washington Post* reporting that the satellites would be launched by powerful Thor-Delta rockets. Nobody ever bothered to ask the Interior Department where it would get hold of all the money, know-how, and hardware needed to start this alternative space program.

Finally, NASA decided that ERTS was a terrible name. ("[It] makes me think of all the wrong kinds of things," complained a top NASA official in a memo on the subject.) The search was on for a new one and after rejecting dozens (including Harvest, Prospector, Ecoscan, Cartos, Reaper, Pay Dirt, Yield, Bonanza, Provender, Sunshine, Terrascope, Ecosat, Harbinger, and all sorts of mythological entries like Hermes, Iris, Mammon, Ceres, and even Yum Kaax, a Mayan harvest god) it decided on *Landsat* in 1972.

"Fab Four" asteroids at the Lowell Observatory in Flagstaff, Arizona, in 1982 and 1983.

Eve. One of a number of names on Venus disputed by the National Organization for Women, which objected to it because it was not the name of a real woman. Before NOW objected, the system had reserved large craters and other major features for mythological figures and small craters smaller than 100 kilometers in diameter for real women. In 1980, the IAU arrived at a compromise with NOW and abandoned the practice of naming all of the large craters after mythological women. Under the terms of the compromise real women, such as French novelist Colette, got craters, but the IAU stuck with Eve for symbolic reasons.

Recently with the arrival of the *Magellan* spacecraft's imaging radar, up to 4,000 new features are now being identified on Venus that will need names. In fact, the Jet Propulsion Laboratory in Pasadena, California, and the U.S. Geological Survey office in Flagstaff, Arizona, in 1991 appealed to the world for suggestions.

There are rules here though. Those immortalized on Venus must be dead at least three years. Some features can be named after goddesses of ancient religions and cultures, while craters and volcanic vents are being given historical names. Positively no 19th- or 20th-century political or military figures or women prominent in any of the six main, modern religions are allowed, which would leave out Joan of Arc, the original Madonna, Indira Gandhi, Margaret Chase Smith, Mother Teresa, and Mary Baker Eddy.

G

George. When Sir William Hershel discovered the seventh planet in 1781, he wanted to name it for George III. He was dissuaded, and the planet was called Uranus, after the oldest god in Greek mythology. *George* would be a welcome relief for schoolteachers who have long suffered students who gleefully treat the name as if it were two words.

H

Hell. A lunar plain which was named for Father Maximilian Hell (1720-1792), a Hungarian Jesuit and astronomer. Billy is another crater named for a Jesuit and not a feature named by President Carter for his brother. Because of their early interest in the moon and its features, the Jesuits named a large number of moon sites after their members.

M

Mare. Sea. There are many of these on the dry lunar surface. Many of the names of lunar features date to a star map published in 1651 by Giovanni Riccoli. The large dark blotches on the moon's visible surface were designated as "maria," the Latin word for seas. Eight larger "seas" are readily visible: Mare Imbrium (Rains), Mare Serenitatis (Serenity), Mare Crisium (Crises), Mare Tranquillitatis (Tranquility), Mare Humorum (Moisture), Mare Nubium (Clouds), Mare Fecunditatis (Fertility), and Mare Nectaris (Nectar). There is even a lunar ocean, Oceanus Procellarum (the Ocean of Storms).

The Unsinkable Molly Brown

A rare space nickname, Molly Brown was the name given to the first manned Gemini mission by astronauts Virgil I. Grissom and John W. Young. It came from the musical comedy *The Unsinkable Molly Brown* and was a back-handed reference to the sinking of Grissom's Mercury Redstone spacecraft after splashdown in the Atlantic in 1961. Such levity was not fully appreciated, and NASA announced that henceforth "all Gemini flights should use…official space-craft nomenclature." Molly Brown was, in fact, mild compared to Grissom's other choice. In his book *Gemini*, published shortly after his death, he wrote that the top brass had taken a dim view of his suggestion to call it Titanic.

In an article in *Spaceflight* magazine, Curtis Peebles points out that Grissom actually had a first choice which was Wapasha, the name of the Indian tribe after

which the Wabash River was named. It was pointed out that this would inevitably get it called "The Wabash Cannonball." This made it unacceptable for family reasons because Grissom's father had worked for the Baltimore and Ohio railroad.

The next Gemini flight had an official nickname (American Eagle) which was never used, but it did get called "Little EVA" because it was the first mission on which an American took a walk in space, known technically as EVA for extra vehicular activity.

Much later Apollo astronauts, starting with the flight of *Apollo 9*, were allowed to code name their command and service (CSM) and lunar modules (LM). The code names were Gumdrop (CSM) and Spider (LM) for *Apollo 9* and Charlie Brown and Snoopy for *Apollo 10*. But these lighthearted names did not fit well with the NASA hierarchy, which decided against casual nicknaming, so it was Columbia and Eagle for *Apollo 11*, Yankee Clipper and Intrepid for *Apollo 12*, Odyssey and Aquarius for *Apollo 13*, Kitty Hawk and Antares for *Apollo 14*, Endeavor and Falcon for *Apollo 15*, Casper and Orion for *Apollo 16*, and America and Challenger for *Apollo 17*.

Mt. Olympus. The largest mountain on Mars, which is three times the height of Mt. Everest and aptly named.

MOUSE. In 1953, well before the space age began, a physicist named S. Fred Singer began talking about a pet idea of his for which he created the acronym MOUSE—for Minimal Orbital Unmanned Satellite of Earth. It would orbit the earth and radio back images that would tell us about the world's weather. However, the first U.S. weather satellite, launched in 1960, was not called MOUSE but TIROS for Television and Infrared Observation Satellite.

O

O.S. The name given to a crater by the *Apollo 15* astronauts because, if their spacecraft landed near it, they would have to say "Oh, shucks, we missed." O.S. was situated across a 1,200-foot-deep rill from the intended landing spot, and one presumes that if they had landed there the expletive might have been stronger than "Oh, shucks." O.S. was one of a number of lunar locations named by NASA planners and astronauts during Project Apollo. Other impromptu names included a crater cluster called Weird, a crater named St. George after the wine drunk by Jules Verne's crew before their trip to the moon, and a hazardous area dubbed Spook. The latter came from the crew of *Apollo 16*, which also gave the moon such good-old-boy names as Smoky, Stone Mountain, Flag, and Gator.

In an article about all of this in the *Smithsonian* magazine, Farouk El-Baz of the National Air and Space Museum points out that the IAU legitimized most of these names despite many objections. For instance, the Soviet Union's delega-

tion was not thrilled with a crater named Lara after the heroine of Boris Pasternak's *Dr. Zhivago.*

S

Sea of Moscow. The large bone-dry "seas" of the moon have always been named for states of mind or nature such as Sea of Tranquility and Ocean of Storms. But when the Soviet *Luna 3* discovered two *mare* on the far side of the moon, they asked that one be named the Sea of Moscow. IAU delegates objected until the Soviet representative declared, "Moscow *is* a state of mind."

The custom of calling these dark regions "seas" started with Galileo, who also called the bright highlands "lands."

Shuttle. For more than a decade, NASA wrestled with the fact that it could not warm up to the name "shuttle" for its reusable space plane.

There are dozens of memos and lists of suggestions in the agency's archives documenting the struggle to come up with a better name. A 1974 memo from George Low, NASA Deputy Administrator, says, "Insofar as the Shuttle is concerned, it is clear that we are not communicating what it is and what it does with its name." Names which were officially suggested included Sequoia, Spaceliner, Spacetanker, Pegasus, Astroliner, Hermes, Astroplane, Skylark, Space Clipper, and Sky King. One memo discusses mythological names including Alborak, the winged horse of Ascension, and Chronus, the lord of the universe. Editorialists got into the act, suggesting names like Firebird and Phoenix and, when it fell behind schedule, Turkey. (Some inside NASA took to calling it the Brick Airplane because of its covering of heat shield tiles.)

NASA even went to the public in 1976 with a ballot which listed Shuttle, Astro Ship, Space Clipper, Star Ship, Star Liner, and Space Liner, which netted a clear public preference for Shuttle (58%). The ballot, given to visitors to the Kennedy Space Center and other facilities, had no place for write-in candidates, but people did write other names on the ballot including Space Yo-Yo, The Good Ferry, and The Good Ship Lollipop.

But it had been called the Shuttle from the beginning and that name simply stuck. As best as can be determined, the first reference to a "man-carrying space shuttle" appeared in an article in the *Christian Science Monitor* of December 8, 1959, by staff writer Courtney Sheldon.

The names of the vehicles themselves were taken from famous ships: *Columbia, Challenger, Discovery,* and *Atlantis*.

The one exception was the *Enterprise*, which was originally destined to be called the *Constitution*. But a massive campaign by fans of *Star Trek* who gathered more than 100,000 signatures convinced President Ford to change it to the name of the spaceship in that TV series. Ford overruled NASA, which was not moved by the "trekkies."

Sputnik. The name of the first man-made satellite, which was put into orbit on October 4, 1957. It is an abbreviation of *Iskustvennyi Sputnik Zemli* or "Artificial Fellow Traveler Around the Earth." The name took hold with such immediate strength that Arthur Minton wrote in *Names*, "Thus with the launching of the satellite the Soviets achieved not only a scientific triumph but (possibly more to their surprise) a philological coup in the penetration of English and other languages by *sputnik*."

When the U.S. tried to launch its own satellite on December 6th of the same year as part of Project Vanguard the slender vehicle rose a few feet off the launch platform, shuddered slightly, burst into flames and collapsed. Its tiny 3.2 pound payload was thrown free of the fire and lay on the ground beeping perfectly. With this failure, a whole new collection of names was created by the press, among them Goofnick, Oops-nik, Flopnik, Dudnik, Kaputnik, Puffnik, Stallnik, If-nik, Stay-putnik, Sputternik, and Pfftnik.

Suddenly, the influence of *Sputnik* was everywhere: *kaputnik, beatnik,* and *nudnik* (which was a boring teacher in the slang of the late 50s and not to be confused with a phoodnik, which was a nudnik with a Ph.D.). By 1960 Professor J.B. Rudnyckyj claimed a list of 200 new "-niks" and told the *Chicago Sun-Times* that the nation was in the grips of "nik-itis." It was not until the era of Watergate that we were to see a new name get so much play in such constructions as *Koreagate, Beiruitgate, Briefinggate,* and *Curtsygate*. The latter was the term that was momentarily used to describe a 1981 flap over whether or not the U.S. Chief of Protocol would curtsy for Britain's Prince Charles (she did). A feeble attempt to pin campaign-financing irregularities on Walter Mondale's organization in 1984 was naturally dubbed "Waltergate."

Starscam. The name, along with *Stargate*, given by astronomers to an enterprising scheme launched by the International Star Registry of Toronto by which anyone with $35 cash (or an acceptable credit card) could have a star named after them. For that sum you get a certificate establishing the new name and a chart on which the star is marked. In addition the name is recorded in a book "copyrighted by the Library of Congress." The Library of

Congress has termed this heavily advertised plan one of its "worst headaches" because it is in no way condoned by the Library. Another outfit, Name a Star Immortality, Inc. of Tarzana, California, linked a similar scheme to the Harvard-Smithsonian Astrophysical Observatory's Star Catalog. The Smithsonian complained to the postal service which in turn threatened to cut off the outfit's mail if it didn't take the Smithsonian out of its ads.

The names are of course *not* accepted by the International Astronomical Union, and several astronomical societies have warned consumers not to be taken in by this bid for immortality. Stars in the IAU scheme of things are all numbered although a few, such as Barnard's Star, are known informally by names. Some are far from romantic. Quoting an article in the *Wall Street Journal* on star names, we find "Alpheratz, in the constellation Andromeda, is Arabic for 'the horse's navel.'

Bright-red Betelgeuse is Arabic for 'armpit of the central one.'"

It seems though that the appeal of getting one's name aloft is still a potent one. In 1994 the Nieman Marcus department store chain took bids starting at $100,000 to paint a couple's name in foot-high letters on the nose of a new United Airlines Boeing 777. The names were to stay on the plane for a year, and the couple would get a year's worth of unlimited first-class travel. Any amount paid over $100,000 would be donated to charity.

T

Titania and Oberon. The queen and king of faeries in Shakespeare's *A Midsummer Night's Dream* and the name of two moons of Uranus. Traditionally all the moons of Uranus have had names from Shakespeare and Pope. When newly discovered moons were named in 1988, they included Juliet and Puck.

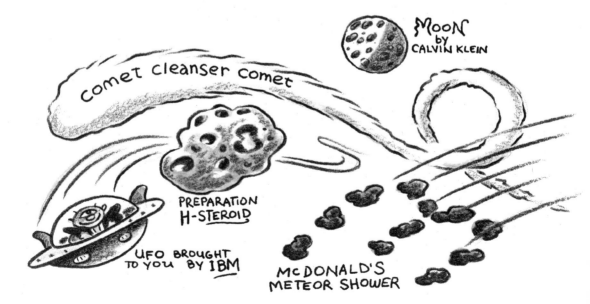

Ballot Names

None of the Above and Other Candidates for Public Office

6

Time was when politicians had great nicknames. These were big, blustery nick-names that usually appeared on the ballot in parentheses in the middle of the candidate's real name. But that has all changed in this era of image consultants and blow-dried hair. Some still have good names, but you have to look for them in those corners of the country where the tradition is still alive. One such place is Louisiana, where candidates deep into the 1980s and 1990s have included men with such ballot names as "Needlenose," "Dookie," "Hamburger," "Goat," "Cow," and "Cookie."

In Texas a good nickname is part of the strategy for winning local office. In April 1995, the *Dallas Morning News* ran an article entitled, "Names of the game: Candidates hope their monikers bring votes," which told of current ballot names like Norris "Stretch" Rideaux, J.W. "Toady" Bearden, and Chuck "Hatchet" Beatty (a former play-er for football's St. Louis Cardinals and Pittsburgh Steelers who got the nickname for his tackling style).

One of the best examples of the unembarrassed nickname is C.W. "Runt" Bishop, an Illinois Congressman who, in the late 1940s, claimed he was the only member of either house to have his nickname on the brass nameplate on his office door. In 1948, when "Runt" was up for reelection, the Illinois ballot also contained such nicknames as

"Coffee Joe," "Butch," "Jellyroll," "Boots," and "Pitt Shoes." One of the few without a nickname was Carl Pretzel.

Even if ballot names have become pretty tame of late, there are occasional wild exceptions such as the following:

B

Bananas the Clown. Les E. Johnson attempted to run for the Salt Lake City council under this name in the 1970s. Despite his argument that "It wouldn't be unprecedented for a clown to be in city government," the city attorney's office denied him the colorful ballot name.

E

E. Z. Million. The real name of a candidate for the Oklahoma legislature in 1968.

Edward T. Indigo. One of a group of names which appear each election on the demonstration ballot—that is, the one used to show the working of the voting machines—when the author goes to vote on Election Day in Montgomery County, Maryland. Since 1984 Indigo has been running for president along with John W. Gray, Thomas W. Scarlet, and Benjamin Ebony, who was from Putting Green, North Dakota. The perennial choice for Senate is between Alonzo Azure and Charlotte Chartreuse. Bertram Bronze, Geraldine Gold, and Steven J. Silver are eternally running for the House, while those running for the Board of Education are Bruce M. Begonia, Rhoda Dendron, Francine Fern, George Geranium, Patsy Jean Pansy, and Terrence Tulip.

G

Gary Hart. It was originally Gary Hartpence, and his reason for changing it actually became an issue in the 1984 presidential primaries. He said he had done it when he was embarking on a political career in 1961 because Hart was easier to say and spell, but that was not enough for those who saw in it some underlying character flaw. Nobody batted an eyelash when, for example, it was revealed that David Dwight Eisenhower had rearranged his name. In her *Washington Post* column Judy Mann said that Hartpence "was a perfect name for a Dickens crook, but not for the U.S. Senate." (She also said that Fritz Mondale sounded like "a broken appliance.")

J

John Calvin Coolidge. One of a number of politicians who have run and served with their middle names. Besides Coolidge, there was Stephen Grover Cleveland and Thomas Woodrow Wilson. Ulysses Simpson Grant was christened Hiram Ulysses Grant but changed it to Ulysses Simpson Grant. The S in Harry S Truman stood for nothing at all, which meant for a long time it was commonly written without a period. When Barry Goldwater ran against the Johnson-Humphrey Ticket in 1964, he insisted on calling the vice presidential candidate by the full name of Hubert Horatio Humphrey. Not only did Humphrey refrain from calling the senator from Arizona by his full name, Barry Morris Goldwater, but finally gamely insisted that he liked being called Horatio.

N

Newt Gingrich. The Speaker of the House from Georgia, who is one of a number of politicians who, over the years, have insisted on being called by a shortened first name on the ballot and in the press. Others who have built careers on clipped names include Jimmy Carter, Sam Nunn, Pete Domenici, Joe Biden, Bill Brock, Al Gore, Sam Ervin, Phil Gramm, Mike Mansfield, Bob Dole, and Bill Clinton.

Dan Rapoport, a writer who has looked into such things, says that once you get an eye on the presidency your name tends to shorten. Robert Dole becomes Bob Dole, Albert Gore becomes Al Gore and so forth.

None of the Above. Luther Devine Knox had his name legally changed to this in order to run in the Louisiana gubernatorial election in 1979. The courts ruled he could not have this name on the ballot as it was "deceptive." Knox said that he took this action because he felt that voters should have a chance to reject traditional candidates in favor of "none of the above."

"None of the above" has done better elsewhere. In 1990 this name came in second in a Nevada Democratic primary with eight percent of the vote. "None of the above" appears on all Nevada ballots as a means of voter protest. A long-shot hopeful who changed his name to Rhinestone Cowboy ran third with 2,308 votes, or three percent.

P

Pat "Family Farmer" O'Reilly. This man won two Congressional elections from Minnesota with this middle name. However, when a woman attempted to use "Prolife" as her middle name in another Minnesota race in 1984, she was told by the courts that she could not use the middle name.

R

Rebecca Robot. An attempt was made to run a robot with this name in the 1984 presidential election by a group claiming that such a candidate would help prepare Americans to live in the world of high technology.

Richard Nixon. Once ran and won as a Waukegan, Illinois, alderman and also raised eyebrows when he, a relative of a Carter administration staff member, was invited to the Carter inaugural. Another Richard Nixon was arrested in Pittsburgh in 1976 for suspected possession of marijuana. Because the arresting officer was named George Washington, the Associ-

ated Press prefaced the story on the arrest with the notation that it was no joke. At the time of the arrest, according to the AP, Washington's usual partner, officer Benjamin Franklin, was home sick.

Robert A. Taft. Would his name have been a liability if he had been elected president when the trend existed to refer to presidents by all three initials? The fad seems to have started with FDR and ended with LBJ, although the initials for First Lady Hillary Rodham Clinton—HRC—have seen some editorial use. Come to think of it, Grant's original name—Hiram Ulysses Grant—would not have done for a general.

S

Sister Boom Boom. One of a number of wild names which forced the San Francisco Board of Supervisors in 1983 to outlaw loony names from the ballot. In 1982 such names as Jello Biafra, James Bond Zero, and Sister Boom Boom had appeared on the ballot for mayor, and names like Artaurus Hamilton 20, Crown Prince Arcadia, and Ronnie B. Foxy were filing for the next election. The need for the law was in part predicated on the fact that Sister Boom Boom attracted 23,121 votes—more than some legitimate candidates.

T

Tarquin Fintimlinbinwhinbimlin Bus Stop-F'Tang-F'Tang-Ole-Biscuit-Barrel. John Desmond Lewis made this his legal name when he ran as a British parliamentary candidate of the Raving Looney Society of Cambridge in 1981. He had done this for two reasons: to set a new record for the least number of votes ever cast in a British election and to have his new name read on television by the Lord Mayor. He attracted 233 votes, far above the mere 20 which was the record, and the name was shortened on TV to "Mr. Tarquin Biscuit-Barrel." Better luck next time. The name, by the way, comes from a Monty Python routine about such a candidate.

U

Uriah Heep-partiet. A Swedish political party with one member. In Sweden the law permits one to write in a party name in parliamentary elections. In the 1991 election there were more than 1,700 parties written in. Some were serious, others questionable. The list as published in the newspaper *Svensk Dagbladet* included: Arnold Schwarzenegger, Bananapartiet, Bart Simpson, Big Brother Party, Cats is mor fun, Cowboy o indianpartiet, Dart Vader, Heavy-matalpartiet, Inkompetens-parti, LSD-partiet, Nobody, Partiet-partiet, Pruttpartiet (the fart party), Robin Hood, Ted Bundy Partiet, and this one: The union of killer pepperonis and mystical girls.

Ballpark Figures

A Baseball Hall of Names

7

The "Babe"

Some names were just meant for baseball. Ernie Banks used to list names fit only for sluggers: Babe Ruth, Mickey Mantle, Harmon Killebrew, Frank Howard, and Ron Swoboda—the name, according to columnist George Vecsey, that Banks "most liked to roll around on his tongue . . . worth 500 home runs in itself, or so it seemed at the time."

It would seem then that many players have fine given names and need no nickname beyond their real name or a natural modification of what appeared on a birth certificate. This is the case with Mel Ott, Reggie Jackson, Rickey Henderson, Maury Wills, Rod Carew, Pete Rose, Lou Brock, Willie McCovey, Darryl Strawberry, Cal Ripken, Jr., and too many others to mention. Ripken's lack of a nickname has been cause for comment. "It's too late now," wrote Phil Jackman in the *Baltimore Sun* on the eve of Ripken's streak of 2,131 consecutive games, "but in keeping with the old-fashioned values Ripken has always brought to baseball, it's strange a nickname was never hung on him. About 80 percent of old ballplayers had nicknames."

Others get just the right touch with the addition of a perfect, tidy nickname. This is clearly the case with Catfish Hunter, Boog Powell, Ty Cobb, Cy Young, Rusty Staub, Sparky Lyle (whose real name is Albert), and Tug McGraw (who insists that his nickname is a throwback to his days as a breastfeeder). Some have been given great baseball names, as Lawrence Peter Berra was turned into "Yogi," Dorrel Norman Elvert Herzog to "Whitey," and the late Alfred Manuel Martin to "Billy."

As many baseball columnists have discovered on slow days, the nicknames are a show in themselves—that is, if one is fascinated with monikers on the order of Bow Wow Arft, Biddie McPhee, Turkey Mike Donlin, Swish Nicholson, Inky Strange, Inch Gleich, Coyote Wet, Foghorn Myatt, Easter-Egg Head Shellenback, Bitsy Mott, Pebbles Glasscock, Possum Belly Whitted, Hooks Wiltse, Piano Legs Gore, Piano Legs Hickman, Bunions Zeider, Slewfoot Butler, Orator O'Rourke, Oyster Tommy Burns, Sea Lion Hall, Pinky Hargrave, Fats Fothergill, Stubby Overmire, Bama Rowell, Arky Vaughan, Popeye Mahaffey, Boob McNutt, Moose Dropo, Four-Sack Dusak, Buttermilk Tommy Dowd, Trolly Line Butler, Ding-a-Ling Clay, Buttercup Dickerson, Battleship Gremminger, Boardwalk Brown, Heinie Meine, Chicken Wolf, Phenomenal Smith, Jumbo Shoeneck, Lollypop Killefer, Sweetbreads Bailey, Beartracks Javery, Bullet Joe Bush, Childe Harold Janvrin, Frosty Bill Duggleby, Nemo Munns, Mountain Music Melton, Poll Perritt, Sabu Schuster, Unser Choe, Zorie Rhem, Tarzan Parmelee, True Gun Hart, Ginger Beaumont, Ubbo Ubbo Hornung, Cannonball Titcomb, and Dandelion Pfeffer.

Names are terribly important to baseball, a point that is underscored in Robert Coover's remarkable novel *The Universal Baseball Association: J. Henry Waugh, Prop.* In the book Henry Waugh creates imaginary teams staffed with players with names like Rag Rooney and Sycamore Flynn. "Henry was always careful about names," wrote Coover, "for they gave the league its sense of fulfillment and failure, its emotion." Later in the book, Coover added, "Names had to be chosen, therefore, that could bear the whole weight of perpetuity."

So it is in the real world. In fact, some names have such impact that they tend to be recalled long after the player's field performance is forgotten. This is true of those rich, hot fudge sundae names like Sibby Sisti, Van Lingle Mungo, Debs Garms and Snuffy Sternweiss. Add to these, names of more recent vintage like Blue Moon Odom, Oil Can Boyd, Storm Davis, and T-Bone Shelby.

There are precious few T-Bones and Oil Cans these days because baseball nicknames seem to be in decline. The impression one gets is that there just aren't as many and the nicknames themselves aren't as colorful. Several theories have been advanced to explain this. C.C. Johnson Spink of the *Sporting News* concluded in 1979 that "The higher a man goes up in the economic scale, the less likely he is to have a nickname. . . . It's that way in baseball . . . now that the players have become big money men." Spink suggested the proper new nickname was "Mister." Another theory which has been bandied about is that they went into decline beginning in 1960 when Bill Veeck first started putting names on the back of uniforms and nicknames weren't needed anymore to help remember players.

Perhaps the most ambitious theory on the decline of baseball nicknames appeared in an article in the *Journal of Sport Behavior* by James K. Skipper, Jr. After demonstrating the decade-by-decade decline, he suggests that it may demonstrate a shift in American society from a *gemeinschaft* model, characterized by a sense of solidarity, to a *gesellschaft* model, characterized by mobility and individualism.

Writing in the *Sporting News,* John Schulian has not only decried the decline of nicknames but also the fall of given names like Enos and Purnal. "It's a pity," he writes, but "what else is there to expect now that the children of the Spock generation are having children of their own? Most of these sensitive creatures would no sooner name a son Vada or Slater than they would wade in quicksand."

All of this is not to say no good given names are coming along or that no new nicknames are being bestowed. A 1980 press release from the Seattle Mariners for instance lists a nickname for almost every member of the team, ranging from such fairly traditional monikers as "Woody," "Blade," "Zelmo," and "Honey" to "Beldar," named for the famed "Saturday Night Live" Conehead, and "Larry, but they call him Larry." The last example was the nickname given for Larry Cox because they say he looks like Larry Fine of the Three Stooges, but was already named Larry. When Gaylord Perry went to the same team late in his long career, he was immediately dubbed "The Ancient Mariner."

But press department sobriquets seldom stick unlike those that come from the locker rooms and press boxes. Ironically, team press offices may be alone in the public relations business in that they regularly issue press releases which make fun of their clients through unflattering nicknames. It is from a 1977 official Kansas City Royals press release that one learns, for instance, that George Brett's nickname was "Mullet-head" and that third base coach Chuck Hiller was called "Hitler." Indeed. This is an abomination which ranks with that of *Sports Illustrated* trying

some years back to hang "Teddy Ballgame" on Ted Williams or *Sporting News* trying to give Ken Oberkfell the nickname "Kayo" while he was still in the minors.

Press agentry aside, there may be another factor at work in the "decline" of the baseball nickname and that is the reluctance of the writers and sportscasters to bring them to the public. In an unsigned article in the 1978 *Toronto Blue Jays Scorebook* entitled "Whatever Happened to Nicknames?" it is concluded, "Most of today's ballplayers carry nicknames, but writers are often too sophisticated, delicate, or unimaginative to publicize them." The article goes on to point out that in the Toronto clubhouse—as opposed to the press office—you are likely to hear names like Buzz, Target, Tarzan, Rocky, The Beeg Mon, Marv, Monk, Sarge, and Bombo.

But beyond all of this the game has a penchant for titling things—people, places, and things. The game creates a seemingly endless and mellifluous list of titles, honorifics and, for the lack of a better term, *noms de press.* The players called Walter Johnson "Barney," but it was the press that called him "Big Train." Any good sportswriter can work a few of these into one great sentence: "Rocket Robert's legal stuff is as formidable as the Great Scott's suspect stuff." (Tom Boswell, the *Washington Post,* October 18, 1986)

The most important single thing to have happened to nicknames of late is the emergence of ESPN announcer Chris "I'll Never Be Your Beast of" Berman, who has created atrocious punning monikers for baseball players. The best of the lot: Burt "Be Home" Blyleven, John "Tonight, let it be" Lowenstein, Eddie "Eat, drink and be" Murray, Von "Purple" Hayes, Julio "Won't you let me take you on a sea"

Cruz, Frank Tanana "Daiquiri," Carlos "One if by land, two if by sea, and three if" Baerga, and Jim "Two silhouettes on" Deshaies.

In 1994, when his book *Chris Names* was published and the long baseball strike was taking hold, Mark Hyman of the *Baltimore Sun* asked Berman about his one-man revival of the baseball nickname.

Q: Was there a "first" nickname, and who was on the receiving end?

A: Either Frank Tanana "Daiquiri" or John Mayberry "RFD," only because both go back to Brown [University], where I was at school. Both found their way onto the air in the summer of 1980, at about 3 o'clock in the morning.

Q: Do players ever get upset with you for dreaming up nicknames they don't like or find insulting for some reason?

A: Not really, because none is derogatory. There are no Mike "Dim" Witt(s). Nothing like that. Not even one or two out of 800. At an All-Star Game, Kevin "Bigmouth" Bass approached me and, with a big smile, said the nickname made him sound like a big complainer. So, we changed it, to "Smallmouth" Bass.

Q: With labor problems so much in the news, are you coming up with nicknames for the negotiators, starting with players union leader Donald Fehr?

A: How about, Don "The only thing to Fehr is Don himself" Fehr?

Q: And owners negotiator Dick Ravitch?

A: Ravitch . . . Ravitch. I'll have to tinker with that. Hopefully, the owners won't "Ravitch" the game.

And now, a collection of pre-Berman classics:

A

Alex the Great. Grover Cleveland Alexander.

The All-American Out. Leo Durocher, so dubbed by Babe Ruth according to Durocher in *Nice Guys Finish Last*. Later applied to a number of players including Jerry Koosman.

The Amazing Mays. Willie Mays.

The Amazing Rickey Machine. Rickey Henderson.

The American Peasant. Umpire George Pipgras.

The Ancient Mariner. Gaylord Perry, who got it when he went to the Seattle Mariners late in his career. Red Smith also put the handle on an older Rabbit Maranville "because of the way he hopped around the infield gathering grounders."

The Apache. Howard Nunn.

The Apollo of the Box. Tony Mullane.

The Arkansas Hummingbird. Lon Warneke.

The Arkansas Traveler. Travis Jackson.

Arriba! Roberto Clemente.

The Astoria Eagle. Hughie McQuillan.

B

Babe Ruth—Fred Lieb, the great baseball writer, once wrote of this nickname, "Babe went as naturally with Ruth as ham goes with eggs." There were several explanations for how Ruth got the name but Lieb said that Ruth told him that it had started when he was a young lad taken to St.

Mary's School in Baltimore. "Some of the older kids picked on him," Lieb reported. "He did considerable crying, so they called him Babe." Yet there is evidence that Ruth was not Babe on the field. As Tristram Potter Coffin points out in his book on the folklore of baseball, *The Old Ball Game,* Ruth "was called 'Jidge' by most of his teammates and 'The Big Monk' or 'Monkey' by most of his opponents."

Babe Ruth's Legs. Sammy Byrd, who was a defensive replacement for the Babe.

The Baby Bull. Orlando Cepeda.

Baby Cakes. Jim Palmer, an allusion to his Jockey shorts ads, say many, but it predated the ads, and it refers to his love of pancakes.

The Bad Boy of the Diamond. Don Black.

Bad Henry. Hank Aaron, from a time when bad meant good, but mainly because he was bad for pitchers. The name was hung on him by Sandy Koufax according to Dan Schlossberg in *The Baseball Catalog.*

The Barber. Sal Maglie.

The Barnum of the Bushes. Joe Engel.

The Base Burglar. Lou Brock.

Baseball's Man of the Hour. Ralph Kiner.

Baseball's Quiet Man. Bill Dickey.

Bay's Ball. The 1989 World Series.

The Beast. Jimmy Foxx.

The Beloved Bums. The Brooklyn Dodgers.

Big Ben. Larry Bearnarth.

The Big Bear. Fred Hutchinson.

Big Blue. The Los Angeles Dodgers.

The Big Cat. Johnny Mize because of his grace and fluid movement.

The Big Donkey. Frank Thomas.

Big Ed. Ed Delahanty.

Big Mac. *The Macmillan Baseball Encyclopedia.*

The Big Mon. Rico Carty.

The Big Moose. Edward Walsh.

The Big O. Bob Oliver.

Big Poison/Little Poison. Paul Waner along with his brother Lloyd. The lore of the game insists that the brothers got these names as someone with the sound of Brooklyn in their voice referred to them as "big person" and "little person." Although almost identical in size, Paul was three years older, making him Big Poison. Others insist that Big Poison was a simple reference to the fact that Paul batted between .321 and .373 during his first dozen seasons.

The Big Red Machine. The Cincinnati Reds during any year beginning with the numbers 197.

Big Sam. Samuel Thompson.

Big Six. Sobriquet of Christy Mathewson, with several different explanations, including that of a powerful typographical trade union known as the Big Six and a famous horse-drawn fire engine of the era known as the "Big Six." Writer Frank Graham, however, studied the matter and concluded that it came from an exchange something like this:

> *First player: How big do you think that big kid is?*
>
> *Second player: Six feet.*
>
> *First player: He's the biggest six you ever saw—a big six.*

The Big Train. Sobriquet of the powerful Walter Johnson, not to be confused with Rufus "Big Train" Johnson. Walter's nickname seems to have been created by Grantland Rice, who wrote in 1922, "The Big Train comes to town today."

Bijou of the East. Fenway Park.

Billy Buck. Bill Buckner.

Billy the Kid. Billy Martin.

The Bird. Mark Fidrych because he cut a figure like Big Bird of *Sesame Street* fame.

The Black Babe Ruth. Josh Gibson.

The Black Ty Cobb. James "Cool Papa" Bell.

Black Magic. Satchel Paige.

The Black Matty. Satchel Paige, an allusion to Christy Mathewson.

Bleacher Bums. Cubs fans in the cheap seats.

The Blimp. Babe Phelps.

Blue Moon. John Odom. "His boyhood friends nicknamed him 'Moon' because of his moon-shaped faced," says Mike Whiteford in *Talking about Baseball*. "Later his professional teammates embellished the nickname to 'Blue Moon' because he often appeared downcast."

Boilin' Boily. Burleigh Grimes.

Boom Boom. Walter Beck who, according to Lee Allen in *The Hot Stove League*, acquired it "one day at the old Baker Bowl in Philadelphia when ball after ball boomed off his delivery and hit the tin of the right field fence."

The Boomer. George Scott.

The Bones Battery. Catcher Connie Mack and pitcher Frank Gilmore, two tall, skinny guys, who worked together in the 1880s.

Born to be a Met. Marvin Eugene Throneberry, whose initials are MET.

The Boston Massacre. The Red Sox' 1978 fade.

Bots Nekola—In a booklet at the Hall of Fame entitled *Ballplayers' Nicknames*, Bots is singled out as one of a handful of baseball nicknames that have stuck to only one player. Others: Cuke Barrows, Ott Stein, Ubbo Ubbo Hornung, Weaser Scoffic, Wock Williams, and Yock Lumley.

The Boy Manager. a. Stanley Harris. b. Lou Boudreau on taking over the Indians.

The Boy Wonder. a. Bucky Harris for managing the Senators to a pennant at age 27. b. Johnny Bench.

The Brat. Eddie Stanky.

The Brew. Harmon Killebrew.

The Broadcaster. Tommy Byrne for his running commentary during games in which he played.

The Bronx Bombers. Traditional sobriquet of the New York Yankees.

The Bronx Zoo. The Yankees since the 1979 book of the same title.

Brother Lo. John Lowenstein.

Bucketfoot Al. Al Simmons.

Buffalo Head. Don Zimmer. See **Loyal Order of …**

The Bull. Greg Luzinski.

Bullet Bob. Bob Feller.

Buy a Vowel. Kent Hrbek.

Bye-Bye. Steve Balboni, who got it when he was hitting homers with great frequency in the minors but soon saw its limitation. Still in the minors, he told *The Sporting News*, "Every time I strike out or fly out you can hear them yelling bye-bye.

I can't seem to stop it so I'm going to quit trying."

C

The Capital Punisher/Capital Punishment. Frank Howard, as a Washington Senator slugger.

Captain Carl. Carl Yastrzemski.

Captain Hook. Sparky Anderson for his reliance on relief pitchers during his years as Reds' manager.

Captain Midnight. Lee Walls.

Casey's Little Bobo. An early Billy Martin.

The Chairman of the Board. Whitey Ford, a name given to him by Elston Howard according to Ford in *Slick*.

The Champ. Harold "Pee Wee" Reese, who was a marbles champ as a kid.

Charlie Hustle. Pete Rose. According to George Vecsey, the *New York Times* July 26, 1985, the title was bestowed on a "sultry Sunday afternoon in Tampa, Florida, in 1963 when two Yankees watched him run during an exhibition." Vecsey continued, "Ah, but the reader already knows that the two fat-cat Yankees, guffawing at the intense rookie, were Whitey Ford and Mickey Mantle."

The Chief. Allie Reynolds, because he was part Creek Indian.

Choke vs. Clutch. The traditional outcome of key series between the Boston Red Sox and the New York Yankees.

Circus Solly. Art Hoffman.

The Clouting Cossack. Lou Novikoff.

The Clown Prince of Baseball. Al Schacht.

The Cobra. Dave Parker who, according to Mike Whiteford in *Talking about Baseball*, got the name because "His coiled batting stance reminded Pirate announcer Bob Prince of a cobra."

The Colonel. Jim Turner.

Columbia Lou. Lou Gehrig.

The Commerce Comet/The Commerce Kid. Mickey Mantle.

The Count. John Montefusco.

Country. Enos Slaughter. To many older baseball fans this ranks as one of the all-time great baseball names along with Virgil "Fire" Trucks and Wilmer "Vinegar Bend" Mizell.

Cousin Ed. Ed Barrow.

The Crab. Jesse Burkett and John Evers.

Crazy Horse. Tim Foli.

The Cricket. Bill Rigney.

The Cry Baby Indians. The 1940 Cleveland Indians who had petitioned the front office to remove manager Ossie Vitt, who the players contended had been mean to them. The team became the laughingstock of the American League and attracted other nicknames including **The Bawl Team** and **The Half Vitts.**

Cy Old. Jim Palmer after winning the Cy Young Award for the third time.

Cy Young—His real name was Denton True Young and Cy was short for Cyclone. Over the years there have been a number of Cy's up to the "Cy Clone" handle attached to Baltimore Oriole Storm Davis because of his resemblance to Cy Young Award-winning pitcher Jim Palmer.

D

The Daffiness Boys. The Brooklyn Dodgers ca. 1936 and the Dean Brothers.

Daddy Wags. Leon Wagner.

Dapper Dan. Dan Howley.

The Dazzler. Arthur Charles Vance.

The Dead End Kid. Pepper Martin.

The Dead Sox. The Red Sox when the offense is failing.

The Dean. Chuck Tanner.

Dear Old Roger. Roger Connor.

Death to Flying Things. Jack Chapman and Robert V. Ferguson.

Dem Bums. Sobriquet of the Brooklyn Dodgers.

Dr. K. Dwight Gooden.

Dr. No. Chuck Hiller.

Dr. Strangeglove. Dick Stuart, whose defensive abilities did not rank with his ability as a hitter.

Double X. Jimmy Foxx, supposedly because he was listed in early scorecards with a single X.

Dreamer's Month. March because, as Bob Uecker puts it in *Catcher in the Wry,* "in March, on paper, every team looks stronger than it did a year ago."

Ducky Medwick—His real name was Joe, and he was one of the 1934 St. Louis Cardinals a.k.a. "The Gashouse Gang," which included such well-named gents as Rip Collins, Dizzy Dean, Pepper Martin, Spud Davis, Lippy Leo Durocher, Tex Carlton, and Wild Bill Hallahan. At about the same time the Detroit Tigers fielded a team with such greats as Flea Clifton, Hot Potato Hamlin, Chief Hogsett, General Crowder, Goose Goslin, Hammering Hank Greenberg, and Firpo Marberry. Medwick, by the way, never liked the name "Ducky," but it stuck and there was nothing he could do about it.

The Duke of Flatbush. Duke Snider, who got the name Duke as a kid.

The Duke of Milwaukee. Al Simmons.

The Duke of Tralee. Roger Bresnahan.

The Durable Dutchman. Lou Gehrig.

Dusty Rhodes—One of a bunch of those guys whose nicknames came as naturally as Sad for Sams and Professor or Specs for players with glasses. Similarly, Collinses have tended to be called Rip, and Gordons, Flash. Time was when all players of Teutonic descent named Henry became Heinie and before World War II it was common to dub big lefthanded pitchers Rube—Rube Waddel, Rube Marquard, Rube Benton, and Rube Walberg who was also known as Swede. There were others named Swede, as well as Greeks, Frenchys, and more than a couple Dutches who took their name from the German name for the Fatherland, "Deutschland." Players with M.D.'s or D.D.S.'s got called "Doc" as in the cases of Al "Doc" Bushong, Mike "Doc" Powers and others. Particularly skinny guys tended to get called "Blade" or "Slats," and if your name was Campbell, they would call you "Soupy."

E

Elmer the Great. Walter Beck.

Eye Chart. Doug Gwosdz.

The Earl of Baltimore. Earl Weaver.

The Earl of Snohomish. Earl Torgeson.

The $11,000 Lemon. Rube Marquard because of his poor showing just after being purchased by the Giants for what was a staggering sum in 1908.

El Espirador. Mario Mendoza. The vacuum cleaner in English and a reference to his ability at shortstop.

F

The Father of Black Baseball. Rube Foster, who organized the first Negro League.

The Father of the Curveball. William "Candy" Cummings.

Fifth Avenue. Lyn Lary.

The First. Jackie Robinson.

The Flying Dutchman. Honus Wagner.

The Fordham Fireman. Johnny Murphy, one of the first great relief pitchers.

The Fordham Flash. Frankie Frisch, a Fordham graduate and one of the rare college graduates of his era in baseball.

The Fowlerville Flailer. Charlie Gehringer.

Frankie the Crow. Frank Crosetti for his chatter.

Fred Flintstone. Fred Gladding.

The Freshest Man on Earth. Arlie Latham.

The Friendly Confines. Wrigley Field.

G

The Gashouse Gang. Sobriquet of the St. Louis Cardinals in the 1930s, especially the 1934 St. Louis Cardinals, an aggregation which also included such well-named gents as Ducky Medwick, Rip Collins, Dizzy Dean, Pepper Martin, Spud Davis, Lippy Leo Durocher, Tex Carlton and

Wild Bill Hallahan. See also **Ducky Medwick.**

The Gause Ghost. Joe Moore of Gause, Texas.

The Gentle Giant. Ted Kluszewski.

Gentleman Jim. Jim Lonborg.

The Georgia Flash. Ty Cobb.

The Georgia Ghost. Ty Cobb.

The Georgia Peach. Sobriquet of Ty Cobb.

Gettysburg Eddy. Edward Plank.

The Glider. Ed Charles.

The Gliding Panther of Second Base. Napoleon Lajoie.

The Good Humor Man. Roy Campanella.

El Goofy. Vernon Lefty Gomez.

Gooney Bird. Don Larsen.

Gorgeous George. George Sisler.

The Grand Old Man of Baseball or **The Grand Old Man.** Connie Mack. This was sometimes shortened to GOM.

Le Grand Orange. Rusty Staub.

The Gray Eagle. A prematurely gray Tris Speaker.

The Great. Art Shires.

The Great Agitator. Billy Martin.

The Great Dean. Dizzy Dean.

The Great Gabbo. Frank Gabler. In *High and Inside,* Joseph McBride says that the name was adapted from the name of the novel by F. Scott Fitzgerald.

The Great One. Roberto Clemente.

Great Scott. George Scott.

The Great Wall. See **The Green Monster.**

The Greatest Day in the Baseball Year. Induction Day at Cooperstown.

The Green Monster. The great wall in the left field at Fenway Park.

The Griffmen. Clark Griffith's Washington Senators.

The Grounded Blimp. Babe Phelps, who was simply the **Blimp** before he refused to fly.

H

Hairs vs. Squares. The 1969 World Series.

Half-Pint. George Rye.

Hammerin' Hank. a. Hank Bauer. b. Hank Aaron. c. Hank Greenberg.

Hankus-Pankus. Hank Greenberg.

Happy Jack. John Chesbro.

Harry the Cat. Harry Brecheen.

Harry the Hat. Harry Walker.

Harry the Horse. Harry Danning.

The Hatchet. Umpire Ken Kaiser.

The Heavenly Twins. Tommy McCarthy and Hugh Duffy.

High Pockets. George Kelly. Damon Runyon pinned this nickname on Kelly, the former New York first baseman, because he had to reach high for his shirt-pocket chewing tobacco.

High Rise. J. R. Richard.

Hit 'Em Where They Ain't. Wee Willie Keeler.

The Hitless Wonders. The 1906 White Sox, who won their pennant with few good hitters and only six home runs all season.

The Home of Baseball. Cooperstown, New York.

Home Run Baker. John Franklin Baker, who won the name in the 1911 World Series.

The Home Run King. Babe Ruth.

The Hoosier Comet. Oscar Charleston.

The Hoosier Hammerer. Chuck Klein.

The Hoosier Thunderbolt. Amos Rusie.

The Hoover. Brooks Robinson.

Hot Rod. Rod Kanehl.

The House that Ruth Built. Sobriquet of Yankee Stadium.

The Human Mosquito. Jimmy Slagle.

The Human Vacuum Cleaner. Brooks Robinson.

The $100,000 Infield. Sobriquet of the Philadelphia Athletics, 1910-1914 with Jack Barry, Home Run Baker, Eddie Collins and Stuffy McInnis.

I

The Idol of Baseball Fandom. Ty Cobb.

The Incredible Heap. Kenny Kaiser.

The Invincible One. Warren Spahn.

The I-70 Series. 1985, the all-Missouri Series which acknowledged the linking of St. Louis and Kansas City by Interstate 70.

The I-95 Series. 1983, between the Baltimore Orioles and the Philadelphia Phillies which are linked by Interstate 95.

The Iron Horse. Sobriquet of Lou Gehrig.

The Iron Man. a. Joseph McGinnity. b. Umpire Bill McGowen for working 2,541 consecutive games over a period of 16½ years.

J

The Japanese Babe Ruth. Sadaharu Oh.

Joe D. Joe DiMaggio.

John McGraw's Boy. Mel Ott.

Jolly Cholly. Charlie Grimm.

Joltin' Joe. Joe DiMaggio, a title stemming from and aided by a popular song with a refrain "Joltin' Joe DiMaggio."

Jumbo Jim. Jim Nash.

K

The Ken and Barbie of Baseball. Steve and Cyndy Garvey.

Kentucky Colonel. Earle Combs.

The Kid. Tommy McCarthy, Norman Elberfield, Charles Nichols, William Gleason, and Ted Williams, among others.

The Killer. Harmon Killebrew as a feared slugger.

The Killer Bees. 1987 Red Sox batting order starting with Burks, Barrett, Boggs, and Baylor with Buckner batting seventh.

The King. a. Harmon Killebrew. b. Alex Kellner.

The King and the Crown Prince. Babe Ruth and Lou Gehrig.

King Carl. Carl Hubbell.

King Kong. Charlie Keller.

King Larry. Napoleon Lajoie.

The King of Clout. Babe Ruth.

L

Lady. Charles Baldwin who is listed in the *Baseball Encyclopedia* as Lady. (Some years back the *Sporting News* suggested a chorus line of baseball players to include Baldwin as well as Lena Blackburn, Tillie Shafer, Sadie McMahon, Kittie Bransfield, Dolly Stark, Goldie Holt, Carmen Hill and the Ryan "sisters" Blondie and Rosie. Then there was Cuddles Cottier who played for the Washington Senators in the late 1960s, Daisy Davis, Bonnie Hollingsworth, Fay Thomas, and Snooks Dowd.)

Larrupin' Lou. Lou Gehrig.

Larry, but they call him Larry. Larry Cox. It took a May 1980, press release from the Seattle Mariners to explain this one: "they say he looks like Larry Fine of Three Stooges fame, but his name is already Larry; thus the qualification in the nickname."

Leo the Lip. Leo Durocher.

The Lightning Lad. Carlton Fisk.

The Lip. Leo Durocher.

Little Eva. Bill Lange, who was so named because he was so unlike the other Little Eva.

The Little General. Gene Mauch.

The Little Giant. Mel Ott.

The Little Globetrotter. Billy Earle.

The Little Miracle of Coogan's Bluff. The New York Giants of 1951 from the point in mid-August when they were 14½ games out of first.

Little Napoleon. John J. McGraw.

Little Poison. Lloyd Waner who, according to his 1982 *Sporting News* obituary, got the name when "an Eastern fan with a Brooklyn accent called him a 'little person' but it came out as 'little poison.'" See also **Big Poison.**

The Little Round Man. Jimmy Dykes.

The Little Steam Engine. Pud Galvin.

Lord Byron. Umpire Bill Byron.

Lou'siana Lightnin'. Ron Guidry.

The Loyal Order of the Buffalo Heads. Sarcastic name for a group of Red Sox who played for Don Zimmer, who was known as "Buffalo Head" to his men.

The Lumber Company. The 1976 Pirates.

Lusty Lou. Lou Novikoff.

M

The McGrawmen. The New York Giants under John McGraw.

McGraw's Boy. Mel Ott.

McLucky. Dave McNally.

M&M Boys. Mickey Mantle and Roger Maris.

The Mackmen. The Philadelphia A's under Connie Mack.

The Macaroni Pony. Bob Coluccio.

The Mad Hungarian. Al Hrabosky.

The Mad Monk. Russ Meyer.

The Mad Russian. Lou Novikoff.

The Mahatma. Branch Rickey, a name given to him by the press.

The Mail Carrier. Earle Combs.

The Major. Ralph Houk.

The Man. Stan Musial.

Man o' War. Sam Rice.

The Man with the Golden Arm. Sandy Koufax.

The Margo Embargo. A ban on coverage of the Wade Boggs-Margo Adams affair put into effect in March 1989 by the Detroit Sports Broadcasters Association.

Marse Joe. Joseph McCarthy.

Marvelous Marv. Marvin Throneberry.

Master Melvin. Mel Ott.

Matty the Great. Christy Mathewson.

The Mechanical Man. Charles Gehringer.

The Meek Man from Meeker. Carl Hubbell.

The Meeker Magician. Carl Hubbell.

Memphis Bill. Bill Terry.

Mick the Quick. Mickey Rivers.

Mickey Mouth. Mickey Rivers.

The Mighty Mite/The Mite Manager. Miller Huggins.

The Million Dollar Baby from the 5&10 Cent Store. Lewis "Hack" Wilson.

The Miracle Man. George Stallings for his stewardship of the 1914 Braves. See

The Miracle Team.

The Miracle Mets. The 1969 World Champions.

The Miracle Team. The 1914 Braves which was in last place on July 19th but went on to win the pennant.

Mr. Ballgame. Ted Williams.

Mr. Baseball. a. Connie Mack. b. Bob Uecker, who in his book *Catcher in the Wry* points out that he is known by this title by "a generation that never saw me play."

Mr. Blunt. Rogers Hornsby, who Bob Broeg once said "must have thought that diplomacy was a respiratory disease."

Mr. Bones. Kent Tekulve.

Mr. Brave. Hank Aaron.

Mr. Candy. Reggie Jackson, after the Reggie chocolate bar made its debut in 1978.

Mr. Cub. Ernest Banks.

Mr. Dodger. Vin Scully, an honor bestowed on the announcer by Tommy Lasorda.

Mr. Impossible. Brooks Robinson.

Mr. Milkshake. Bill Virdon.

The Mistake by the Lake. The Cleveland Indians.

Mr. Moist. Gaylord Perry.

Mr. October. Reggie Jackson. In his autobiography *Reggie*, Jackson says that it was given to him by Thurman Munson at the beginning of the 1977 Series, and it was meant sarcastically because Jackson had done so badly during the playoffs against the Royals.

Mr. Shortstop. Marty Marion.

Mr. Sunshine. Ernie Banks.

The Mole. Rod Kanehl, for his fascination with the New York subways during his Mets years.

The Monsignor. Vada Pinson because players confided in him.

The Monster. Dick Radatz.

The Moon Man. a. Jay Johnstone. "I'll tell you how [he] got his nickname," Expos manager Bob Rogers explained on more than one occasion: "One day he lost a ball in the sun, but when he came back to the bench he said, 'I lost it in the moon.' After that we called him Moon Man." b. Steve Hovley. c. Mike Marshall. d. Mike Shannon.

Mountain Music. Cliff Melton.

The Mullethead. George Brett.

The Mummy. Joe Coates.

Murderer's Row. a. The heart of the 1927 New York Yankees batting order—Tony Lazzeri, Lou Gehrig, Babe Ruth, Earle Combs, and Bob Meusel. "Murderer's Row wasn't named for me as so many people think," Babe Ruth recalled later. "I just joined the Row when I joined the Yankees." b. The heart of the 1919 New York Yankees batting order—Ping Bodie, Roger Peckinpaugh, Duffy Lewis, and Home Run Baker.

The Mustache Gang. The Oakland A's of the early 1970s.

My Favorite Martian. Jay Johnstone.

The Mysterious Dr. Lau. Charlie Lau.

N

The Nashville Narcissus. Red Lucas.

The New Breed. Early Mets fans from the 1961-1962 ABC television series of the same name.

The Nickel Series. Series between New York teams when the cost of a subway ride was $.05.

The Noblest Roman. Charles Comiskey.

O

The Octopus of Baseball. Marty Marion.

Oil Can. Dennis Boyd, who got the name, according to a *USA Today* interview of February 28, 1988, "for draining beer cans in his hometown of Meridian, Mississippi, where beer is called oil." He has attempted to shed the name which sometimes led to unfortunate word play. ("The Can is leaking," said Vin Scully during the 1986 World Series when Boyd got into trouble.)

Oil Can Harry. Ray Oyler.

Old Aches and Pains. Luke Appling.

The Old Arbiter/The Old Arbitrator. Bill Klem.

The Old Bear. Fred Hutchinson.

Old Biscuit Pants. Lou Gehrig.

The Old Fox. Clark Calvin Griffith.

The Old Hoss. Charles Radbourn.

Old Man River. Connie Mack.

The Old Master. Bob Gibson.

The Old Meal Ticket. Sobriquet of Carl Hubbell.

The Old Perfessor. Casey Stengel who, like Babe Ruth, may have had the perfect baeball nickname because not one fan in a dozen knew that his real name was Charles and that Casey stood for the initials of his home town Kansas City. Fred Lieb once commented on natural nicknames like Casey: "nicknames must be spontaneous, as they rarely can be manufactured." Early in his career he was called Dutch.

Old Pete. Grover Cleveland Alexander.

Old Reliable. Tommy Henrich.

The Old Roman. Charles Comiskey.

Old Second Inning. Tim McCarver. Bill Lee gave him the name which, he explained in his autobiography *The Wrong Stuff*, was "due to his habit of having to take a dump in the john between the first and second inning of each game."

Old Soupbone. Carl Hubbell.

Old Stubblebeard. Burleigh Grimes.

Old Tennis Ball Head. Steve Hovley.

Old Tomato Face. Nick Cullop, whose face tended to redness.

The Old Warhorse. Enos Slaughter.

The One and Only. Babe Ruth.

The Only Del. Edward Delahanty.

The Only Nolan. Edward Sylvester Nolan.

Orang-Outang. Earl Averill.

Orator Jim. James O'Rourke.

The Other Babe. Babe Herman.

P

The Pale Hose. The White Sox.

The Peerless Dutchman. Honus Wagner.

The Peerless Hal. Hal Chase.

The Peerless Leader. Sobriquet of Frank Chance, from which Red Smith derived his **The Practically Peerless Leader** for Leo Durocher.

The Penguin. Ron Cey.

The People's Cherce. Dixie Walker.

The Perfect Ballplayer. George Sisler.

Pete the Hustler. Pete Rose.

The Phantom. Julian Javier because, as is explained in Bob Gibson's *From Ghetto to Glory*, "he makes the double play so quickly and gets out of the way of the runner so fast, he's like a phantom."

George "Pickles" Gerken—One of those irresistible nicknames like "Pickles" Dillhoefer.

Ping Bodie—One of a number of examples where early sports writers compressed names to fit headlines and roll off the tongue. Bodie's real name was Francesco Pezzolo. Another case was that of Rinaldo Angelo Paolinelli who was trimmed down to Babe Pinelli. Writing in 1974, Fred Lieb took a look at the new crop of players—men with names like Bob Apodaca and Al Hrabosky—and asked, "What would the writers of the days of Ring Lardner, Damon Runyon, and Charlie Dryden have done with such names?"

The Pirate's Second Shortstop. Pie Traynor.

Pistol Pete. Pete Reiser.

Poosh 'Em Up. Tony Lazzeri.

The Pretzel Battery. Ted Breitenstein and Heinie Peitz.

The Pride of the Yankees. Lou Gehrig.

Prince Hal. Hal Schumacher.

The Principal Owner. George Steinbrenner.

The Puker. Umpire Paul Pryor because he once threw up on catcher Johnny Roseboro at Dodger Stadium.

Q

The Quakers. The early Philadelphia Phillies.

R

The Rabbi of Swat. Moe Solomon.

Rabbit. James Maranville who, depending on your source got the name from (a) his pep and the way he hopped around the bases, or (b) his willingness to wiggle his ears for the fans. (According to reporters, when Maranville toured Japan the fans went crazy wiggling their hands against the side of their heads like rabbit ears. He, of course, reciprocated.) Or (c): as Leo Durocher puts it in *Nice Guys Finish Last*, "The Rabbit was a little fellow, that's how he got his nickname."

The Rajah. Rogers Hornsby.

The Rape of the Red Sox. The period from the championship years of 1915-1916 to 1923 when they were in the cellar.

Rapid Robert. Bob Feller. Roy Blount, Jr., writing in *Inside Sports*, had this to say about the name: "The world will always know Bob Feller as 'Rapid Robert,' but his fellow Indians called him 'Inky' because he had himself incorporated."

The Roadrunner. Ralph Garr.

The Reading Rifle. Carl Furillo.

The Red Rooster. Doug Rader.

Reggie Jackson. He has been known as Reggie for so long that people forget he is actually Reginald Martinez Jackson. When he hit three home runs in the last game of the 1977 World Series, sports writers in New York speculated that every male born within 100 miles of the city that day would be named Reggie. The process may have started before that, given the number of younger Reggies now making a name for themselves in sports.

Reggie's Regiment. Fans who came to the stadium to see Reggie Jackson hit home runs in Oakland.

The Rock of Snohomish. Earl Averill. See also **Earl of Snohomish**.

Rocket Man. Roger Clemens, from his style of delivery.

The Ruppert Rifles. The New York Yankees under the ownership of Jacob Ruppert.

S

The Say Hey Kid. Willie Mays.

Scrap Iron. a. Ed Beecher. b. Clint Courtney. c. Bob Stinson. d. Phil Garner.

Schoolboy. Lynwood Rowe.

The Scot Heard Round the World. Bobby Thomson.

The Screaming Skull. Sal Maglie.

The September Massacre. What happened to the Red Sox in 1978.

The Series by the Bay. The 1989 World Series between Oakland Athletics and the San Francisco Giants.

Sgt. Hank. Hank Bauer.

Shoeless Joe. Joe Jackson.

Shot Heard 'Round the World. Bobby Thomson's 1951 playoff home run.

The Shuttle Series. The 1986 World Series, an allusion to the fact that Boston and New York are linked by two air shuttle services.

The Silent Captain of the Red Sox. Bobby Doerr, a title given to him by Ted Williams.

The Silent Pole. Harry Coveleski.

The Silver Fox. Duke Snider.

The Singer Throwing Machine. Bill Singer.

Sir Timothy. Tim Keefe.

Sky King. Denny McLain, given when he took flying lessons.

Sky Young. Denny McLain, given to him when he won the Cy Young Award.

The Skydome Summit. The April 10, 1990, meeting of President George Bush and Prime Minister Brian Mulroney of Canada in the Toronto Skydome. The meeting was followed by a Blue Jays—Texas Rangers game.

Sliding Billy. Bill Hamilton.

The Snake Man. Moe Drabowsky.

The Space Man. Bill Lee.

The Southside Hitmen. The Chicago White Sox when they are hitting.

The Splendid Splinter. Ted Williams, who was given the name before he shattered a jet in Korea in a crash-landing.

The Sport of Eggheads. Baseball.

The Squire of Kennett Square. Herb Pennock.

Stan the Man. Stan Musial. In the *Baseball Life of Sandy Koufax*, George Vecsey says: "How Musial used to murder those Bums! Every time he came to bat, the fans used to groan, 'Here comes that man again! Stan the Man!' Now everybody in baseball called him 'Stan the Man.'"

Stan the Man Unusual. Don Stanhouse, also called *Full Pack*, for his spaceyness. Writing on the topic of names in *Inside Sports*, Roy Blount, Jr. said that this one was so good that it deserved its own title *The Splendid Sobriquet*. It was originally created by Mike Flanagan, whom Blount dubbed *The Dubber*.

The Staten Island Scot. Bobby Thomson.

Steady Eddie. Ed Kranepool.

The Stick. Candlestick Park.

The Straw that Stirs the Drink. Reggie Jackson.

Subway Series. Any World Series in which two New York teams participate. As of this writing the last one took place in 1956 between the Yankees and the Dodgers.

Sudden Sam. Sam McDowell for the fact that when opposing batters were asked how his fastball approached they would say something like, "All of a sudden, man, all of a sudden."

The Suds Series. 1982, which saw two teams, the Brewers and Cardinals, from cities with strong links to beer. The Milwaukee team is named for that city's production of beer, and the St. Louis team is owned by the Busch family of the Anheuser-Busch breweries.

Suitcase. Harry Simpson. Two good explanations for this nickname: that he was an oft-traded player who lived out of his suitcase and that he had big suitcase-sized feet. Take your pick.

The Sultan of Swat. Babe Ruth. Leonard R.N. Ashley, an English professor at Brooklyn College, said at a recent conference on Babe Ruth that the name comes from 19th-century comic verse about Indian royalty from Swat. (No, not the Cleveland Indians.) Variations on this theme of royalty that were attached to the Babe in addition to the Sultan included The Caliph of Clout, Wazoo of Wallop, Potentate of the Pill, and Bazoo of the Bang.

The Sultan of Swish. Dave Nicholson.

Super Joe. Joe Charboneau.

The Swamp Fox. Al Dark.

Sweet Juice. William "Judy" Johnson.

Sweet Lou from Peru. Lou Pinella, who actually hailed from Tampa.

T

The Tabasco Kid. Norm Elberfeld.

Taj O'Malley. Dodger Stadium.

The Tall Tactician. Connie Mack.

Tanglefoot Lou. Lou Gehrig, early in his career.

The Tater Man. George Scott.

Ted Threads. Ted Williams as manager of the Washington Senators, so named, according to the June 6, 1971, *Washington Star*, "by his charges, who are amazed at his casual wardrobe."

Teddy Ballgame. Ted Williams. In *My Turn at Bat* Williams says that he got this from the son of a friend who met Williams at age two and several years later said he wanted to go back to Fenway Park to see Teddy Ballgame.

Ten to Two. Art Fowler because, as Sparky Lyle points out in *The Bronx Zoo*, "that's the way his feet point."

The Thin Thunderbolt. Ted Williams, so called by Bob Feller in *Strikeout Story* and elsewhere.

Three-Finger. Mordecai Brown.

The Time Zone Without a Team. The Mountain Time Zone. The sobriquet was used in promoting the idea of a team in Denver.

Tobacco John. John Lanning.

Tom Terrific. Tom Seaver.

The Toy Cannon. Jim Wynn.

Toys in the Attic. Frank Bertaina, a name given to him in Baltimore by Moe Drabowsky.

The Tribe. The Cleveland Indians.

Truthful Jeems. Jim Mutrie.

The $25 Million Dollar Man. Dave Winfield, so called by Reggie Jackson in *Reggie*.

Twinkle Toes. George Selkirk for his distinctive way of walking. He only stole 49 bases in his career despite the name.

Two Head. Babe Ruth. Baseball historian Robert Smith has noted that this name was used by other players and that it drove him wild. It alluded to the fact that his head seemed twice normal size.

The Ty Cobb of the National League. Honus Wagner.

U

Uncle Robby. Wilbert Robinson, whose team in Brooklyn was known as "The Robins" in his honor.

Uncle Tired. Tommy Davis.

The Unholy Trio. Mickey Mantle, Billy Martin, and Whitey Ford.

The Union Man. Walter Holke.

The Unknown Soldier. Commissioner General William D. Eckert.

V

Venus de Milo Outfield. Any that is beautiful but has no arms.

Vincent Van Go. Vince Coleman.

Vinegar Bend. Wilmer Mizell. After being elected to the House of Representatives from North Carolina in the 1960s, he explained the name, which was also the name of his hometown: "A railroad was being built in that part of Alabama a long time ago. The diet of the railroad workers included sorghum molasses. A barrel of the molasses soured into vinegar and was poured into Escatawapa River at a place where it makes a bend, and ever since the place has been called Vinegar Bend."

The Vulture. Phil Regan, during his Dodger days, when he came into a game as a relief pitcher and picked up a win.

W

The Wahoo Barber/Wahoo Sam. Sam Crawford.

Wamby. Bill Wambsganss, who had a true *nom de press*. He was rewarded for the feat of completing the only unassisted triple play in World Series history (1920) by having his name cut to Wamby by typesetters. Modern record book compilers have put his name back together. (Wamby was one of a number of examples where early sports writers compressed names to fit headlines and box scores. See also **Ping Bodie** for more examples.)

The Waterbury Wizard. Jimmy Piersall.

The Weatherman. Mickey Rivers for his ability to predict the weather.

Wee Willie. Willie Keeler.

What's the Use. Pearce Chiles.

The Wheeze Kids. The 1983 Philadelphia Phillies, who one preseason observer said was composed of veterans destined to make cameo appearances at Old Timers' games.

The Whip. Ewell Blackwell. Also called *The Buggywhip.*

The White Gorilla. Goose Gossage.

The White Rat. Whitey Herzog.

The Whiz Kids. The 1950 Phillies.

Why Me? Danny Cater, who asked this question everytime he was put out on a great play.

Wiggly Field. Candlestick Park after the 1989 World Series earthquake.

Wild Bill. Bill Donovan.

The Wild Hoss of the Osage. Sobriquet of Pepper Martin.

The Wizard of Gauze. Trainer Jim Dudley.

The Wizard of Oz. Ozzie Smith.

The World Serious. The World Series. A phrase made famous by Ring Lardner, but heard much earlier (first) from the lips of New York Giant Josh Devore in 1911 by Fred Lieb.

Y

The Yankee Clipper. a. Long established sobriquet of Joe DiMaggio, but it was also used derisively for **b.** George Steinbrenner, who insisted that his players be clean shaven.

Ye Childe Harold. Pete Reiser.

The Year of the Asterisk. The strike-interrupted 1981 season when most records and statistics were marked with an asterisk.

The Year of the Lockout. 1990.

The Year of the Rookie. 1986 (Canseco, Joyner, et al.).

The Year of the Zero. 1968.

Yogi. Yogi Berra.

Young Cy Young. Irving Young, who pitched for the Boston Nationals while Cy Young pitched for the Boston Americans.

Yogi Berra

Admittedly, some of the names in this chapter are not among the most famous in baseball, but the following are. Here is a selected listing of nicknames of players who have been elected to the Baseball Hall of Fame. If you can identify 40 of them you are an expert and if you can get beyond 50 you are a true authority.

1. Ban. 2. Beauty. 3. Big Ed. 4. Big Poison. 5. Big Sam. 6. Big Six. 7. Big Train. 8. Bucketfoot. 9. Bucky. 10. Candy. 11. Chick. 12. Chief. 13. Cocky. 14. Connie. 15. Cool Papa. 16. Cousin Egbert. 17. Crab (two of them). 18. Cracker. 19. Mr. Cub. 20. Dazzy. 21. Deacon. 22. Ducky. 23. Duke. 24. EE-Yah. 25. The Fordham Flash. 26. Gabby. 27. The Georgia Peach. 28. Gettysburg Eddie. 29. Goose. 30. Gorgeous George. 31. Happy Jack. 32. Heinie. 33. Home Run. 34. Honus. 35. Husk. 36. Iron Horse. 37. Iron Man. 38. Jackie. 39. Jephtha. 40. Jocko. 41. Judge. 42. Judy. 43. Kentucky Colonel. 44. Kiki.

45. King. 46. King Carl. 47. The Knight of Kennett Square. 48. Lindy. 49. Little Napoleon. 50. Little Poison. 51. Mahatma. 52. Marse Joe. 53. The Mechanical Man. 54. Mighty Mite. 55. Miner. 56. Monte. 57. Old Arbitrator. 58. Old Fox. 59. Old Hoss. 60. Old Roman. 61. Old Stubblebeard. 62. Orator Jim. 63. Pie. 64. Pud. 65. Rabbit. 66. Rajah. 67. Rapid Robert. 68. Sandy. 69. Satchel. 70. Schoolboy. 71. Scoops. 72. Slug. 73. Spoke. 74. Sunny Jim. 75. The Kid. 76. The Man. 77. Uncle Robby. 78. Wahoo. 79. Wee Willie. 80. The Yankee Clipper.

The answers:

1. Byron Johnson. 2. David Bancroft. 3. Ed Delahanty. 4. Paul Waner. 5. Samuel Thompson. 6. Christopher Mathewson. 7. Walter Johnson. 8. Aloysius Simmons. 9. Stanley Harris. 10. William Cummings. 11. Charles Hafey. 12. Charles Bender. 13. Edward Collins. 14. Cornelius McGillicuddy (Connie Mack's real name). 15. James Bell. 16. Edward Barrow. 17. Jesse Burkett and John Evers. 18. Raymond Schalk. 19. Ernest Banks. 20. Arthur Vance. 21. William McKechnie. 22. Joseph Medwick. 23. Roger Bresnahan. 24. Hugh Jennings. 25. Frank Frisch. 26. Charles Hartnett. 27. Tyrus Cobb. 28. Edward Plank. 29. Leon Goslin. 30. George Sisler. 31. Jack Chesbro. 32. Henry Manush. 33. Frank Baker. 34. John Wagner. 35. Frank Chance. 36. Louis Gehrig. 37. Joseph McGinnity. 38. Jack Robinson. 39. Eppa Rixey. 40. John Conlan. 41. Kenesaw M. Landis. 42. William Johnson. 43. Earle Combs. 44. Hazen Cuyler. 45. Michael Kelly. 46. Carl Hubbell. 47. Herbert Pennock. 48. Frederick Lindstrom. 49. John McGraw. 50. Lloyd Waner. 51. Branch Rickey. 52. Joseph McCarthy. 53. Charles Gehringer. 54. Miller Huggins. 55. Mordecai Brown. 56. Monford Irvin. 57. William Klem. 58. Clark Griffith. 59. Charles Radbourn. 60. Charles Comiskey. 61. Burleigh Grimes. 62. James O'Rourke. 63. Harold Traynor. 64. James Galvin. 65. Walter Maranville. 66. Rogers Hornsby. 67. Robert Feller. 68. Sanford Koufax. 69. Leroy Paige. 70. Waite Hoyt. 71. Max Carey. 72. Harry Heilmann. 73. Tristram Speaker. 74. James Bottomley. 75. Theodore Williams. 76. Stanley Musial. 77. Wilbert Robinson. 78. Samuel Crawford. 79. William Keeler. 80. Joseph DiMaggio.

Calling All Cars

The Floating Bull, American Chocolate, and Other Automobile Nameplates

8

C ar names tend to be important to people. Well-heeled suburbanites like to talk of their Volvos, the Beach Boys sing of their little GTOs, Volkswagen owners speak affectionately and defensively of their Rabbits, and there is no quicker way to evoke nostalgia than to name cars no longer in production, whether they be Hudsons and Hupmobiles or Marlins and Monzas.

The folks in Detroit, Tokyo, and other automotive centers know this, and lots of time and money go into what a car is to be called. Once the only thing that a company had to worry about was its basic name, but then came *series* names so that one no longer talked about a Pontiac but about a Phoenix, Firebird, or Grand Prix.

Broadly speaking, cars were first named for their builders or designers. John and Horace Dodge, the Maserati brothers, Henry Ford, David Dunbar Buick, Louis Chevrolet, Ransom Eli Olds, Karl Benz, Enzo Ferrari, Ferdinand Porsche, Ferruccio Lamborghini, and Pierre Renault are all gone, but their names live on.

But after World War II, the series name started, with an emphasis on glamorous destinations like Monte Carlo, Malibu, Bel Air, Greenbriar, Sun Valley, Pinehurst, Biarritz, Monterey, Biscayne, Riviera, Catalina, Newport, and Capri. Then came a menagerie of things that flew, ran, and swam including the Impala, Cobra, Sting Ray, Marlin, Cougar, Wildcat, Thunderbird, Mustang, Firebird, Road Runner, Bobcat, and Super Bee.

Next came a sudden burst of appropriate names for the early days of the space age, among them Starfire, Galaxy, Meteor, Nova, Satellite, Polara, Golden Rocket, and those models, like the Olds F-85 and Ford 500-XL, that sounded much more like jet fighters than cars. In fact, the F-85, brought out in 1961 by Oldsmobile, was only one digit removed from the Air Force's F-86 Sabrejet fighter.

For a while, numbers played an important role in the naming of models. Oldsmobile, for instance, used names like 4-4-2 (a Cutlass with 4-on-the-floor, 4-barrel carb, and dual exhaust), Ninety-Eight (always spelled out), and various 88's. The eights used in most Olds numbers originally referred to the V-8 engines, and the occasional six stood for six-cylinder models. The many Delta models got their name from the time when delta wing planes were first being discussed as the wave of the future.

Of late, there has been a trend to euphoniously named cars with no real or clear car-directed meaning, like Tercels, Sentras, Quantums, Integras, Celicas, Cieras, Preludes, Supras, Accords, and Cressidas. Cressida? The Trull of Troy in Shakespeare's *Troilus and Cressida*.

Some of these work and some don't. Despite a decade of use, Stanza never really worked and it is now an Altima. Accura, a neologism if there ever was one, suggests precision, which is exactly what Honda was pushing: precise engineering.

The mania for odd suffixes, which is still very much with us, hit hard in the late 1980s. "These days, model suffixes are the rage," wrote Preston Lerner in the *Dallas Morning News* on January 24, 1988: "People no longer buy a Pontiac Bonneville. They buy a Pontiac 6000 STE-AWD, a Mitsubishi Starion ESI-R, or a Ford Escort EXP. Besides sounding European, these suffixes also alert buyers

to the special features of the cars, whether all-wheel-drive or a turbocharged engine. But what started as a marketing device and simplification tool has turned into a nightmare of growing complexity. The problem is that automakers worldwide have come up with their own suffixes, but few share common meanings. Many of them, in fact, mean nothing at all."

A sampling of the 1988 bumper crop of suffixes included D, DL, DX, E, ES, ESI, ESI-R, EXP, G, GL, GLS, GLX, GS, GT, GTA, GTB, GTS, GXE, i, is, iX, IROC-Z, L, LE, LS, LSC, LT, LX, MT-5, RS, S, SC, SD, SE, SEC, SEL, SL, SS, SSE, STE, STE-AWD, STX, SW8, SX, T, TD, TE, TSi, T-Type, X, XE, XR-7, Z and ZX.

Moving right along, we come to a traffic jam of makes and models with names worthy of comment. It is, however, just a small sampling from the more than 3,000 makes of cars and trucks that have been produced by some 1,500 manufacturers since the turn of the century.

A

A is for Alliance (what better name for a car built by a partnership between a French company, Renault, and an American one, American Motors), Arrow, Alvis, Auburn, American, Accord, Ambassador, Audi, Avanti, Aspen, and Aries, along with the:

Accura. Neologism suggesting precision, created by a consulting company, with the understanding that one of Honda's desired hallmarks for the brand was precise engineering.

Achieva. A computer-generated name, or neologism, that doesn't mean anything but suggests achievement. Oldsmobile originally called the car Achiever, but softened it to Achieva to remove the stigma of a young urban professional who had "made it."

Altima. A neologism that hints at the ultimate or best but doesn't have a real meaning. Replaced the Stanza, a name that never caught on with the public in a decade of use.

American Chocolate. A bygone American automobile which was unusual in that the name appeals to the sense of taste. It was built between 1902 and 1906 in a plant that had made machinery for making chocolate. This and the next car on the list are examples of cars which were the sole offerings of their manufacturer.

Aurora. Rare case of a model name divorced from the brand name. The all-new 1995 Aurora did not bear the Oldsmobile name on its exterior. The company decided it did not want to risk turning away import buyers, who might not buy an Oldsmobile. Oldsmobile borrowed the name from a Cadillac concept car displayed at the North American International Auto Show in the late 1980s.

Average Man's. An early car from Kansas which—along with Everybody's and People's—tried for broad appeal with a name.

B

B is for the Buick, Bug, Bugati, Bantam, Bearcat, Blazer, Brush, Beretta, Benz, Barracuda, Brougham, and Bentley, along with the:

Blood. A car from the Michigan Automobile Co. produced by the Blood brothers from 1903 to 1908. If the Blood seems improbable consider the Kidney, which came out in 1910.

BMW. The Bavarian Motor Works, or Bayerische Motoren Werke in German. There are those who insist it stands for Bust My Wallet.

Bonneville. This Pontiac is one of the few with a name that actually has something to do with the history of the company. The name was taken from the Bonneville Salt Flats, where Pontiac set 24-hour endurance records in 1956.

Bugmobile. There really was a car of this name, ranking with the likes of the Lu-Lu and Pungs-Finch for claim to oddest early car name. Some years ago James S. Pooler of the *Detroit Free Press* came up with his own list of unusual car names: Abenaque, Acorn, Aerotype, Balboa, Beacon Flyer, Car-Nation, Couple Gear, Cucmobile, Dan Patch (who was also a horse), Dewabout, Dudgeon, Electronomic, Emancipator, Flexbi, Gadabout, Goodspeed, Nance, Old Reliable, O-We-Go, Pastoria, Pneumobile, Prigg, Simplicity, Thorobred, Zentomobile, and Zip. Others not on Pooler's list include the Seven Little Buffaloes, Red Bug, American Underslung, Little Mac, Gas Au Lac, and Drednot.

C

C is for the Columbia, Cord, Cunningham, Crosley, Case, Chalmers, Checker, Civic, Corolla, Celica, Cavalier, Corvette, Caprice, Calais, Century, Cougar, CRX, Corsica, Charger, Conquest, Chrysler, Cordoba, Cressida, Carrera, and Citroen, as well as the:

Cadillac. Named for Le Sieur Antoine de la Mothe Cadillac, founder of Detroit.

Camaro. It means *nothing* in Spanish and is part of the stable of Chevrolets which begin with C, including the Celebrity, Citation, Caprice, Corvette, Chevette,

Cavalier, Corsica and—stretching it a little—the Monte Carlo. The first Chevrolet was a Classic 6, brought out in 1911. There have been Chevrolets that do not begin with C—like the Lumina, Tahoe, Blazer, and Malibu—but they are in the minority. Nor is Chevrolet alone in the C-practice, given names like Calais, Cougar, Celica, Corolla, Colt, Caravan, Century, Coronet, Cimarron, Coupe de Ville, Concord, Charger, Crown Victoria, Cutlass, Corona, Capri, Civic, and Continental. Five of the top 10 selling cars of 1983 started with C and a sixth, the Sentra, had the C-sound. Then, of course, there is Chrysler, which is named for company founder Walter P. Chrysler.

The only letter that begins to approach the C is T as in Tempo, Tercel, Town and Country, Turismo, Trans Am, Topaz, Thunderbird, and Triumph. The case can also be made for V-names, which are not as popular as C's or T's but tend to be good solid car names, like the Valiant, Ventura, Volare, and Versailles. Because the author found himself seriously considering the Vista, Vanagon, and Voyager before settling on the latter when he last bought a new car, he confesses to a deep V-preference.

Caravan. Name for the Dodge minivan which is not only a good nomadic image but also not a bad pun for this hybrid—is it a CAR? A VAN?

Chevrolet. Named for Louis Chevrolet, designer and race driver for Buick, who founded the company with GM founder Billy Durant. The first cars turned out by the company were called Littles, after another executive of the company, but a merger changed this and the Chevrolet name survived. Durant once told an interviewer, after its namesake had left the

company, that the name meant "little mountain goat."

Ciera. At one time "the most thoroughly researched name in Oldsmobile's long history." Like other recent series it has a name that you won't find in any dictionary. In this case, Oldsmobile had these criteria:

- *Specific interpretation or meaning was not necessary; name should be open to individual inferences.*

- *No negative implications.*

- *Broad appeal.*

- *Must complement Cutlass name/image.*

Using these criteria, the company took a year to narrow a list of hundreds of names down to a final 50 which were then narrowed down to one, Ciera, which was deemed to have the greatest customer appeal.

Cleveland. This was one of the most popular names of all time as there were at least five separate Clevelands, each manufactured by different people. The number of Clevelands underscore the early trend to name cars either after their builder or the place where they were built. The name American shows up in nearly 30 car names, and there have been at least a half-dozen with Michigan in their title.

"Cloud cars." Chrysler Cirrus and Dodge Stratus passed muster for image-making and advertising. But Chrysler Corp. marketers were stumped for a name for the Plymouth version of their new compact-midsize sedan. So they asked the company's employees for suggestions. More than 1,000 submitted names and more than 2,000 names were considered before decision-makers settled on Breeze.

Colt. Ford backed away from this as a model name because, according to the *Detroit Free Press,* studies showed that too many consumers associated the name with a gun. That did not deter Chrysler.

Corvair. A blend of Corvette and Bel Air given to Chevy's rear-engined car brought out in 1960. This name was one of those first given to "dream cars" shown in GM Motoramas of the 1950s, including the Biscayne, which was named for the Key Biscayne site of the Motoramas. Other "dream car" names were the Impala and the Corvette.

Cutie. One of a special line of "women's" models sold in Japan by Toyota, which, besides the Tercel Cutie, has offered the Corsa Sophia, Corolla II Lime, and Sprinter Lise. Nissan offers the Gloria and Fairlady as special women's cars for the home model. Commenting on this, Paul Lienert of the *Detroit Free Press* asked, "How many macho American drivers would buy the Datsun 280ZX if they knew that model was called the Fairlady in the home market?"

D

D is for the Duesenberg, Delage, Detroit Electric, Duryea, Daimler, Darracq, duPont, Delahaye, De Tamble, Dodge, DeSoto, Dakota, Dynasty, Daytona, and de Ville, along with the:

Datsun. Name with high degree of recognition in North America and Europe which has been abandoned at great cost in favor of the name Nissan. This was done—at an estimated cost of $50 million to $100 million—so that the company could consolidate its worldwide marketing under a single name.

Originally called the Dat from the initials of the company's three founding investors, a small 1931 Dat was dubbed *son of Dat* and later evolved into Datsun.

There is a popular folk version of how the Datsun got its name, which goes like this: Nissan had created a new car in a short period of time and realized that they had no name for it. They knew the Germans were good at names so contact was made with a consulting firm there. The Japanese said their car had been created in a very short time and expected the Germans to come up with a name within a day. "Ach, my goodness!" said the German on the other end of the phone, "Datsun!"

Dictator. One of the worst car names of all time, this is the name that the Studebaker Corporation of America gave to its lowest-price car in 1927. The expensive Studebaker was called the President. The Dictator was part of the line until 1938 when the low-cost model was named the Champion. In Britain the name was unacceptable from the outset and the car was sold there as the Director 6.

E

E is for the Excelsior, Erskine, Essex, Encore, Eagle, Escort, and Excaliber, along with the:

Edsel. Named for Edsel Bryant Ford, son of Henry Ford, this car made its debut in 1956 and died after a mere 110,000 cars were built and sold. In his paper "Of Edsels and Marauders," D. B. Graham of the University of Texas observed with irony, "If history is bunk, as his father told us, what then of Edsel's name, Edsel who died in 1943, and who in 1956 could hardly be said to live in the consciousness of many Americans?" Ironically this ill-suited name—a Ford executive later said it would have better fit a tractor—for an ill-fated car was the result of a massive search for a suitable name. Because this was no mere series but a totally new car to ride alongside the Ford, Mercury, and Lincoln, the company used no less than 300 outsiders, including poet Marianne Moore. The Brooklyn poet later published her correspondence with Ford in the *New Yorker*, where she revealed some of her suggestions: Turbotorc, Thunder Crester, and Utopian Turtletop. Finally, the company wrote back telling her that it had settled on a name with an air "of gaity and zest," chosen from close to 18,000 candidates. Runners-up to Edsel in the final balloting: Corsair, Ranger, Pacer, and Citation.

"After Edsel, Ford did better," wrote Professor Graham in his paper. "They returned to the great tradition of Thunderbird. Falcon, Mustang, and Maverick were all superior to Edsel."

F

F is for the Fleetwood, Fredonia, Fleetline, Ford, Festiva, Fiero, Fraser, Ferrari, and Fiat, as well as the:

Fiesta. It is notable because it was to be called the Bambi until Ford chairman Henry Ford II stepped in at the last minute to rename the subcompact.

G

G is for the Galant, Grand Am, Graham, Gerald, and Grand Prix, along with the Goliath of car names:

General Motors. How did this giant get its name? According to Lawrence R. Gustin, manager of internal communications for that company and biographer of GM founder William C. Durant, "The name was selected by...Durant in September 1908, after he learned he could not use the names International Motor Car Co. or United Motors because of prior claims on those names." The firms with the preferred names are long gone. Durant also picked the name Buick, which originally belonged to a Scot named David Dunbar Buick who developed the original Buick and whose ancestors changed it from the original *Buik*. Durant liked the ring of the name although he momentarily feared people would pronounce it "Booick." The man Buick sold out early and, according to Terry Dunham in his book *The Buick: A Complete History*, lost a fortune and "in old age he was so poor he could afford neither a telephone or a Buick."

Geo. The lineup of small vehicles sold in Chevrolet dealerships. *Geo* is a morpheme, the smallest meaningful language unit, which means "world" in many languages. Geos are imported from Japan, built in a General Motors-Suzuki joint venture in Canada and a GM-Toyota joint venture in California.

Gremlin. A provocative naming move by American Motors because the gremlin is a notorious troublemaker. It was replaced by the Spirit as American Motors' subcompact in 1978. A precedent for the Gremlin was Imp, a car that rolled in the days before World War I.

GTO. Pontiac began using this name which had been used by Ferrari. It stands for Gran Turismo Omologato, which means "grand touring car in production."

H

H is for the Holley, Hispano-Suiza, Horch, Haynes-Apperson, Hawk, Horizon, Honda, Hupmobile, Hillman, Humber, and Holiday, as well as the:

Hudson. Produced from 1909 to 1958, this American classic was named for J. L. Hudson, famed Detroit department store owner, who was one of eight Michigan businessmen who banded together "to produce an automobile that would sell for less than $1,000."

I

I is for the Impala, International, Imperial, Invicta, Imp, and Infiniti, as well as the:

Isuzu. The name means "50 bells" in Japanese.

K

K is for the Kissel, Knox, King, and Kaiser, along with the:

K-car. Back in 1979 and 1980, Chrysler Corp. was asking Congress to help save the company, and it said it had an as-yet-unnamed car with the internal code name of K that would revive the company. The K's came out named as the Plymouth Reliant and Dodge Aries, but the K stuck and then GM cars began being referred to by their code letter. According to an article in the *Wall Street Journal* on June 8, 1984, the situation came down to this: "GM's current models include A, B, C, D, E, G, J,

T, X, and Y cars, with H, N, W and some others on the drawing boards. Chrysler's lineup includes the CV, E, J, K, L, M, Y and T." Detroit is almost out of these names but as the *Journal* article pointed out, "So far nobody is credited with an I, O, or U car." Ford, by the way, uses animal code names like Fox and Panther.

L

L is for the Lincoln, Lynx, Lamborghini, LaSalle, Lark, Lumina, Legacy, Locomobile, Lafayette, Lozier, Lavil Log, LeMans, and Limited, along with the:

LeSabre. When Buick brought out its "revolutionary" new 1959 line, the cars had starkly new names starting with LeSabre (French for "the sword), along with Invicta (Latin for "unconquerable") and Electra (Greek for "brilliant"). These had been picked from a list of more than a thousand choices and seemed to cross a new line into its hard-edged names, paving the way for Spoilers, Marauders, Lasers, and Cutlasses. Now over 25 years old, the LeSabre and Electra are two of the longest-lived series names around.

Lexus. In 1988 Toyota's new Lexus luxury-car division was sued by LEXIS, the information-retrieval service owned by Mead Data Central Inc. A federal court restrained Lexus from national advertising, saying it would dilute the effect of LEXIS's name. An appeals court reversed the decision. In 1992 Nissan was challenged by Altima Systems Inc., a Concord, California, computer business that claimed it had the name Altima first. They reached a confidential settlement. Altima the car is now one of Nissan's hottest sellers.

Loyale. After rejecting more than 500

"Go Anywhere, Do Anything"

J is for the Jaguar, Jetta, Justy, and Jordan, and what is perhaps the most beloved of all car monikers:

Jeep. Army car in general use in the U.S. Army during World War II and thereafter for many years. The term gained immediate approval and seems to be as universal 50 years later and is applied to a number of jeep-style vehicles, including some made by folks who were America's enemy in World War II.

As A. Marjorie Taylor reports in *The Language of World War II,* "The car itself was not invented by any one person, but evolved gradually, a need for such a type of car being felt in World War I. The earliest experimental models (made by Willys-Overland, American Bantam, and Ford) were nicknamed Beep, Bug, Blitz, Buggy, Chigger, Midget, Puddle Jumper, Peep, etc."

Several sources, including *American Speech,* February 1943, give this account of its nicknaming: The first Willys model was nicknamed Jeep and this name stuck. In February 1941, the Willys car was being put through some tests in Washington, with Katharine Hillyer, staff writer for the *Washington Daily News,* as a passenger. Someone asked the driver the "name of that thing, mister" and was told "It's a Jeep." A picture of the Jeep with its name in the caption appeared in the *Washington Daily News* on February 19, 1941.

The term *Jeep* appeared in the Popeye comic strip as early as March 16, 1936, and may have been the genesis of the term as it was known in World War II. This letter of June 23, 1944, to lexicographer Peter Tamony, quoted in part, from William Howlett, Carl Byoir and Associates, Inc., provides the official explanation:

"We feel that the word originated with [Elzie C.] Segar, King Features cartoonist, who until his recent death wrote the Popeye strip. You will recall that in this feature there was a character called the *Jeep* which lived on orchids and could go anywhere and do anything. It is our contention that the boys in the service picked this name up from Segar and applied it to the Willys vehicle which has many of the 'go anywhere, do anything' characteristics of the Popeye character."

However, two other items in the collection of Peter Tamony at the University of Missouri provide an alternative explanation:

1. "Do you know why those swift little army cars are called *jeeps?* It's Model G-P produced by that automobile manufacturer—and G-P easily becomes *jeep.*" (An item in the *San Francisco Call-Bulletin,* November 22, 1941, "This is the Life" by Marsh Maslin.)

2. "The pronunciation of initials sometimes gives the English language a brand-new word. This is what happened when a new kind of United States Army vehicle was officially named *General Purpose Car.* It was first referred to by its initials, G.P., and you can easily see how this became the very popular *jeep.*" (From Robert L. Morgan, *Why We Say...* [New York: Sterling Publishing Co., 1953])

Today, the name **Jeep** *is a registered trademark of the Chrysler Corporation.*

names, this is what Subaru chose to name a four-door family car. The development of this name was charted by Robert Johnson of the *Wall Street Journal*, who termed the final choice "about as exciting as a lug nut." Johnson was intrigued by some of the losing names and the reasons they were rejected. Asteroid, for instance, was rejected because it might remind people of their hemorrhoids. The title of the article announcing the Loyale pick, a name picked to reflect customer loyalty, was "Soe Thise Ise Whate Consultantse Doe Toe Earne Alle Thate Moneye."

LSD. A car of the Coolidge era. Three-letter combinations seem to be the rule with initial-named cars: BMW, GTO, LTD, AMX, GTX, XJS, and GLC. The much loved MG, for Morris Garages, is one of the few exceptions.

M

M is for the Mercury, Marmon, Model A, Model T, Merkur, Maytag, Maxwell, Minerva, Morgan, MX-6, Monte Carlo, MG, Monza, Mustang, and Maxima, which appears to be a rare plural car name (what is more than one maximum?), as well as the:

Maverick. Unbranded stock or a nonconformist, both meanings from Texas lawyer Samuel Augustus Maverick (1803-1870), who was notably careless about branding his cattle, and the name of a Ford model which came out in 1969. The name was unusual but not as unusual as the names for the colors it came in: among others, Hylla Blue, Original Cinnamon, Anti-Establish-Mint and Thanks Vermillion. According to a 1969 item in *Automotive News* these names originally came from an Eagle Shirtmaker contest for new color

names which included Mason Dixon Lime, Bringembak Olive, and Tuckered Out Plum.

Mercedes-Benz. Named in 1900 for Mercedes, daughter of Emil Jellinek, diplomat and financier with interests in the company. In 1956 Leo Donovan of the *Detroit Free Press* wrote in his column, "Strange no car is named after a woman." Readers immediately pelted him with names, starting with Mercedes and including the Dolly Madison, the Diana, the Henrietta, the Maja, the Lorraine, the Delia, the Alma, and, of course, the Tin Lizzie.

Mitsubishi. It means "three pebbles" in Japanese, but the company has changed that to three diamonds in its logo.

N

N is for the Northern, New Yorker, Nissan, Nash, and Nova, as well as the one and only:

Nucleon. Ford's prototype nuclear-powered car, which was all but forgotten until it was featured in a 1984 Smithsonian exhibition called "Yesterday's Tomorrows: Past Visions of the American Future."

The Nucleon

O

O is for the Oakland, Overland, Oldsmobile, Opel, and Omni, along with the aptly labeled:

One of the Best. A British car manufactured from 1903-1906. It was modestly named compared to the Only, which was made by the Only Motor Car Co. of Port Jefferson, New York, from 1909-1915.

Otto-Mobile. An early puncar along with Ottokar and Otto.

P

P is for the Pinto, Pontiac, Peugeot, Packard, Pennington, Pierce Arrow, Phantom, Phaeton, Phelps, Polo, Prescott, Porsche, and the one-user Popemobiles, specially rebuilt Mercedes-Benz trucks created to display and protect Pope John Paul II after a 1981 assassination attempt. Also:

Plymouth. The brainchild of Walter Chrysler, this line of cars which debuted in 1928 was named to evoke the endurance of the Pilgrims who settled in Massachusetts.

Probe. Deemed by one writer as the most fascinating of all modern car names. Writing in the *Washington Times* on the topic of car names in 1989, Jennifer Harper asked what this name was all about: "As in space probe? Dental probe? Security probe? Conscience probe? Probe-oscis?"

Q

Q is for the Queen, Quick, Quinsler, Quo Vadis, and the Quantum.

R

R is for the Reo, Ruxton, Rohr, Riley, Roadmaster, Regal, Reatta, Rolls-Royce, and Reliant, as well as the:

Rambler. First a bicycle name, it has figured twice in automotive history—first, in 1902, as one of the first mass-produced automobiles, and in 1950 as a new breed of compact car in an era of ostentatious monster cars with useless fins.

Reliant. This Chrysler is oddly named when you recall that *reliant* describes someone or something that is dependent, that depends on another, a hanger-on. The oddness of Reliant as a car name was pointed out in the *Chicago Tribune* by Dan Tucker, a former English major led to muse on such things while stuck in a traffic jam, who was also puzzled by American Motors' Renegade, which means, "one who rejects his religion, cause, allegiance, or group for another; a traitor." The case can be made that the Chevrolet Citation is a peculiar name for two reasons: 1. Traffic tickets are often referred to as citations. 2. One model of the ill-fated Edsel was called the Citation.

Rockne. For its 1932 season, Studebaker launched a new car with a new name in honor of Knute Rockne, the great Notre Dame football coach who died in a plane crash in 1931. There were Rocknes in 1932 and 1933, but it never caught on and was discontinued at the end of 1933. Sticker price for a Rockne: $585.

Rolls-Royce. Named for Sir Henry Royce, who started the company in 1903, and for Charles Stewart Rolls, who promoted it. Rolls was the first Englishman to be killed in an airplane.

It can be argued that the name is the most prestigious product name in the world, while the individual model names are the stuff of dreams for those who would like to be rich. There have been Wraiths, Phantoms, and various Silvers—Silver Ghosts, Silver Dawns, Silver Clouds, and, most recently, Silver Spirits and Silver Spurs. The only two that do not seem to fit are two models introduced in the 1970s, the Corniche and the Camargue, which sound like expensive Chevrolets.

S

S is for the Shadow, Sundance, Simca, Saab, Studebaker, Stanley Steamer, Samson, Staley, Stutz, Scout, Sentinel, St. Louis, Scripps-Booth, Stoddard-Dayton, Simplex, Sears, Snell, Sable, Sierra, Supra, Sunny, Sunbeam, Siva Llama, and Seat, as well as the:

Saturn. In early 1985, General Motors announced the first new line of cars in 67 years, called the Saturn, giving the planets a boost they haven't had since the Mercury came along.

Sentra. This Nissan model was named by Namelab Inc. of San Francisco, a company in the business of naming products and companies. Ira Bachrach, driving force behind the naming company, was quoted in *American Way* magazine on how he came up with Sentra: "It's the company's mainstream, or central, car, and they wanted consumers to understand that it was quite safe even though it was small. The word *Sentra* sounds like *central* as well as *sentry,* which evokes images of safety."

Subaru. It means "the Pleiades," which is the constellation of stars which appears on the car's logo.

Sunbird. As if to prove that all modern model names are not the product of massive research efforts, the name of this Pontiac was suggested by Edith Jones, secretary to a Pontiac general manager. Similarly, Chevy II—predecessor to the Nova—was simply doodled on a tablecloth by a sales executive and an ad man at a lunch in the 1960s.

T

T is for the Tempo, Topaz, Talbot, Toledo, Tudor, Thomas, Terraplane, Toyota, Targa, and Town and Country, as well as the:

Taurus. The late Lew Veraldi, vice president of Ford car product development, and John Risk, a top engineer, determined that both their wives were born under the Taurus sign of the zodiac. Taurus was the project code name that eventually became the name of the car.

Toronado. One of the pioneering uses of a name that implied something but was new coinage. In the mid-1980s, Helen Jones Earley of Oldsmobile's Public Relations department in Lansing, Michigan, explained how the Toronado was named, thereby giving us rare insight into the ritual:

"The front-wheel drive Toronado was introduced in late 1965. Our engineering staff went through thousands of names in order to appropriately determine which would best fit this Oldsmobile model. This included animals, birds, fish, etc. In the pure Spanish concept, the word comes out to *the floating bull.* Of course, this has no reference to the car and has no meaning. We simply felt that Toronado would aptly describe the most unique car in the automobile world at that time."

U

U is for the Ultra, Umog, U2, UAZ, Ultima, Ultramobile, Unic, Union, Unipower, Unique, Unit, United, Universal, and Upton, along with the:

Urbmobile. One of a number of names given to prototype electric cars which never sound like real car names. Others: Amitron, Lectric Leopard, and Markette.

V

V is for the Volkswagen, Vim Suburban, Victoria, Victory, Voyager, Vauxhall, and Valiant, along with the:

Villager. Picked as the name for Mercury's minivan; the name Columbia was a finalist. Mercury liked it because of the symbolism of the space shuttle. It was scrapped when consumer research suggested a link with drugs, as in Colombia's cocaine trade.

Volvo. Latin for "I roll" is appropriate, but it originally came from the name of a ball-bearing company subsidiary where the two founders once worked. Commenting on the name in his *Dictionary of Trade Name Origins*, Adrian Room says, "The name with its two *Vs* and two *Os* is visually and graphically memorable, and a good international name—but is its resemblance to an anatomical term a potential embarrassment?" Room cannot resist answering his own question: "Doubtless *Volvo* [is] aware of this—yet the logo on the cars shows the name in the centre of a circle with a top-right out-pointing arrow—the astronomical sign for Mars or the male!"

W

W stands for the Willys, Wasp, White, Winton, Westminster, Waverly, and the Waterloo, which was unveiled in 1902 (this defeatist name was followed later by a car called the Napoleon), along with the:

Windstar. Ford's minivan companion to its Aerostar. The goal was a name that kept a family relationship to the Aerostar but was different enough to persuade buyers it was a new vehicle.

X

X is for the XKSS, XJS, Xenia, Xian-Jin, and Xtra.

Y

Y is for the Yugo, Yale, Yankee, Yank, Yenko, and YLN.

Z

Z is for the Zephyr, ZAZ966, Zastava, Zagato, Zip, Zil, Zim, Zin, Zis, and the:

Z3. This 1996 BMW Roadster proved that a letter name at the end of the alphabet was acceptable to buyers—at the end of 1995, two months before it came out, there were orders for 8,500 of them. The reason for the boom was in part due to the fact that the Z3 was the car driven by James Bond in the movie *GoldenEye*.

Collector's Showcase

Featuring Items from the John Q. Raspberry Memorial Collection of Names

9

ADELINE DINGLEDINE

NELIOUS KEE

OTIS PEBBLES MOTLEY

ZICKAFOOSE

OPAL LIVELY

MEBA ULCH

One morning almost 45 years ago someone telephoned Leland Hilligoss, a reference librarian at the St. Louis Public Library, to see if he could help locate a man named John Q. Raspberry. Hilligoss quickly found Raspberry in the phone book, but the name stayed with him, and a short time later when he started a collection of colorful and unusual names, he decided to name the collection after Raspberry. Soon he was adding all sorts of names to the collection: names that seemed to describe something else, like Holland Tunnell and Christian Bible, names that seemed reversed unless they were first spotted in the telephone book, like Cookie Fortune, Prey Lettuce, and Rush Gold, and names, like John Q. Raspberry, that were meant to be savored.

Over time Hilligoss enlisted other librarians and friends in the search and carefully avoided anonymous contributions or those from people he did not know in order to avoid fakes. By the mid-1980s, when it was shown to the author of this book, there were thousands of names in the collection which was housed in a giant battered manila envelope with THE JOHN Q. RASPBERRY MEMORIAL COLLECTION OF NAMES printed boldly across its front. Inside the envelope were hundreds and hundreds of small slips of paper containing names and their sources. Hilligoss, whose avocation is heraldry, found many antique names in old records. All sorts of things show up on the little slips of paper, including these quoted as found:

James W. G. T. C. H. K. A. G. E. Smith (1 year old) 1850 Ala. Census.

Olive Green married a Branch and became Olive Branch.

Xenerious Cherkinbower, 1850 St. Louis Census.

The Barons MacPhunn (alias M'Funie) of Dripp, from *Vassals of the Campbells in Scotland.*

One slip has a number of names collected from an old metropolitan phone book which includes Edy the Bagel and Wee Lox. Generally there are few Germanic or Native American names, but when found, they tend to be on the order of Lieut. Baron von Figyelmessy, a pilot, and Montgomery Ward Two Bellies. Some items defy categorization, such as the one from a North Carolina phone book for "Nixon's Funeral Home" followed by "If no answer dial Nixon's WB Cafe."

There are a number of knights, barons, and other titled individuals in the collection, including the Omugabe of Ankole, Sir Anthony Wass Buzzard, Sir Dingle Foot, Sir Bernard Thumboo Chetty, Sir Geoffrey Cuthbert Allchin, Rear Adm. Sir Leighton-Seymour Bracegirdle, and Adm. the Hon. Sir Reginald Aylmer Ranfurly Plunkett-Ernle-Erle-Drax, Knight Commander of the Bath.

Hilligoss, an extraordinarily generous and trusting man, loaned the collection to me for use in the first incarnation of this book with the provisos that (1) people

would not be identified by hometown and that (2) I add a few names to the collection as I worked through it. Many, many hours after opening the hallowed envelope, I settled on a selection of the most fascinating and colorful, and I will present them shortly.

As my part of the deal, I have added several dozen of my own discovery as well as scores which were given to me by a number of other collectors, most notably the late Barbara "Rainbow" Fletcher, author of *Don't Blame It On the Stork;* Jay Ames; Ben Willis; Joyce Rizzo; and Margaret Whitesides, who collected names for many years from her vantage point on the city desk of the *Chicago Daily News.* A number came from various items on name collecting published in the *Bulletin of the American Name Society,* from columns from the old *Washington Star* on file at the Martin Luther King Library (notably columns by Philip H. Love, Tom Dowling, and Charlie Rice), and from sources as diverse as H. L. Mencken (who discovered Dagmar Sewer) and the *Manchester Guardian* (which occasionally produces lists of names on the order of Thomas Strangeways Pigg and Mona Lisa Gooseberry).

It bids, again, to be one of the most colorful and fascinating list of real names ever set into print. As far as can be determined, all of the names are real and almost all were collected in North America and the British Isles. The purpose of the list is to celebrate the rich and remarkable diversity of names. It is separated into two sections: a general collection and a list of complementary names, or those which were created by parents—or marriage—with the resulting juxtaposition of an Ann Teak or a Hearty Meal.

From Leafy Beagle to Vera Necessary

A

Preserved Algar
Goldie Ambush
Cheerful Hyacinth Apple
Threepersons Appleyard
Broadus Arrowhead
Blaise Arsement
Anita Askew-Bawl

B

Magdalena Babblejack
Braser Bacon
Lucious Bacon
Taffy Sidebottom Ball
Beatrix Meats Balls
Dewey Barefoot
The Rev. Buzzard Barnes
True Batts
Quarteen Baxton
Leafy Beagle
C. Shovine Bean
Sessel Bean
Olga Beanblossom
Augdon Beasley
Twatie Beodath
Phoebe B. Peabody Beebe
Oneta Beeny
Madonna Beers
Wilburn R. Beerwart
Didier Begat
Sosthenes Behn
Pebble Belcher
Silence Bellows
Pud Berry
Callie Bess-Bogle
Uneeda Bias
Sibyl Bibble
Christian Bible
Hardin Biggerstaff
Dorinda Biggot
Benoni J. Bippus

Zirl D. Birge
Lenoir Black
Dionioush Blackshear
Virtue Blaring
April Blathers
Morticia Bloodsaw
Pinkie Mae Blowe
True Ralph Blue
Zerubabel Blunt
Fleno Bobo
Gromer D. Bobo
Lawnsey Bobo
Ormond Bobo
Plummer Bodily
Yolanda Bologna
Dimple Bonds
Wincenty Bonk
Zular Mae Bootchec
Luther O. Booze
Waynard Bopp
Elmyrtice J. Boshaw
Winter Ball Bottom
Little Botts
Minnie Minor Botts
Vital Bourgeois
Urbin Bowels
Billie Ann Bowlegs
Oofty Goofty Bowman
Ivory Box
Delicia Bracegirdle
Blanch Branch
Lamentation Brazil
Ulus Breedlove
Clorine Bright
Ferrel Bugg
Sereatha Bugg
Tee Olivure Buggs
Romaine Bumb
Orlando Furioso Bump
Barbara Bumpers
Gentle Bunch
Jewell Bunion
Loudies Burris
Blazy Busno
Relius Bussie

Coit Bustle
Virgil Bustle
Awful Butler
Charles Butterfuss
Berdina Buzzard
Whimper Jo Bynum
Orbenzender Byrd

C

Zetta Cabbage
Lunis Cansler
Oddy Carbona
Clifton Carnal
Burgoone Carnes
Ace Case
Hiawatha Cathcart
Onezine Champagne
Ulepses Champion
Vasedoza Chatmon
Haddassah Mae Cheatum
Tensil Cheesebrew
Toni Chickaloni
Chuck M. Chin
Sylvia Chinchilla
Ewhen Chorny
Oldiest Christmas
Kidnorked Cinsoete
Wooloomooloo Cleaves
Nuble Van Cleve
Brooksie Sue Click
Cletus Clodfelter
Ethel Cluck
Muddy Cockrell
Rodney Codpiece
Sinbad Condeluci
Alonzo Coots
Orie Corn
Youal R. Corn
Robert Cow
Clum Crane
Homer Crotts
Swanora Crudup
Margueryte Crum

Lovie Crumblie
Craven Crump
Manzy Crunk
Elmer Cudd
Macy Cuff
Fremont Curd
Naughtybird Curtsey
Rosebud Custard

D

Nancy Dancy
Blose Darcy
Zip A Dee Doo Daub
Philomena Deer
Neely C. Derryberry
Tisha Desha
Theo Despot
Hoke Dew
Dorn Dibble
Dimple Dilley
Isadora Ding
Frizelle Dingle
Adeline Dingledine
W. French Dingler
Oddie Dinkins
Dutch Dipple
David Disco
Tivoli B. Disharoon
Question Disnute
Valley Ditch
Abdoo Divis
O. K. Arthur Doak
Ola A. Dock
Verbal Dockery
Amanda Dove Doody
Ota Dossett
Crescent Dragonwagon
Ivory Drybread
Trufly Dubey
Drucella Duckworth
Wadley Duckworth
Flash Dumdum
Zanis Dumpis
Tatsumbie DuPea
Ike K. Dye

E

Margaret Rose Early
Rotten Earp
Calliroe Economu
Jemima Egge
Ed Ek
J. Crum El
Ocellous Ellis
Coyness L. Ennix
Foil Essick
Mrs. Weejane Estep
Kincheloe Ezell

F

Mrs. Palaladdey Faison
Argyle Faith
Anthony Falsetto
Wilbert Fangman
Wilson Fankboner
Elder Woodrow Fann
Faramarz Faramarpour
Finis Farr
Parvin Feaster
Binkley Fidge
Zeecozy Finney
Delbert Fireline
Mrs. Florida Fish
Wanda Fish
Windol Fiveash
Olga Flabbi
Lotawanna Flateau
Gerri Flatequal
Gaither Flatt
Byford L. Fleehart
Cassandra M. Flipper
Luster T. Flippen
Elzora Flitt
Waldemar Floggie
JoAnn Floozbonger
Ewing A. Flu
Felix J. Fluck
Bishop Flucker
Lentilhon Fluegge
Mazola Fluelen
Beatrice Flunder
Urban Flusche

Shannon Flyrear
Effie Fogg
Goble Fogle
Willa Babcok Folch-Pi
Epcy Fooshe
Santee Foppee
Prudie E. Forcum
Cookie Fortune
Filbain Fotler
Xenophone Foukas
Odious Foust
Burpee Fox
Pearlie Frogge
Fritioff Q. Fryxel
Foster Fudge
Itzhak Fuf
Justus H. Fugate
E. Vercel Fuglestad
Phifer Fullenwider, Jr.
America Funk
Ina Funk
Cashmere Funkhouser
Kenneth Funmaker
Capers C. Funnye
Fairy Furlong
Calvina Raye Furnace
Cash Furr
Wendekk Hinkle Furry
LaVon Futch

G

OK Pun Gassett
Quo Vadis Gates
Cleoletta Gee
Hilbert Gitchuway
Thap Glapthorne and
   Thack Glapthorne
L. E. Vontilzer Gleaves
Rudo S. Globus
Aage Glue
Asbury Glymph
Bing W. Go
Nice Go
Arthur Goatee
Delmus Gobble
Geranium Gobble
Loney Gog

President Goggins
Bubba Gong
Garnett Gooch
Colon B. Goodykoontz
Ryan Googoo
Felty Goosehead
Mrs. Methyl A. Goss
Veneta Grapes
Emcee Gray
Neniah Greathouse
Birdie Greenhouse
Powhatan Grevious
Roman Guck
Regula Gut
Elmer H. Gutzlaff

H

Coy Ham
Rusty Hammer
Zuedora Hare
Mrs. Ruth Hogwood Harp
Alyoysius Leroy
    Hasenfratz
Mona Lisa Sonia
    Danielle Hawk
Miss Wixie Herring
King Hero
Condo Hester
Sports Model
    Higenbotham
Leneva Hippe
Mrs. Lucky Lulu Hoar
Gum Shu Hom
Icy Macy Hoober
Zola G. Hooberry
Rev. Dunk Hooker
Square Horn, Jr.
Birdie T. Hospital
Monika Brigitta Houselog
Howard Harold Howard
Romany Huck
Zeffer Hull
Miss Fairy Hunt
Mrs. Mossie Husbands
Folks Huxford

I

Waugaman E. Ickes
Mrs. Eldris Idol
Calamity Iffershort
Elizabeth Hogg
    Ironmonger
Urwanda Island

J

Mingtoy Johnson
Joy Jolly
Karma Jukes
Birdsell Just
Hague C. Justice

K

Bloomie Kanipe
Jingle-Bells Kaplan
Mr. Oriole Katt
Nelious Kee
Hearn Kernodle
Texas Kidd
Forrest Kidney
Pebble Kirchmaier
Epluribus Kitchen
Coy Kitchens
Arvel Knuckles
Norbeth Koonce
Yvette Boasso Kopp
Tarzan Kush
Kasper Kwak

L

Fannie LaFata
Latitia LaFauce
Romeo LaGore
Ignatz Lafnitzegger
Dallas Utah Lamastus
Rose Larose
Velvet LaSane
Bebezene Lawless
Dr. Illtread W. Lecher

Lubertha Lemon
Tangerine Levy
Areagus Likely
Evelyn Liptrap
Earless Littlejohn
Daisy Lobster
Fanny Longbottom
Tuck Longest
Varnard P. Longhibler
Rolla Longnecker
Iwanna Looney
Cleyon Loonsfoot
Birdie Loose
Furbish Lousewort
Blessed Mary Love
Ducky O.L. Love
Pink Lovelace
Mrs. Beaver Luckey
Bolivar Lugg
Irma Lumber
King Charles Lumzy
The Rev. Vicesimus Lush
Rose Luster
Sethyl Lux

M

Althea Foss
    McBiddlewhiskers
Lesterine McCurine
Ophelia McFashion
Lun-Ye McGee
Perpetua McGurk
Projectus Machebeuf
River Rue Mack
Esterline McKnuckles
Sterling B. McSwine
Marcellous McZeal
Cleveland Maiden
King Mama
Kissia Mammon
Marilyn Joy Mankiller
Channing Manning
America Mantilla
Duel Maroon
Marvin Masoncup

Euthemia Matsoukas
Pea P. Matuu
Bugzester Maxim
Nita Maytubby
Gun-Britt Mbuthia
Gerald Measels
Maryland R. Midgett
Fuller Milsaps
Heavenfeather Miller
Sedonia Minneweather
Harold F. Mishmash
Berneal Misplay
Luch V. Moga
Pung Elba Molina
Lee Fat Mon
Beveridge Moose
Elteaser Mormon
Mrs. Feddo Mos
Otis Pebbles Motley
Marty Mouse
Skidmore Mousey
Emma Mutton
Oscar Muck
Otis Muckenfuss
Mrs. Eredon Muckle
Madonna Mudd
S. D. Muggleworth
Rains Munday
W. S. Mushrush

N

Voltaire Nails
Spurgeon Nanney
Ona Nation
Mabel Nebel
Esker New
Olney W. Nicewonger
Thela Idyl Nipper
Farke Nitzberg
Ney Nun Nix
Harmless Noland
Nayni Notion
Veto Noto
Dovie Lou Nuckles
Nall Nuckolls
Belle Nuddle
J. Lunchnet Nudy

Thomas J. Numnum
Osco Nunnery
Clovis Nutt
Minzo Nutt

O

Cecil O'Dear
Cleteel Odom
Dewey Odor
William Off
Flora Offel
Venus Officer
Olga Ooglaoga
J. J. Oladipupo
Ethel Oink
Pun On
Lovene Onutz
Marvin Oonk
Atilla Orhun
Ephraim Very Ott
Lester Ouchmoody
Orphia Outhouse
Ocal O. Overpeck
Esther Oyster

P

Monique Pancake
Corney Papp
Ovid F. Parody
Crouch Parrott
Goldus M. Parsley
John T. Parsnip
Sip T. Passwater
Horace Pea
Blondina Pee
Marshall Peace
Mrs. Uncas Peacock
Luda Peeler
Reveille Peepless
Groucher Peet
Romy Pellemounter
Loveless Pelt
Dean Pencil
Travis Penix
Tristram Tupper Penn

Berry Perry
Per Person
Heavenly Peterson
Flem D. Pettyjohn
Farce Pickle
Madge Pickup
Temple Pie
Silver W. Pigg
Primace Piggie
McCoy Pighee
Burris A. Pigman
Boise A. Pillow
Bertha Pimpell
Marinka Pinka
Grace Pinkapank
Postal Pinkston
Nay Pinnegar
Flodene Pippert
Goldie Pisk
Marily Schmitt Plankers
Wayland Plaster
Valli Plog
Lamoine Plopper
Nelson Pluff
Petway K. Plunk
Rollo G. Plunk
Noble Pluntz
Esse Poke
Evangelist Polite
Zeal Pong
Flikker Poot
Minerva Porch
Gardiner L. Porcupile
Amarindo Portfolio
Craspius Pounders
Merlin Prance
Lisoon Pretty
Oral Prffitt
Creola Pribble
Laura Adelaide
   Van Winkle Prigg
Rome Privet
Blanche Pubis
Clotilde Puffe
Noble Puffer
Elmer Puffpuff
Desire Pugh

Curt Puke
Slipp Punches
Fawntreba Pyrtle

Q

Loyce Quattlebaum

R

Peter J. J. Rabbitt
Les Rainey
Hillious Rather
William Plain Reason
Clay Reddish
Cub M. Riddle
Viva Riffle
Spaulding Ringo
Cato Roach
Tahiti Robaire
Plymouth Rock
Burger Rocket
Melon Roof
Silver Roofer
Maudlin Rose
Rulax Rowe
Roy L. Royalty
Freelove Rust

S

Goldie Sacharin
Quenel Saucier
Aurelian N. Schexnayder
Twila Schkithance
Fermine Schlag
Sylvester Schnoring
Doplhin Schrum
Excell Henry
  Schwinegruber
Goolsby Scroggins
Ocean Scupeen
Shruble Seeds
Quintes E. Self
Delta Seupersad
Miss Canola Shaddix

Starlight Cauliflower
  Shaw
Obediah Shegog
Ona Shopbell
Miss Mopsie Shott
Geneva Shrapnel
Ottan Skidstart
Marriable F. Skipper
Creed Skull
Norval Sleed
Armella Smerge
Okla Homer Smith
Murthy D. Sn
Alvin Snake
Elmore Snapp-Trappe
Berlina Snipes
Nettie Faye Snoddy
Uzell Snook
Leo Snozzie
Wilfred Snoozy
Alfred Snurpus
Mee T. SooHoo
Mrs. Gum Southard
Ace Speed
Ora Speegle
Ant Spino
Joop Spit
Denys Spittle
Odessa Spore
Odolfus Stamps
Ignas Stankus
Oystein Stole
Stella Stoops
Phoney Stout
Pepper Strain
Ruby Strawberry
Tyress Stubbs
Mowyer C. Stump
Exzera Suggs
Loving Suggs
Leo Tard Sullivan
Rebecca Sunnybrook
Michael Superman
Rodney Surprise
Clara Belle Sweat
Perley Swett
Tyco W. Swick

T

Zennus Tabbutt
Richard In Tang III
Craven Tart
Alf E. Tarwater
Johnson Teehee
V. D. Teet
Joe Terror
Irutha Fann Tew
Barbara Threefoot
Marvin Threewits
Ends T. Throop
Terrence Tickle
Fonzo Tidwell
Birdie Tinkle
Taffird J. Tinnius
Cosmo Tisbo
Otto Tittlefitz
Eloise Tittlekitty
Hiram Toadflax
Goodsel Toadvine
Ivory Tookas
Olive Toothaker
Huba Z. Topai
Oddie Tribune
Uldene Trickett
Korner Trinklet
Advance Triplett
Farrah Trostle
Loyal Trout
Elton Truss
Saving Tucker
Albirdia Tuggle
Nausica Tumbleson
Guvis Tumblin
Helen Tummy
Zealious Tunstle
Georgiana Turnipseed
Randy Turtle
King Tutt
Cooper J. Twaddle
Hogjaw Twaddle
Trina Twaddle-Montmayer
Sherman Tweet

U

Wyoma Ubelhor
Finely S. Uber
Ida Ubogy
Meba Ulch
Rufous Ullage
Dorothy Unnewehr
Boobpha Upthumpa
Mrs. Epsa Uren
Belle Utt
Erla Utter
Chippe Uy
Union Uzzle

V

Coy Valentine
Kong Vang
Marian Karian Varian
Mrs. Ovie Veale
Beedie Venable
Icy Vermillion

W

Rot C. Wack
Dolly Waffle
Mayblossom Wall
Woollen Hands Walshe
Doodle Dangle Wang
Walter Wart
Leonard Waxdeck
Anthropomorphic
    Westphal
Irwin Wetnight
Hannah Whisker
Percy A. Whynott
Brudder Widdo
Dimple T. Wiggins
Kimberley Wimberley
Minus Wingo
Gwendolyne Winklepleck
Crit Wolf
Herbert Wolf-
    eschlaegelsteinhausen-
    bergerhaufstedt
Bunyan Snipes Womble

Wendall Womble
Ting Wong
Wing Wong
Cozy Lee Woolfolk
Ursula Woop
Clifteen Wooters
Knud Word
A. Toxin Worm
Leander Worm
Serepta Worms
Peregrine Worsthorne
Onufry Woyak
Biddy Wrinkle
Gayla Wurl
Batt Wyche

Y

Anastasia Yabanobolous
McDonald Yawn
Joseph K. Ah Yet
Duck Yoo
Xavier Yopp
Wickiup Yurt
Otie Yutz

Z

Tosca Zerk
Vera Zero
Opal Lively Zickafoose
Jot Zed Zillion
Minnie Zips
Trougout Zumm

Complementary Names.
Since these are "of a piece"
they are listed alphabetically
by first name.

A

A. Forest Ranger
A. Lightfoot Walker
Adam Baum, the Rev.
Arch Virtue
Asia Minor
August Sunday

B

Barry Kuda
Becautious Hunter
Bent Korner
Berry Creamer
Berry Hunter
Berth Day Suter
Blossom Dew
Brite Rash

C

Candy Truss
Canon Ball, the Rev.
Champ Stonebreaker
Charity Fullilove
Charlotte Roos
Concepcion Love
Constant True Love
Cort R. Oi

D

Daily Swindle
Dimple Monger
Dirk Stikker

E

Earthmother Freeborn
Eaton Cotton
Etta Cherry

F

Fairest Price
Fair Hooker (former
    Cleveland Browns
    wide receiver)
Fannie Plenty
Fern Ivy
Fish Hook
Forrest Green
Pvt. Free Love
Friday Knight
Frieda Egg

G

Grave Heaven

H

Hard Bricker
Harmony Glory
Holland Tunnell
Honest Peek
Humann Klumpp

I

Ideal Snow
Innocent Babe
Ivy Snow Frost

J

Jerzy Kowski

K

King Edward Fears

L

Loveless Savage
Lowe Gear

M

Mac Aroni
Magnolia Flowers
Maida Swindle
Major Hill
Mary A. Christian
Mary Mea
Mary Rhoda Duck
Matt Adhoor
Melody Toot
Merie Spearman
Merry Holliday Koo
Missouri Streets
Morning Dew
Moody Mask

N

Neva Raines
Nile Green
Noble Waddle

O

Only Human
Oral Musick
Original Bugg
Overland Driver

P

Pansy Potts
Pleasant Vice
Pool Hall
Preserved Fish

R

Ray Gunn
Red Wall
River Jordan
Rivers Rush
Rollin Stone
Rose Cologne
Rowdy Group—This
name shows up several
times in the Raspberry
collection as well as in
other collections and is
always noted as a phone
book listing. Could this
be a collective name for
a group of, say, college
students?
Rum Tapp

S

Safety First—"Every time
I get a traffic ticket I get a
column in the newspa-
pers," he once told a
reporter. "I've been in
Ripley's three times."
His sister's name: June.

Sally Forth
Scott Towle
Seaborn Moss
Serious Misconduct
Sherry Moonshine
Solomon Mines
Spring Wheat
Stella Star
Summers Long

T

Temperence Going
Tin Cans
Tiny Stamps
Tom N. Gerry
Truly Hardy
Truly Irish
T. V. Button

V

Valentine Card
Vanity Fair
Vera Necessary

W

Watt Cheek
Wealthy Driver
Weary Willie
Wellington Boot
William Shake Spear
Mrs. Wood Sapp
Woodie Lott
Worth Price
Worthy Brown

A list like this suggests that there should be a central clearinghouse for name collections. Several major collections have been lost over the years while others remain tied up in estates or otherwise unavailable to the public. The fact is that there are some fantastic collections around that rival the full Raspberry Collection. Hard to believe? Consider these:

The Hubbard Collection. One of the greatest collections was put together by the late George Hubbard of New York City, who once wrote an article on his collection for *Hobbies* magazine under the pen name of Suffern Catts: he seems to have collected in just about every category but always sought the full name. He once told an interviewer that his favorites from his accumulation of 10,000 included Oscar Asparagus, Three Persons Appleyard, Aphrodite Chackess, and Sistine Madonna McClung. Hubbard was once quoted in the *New York Post* on the ideal nature of a name collection: "You don't have to polish it, dust it, or wash it, and no one is going to steal it from you, so you don't have to insure it. It's the easiest kind of collection and the most charming. It doesn't cost anything, and it doesn't require labor."

The Rainbow Collection. The vast collection put together over a period of more than 25 years by Barbara Rainbow Fletcher of Seattle. Much of this collection is contained in her fine book *Don't Blame It On the Stork,* and it is arranged by category. For instance, under the heading "Is a Rose as Sweet by any Other Name?" she lists more than 50 Roses including these real names: Rosie Butts, Rose Bloom, Rose Rose, and Rose Bud. Her list of Mays include Hilda May Falter, Helen May Buck, Hazel May Call, and Jennie May Shove. There is even a major sub-collection of "X-Rated" names. A small sampling: Seymore Astern, Bernard Sexfinger, Helen Zahss, Hyman Ballbinder, and Lemaza Hotballs. Because of the exhaustive thematic work she has done, it may be a unique collection.

SVEFNAP. Another great North American collection is in Canada and is under the aegis of the one-man Society for the Verification and Enjoyment of Fascinating Names of Actual Persons. Founded many years ago by Clive Gilmore of the *Toronto Star,* now its Founder Emeritus, the new curator is Allan Fotheringham, of the *Vancouver Sun* and *MacLean's Magazine.*

Fotheringham has written that SVEFNAP has "stern standards" and will not accept names like Jack Knife and Mary Christmas but demands "verve, imagination [and] a certain insane courage in naming the progeny." Examples he gives which are up to SVEFNAP standards include Lawrence Flewelling Grumbly, Gerbert Harmston Frudd, and Zilpher Spittle.

There are other collections, including that of the Hobart Clonch, Jr. Memorial Funny Name Society.

Corporate Names

T ime was, a company went into the molasses business, called itself American
Molasses and kept that name as long as the molasses kept flowing. Then beginning in the 1960s, the idea took hold that a quick name change was good for the
corporate image. Merger mania dictated more changes, and soon it was hard to keep
track of who was and who used to be who. *If* there had been an American Molasses, it
would have become Amolco in 1968, turned into AMPCO in 1975 after its merger with
Pizza Chalet, and since 1984 would have been known as Amptech Group.

If the 1980s saw the high tide of name-changing for corporate America, the 1990s
have been a period in which the trend has slowed. One reason may have been that the
general population that knew what U.S. Steel was all about wasn't at all sure about USX.
One study made in 1988, two years after the change to USX, revealed that consumers
held USX in low esteem (the lowest 5 percent in ranking) and U.S. Steel in high regard
(in the top half).

USX was not alone. International Harvester, whose roots go back to the 1830s,
became Navistar International Corp.; American Can became Primerica; Datsun became
Nissan (at a cost of $50 million or more); United States Gypsum became USG Corp.; and
Libbey-Owens-Ford became Trinova.

Here are some of the major trends in modern corporate naming, which went into high gear in the late 1980s, with one from the 1990s:

The Big Buck Change. The most famous of these took place when the Esso tiger told us, "We're changing our name but not our stripes." The change to Exxon, which took place in 1972, climaxed three years of linguistic and marketing tests and ended up costing the company more than $100 million. Signs and logos were changed at 65,000 locations.

Operating under the code name of Project Nugget, the company looked at more than 10,000 names in order to come up with one that was (a) short, (b) had no actual meaning, and (c) had no vulgar or negative connotations in any of the world's major languages. *Barrons* reported that some stockholders were pleased because to them "double X means double excellent" while others saw it as a double cross.

Exxon takes this all very seriously and has gone as far as to sue the Exxene Corp., a tiny Illinois firm, for trademark infringement. Exxene countersued and won, although that decision was appealed by Exxon. This yielded the following headline in the *Wall Street Journal* in 1981: "Exxon, Schmexxon, Says the Jury, Score This Round for the Little Guy." Meanwhile, others have decided they like the double-*x*—for instance, in 1984 Simplicity Patterns became the Maxxam Group. *Maxxam*, like *Exxon*, means nothing but has the added advantage of being a palindrome.

Forbes noted in the early 1970s that "X-names are highly prized." The magazine added that the greatest of all the X-names, Xerox, almost didn't make it, as the company's late president, Joseph Wilson, was afraid people would pronounce it "Ex-rox" and mistake it for a laxative.

Today the double-*x* in business names is commonplace—as with Maxxam, Nexxus, T. J. Maxx, and a telescope maker named Lynxx—and there is a pornographic cable channel known as the Exxxtasy Channel sporting three *x*'s.

The Exxon change cost a bundle, but it is hardly alone in that regard. In 1969, Gulf Canada Ltd. announced that it had spent close to $14 million to change its name from the British American Oil Co. Ltd., and in 1979 Allegheny Airlines became USAir for a mere $3 million. Given this, a change costing less than a million is considered a bargain.

Compressions. Everywhere one looked in the 1990s, one found names with a missing space and a capital letter in the middle: USAir, FedEx, HarperCollins, MasterCard, NutraSweet, ComputerLand, and so many more jammings.

Descriptive Names. Small business still retains much of this spirit; a moving company in Iowa which calls itself Two Men and a Truck, and Wreck-a-Mended, which is a Florida family-owned auto body shop, are among those which have won awards for their aptness.

Initials. It started in the 1960s when fine old names like Smith-Corona became SCM, Thompson-Ramo-Woolridge became TRW, and the Republic Aviation Corp. became RAC. The Hamilton Watch Company became HMW Industries, PPG was once Pittsburgh Plate Glass, GAF was General Aniline and Film, CPC was Corn Products Corp., and Swift and Co. became Esmark, Inc. The colorful Batten, Barton, Durstine & Osborne—once said to sound like a trunk falling down the stairs—is now blandly known as BBDO International.

Some of these work better than others. IBM, 3M, and RCA—all official names for those companies—get away with it, but what of M/A COM Inc., which the *Washington Post* termed the worst named company in the Washington area?

Most disconcerting: trucks in my neighborhood with the large letters G.O.D. on them—it stands for Guaranteed Overnight Delivery.

Merger Names. Some of these take something from the name of each company merged (Connecticut General and INA merged into Cigna Corp.) while others become something new. An interesting example of the latter is that of the Sovran Bank, which was created after two Virginia banks merged in 1984. It is a variant spelling of the word *sovereign* which hasn't been much used since the 17th century and which sounds more like the name of a brand of instant coffee than of a bank. Some other strange names emerge from all of this. It began as the Bank of Ohio, but after 36 mergers, it had become the Fifth Third Bancorp. When Burroughs and Sperry Corp. merged in 1986, employees were asked to come up with a name for the pairing. There were 31,000 suggestions from which *Unisys* won. The winner was paid $5,000. The combination of United Airlines, Hertz, and Westin Hotels became Allegis in 1987.

Oxymoronic Names. United Diversified, Ideal Basic, and Monument Energy are three of those self-contradicting names pointed out by Steele Commager in a 1983 *New York Times* article on the subject. He also pointed to companies which could dispirit potential investors, including Zero Corporation, Limited Stores, and Sunset Industries. Speaking of bad names, consider such airline names as Kiwi (a

bird that cannot fly), Coffin Air Services, and Ransom Air.

Personifications. Popular among franchising groups who offer people a new livelihood as the owner of a Dr. Vinal, Dr. Personnel, Sir Goofey (of Sir Goofey Golf), Sir Beef, Dr. Nick (of Dr. Nick's Transmissions) franchise and many more.

Apparently this can work wonders. Thixo-Tex, a moderately successful rustproofing product from the Matex International Corp., did not take off until it was renamed Rusty Jones. Chessie System Inc., named for the C&O kitten, came along to replace the awkward C&O/B&O which was pronounced "Ceenobeeno."

Staccato Names. Some fine old names have been rendered punchy and zappy. International Nickel is now Inco, the Old Utica Drop Forge and Steel Co. became Utco, and the American Smelting and Refining Co. was turned into Asarco. Commenting on names of this type in the *Washington Star*, when they first began cropping up, Bob Swift said, "They sound impolite to me, like someone committing a social error." Some don't sound quite so bad. Just after Hart Schaffner & Marx announced it would become Hartmarx, an article in the *Wall Street Journal* said it sounded "a little like a brother of Groucho and Zeppo."

Occasionally one doesn't make it. Back in the 1950s the Socony-Vacuum Oil Company seriously considered becoming Sovac until market researchers found that the public associated the new name with Soviet Russia and communism. It chose Mobil instead.

This trend continues, especially among utilities. The Indianapolis Power and Light Co. became Impalco Enterprises and the Tampa Electric Co. is now the TECO Energy Corp.

These clipped names are often the subject of great thought and deliberation. *Citgo*, for instance, was one of 100,000 computer-generated choices offered for the old Cities Service Corp.

Troublesome Names. When Sam Battistone and F. Newell Bohnett founded a fast-food chain, they took one man's first name and the first two letters of the second man's last name to get *Sambo's*. The name offended because of its suggestion of *Little Black Sambo*. The city of Toledo tried unsuccessfully to block the opening of a restaurant there in 1978, and community pressure in Reston, Virginia, and several other locations got the name of the restaurant changed to the *Jolly Tiger*. The name has not helped and in 1981, the company began experimenting with *No Place Like Sam's*. At that point, *Time* magazine said the company's name had given it "a major image problem."

Wang Laboratories Inc. has had name problems of a different kind as people have not been oblivious to the fact that *wang* is one of the many slang terms for the male sex organ. When a Washington, D.C., radio station, WASH, aired a gag commercial for Wang with obvious play on the sexual meaning of the name, the company was not amused. Wang, in 1984, sued WASH for $10 million.

Unbankish Names.

For decades you could rely on stolid, unchanging bank names, but no more. Banks, like utilities, are moving away from the basics and giving themselves names which are more reminiscent of high technology than finance, as with Banco, Unibanc, Bank One, Citicorp, and the aforementioned Sovran, which are a far cry from First National. There were, in 1986 exactly 1,681 with First National in their name. Through merger and name change, few remain.

Maybe the best of the new bank names is that of Tightwad Bank of Tightwad, Missouri. It is actually a branch of the Citizens Bank of Windsor, Missouri, and changed its name officially in 1984 in an effort, according to the *Wall Street Journal*, "to appeal to penny pinchers everywhere."

Our motto:
"We threw away the keys to your money."

Vague Names. As companies diversify, the trend has been to have a less specific name. When, for example, National Theaters Inc. expanded beyond a chain of theaters, they became the National General Corp. Ditto for Signal Oil, which became the Signal Companies after diversification, and the U.S. Rubber Co. which is now Uniroyal. What these companies have in common is that they don't give you a clue about what they actually do—e.g., Coradian Corp., Camelot International, Elscint Ltd., Conwed Corp., Cyclops Corp. One of the more recent cases of going from the specific to the vague was General Tire and Rubber, which is now known as GenCorp.

The trend merited comment in the *Bulletin of the American Name Society:* "The fine old names, full of flavor, are gradually vanishing from the scene, replaced by bland and colorless appellations." This was written before AT&T spun off regional phone companies with the names *Ameritech* and *Nynex*, the latter deemed to be the worst name of any company in America by the publisher of *Advertising Age*. What does it sound like? It has been variously suggested that it sounds like the rating for a very dirty movie, the middle name of a Muslim boxer, and the brand name of a hair restorer.

Ironically, one of the places where corporate names are refreshingly direct is on the ticker tapes of the major stock exchanges where the symbols are often models of clarity. Anheuser-Busch is BUD, Dr. Pepper Co. is DOC, Magic Marker Industries is PEN, After Six Inc. is TUX, Nutrition World Inc. (a health food chain) is NUTS, Seagram Co. Ltd. is VO, a restaurant chain featuring potatoes, called 1 Potato 2 Inc., shows on the tape as SPUD, the Boston Beer Co. is SAM (it makes Sam Adams Beer), and the Cheesecake Factory is CAKE.

Cybernetic Baptism

Dear Book Reader,
You and other members of the Reader family may have already won $500,000....Like your neigh-
bors the Page Turners, you have been carefully selected....

So they come in from the magazine sweepstakes czars, political fund-raisers, and just about anyone else who can figure out how to get a bulk mail permit, buy some mailing lists, and fire up a computer.

All sorts of things then start to happen. New people are created—my name, Paul, was once erroneously listed as Paula in the phone book, and she began getting letters from *Redbook* and *Ms.* She has not been allowed to die, offering an odd cybernetic immortality, because every time I think that Paula is gone, she comes back again. Suddenly in 1984, she got a pile of mail from the Mondale-Ferraro election committee while the real me was totally neglected by the Democratic National Committee, despite the fact that I was a registered Democrat.

Since the 1984 election she has been made a doctor and presumably married one. A December 5, 1984, form letter from Geraldine Ferraro is addressed to Dr. and Dr. Paula Dickson. Even more remarkably she is thanked for her "generous contribution" to the campaign. At the beginning of 1985, she had become just plain Ms. again in a letter from the DNC asking for money, in addition to her generous 1984 contribution. As this is written in 1996 her mail has dwindled, apparently because the word is out that she is not a generous soul. Dr. Paula is now 22 years old and will doubtlessly outlive me, especially after this appears in print.

Meanwhile my wife, who has actually given money to the Democrats, has been getting mail for some years now addressed to Mr. Nancy Dickson. They have also called for Mr. Nancy at dinner to thank him for his contribution.

People do seem to live forever in this realm. The *Washington Post* noted a while back that David W. Taylor, whose name is on the David W. Taylor Naval Ship Research and Development Center, had been dead for 44 years, but that didn't stop the Book-of-the-Month Club from occasionally asking him to join. If there is a liberal attitude towards death here, it does not extend to long names. Many people have had their names chopped off by computers which have been programmed not to tolerate names with more than 12 letters and simply lop off the extra letter. Others have reduced all middle names to an initial and refuse to have anything to do with Jr.'s and III's.

As the computer age grinds on, the opportunity for collecting these *automonyms* (a coinage created for this automated naming) will grow. For starters here are some examples that I have collected. All are from computer-generated letters, many of which were sent out asking for contributions to candidates for election.

Dear Mr. Boys (to parents who had sent a subscription to a sports magazine for their sons as "The Haley Boys")

Dear Mr. Cncl. Rep. Wmn. (to a local Council of Republican Women)

Dear Mr. Co.

Dear Ms. Credit

Dear Mr. Electronics

Dear Ms. Farm

Dear Mr. Inc.

Dear Ms. Marketing

Dear Mr. Mfg.

Dear Mr. Of (letter addressed to Austin Texas City Of)

Dear Mr. Office

Dear Mr. The

Dear Mr. Trust (to an oil trust)

Dear Ms. Wash (to a car wash)

And, saving the best for last, a letter addressed to **Dear Mr. God** (to the Church of God).

Sometimes it is not just the name but the contents of the letter which make these gaffs amusing. The *Reader's Digest* reported on a letter to the Public Service Co. of Oklahoma which began:

Dear Mr. Serv.,
Did you know that the Serv. family name was recorded with a coat of arms in the heraldic archives—and while there are 60 million households in the United States, fewer than 212 of them are Serv. households?

The letter goes on to offer Publ. Serv. a coat of arms and a report on the Serv. family—all "suitable for framing."

All of this is not to say that the senders are always at fault. A friend puckishly wrote "Clearly" in a form that stated "Name, please print clearly" and takes great pleasure from the mail that he is getting as Mr. Clearly.

All of this will probably only get worse before it gets better—unless of course you collect automonyms and then it seems we are entering a Golden Age.

Goodnight, Ms. Wash, wherever you are.

Dutch Dictionary

Slur Names 12

Dutch Nose Job

Dutch Door

The first list came from J. van de Weyer, who now lives in Iowa but is from the Netherlands—in other words, a Dutchman. He thought I'd be interested in what had been done to his people in English, and his Dutch dictionary included these examples:

the Dutch act = suicide.

Dutch courage = bravery inspired by drinking. As far back as 1625 the British poet Edmund Waller wrote:

> *The Dutch their wine and all their brandy lost,*
> *Disarmed of that from which their courage grows.*

Dutch defense = surrender, no defense at all.

Dutch nightingale = a frog.

Dutch reckoning = guesswork, or a disputed bill.

Dutch treat = a treat whose price is shared by host and guest(s).

Dutch uncle = a severe, disciplinary man.

Dutch widow = a prostitute.

to be in Dutch = to be in trouble.

This led to a search for as many Dutch terms as possible and some explanation for why the good people of the Netherlands have been made to suffer so in English. By all accounts, the pejorative use of the word *Dutch* dates back to the 17th century when the British and the Dutch fought over control of the sea and parts of the New World. Not only did the British start the tradition of hostile Dutch slurs but actually wiped out Dutch names when territory changed hands. New Amsterdam became New York as soon as the British took over in 1664. In *The American Language: Supplement I*, H. L. Mencken traces the English use of the derisive *Dutch* back to 1608, but adds that many of the slurs started in the United States where some may have been aimed at Germans, who have been "Dutch" for generations. This came about as early immigrants referred to themselves as *Deutsch.* Those with the nickname "Dutch" were, in fact, seldom from the Netherlands but of German background. For this reason, many a Dutch immigrant referred to himself as a Hollander or Netherlander.

One Dutch term, *Dutch courage,* appears to have come from an actual facet of Dutch life rather than from a generalized dislike. In their *Naval Terms Dictionary,* John V. Noel and Edward L. Beach give it this definition: "The courage obtained from drink. Comes from the custom initiated by the famous Dutch Admirals, Tromp and de Ruyter, of giving their crews a liberal libation before battle with the English. The practice was naturally belittled by the English, who nevertheless were forced to admit to the effectiveness of the Dutch Navy."

After consulting slang dictionaries dating back to 1811 and a number of specialized dictionaries, I now appreciate how pervasive this longstanding Dutch slur has become and how it continues to be the most multifaceted semantic injustice. Writer Richard Lederer, who took a hard look at the slur after marrying Simon

van Egeren, a woman of Dutch descent, concluded that the collective Dutch compounds and expressions amount to a depiction of people who are "cowardly, cheap and deceitful." In an attempt to turn this slur around Lederer wrote of his wife in one of his "Looking at Language" newspaper columns, "Throughout my relationship with my Dutch treat, I've been enjoying saucy Holland days."

The List:

double Dutch = gibberish; also a jump rope term for jumping with two ropes.

Dutch auction = one which starts with a high bid and works down.

Dutch barn = a barn without sides.

Dutch bath = an acid bath used in etching.

Dutch book = a bookmaker's account book.

Dutch brig = a cell in which punishment is meted out.

Dutch build = a squat person.

Dutch cap = a condom.

Dutch cheese = baldness.

Dutch comfort = consolation typified by the line, "It could have been worse."

Dutch concert = a concert in which everyone plays a different tune.

Dutch daub = a mediocre painting, ironic since there were so many great Dutch painters.

Dutch drink = emptying a glass in one gulp.

Dutch elm disease = not the same kind of slur as the others, but it goes to show how unlucky the Dutch are when it comes to naming.

Dutch feast = a dinner at which the host gets drunk before the guests do, or worse yet one where the host is drunk before the guests arrive.

Dutch fit = a fit of rage.

Dutch gleek = liquor.

Dutch leave = to be AWOL, a term which became popular during the Spanish-American War.

Dutch nightingale = a frog.

Dutch palate = coarse taste.

Dutch pink = boxer's term for blood.

Dutch pump = sailor's punishment in which he is thrown overboard and must tread water to keep from drowning.

Dutch rod = a Luger pistol.

Dutch row = a faked altercation.

Dutch roll = a combined yaw and roll in an aircraft, something to be avoided because it can cause a plane to go out of control. This term shows that some of these Dutch words are new, since the earliest reference I could find to it was in a 1950 issue of *Popular Science.*

Dutch route = suicide.

Dutch rub = an intensely painful rubbing usually to the scalp.

Dutch silver = silver plate.

Dutch steak = hamburger.

Dutch tilt = a television and movie term for a camera which has been tilted from the horizontal for dramatic effect.

Dutch wheelbarrow = taking someone by their legs as they walk with their hands.

Dutch wife (or **Dutch husband**) = a feather pillow, a poor bed companion, more recently an inflatable rubber sex partner.

Dutchman's headache = drunkenness.

Dutchy = slovenly.

In addition there are Dutch phrases:

as drunk as a Dutchman

Well, I'll be a Dutchman's uncle = an expression of surprise.

to get one's Dutch up = to arouse one's temper. Charles Earle Funke points out in his book *Heavens to Betsy* that this in fact refers to the Pennsylvania Dutch, who are of course not Dutch but German.

The Dutch have done little to fight back. Noah Jacobs tells us in his book *Naming Day in Eden* that they do refer to a dirty trick in the Netherlands as a "German trick" and have been known to use *Scotch* in references to extreme cheapness. The only other response, according to Stuart Berg Flexner in *I Hear America Talking*, was in 1934, when the government of the Netherlands ordered its public officials to stop using the term *Dutch* because of its connotations and stick to *the Netherlands.*

If there is any consolation for the Dutch, it is that they have been left out of the recent round of ethnic jokes (Newfie, Polack, Aggie, etc.) and that there are other slurs and characterizations. In 1944 Abraham Roback published a book entitled *A Dictionary of International Slurs*, which contained scads of them. Of course many of these ethnic and geographic terms are not slurs but descriptions used in everyday speech (*French toast, Danish pastry, Chinese checkers, Siamese twins, Cuban heels, Canadian bacon, English muffins,* and so forth). Many of these are misnomers—Danish pastry is Vienna bread in Denmark, and the English are unfamiliar with American English muffins—but they are hardly negative.

Borrowing a few from Roback and adding many of more recent vintage, here is proof that the Dutch have company:

American tweezers = burglary tools.

Bronx bagpipe = a vacuum cleaner.

Bronx cheer = flatulent razz.

Chinese fire drill = pandemonium.

Chicago majority = 105 percent of the vote.

Chicago piano = a machine gun.

Chicago rubdown = a thrashing.

Colorado Kool-Aid = Coors beer.

English disease = chronic discontent.

French disease = syphilis.

French letter = a condom.

German tea = beer.

Indian gift = a gift which one expects to have returned.

Irish confetti = bricks.

Irish dividend = an assessment.

Irish draperies = cobwebs.

Irish parliament = a noisy argument bordering on a free fight.

Irish pennant = a loose thread.

Italian perfume = garlic.

Jewish penicillin = chicken soup.

Mexican standoff = confrontation that cannot be resolved.

Mexican strawberries = beans.

Norwegian Jello = lutefisk, so called because it is rubbery and gooey before cooking. It has been called far worse names.

Russian boots = leg irons.

Scotch organ = cash register.

Spanish padlock = chastity belt.

Swedish fiddle = a crosscut saw.

Turkish medal = an unbuttoned fly.

Of course, many of these pairings are much more hostile, and I will refrain from using them lest I get in Dutch, which is hard to avoid. In 1993, for example, a lawsuit was filed by Welsh-Americans against *Newsweek*, the *Wall Street Journal*, the *Los Angeles Times*, Universal Press Syndicate, and NBC, because each has used the term *welsh* when referring to cheating on debts. Days later the *Washington Post* carried a front-page story on the misfortunes of Homestead, Florida, which had recently been hit by everything from a hurricane and winter cyclone to clouds of mosquitoes. In the article, *Post* reporter William Booth reported, "Homestead Mayor [Tad] DeMilly fears the government and President Clinton may welsh on promises made to help south Dade County recover."

MORAL: Old slurs are hard to break.

Dutch Nightingale

Eponymous Beats Anonymous

Leotards, Chauvinists, and Begonias Have One Thing in Common

13

Mr. Guppy meets Big Bertha

The odds against having your name become a word are in the tens of millions-to-one category. It is as likely as living to be 115 years of age or getting the top off a childproof medicine bottle in less than a minute.

Despite this, some might have preferred that the honor had passed them by, because they are remembered for a rather small thing, while their great deeds are all but forgotten. This was true of Prime Minister William Ewart Gladstone, who for decades was remembered more for the baggage he carried than for his great statesmanship. For others, great disasters are forgotten in light of what was, at the time, a minor detail. Consider the Earl of Cardigan, who led the ill-fated Charge of the Light Brigade but today is more likely to be remembered for the woolen sweater he designed to keep his troops warm in the Crimea or, for that matter, Cardigan's commander Lord Raglan, who ordered the Charge. He is now more likely to be recalled for his oddly configured sleeves than for a military disaster.

Then there are those whose names get attached to unpleasant things. Consider the case of Dr. Joseph-Ignace Guillotin, who went to his grave protesting the fact that *they* had put his name on that machine which he did *not* invent. All the poor doctor had done was to give a speech advocating a more "merciful" means of execution to replace the noose and ax then in use. Others just missed such ignominy: Thomas Edison once suggested that the process of legal electrocution be called *westinghousing* after George Westinghouse, who had worked to develop and exploit alternating-current electric power.

Yet for most of us, the prospect of becoming a lowercase noun or verb is to be offered near immortality. A hint for those hoping for this ultimate honor: your odds improve if you hang around people who name plants and flowers or if you breed a new one yourself. Michel Bégon (*begonia*), Major John Bibb (*Bibb lettuce*), Olaf Bromelius (*bromeliad*), Anders Dahl (*dahlia*), Dr. Alexander Garden (*gardenia*), Timothy Hanson (*timothy grass*), Pierre Magnol (*magnolia*), Joel Robert Poinsett (*poinsettia*), Johann Gottfried Zinn (*zinnia*), Joseph Woods (*woodsia*), and Caspar Wistar (*wisteria*) are a few of many such cases.

Such words are called *eponyms,* and they refer to people and places which have become words. Here is a roll of some of the people and a few places which made the leap. It leaves out some of the more famous examples—Louis Braille, Rudolf Diesel, Daniel Gabriel Fahrenheit, and Vidkun Quisling—in favor of the lesser-known likes of:

A

Academus. A hero of Greek mythology who gave his name to a grove near Athens where Plato taught.

B

Berserk. A word that describes one who is raging or crazed. The original Berserker was a warrior in Scandinavian mythology who was so reckless and driven that he fought in skins rather than armor. In Old Norse the term means "bear shirt." *Berserk* is now, among other things, the name for a video game in which the player defends himself from robot attackers with a laser gun.

Bikini. The bikini bathing suit was introduced at a Paris fashion show and was named after the atomic explosion which took place on the Bikini Atoll in the Pacific four days earlier, on July 1, 1946. It stands as one of the oddest and quickest jumps in the history of eponyms: from an atoll to almost nothing at all.

Amelia Jenks Bloomer (1818-1894). She was a well-known women's rights advocate, temperance crusader, and abolitionist who neither invented nor first wore bloomers but spoke in favor of bloomers as an alternative to the hoop skirt. It is one of the rare female eponyms.

Charles Cunningham Boycott (1832-1897). He was an Englishman who farmed and acted as a land agent in 19th-century Ireland. In 1880 he was singled out by a local group of land reformers who saw him as an oppressor of the poor. Specifically, there had been two years of bad potato harvests and three of his tenant farmers demanded rent reductions. Boycott said no emphatically and tried to have one of the tenants evicted. The tenants and the reformers then launched a campaign against him. As he wrote in a letter to the London *Times,* his crops were carried away, his servants intimidated, his livestock driven off, and local merchants refused to sell him goods. He couldn't even get his mail delivered. He finally had to bring in his harvest with the aid of armed guards and was eventually hounded out of Ireland.

There is a 1982 book on eponyms entitled *Batty, Bloomers and Boycott* by London journalist Rosie Boycott, who is the great, great niece of Capt. Boycott. In the book she attempts to pinpoint the moment when the name became a generic word. She believes that moment occurred when a local priest who was supporting the tenants was talking with an American journalist named James Redpath. Reportedly, Redpath turned to the priest and said, "I'm bothered about a word. When people ostracize a land-grabber we call it *social excommunication*, but we ought to have a different word for a landlord or agent like Boycott....*Ostracism* won't do. The peasantry won't understand." The priest thought for a moment and replied, "How would it do to call it to *boycott* him?" Within six years after that first boycott, the name *Boycott* was appearing in the newspapers with a lowercase *b*.

Steve Brodie. "To pull a brodie" is to flop or blunder or take a wild chance. Brodie was a New York newsboy who survived a leap off the Brooklyn Bridge in 1886. He did it to win the $200 that he had been offered to make the jump by friends. He was arrested the following day for attempted suicide but was also offered $100 a week to exhibit himself at a Brooklyn museum as the world's most courageous man. Ironically, *brodie* is associated with a blunder when, in fact, the real Brodie parlayed his jump into long-lasting fame. He was played by George Raft in the movie *The Bowery*.

General Ambrose Everett Burnside (1824-1881). A Civil War Union general more conspicuous for the conspicuous whiskers above his shaved chin than for his leadership (he won no great battles). His *burnsides* grew into *sideburns*. A recent advertising campaign by Hammermill Paper, emphasizing the importance of names, based an ad on Burnside which was titled, "How a Civil War general's name changed the face of Rock 'n' Roll."

Nicholas Chauvin. A soldier in the army of Napoleon whose loyalty was so intense that he was mocked by his comrades and recalled in the word *chauvinism*. In recent times, the term got a good workout applied to male chauvinists—or those excessively loyal to their gender.

Tom Collins. A 19th-century bartender who worked at Limmer's Old House in London. Others whose names live at the cocktail hour include Scottish outlaw Robert Macgregor of the Rob Roy, Queen Mary I of England in the Bloody Mary, and Washington lobbyist Joe Rickey, who invented the Gin Rickey.

The story behind the last discovery bears retelling. Rickey was in a Washington bar, Shoomaker's, one hot day just before the turn of the century and overheard a patron saying that a cooler that the bartender had made was not cooling him. At that moment a wonderful coincidence took place. A fruit vendor entered the bar and the resourceful Rickey grabbed a handful of limes, experimented with them, some gin, and some soda water and added ice. The bartender, George Williamson, gave it the name and within days it was being offered in every bar on Pennsylvania Avenue.

H. L. Mencken traced the martini to the year 1899 and the name on the Martini and Rossi vermouth bottle, but other explanations abound. Two other theories appear in Robert Herzbrun's *The Perfect Martini Book:* (1) that it was named for the town of Martinez, California, where it was first served or (2) that it was named for a British rifle, the Martini and Henry, because of its accuracy and kick.

Dr. Condom. It is alleged that a Dr. Condom who lived in the time of Charles II of England created and gave his name to the prophylactic device. It has never been proven or disproven, and those in the business, according to a source at the company which manufactures Trojans, refer to it as "legend." In 1986 archaeologists discovered five *condoms* made of fish and animal intestines from the 1640s, the right era for Oliver Cromwell, proving that they predate the era of Charles II. Perhaps the elusive Dr. Condom named them. The first use in print, according to *Merriam-Webster's Collegiate® Dictionary, Tenth Edition,* which lists the term as "origin unknown," is ca. 1706.

With final proof still lacking, there are two alternative theories: (1) that it somehow comes from the name of the French town of Condom in Gascony or (2) that it originated in the Latin word *condus* for "guardian." Another individual credited with the invention of the condom was Gabriele Falloppio, who appears shortly.

Johnny Crapaud. This was an alias of New Orleans gambler Bernard Marigny, who, according to legend, brought the first dice to that city, making the first *craps* game possible. He is not to be confused with:

Thomas Crapper. The Englishman who developed the modern flush toilet as Crapper's Valveless Water Waste Preventor. In Wallace Reyburn's biography of him, *Flushed With Pride,* we are told that it is the Americans who have referred to the toilet as the *crapper* while the British themselves have not used the term. "Never has the saying 'A prophet is without honour in his own land' been more true," writes Reyburn: "Here was a man whose foresight, ingenuity, and perseverance brought to perfection one of the great boons of mankind."

Crapper's name, by the way, does not give us *crap* as many have wrongly assumed. Robert Henderson points out in *Human Words* that it is a much older word coming from the Dutch word *krappe* for "scraps."

D

Goodman Derick. Executioner at Tyburn in London who dispatched more than 3,000 people, the most notable of whom was the Earl of Essex, who was executed in 1601. For centuries any hangman or gallows was referred to as a *derick* or, later, *derrick.* Big cranes resembling gallows are called *derricks* because of Goodman Derick the hangman.

John Duns Scotus (1266-1308). He was an Oxford philosopher who took issue with the teachings of Thomas Aquinas. His followers variously called themselves *Scotists, Dunsmen,* and *Dunses.* Soon *dunce* was used for a person who opposed philosophical progress. When Scotus died in 1308, he had no idea that his name would live on as a mark of stupidity.

F

Gabriele Falloppio (sometimes Gabriel Fallopius; 1523-1562). An Italian anatomist who is given credit for discovering the function of the ducts leading from the ovary to the womb which have since been called *fallopian tubes.*

Leonhard Fuchs (1501-1566). A German botanist who became both a flower and a color, *fuchsia.*

Capt. Fudge. In 1881 Eliezer Edwards published *Words, Facts and Phrases: A Dictionary of Curious, Quaint, & Out-of-the-Way Matters* in which he proposes that the term *fudge*—as in, fudging the figures—came from a 17th-century ship's captain who was known widely for his ability to lie and love of doing so. Thereafter whenever a sailor heard a bold lie, he would cry out, "You fudge it!" (Etymologists at Merriam-Webster remain unconvinced and list this term as "origin unknown" in *Merriam-Webster's Collegiate® Dictionary, Tenth Edition.*

G

Rube Goldberg (1883-1970). The late cartoonist's name is now broadly applied to any intricate mechanical contraption which has a simple mission.

Sylvester Graham (1794-1851). Reformer of the last century who advocated an alcohol-free, vegetarian diet which included a whole-wheat cracker that bears his name today. On the opposite side of Graham was James H. Salisbury, an advocate of red meat who left his name on *salisbury steak.*

R. J. L. Guppy. A native of Trinidad and the president of its scientific association who presented the British Museum with a specimen of a tiny tropical fish in the late 19th century.

Button Gwinnett. Something that is "rarer than a Button Gwinnett" is rare indeed. The expression refers to his autograph, which is worth something on the

order of $150,000. Gwinnett was one of three Georgians to sign the Declaration of Independence. He didn't sign much more after that because he was killed in a duel less than a year later. Because a number of autograph collectors have sought to get a full set of signatories to the Declaration of Independence, a Button Gwinnett has taken on extraordinary value.

H

Haile Selassie (1892-1975). Before he became emperor of Ethiopia, his name was Ras (Prince) Tafari, which has been incorporated into the name *Rastafarian.*

Oliver Heaviside (1850-1925). Scientist who predicted the Heaviside layer in the upper atmosphere, now known as the ionosphere. This is one of those rare eponyms that sound as if they were named logically (as for the heavy side) rather than eponymously.

Hermes. The god of secrets gave his name to *hermetically,* as in "hermetically sealed." A rare double eponym occurs in *hermaphrodite* which is *Hermes + Aphrodite. Aphrodite* also lives in *aphrodisiac.* Other ancient gods live on in such words as *atlas, jovial, Dionysian, panic, morphine, fauna, flora, mercurial,* and *volcano.*

Gen. Joseph Hooker (1814-1879). It has been long and often asserted that the term *hooker,* meaning a prostitute, came from the general whose Civil War garrison in Washington included a red-light district. A while back the *Washington Post* retold this story and was challenged by a reader, Ronald C. Semone, who found it in John Russell Bartlett's *Dictionary of American-*

isms as far back as 1849, and in the 1976 supplement to the *Oxford English Dictionary* which says it was used as early as 1845. Said Jack Eisen of the *Post* when confronted with the new evidence, "[my] guess is that local wags during the Civil War chortled at the symbolic relationship between Hooker's Division and the other activities in the neighborhood, and the connection mistakenly became local lore. Heck, it was such a good myth while it lasted."

Despite this, the Civil War story is retold routinely in print where it is routinely refuted by alert readers. In August 1994, the Ann Landers newspaper column provided a fresh locale for repeating the myth and then published its debunking. Landers got a lot of mail from students of language, occasioning her comment: "I didn't realize there were so many scholars who were interested in hookers."

K

Bertha Krupp (1886-1957). She, the eldest daughter and sole heiress to Krupp arms, gave her name to *Big Bertha,* the German Army's mammoth rifle cannon, with which the Germans shelled Paris from a distance of up to nine miles in World War I. Her full name: Bertha Antoinette Krupp von Bohlen und Halbach.

L

Jules Leotard. The French trapeze artist who advocated "more natural garb, that does not hide your best features." Somewhere along the line the name for that garb became pluralized. Superman, for example, wears *leotards,* not a *leotard.*

M

J. L. McAdam (1756-1836). The inventor of a material for repairing roads. It is now *macadam*—tarmac when mixed with tar—and the verb is *macadamize.* He is not to be confused with John Macadam, an Australian chemist (d. l865), after whom the *macadamia nut* is named.

Nicolas-François Mansart (1598-1666). A French architect who gave his name to the jointed roof which is steep on the lower half. He did not invent it—some were built before he was born—but he used them a lot, and his name got attached to that kind of roof.

Jean Martinet. A 17th-century French army officer in the service of Louis XIV, Martinet maintained that it was good for military discipline to have soldiers march for long periods of time. His name is now used to describe petty disciplinarians.

Helen Porter Mitchell (1861-1931). She was an Australian opera singer who changed her name to Melba to honor Melbourne, her birthplace. Her fame spread because of her voice and her taste in food, which included *Melba toast* when dieting and *peach Melba,* which was created in her honor. She is one of the few people to score double eponyms.

N

Jean Nicot (1530?-1600). He introduced tobacco in France after sampling it in Portugal. He gave France a persistent cough and the vocabulary the word *nicotine.*

P

Panacea. Daughter of the Greek god of medicine, Asclepious, her name means "all healing."

Dr. George Papanicolaou (d. 1962). The physician responsible for the *Pap smear* test for uterine cancer.

R

Charles F. Richter (1900-1985). Scientist who spent his professional life studying earthquakes and discovered, along with Beno Gutenberg, a scale to measure the size of earthquakes. Over his objections it became known as the *Richter scale.*

Cesar Ritz (1850-1918). A Swiss innkeeper and restaurateur, who ran swank European hotels, notably the Ritz hotels in London and Paris. The term *ritzy* came into the language in 1920 as a term for anything fashionable, posh, ostentatious. Irving Berlin's classic song "Puttin' on the Ritz" first became a hit when sung by Fred Astaire.

S

Daniel Edward Salmon (1850-1914). His reward for finding the *salmonella* bacteria was to have it named for him.

Henry Shrapnel (1761-1842). British inventor whose shell filled with shot was credited with helping to turn the tide of battle in the final defeat of Napoleon in 1815.

John Batterson Stetson (1830-1906). A hatmaker born in New Jersey, whose name stuck to a wide-brimmed model favored by American cattlemen.

Syphilis. The hero of a 16th-century poem who suffered the disease. Generally speaking, real individuals and groups tend not to want to get their names on diseases. The American Legion has protested the fact that Legionnaires' disease is now named for it just because it happened to break out in the hotel where it was having a convention.

V

Edward Vernon (1684-1757). English admiral who got the nickname "Old Grog" from his grogram coat. Grogram is a coarse mix of wool and mohair. He is remembered because he ordered his sailors to dilute their ration of rum with water, a mixture which became known as *grog.* From *grog* the drink, came *groggy* the condition.

W

Charles Wenburg. According to one story, this shipping magnate of the last century walked into Delmonico's restaurant in New York one night with a new way of preparing lobster that he had discovered in South America. Lorenzo Delmonico prepared it, loved it, and immediately placed it on the menu as *lobster Wenburg.* It stayed like this on the menu until the fateful night a few weeks later when Wenburg got in a fist fight in the restaurant and had to be thrown out. The next day the dish reappeared on the menu as *lobster Newburg.* The letters *w-e-n* had been reversed as a punishment. Lorenzo himself was able to get his name to stick to the *Delmonico steak.* (As with *fudge,* Merriam-Webster etymologists are not convinced and list the term as "origin unknown" in *Merriam-Webster's Collegiate® Dictionary, Tenth Edition.*)

Z

Zoilus. A bitter, envious critic of the 4th century B.C., who has become a generic term for a faultfinder—a *zoilus.* To use it in a sentence: "Anyone who expresses dislike of this book in print is a *zoilus.*"

And this is just the beginning. In Robert Hendrickson's *Human Words* more than 3,000 eponyms are listed, and he stands clear of mythical and dubious examples. Some 1,500 show up in Willard R. Espy's *Thou Improper, Thou Uncommon Noun.* But there are infinite possibilities for a next generation of eponyms. *Time* magazine has, for example, suggested the verb to *plimp* (after George Plimpton) for "the participatory journalism…in which the amateur ventures lamblike among the wolves of professional sport—and then writes about how to be a lamb chop." An *armstrong* has gained some ground as a word for a high trumpet note (from Louis "Satchmo" Armstrong). Also *edsel* (after Edsel Ford and the car named in his honor) is showing strength as a noun for commercial disaster, and it would seem that *moonie* (Reverend Moon), *goldwynism* (Sam Goldwyn), *orwellian* (George Orwell), to *gallup* as a stand-in for polling (after George Gallup), and to *disneyfy* (from Walt Disney) are coming on strong.

Willard Espy has come up with the fascinating game of trying to figure out the names from this era that will be words a hundred years from now. Among the possibilities he suggested in a 1978 magazine article are the following, based on the names of strongman Idi Amin, CBS anchor Walter Cronkite, and Egyptian leader and Nobel Peace Prize co-winner Anwar el-Sadat: *aminate*—to eliminate political opponents by violent means (synonym: *idify*); *cronkite*—a heavy-duty anchor, immobile in the fiercest storms; *sadate*—to pacify a hostile country by unexpectedly declaring peace instead of war.

It is a marvelous notion which leads one to other possibilities, including *espy*—to use words and names recreationally, as in "She was *espying* with the dictionary."

In 1993 the *Washington Post* ran a contest to coin a new crop of eponyms and two of the winners were: *Clin ton.* n.—A bulk unit of fast-food hamburgers, usually 2,000 pounds, and *Limbaughger.* n.—A huge, soft white cheese with a very strong odor and flavor. Hard to digest.

Another game of sorts is to imagine what it would be like if eponymous people were mixed at birth and the Earl of Sandwich ended up in the bassinet reserved for the Shrapnel baby and vice versa. Or what about mixing the infant Guillotin and Cardigan babies? What if Roquefort had grapes instead of sheep's milk and Champagne was long on ewes and short on vineyards? Would a bubbly glass of Roquefort taste the same as a plate of Champagne and crackers?

Extraterrestrial Names

An Alien Census from the Ufological Literature

14

I'm naming her after you, QEBSFEUF.

It would be hard to find an odder list of names than that which you are about to encounter. It was compiled and sent to the author in small annotated clusters by Martin S. Kottmeyer, who has combed the many stories in which people have reported meetings with entities from other worlds either through physical contact or through a medium. The lists, which began arriving in the early 1980s, have been updated through the end of 1995, when Kottmeyer, who has slogged through mountains of UFO literature, admitted, "As long as this list is, I have no feeling it is comprehensive, because I am frankly long behind in my reading." He adds, "Still, I am confident nobody else would have the perseverance to come up with a list this long."

In alphabetical order, with a minimum of asides and comments, we have these e.t.'s:

A

Aatenset
Acorc
Actar
Acva
Adam
Adela
Adelpho
Adoneides
Adu
Affa
Agar
Ageeka *or* Ohgeeka
Agfar Affa
Aglios
AGU 28
Agva
Ahab
AIN 368
Ainini Nikanine
Aiwas
Akilias
Akilovan
Akon
Akrim Vesta
A-lan
Alen-Adar
Aleva
Alexander
Algarr
Algenyon
Algran-Eltar
Alioth through Phrado
Alna
Alomar
Al Padgett
Alpha La Zulu (*or* Zooloo)
Alten
Alton
Alyn
Amano

Amenhi of the Flashing
  Knives
Andantio
Andon
Andre-Kael
Andrew (This is the name
  of the author's oldest son,
  who was relieved to find
  out that this was a good
  alien, according to the
  report on him in the June
  15, 1982, issue of the
  National Enquirer, although
  he was reported to be
  "opinionated and
  sarcastic.")
Andromeda Rex
Andromeda Rey
Ankar-22
Anna
Anouxia
Antares
Anta-Verron
Anton
Antron
Aphloes
Apol
Apollo
Arta-Dorrec
Artok
Arturo Senziadorro
Ashtar
Ashtar Rayonda
Asket
Asmitor
Asmiz
Asoki
ASOO 3
Astana
Astané
Asteron
Astra
Astrae
Astraelda
Astra-Lari

Atra
Aupho, a Kawpo from
  Awura
Aura Rhanes
Aurora El-Legion
Ausso One
Avec
Awa
Awis
Ayling
Azuba

B

Balmiston
Bashar
Becoval
Beelzebub
Bellarian
Bellarion
Benen
Bernard Kaiser
Bertan
Bet Man (This name was
  explained in the article
  "UFOs in Trouble," in *UFO
  Report:*

Alien: If you think we
  would let anyone take one
  of our craft, you are mis-
  taken. Before you get back,
  this craft would be gone.
  And you, John Olter,
  would look like a fool.

John: It's not Olter, it's Alter.

Alien: I am sorry, John Alter,
  I misunderstood. You have
  nothing to fear from us. Do
  you wish to see the inside
  of our craft?

John: You bet, man!

Alien: I do not understand
  "you bet man." I am not a
  man. My name would
  mean nothing to you but if
  you wish, you may call me
  Bet Man, John Alter.)

Beuldine Vauss
Biaca
Biimos
Bilakka
Blaroc
Blorah
Bo
Bob Solomon
Borealis Telano
Bullié

C

Cabalà
Caellsan
Calagastia
Caldon
Calliope Callisto
Captain Comtah
Captain Cosmowobsy
Captain Linda-Ray (One of
the few aliens whose name
appears to be female. This
would seem to follow
science fiction tradition.
In a 1961 article in the
journal *Names* entitled
"Names and Roles of
Characters in Science
Fiction," Robert Plank
concludes after analyzing
a number of science fiction
magazines, "The most
conspicuous feature
concerning sex is the
paucity of female charac-
ters.")
Captain Video and "The
Boys from Clarion."
Carlinna
Carmen del Playa
Carpathia
Cedalda
Ce-fn-x
Ceres
Ciro Nelhemious

Cjork
Claron
Clatu
Cloe
Clota
Clyveen
Commander Marivonch
Felchar
Conard
Condor
Coner
Control
Corean
Cosentia
Cosmos
Craeton
Crellritus
Crill
Croris
Crpros
Cryxton
Cuza

D

Damon-Rel
Danel-Vordek
Dar-ma-ledge
Darrin Sen
Daryl Clinnel
Dayton
DEI 98
Demo
Demo Hassan
Descla
Deska
Dhanne
Dion
Diophantes
Dividia
Djemion
Dodd Hendricks
Don Alvaredo Quevada
Donestra

Donn
Donnelle
Dora-Ray
Dorca
Dreali
Dr. Madcana
Dr. Thrishna
Dryzek
Dr. Zeno from Alpha
Centauri
Dulac
Dzezd

E

Echo Leia
Eeso
EIEEUEE 7
Elcar
El Elyon
Elen
Elex
Ellanora
Ellsworth
Elor Korrel
Elvane
Emo
Empusas
Enados
Enoch
Eone
Epaminondas
Epamondas
Eros Urides
Esansale
Estralon
Esu
Etelgen

F

Faun

Filo
Fir Kon
Fitozooloplanetologeica

G

Gakko
Gamaah
Gamal
Garcia Sai
Garr
Gary-Sol
Gensan
Gerard
Glon
Gmm
Go'Bo (Nummo from Typhara)
God (resident of Alpha Centauri)
Goldar
Grandfanda
The Great Master
Gregorno
Gutao

H

Harold
Hatonn
Haurrio
Helios
Herod
Herronoah
Higlio Hogag
Hilarion
Holarian
Holeah (than thou?)
Honitur
HONOR
Hshames
Hua

Hulda
Hweig

I

I-am-that-I-am
IAUDA 3
Illmuth
Indrid Cold
Inkra
Inondas
Ishkomar
Itan
IXEEI 4

J

Jarron
Jay
Jehovah
Jemi
Jill
The Jilsron
Jitro Cletaw
John
Jonah
Joohop
Joopah
Joseph
Julio Sangilly
Julo
Jupiter-92

K

Kadar Lacu
Kadar Sutko
Kagmon
Kalaal
Kalah
Kalen-Li Retan
Kalna

Kaloran
Kalsando
Kanet
Kanto
Karas
Kareeta
Karl Ardo
Karl Marx (yes, *the*)
Karma
Karne
Karya
Kashendo
Kela
Kel-Ran
Kemi
Kepton
Keri-Aldek
Kerrull
Ketutsen the Torturer
Khauga
Khyla
Kialda
Kihief
Kilestra
Kimi
Kimilis
Korton
Krain
Kren-Lor Altor
Kresulon
KRO
Krona
Kronin
Kryon
Kumar
Kyros

L

Laactiped
Lady Master Meta
Lalar

Lanaforge
Lanonandek
Lanto
Laskon
Lata
Latamarx
Latu
Launie
Lax
Leah
Leektow
Leita
Lelan
Lena-Ray
Len-Myr
Leo
Lesuron
Lexitron
Lia
Lideo
Lin-Erri
Little Bucky of Venus
Locktopar
Lomec
Lord Kuthumi
Lord Linette
Lord Somar
Lucifer
Luno
Lupon
Lut
Lutbunn
Luu
Lyra

M

M (not James Bond's)
Maha
Majestron
Malnu
Mank-Ton
Manotra
Mantutia Melchizedek

Mara La Aspara
Marla
Marma
Mars
Martok
Mary (from Mars)
Master Aetherius
Master Truth
Master Yogunda
Matton
Maxiomone
Maxslow
Maya
Mayan
Maynell
Mazeru
Me
Meck-Tau
Mek
Melchizedek
Mengus
Mentar
Mercury
Merku
Meron
Merton
Metatron
Michael (One of several, Kottmeyer notes, that are the names of angels. He comments, "Such borrowings are to my mind appropriate.")
Michael El-Legion
Mida
Mika
Mik-ael
Mister Zno
Mitis
Mitzar
Mogwan
Mohada of the Galaxies
Molca
Mond

Monda
Mondra-o-leeka
Monka
Monn
Mono
Montag
Moolana
Mora
Moroni
Mr. Ohoulihan
Mrs. Ecks Edrean
Mrs. Neptuniandustireceas
Mrs. Saturnicusbalsan
Mr. X
Muello
Muhutani
Murial

N

Nah-9
Nalama
Nassaveh
Necoma
Neferu
Nementu the Slaughterer
Neola
Neptune
Nokyle
Noma
Noot
Norbol
Noro
Novak
Nug
Nyochka

O

Oara
Oba
Oblow
OEOE 91
OEOE 95

Ogatta
Ohneshto
Olgar
Omee
The One
Onleel
Oomaruru
Opthanim
Oran
Orbon
Orejano
Orenox
Orii-Val
Orion
Orlon
Orme
Orthon
Orvin-Selat
Othra
Otto Von Mobile
Oxal
Ox-Ho
Ozzo

P

Panion
Parpi (a Keepho from
  Parnhos)
Parz
Pencilava
Perlizar
Phammon
Phusantheas
Plaja
Plura
Plut
Plutana
Pollious
Ponnar of Hatoon (an
  entity distinct from Ponnar
  of Mercury who was also
  reported)
Ponnar of Mercury

Portla
Pouzé
Prince Neosam
Princess Moon Owl
Princess Negonna
Professor Svenboydgol-
  lybros
Ptaal
Pyslavon

Q

Qebsfeuf
Qel
Quamquat
Quazgaa
Quazgaw
Quen-Koll
Quentin
Quetzal

R

Ragon
Rama
Rama Desk'ka
Rama Desk'la
Rama Ka Lo
Ramu
Rani
Ran Kar
Raymere
Rea
Regga of Masar
Remon-Torek
Renton
Retsim
Revance
Rhombus 4-D
Riaus
Rita-Ray
Ro (not the ensign from
  Star Trek: The Next
  Generation)

Robert
Robert F. Six
Robert McNamara (yes, the)
Rolf
Rouee
Rubinako
Rynjavi
Ryr

S

Sadat
Saine
Saint Goo-Ling
Saliano
Saloma
Salvatore
Samu
Sananda
Sanat Kumara
Sandi
Sarad Uris
Sarafulgus
Schonling
Sebah
Sedat
Seexo
Selah
Selorik
Semjase
Sen-Kor (Kottmeyer points
  out that this is also the
  name of an agricultural
  herbicide.)
Serilius
Serkilias
7171
Seyen
Sfath
Shannondoan
Sharon
Shovar
Sidirurgico
The Source

Spig
Starday
Ston
Suna
Sunar
Sut-ko

T

Tabamantia
Tahita
Talayan
Tana
Tanoun
Tarngee
Tarso
Tauri
Taylanz
Teel
Teiau
Telione
Tellay
Terra
Tesla
Thermatta
Thonn
Thoth
Thrishna
Tibus
Timot
Tolta
Tom
Tombo
Tonados
Toni
Tonla
Torado
Totalmon
Touka
Traellison
Tregon
Trena

Tuella
Tukari
Tut
Tweeter
Twitter
Tyora

U

Ulatima
Ulo
Um (Zo's wife)
Umar
Uniah
Uresi
Uriel
UUOO 120
Uxiaulia

V

Vadig
Valdar
Val-Thor
Van the Steadfast
Vax Noah
Vega
Velas
Velia
Venutio
Verim-Quell Hann
Vestra
Vi-Dal
ViVenus
Voltar
Voltimar Karendo
Voltra of Venus
Vonason
V-O-R
Vorondadek
Vurna

W

Walkala
Wan-4
Whobiggerwah
Wolco
Wy-Ora

X

Xan
Xeno
Xenu
Xiti from Itibi Ra II
Xyclon

Y

Yahshua Hamashita
Yamski
Yano
YU 1

Z

Zagat
Zagga of Zakton
Zago
Zandark
Zandor
Zar
Zayron
Zdeen Alexander
Zeeno
Zefta the Thief
Zeiter
Zelas
Zemkla
Zenta Linojucej11
Zio
Zoltar

As a final comment on his collection, the skeptical Kottmeyer says, "I suppose if you are an extraterrestrial and must have a name these are as good as any. I must say, however, it is somewhat difficult to take seriously aliens with names like Knut, Oomaruru, Quamquat, or Luno. And would you want Caldon to take you away? I know I wouldn't. There are a number of them that do seem somehow appropriate names for aliens, yet I must register my impression that aliens are much better off going without names altogether. The instant I encounter a name the whole story loses its alien character and becomes one more science-fiction tale and one must actively suspend belief to finish it. In the truly interesting UFO cases the alien is always nameless."

A case in point is the alien encountered in Dino Kraspedon's *My Contact with Flying Saucers*, in which his response to the question of his name is answered this way: "I have no name in your sense of the word. On my planet, names are a picture of the character of the individual. Through them we know a person's merits and shortcomings, even if he is unknown to us."

Bill Tammeus of the *Kansas City Star*, who reviewed part of Kottmeyer's list, concluded, "Boy, I can see how easily you get the wool pulled over your eyes. Those alleged UFO commander names aren't UFO commanders at all. Every one of those guys at one time or another has played infield for the Chicago Cubs."

There is one interesting postscript to all of this, which is that another student of ufology, John Keel, has written an article in which he asserts that humans with uncommon names are singled out for contacts while those with common names are avoided. In his article "The UFO Name Game" in *Pursuit* magazine, Keel asks, "Why do the Allens, Hills, Reeves, Heflins, and Wamsleys see more of these things than the Smiths, Johnsons, and Browns?" and concludes, "We are obviously dealing with something much more complex than simple coincidence."

Indeed.

Garcia sai

First Name Fashions

John and Mary Meet Jessica and Matthew

15

Having been born in 1939 it was preordained that I, Paul, would grow up with Johns and Marys, have close friends named Richard, Joseph, William, and Robert (Dick, Joe, Bill, and Bob, actually) and marry an (a) Carol, (b) Barbara, or (c) Nancy. As it turned out, all of this was true, including marrying (c). People my age, I roughly reckon, grew up with six Roberts, five Carols, two Phyllises, and a Tom, who would punch you in the nose if you called him Thomas—that is, unless you were Charlie or Tony, and then you could call him whatever you felt like.

These folks had babies who answer to such names as Mark, Joshua, Stacy, and Melissa and tend to prefer the long form to the short as in "The name is Matthew not Matt."

Nothing strange here, as first names are linked to time as closely as the width of ties and the length of skirts. In the 1960s, for instance, we got away from the traditional English and biblical names and have the names to prove it. We called our flower children Harmony, Peace, and Rainbow. The late Frank Zappa named his daughter Moon Unit and his son Dweezil. Sonny and Cher called their daughter Chastity. Johnny Cash had a hit song called "A Boy Named Sue."

In the 1970s, we got cute with Jason and Jennifer and Ashley. In the 1980s, we got ethnic by choosing names with African or Islamic roots. Many black parents took ethnic-sounding names and added prefixes such as La and Sha.

These lists of the top names from New York City birth records underscore the point:

GIRLS

1898
Mary, Catherine, Margaret, Annie, Rose, Marie, Esther, Sarah, Frances, and Ida.

1982
Jennifer, Jessica, Melissa, Nicole, Tiffany, Elizabeth, Michelle, Stephanie, Christina, and Danielle.

1948
Linda, Mary, Barbara, Patricia, Susan, Kathleen, Carol, Nancy, Margaret, and Diane.

1994
Ashley, Jessica, Stephanie, Samantha, Amanda, Nichole, Jennifer, Michelle, Tiffany, and Melissa.

BOYS

1898
John, William, Charles, George, Joseph, Edward, James, Louis, Francis, and Samuel.

1982
Michael, Christopher, Jason, David, Joseph, Anthony, John, Daniel, Robert, and James.

1948
Robert, John, James, Michael, William, Richard, Edward, Thomas, George, and Louis.

1994
Michael, Christopher, Kevin, Anthony, Jonathan, Daniel, Joseph, Matthew, and David.

From the perspective of the mid-1990s, it is apparent that some of the hot names of the recent past are fading as classic names such as Caroline, Madeleine, Sara, and Grace are becoming popular. (For boys, Jacob, Tyler, and Austin are in and Andrew, Joseph, and Daniel are fading.) In the 1990s we are into everything from the seasons to geography. We have Summer and Spring, Paris and Dakota. We have an abundance of gender-neutral names, such as Jordan and Taylor. As if to drive teachers crazy, parents sometimes change the spelling of common names: Madlyn, Alyn, or Keven.

The time-linking of first names has always fascinated me, and for years I have been collecting those back-of-the-paper clippings on the ranking of names as determined by local birth records. I now have a box full of them, dating back to the days of items with early American pre-Jennifer headlines like "John Rates No. 1 as Name for Boys—Mary for Girls." I dumped all the clippings on my desk and from them tried to distill a list of the most noteworthy names of the last few decades. I have tried to keep the list updated through the mid-1990s. Many have helped me bring sense to the list, including Cleveland Kent Evans, Ph.D., who in a 1986 letter shared much of his research on name history. The result is this directory filled with the information you never find in the scores of books with variations on the title "Name Your Baby."

A

Amy. Rose to a strong second place among girls' names in the United States in the mid-1970s and then lost strength. Amy, like a number of other girls' names, underscores the conclusion that fashions in girls' names change more often than in boys', although boys' names move in and out of style more rapidly than they used to.

Anthony. A solidly popular name through the 1970s and into the 1980s.

Ashley. A 1984 article in the *Ottawa Citizen* about a woman who studies birth records called this *the* trendy name for 1984. She is to 1984 what Angela was to 1974. Ashleys will be the 92-year-olds at the U.S. Tricentennial. After being a clear number one in the early 1980s in many places, including the official West Virginia list, Ashley really came into her own in the 1990s when she was number one on the New York City list for 1992, 1993, and 1994.

B

Bailey. Girl's name that began to move in about 1990.

Betty. One of those solid names once so popular but now out of fashion. As Russell Baker wrote in *Growing Up:* "Good women were not Mimi or Fifi or Lulu, they were Betty and Mary and Gladys and Lucy and Elizabeth."

Brad. Not a top-ten name but one of those short male names which seem to be coming into their own in the 1980s. Others are Todd, Scott, and Duane, which have been typified by Kelsie Harder of the American Name Society as tough "linebackers' names." Kyle, Chad, and Ryan are all showing strength.

Brandon. Strong 1990s name for boys especially in the West.

C

Cameron. One of the hot gender-neutral girls' names for the 1990s: "Ultrafeminine names for girls are passé. The hot names are ones that feminist and career moms think will look good on their daughters' résumés," reports Pamela Redmond Satran, who has coauthored, with Linda Rosenkrantz, *The Last Word on First Names* (St. Martin's Press, 1995). Hot girls' names for the 1990s, she told a reporter for the *Chicago Tribune,* are gender-neutral, such as Jordan and Morgan, as well as last names used as first names, such as Mackenzie and Cameron.

Chelsea. Noted in a few surveys as having a good boost in 1983 attributed to Jane Fonda's character in the movie *On Golden Pond.* It has continued to be popular.

Christopher. Second on one 1982 list, it was not even in the top fifty in 1925. Along with Christina and Christine, it is a clearly religious name which seemed to rise in popularity as church memberships declined. The 1990s have been as kind to Christopher as the 1980s: it was, for example, number two in both 1993 and 1994 on the New York City Health Department top-ten list.

Courtney. A name that became popular in the mid-1980s with many alternative spellings: Kortnee, Kourtni, Kourtney, and Cortni.

Craig. A common baby boom name. Because of his age, Craig is now likely to be active in the PTA along with Susan, Phyllis, Marcia, Dale, Dennis, Phillip, and Sharon. They all know people named Laura, Joyce, Kevin, Neil, and Valerie.

Crystal. A name that rose with the popularity of *Dynasty* and a character of that name on the show.

D

Danielle. A strong name in the 1970s and 1980s. William Safire has pointed to this name, among others, and noted, "Curiously, at a time when many women resent the idea of Adam's ribbing, girls' names of the 80's are often derived from boys' names." The pattern is odd: it was on the New York City Health Department top-ten list in 1986, 1989, and 1994.

Diana. It leapt forward in 1982—Princess Di's year to shine.

F

Fallon. When this girl's name began showing up in 1983 some tabulators couldn't figure it out. They had never watched *Dynasty.*

Fred. Good enough for Fred Mertz, Fred Astaire, and Fred Flintstone, it had fallen into such disrepute that the Fred Society came into being in the late 1980s. One magazine described the Society as "a feel-good group for all those poor guys— and the possible Frederica or two—who were saddled with the name at a time when they couldn't object." The group has distributed a number of pro-Fred bumper stickers, including:

BETTER FRED THAN DEAD.

NAME YOUR NEXT CHILD FRED.

I NEVER MET A FRED I DID NOT LIKE.

G

Gary. A rarity until 1951, when the popularity of Gary Cooper put the name on some top-ten lists.

Gregory. A name that became very popular in the early 1950s when the big actor was Gregory Peck. It still shows up on occasion. A 1987 name survey run by Gerber Products showed it number one in the eastern states—at a time when Brandon was the first in the West.

H

Harriet. So negative is the media stereotype of this name that a few years ago a publicist and writer named Harriet Modler threatened to form a group called CASH (Citizens Against Stereotyping Harriet). TV characters have helped make this a rare name for anyone under forty, which could also be said about the next name.

Harvey. A male name that fell on hard times in the 1960s when it dropped to 197th place on one list. At that time Harvey was a name used in TV commercials for doltish men, and a group of Harveys formed a society to fight such stereotyping. When Madison Avenue finally let up on Harvey, it seemed that Harry and Harold became the new dolt names.

Heather. Very strong girl's name through the 1970s—ranking as high as second in one 1972 tally—despite the fact that other flower names (Lily, Violet, Rose, Daisy) were clearly out of favor. On one 1983 list, Heather had fallen to 18th place. In 1981,

Margaret and Thomas Brown, the compilers of the *Times* of London annual list, noted that flower names were beginning to show an increase in popularity, although they were still far out of the top ten. Holly looks like it could grow in popularity, as it has just appeared on one top-50 list in 49th place.

In his book *The Professor's Book of First Names*, Thomas V. Busse looked at the names that had risen fastest in popularity between 1880 and 1980 and then asked students to associate them with people, places, events, and characteristics. Heather, the seventh-fastest-rising girl's name, was stereotyped as "pretty, blond, and bitchy" and linked to a character, Heather Webber on the TV show *General Hospital*, who fit that description.

I

Ian. A steady rise in popularity through the 1970s for this name, which is a variation on John. It seems that this and other variations (Jon, Jonathan) have risen as John has slipped.

J

Jacqueline. A slowly falling girl's name since the 1950s that was given a revival when Jacqueline Kennedy was first lady.

James. For years it topped the list of boys' names in the births column of the *Times* of London. It was knocked out of the top spot in those rankings in 1981 by Thomas but was back on top again in 1982. Although no U.S. list has shown James in a first-place position, it shows up on most of the top-ten lists since 1898.

Jason. A name that began to show remarkable strength in 1972, when, for example, it jumped from a 1971 ranking of tenth to second place in a compilation made by the Commonwealth of Pennsylvania. Still relatively strong, but not helped by the villain of the "Friday the 13th" movies.

Jamie. For girls this name came into its own with Jamie, of television's *Bionic Woman*. The influence of this show was such that it increased the popularity of the name Lindsay, which was the first name of the woman—Lindsay Wagner—who played Jamie.

Jane. A good solid name but one that has yet to have been attached to a single *Playboy* Playmate of the Month in the 400-odd months since the first centerfold. Big names for Playmates run to the likes of Kim, Kerri, Kimberly, and Brandi.

Jenna. The name of a character on *Dallas*, Jenna will be linked to the early to mid-1980s for some time to come. C.K. Evans's research suggests that this is a clear case of TV creating a name, as its popularity quadrupled with the introduction of the character on *Dallas*.

Jennifer. Down on lists in the 1920s and 1930s until the novel and movie *Love Story* came along with a dying heroine named Jennifer. It has been hot ever since and in first place in New York City and other areas since 1972. In *The Name Game* Christopher P. Anderson says that a Donovan song ("Jennifer Juniper") and a Jennie Churchill vogue (a popular book and a TV series) helped.

Jeremy. Humorist Ed Lucaire wrote: "The fact is that all Jeremys are to grow no taller than 5'8" (unless they are British like actor Jeremy Irons), but they do go to law school before becoming agents for William Morris."

Jessica. Strong 1970s name that got even stronger in the early 1980s. In second place on some recent lists, it could challenge Jennifer for first place someday soon.

John. A timeless boy's name which appears on *all* 20th-century lists in the United States up until the 1990s. The New York City Health Department did not have John in 1991 and 1994. It leads most lists before 1900, including one tabulation of names in colonial Virginia which appeared in *Names* magazine and a study of names used in colonial Connecticut. Although it is still commonly believed that John and Mary are paired as the most popular American names, the last time they were both the most popular on the list maintained by the New York City Health Department was in 1928.

Long popular in the British Isles, John has fallen far out of the top ten in England and Wales. In *First Names First*, Leslie Dunkling points out that it is still a very popular Scottish boy's name, along with James and William.

Jordan. Hot gender-neutral name for girls in the 1990s along with Taylor and Bailey.

Joseph. Along with John and James, it has never been off the list of top-ten male names on the New York City list since they started compiling such lists in 1895.

Joshua. One of the *J* names that have risen in recent years, it broke into one top-ten list in 1983. Other *J*'s on the move are Jesse, Jeremy, Justin, and Jill.

K

Karen. Popular 1950s name along with Pamela, Debra, and Kathy.

Katherine. A name with greater strength than the lists would show because Catherine is counted separately. The *Times* of London list for 1980 counted Sarah in first place but noted that if Katherine and Catherine had been counted as one, it would have edged Sarah out of the top spot. In 1981 Katherine took over first place in the *Times* ranking without any help from Catherine.

Kelly. It began to come on strong in the 1970s as traditional Irish names like Margaret and Patricia went into decline, but has dropped in popularity since.

Kimberly. A truly fascinating name in that it seemed to come out of nowhere and land on top-ten lists in the early 1960s. It was, for example, so rare earlier that it does not even appear among the 2,400 names in Elsdon Smith's tremendously popular *Naming the Baby,* originally published in 1943, and was extremely rare into the 1950s.

A 1991 survey of *Playboy* Playmates of the Month indicated that there had been five Kimberlys (that is, if you count one Kymberly and a Kimberley).

Kirsten. After some early 1970s strength, she was fading gradually until 1981, when a *Dallas* character named Kirsten (a suspect during the summer of 1981 when America asked, "Who shot J.R.?") boosted the name into fourth place on a Detroit area list.

L

Linda. The top-ranked girl's name in New York in 1948, she has dropped off virtually all the top-ten lists.

Lindsay. A name with a television inspiration, or, as it was put in a 1987 *USA Today* article on names, "A whole generation of little Lindsays sprung up on the heels of *Bionic Woman* Lindsay Wagner...."

Lisa. Number one girl's name in New York City for the first time in 1964. It slowly dropped and had fallen off the top-ten hit parade by 1982.

M

Mark. A strong name in the mid-1960s on both sides of the Atlantic, it has slipped dramatically since. One 1983 list showed it tied with Benjamin for 26th place.

Mary. In 1981, for the first time since New York City first began keeping name records in 1898, it dropped out of the top ten and crashed to 37th place. It seemed that this would be one of the few girl's names that would never become dated, but now it has.

Matthew. A fast-riser which ranked second in the Pennsylvania statistics in 1982 and ranked as the top boy's name in the 1987 Gerber Products Co. ranking.

Maud. A good bet is that if your name is Maud you are a grandmother. Ditto for Martha, Ida, Alice, Esther, Dorothy, Edith, and Viola.

Megan. This name began finding its way onto top-ten lists in 1983 for the first time.

Melissa. Solid performer, 1975-1985. Researcher C. K. Evans of Bellevue College suggests: "One reason for her solid performance may have been that *Little House on the Prairie* featured both Melissa Sue Anderson and Melissa Gilbert as stars."

Melvin. When this name dropped like a rock in the 1950s, it was attributed to a Jerry Lewis character of ultimate jerkiness.

Michael. He has had such strength in recent years that a young *Baltimore Sun* columnist worried that the name "seems to be surging, carried on by a tide of momentum, until the inevitable day when I will know no one *not* named Mike." Since 1964 it has topped every U.S. and Canadian list and in some cases Michael has been used for twice as many boys as the second-place names. Its popularity is also cross-racial, as it appears at the top of both lists when broken down into white and nonwhite. When the 1994 New York City Health Department list was made public in 1995, Michael was number one for the 13th straight year.

Michelle. In their book *Name Me, I'm Yours*, authors Joan and Lydia Wilen say this name was a rarity until 1965 when it came on strong after Paul McCartney rhymed the name with "ma belle." It has been in the top ten in the United States ever since and has ranked as high as number one in Australia.

N

Nicholas. In his *Professor's Book of First Names,* Thomas Busse notes that this fast-rising name was associated with Nicholas Bradford on the long-running television show *Eight is Enough.* It is one of a number that he was able to link to television characters.

Nicole /Nichole. When the District of Columbia did its first compilation of names in 1977, this name was the most popular for girls born to residents of the city (Jennifer led among suburban babies born in city hospitals). Another study pegged it as the second-fastest-rising name for girls between 1970 and 1980. Erma Bombeck noted that "in the year 2057 nursing homes will be inhabited by the likes of Nicole, Megan, Lauren, Jason, Ryan, and Lindsay."

Patrick. Strong into the 1940s, it fell with the baby boom. In 1947 the *Boston Globe* noted with surprise that it had dropped to 45th place in that heavily Irish city.

Penny. In Busse's study this name fell the fastest of all girl's names for the 1970-1980 period, followed by Martha, Betty, Brenda, Peggy, Bonnie, Mary Jo, Wanda, Bunny, and Jane.

R

Richard. A top-ten name through most of this century, it plummeted to 25th on one list in the Watergate era, when Richard Nixon was having monumental problems.

The popularity of this name was probably not helped by the late Richard Burton, who said that the diminutive of Richard was an appendage and not a name.

Robert. This was the most popular boy's name for a period between the fall of John and the rise of Michael. A very strong baby-boom name, it was tremendously popular from 1946 to 1950.

S

Samantha. A television-linked name of the 1970s, Samantha was a character's name in the series *Bewitched*. Writing in the *Times* of London, Philip Howard reports that this was as true in Britain, where the series was also popular, as in the United States. Howard adds that it also became a popular cat name. In 1986 C. K. Evans made this comment: "This name really didn't catch on very well during the run of *Bewitched* in the U.S. even though it did achieve great success in both Britain and Australia because of the show. It is only now [1986] beginning to appear regularly in American top 50s. Perhaps American parents were more reluctant to give their daughters a name linked with witchcraft than British parents were, and it is only now that the *children* who watched the program are having kids of their own that the name is catching on."

Sarah. Great strength in England, where in 1980 and 1981 she was paired with James at the top of the *Daily Telegraph* list. It is a name with remarkable strength in the United States, drifting on and off top-ten lists since the 1890s. A study of names in colonial Connecticut found it to be the most popular (followed by Mary, Elizabeth, Ann(e), Hannah, Abigail, Esther, Submit, and Lydia).

Sean and **Shawn.** Fast-rising names in the 1970s, helped no doubt by Shawn Cassidy.

Shirley. Hard to believe now, but this was once an exclusively boy's name. As Fritz Spiegal, *Wordplay* editor of the *Weekend Telegraph*, put it in a 1993 column, "Before the child-star Temple, Shirley was an English boy's name."

Stephanie. A name that first hit some top-ten lists in 1982.

T

Tammy. A 1950s name which rose and fell with the popularity of the Tammy movies, such as *Tammy and the Bachelor*. Soon it will be hard to find a Tammy who is under 35.

Tara. Came on big in the 1970s and linked by several observers to Tara Martin on the TV show *All My Children*.

Tiffany. This name showed up for the first time on the New York City top-ten names for girls list in 1980, while Tiffany Welles was a character on the TV show *Charlie's Angels*. It jumped into fifth place in 1982 and became one of the biggest names of the 1980s. C. K. Evans argues that the linking of this name with *Charlie's Angels* is probably a coincidence, as the name had been steadily rising by that point and was already extremely popular in the black community.

Like Kimberly, it was unknown to previous generations (except as the name of the famous jewelry store) and is not even listed among the 2,400 names in Elsdon Smith's *Naming the Baby*.

Tracy. A top-ten name for girls in the early 1970s, it had dropped to such a degree that it is missing from top-50 lists compiled in the early 1980s. Stacy, on the other hand, has shown more staying power.

Tyler. Powerful boy's name in the 1990s—head of the list in some areas.

W

William. When the British initiated compulsory registration of baptism in the 16th century, 22.5% of boys registered were named William. Strong until recently when it has been conspicuously absent from local top-ten lists in the United States. Still very strong in Great Britain.

Z

Zachary. A seemingly outdated name a few years ago, it climbed to 43 on one 1983 list. Other old-fashioned male names which have climbed into the top 50 in recent years: Aaron, Justin, Jared, Tyler, and Jacob.

Beyond these hot names are those which were once popular but which have definitely gone out of fashion, such as Emma and Bertha for girls, and George, Henry, and Albert for boys. Yet even for these names there is hope, as Emma, long out of favor in England, has risen as high as second place on popularity rankings, and the *Times* tabulators have seen Peter, Eleanor, George, Patrick, and Margaret show renewed strength. On the other hand, Fiona, once a popular name in England, has been in trouble of late because, according to one report from London, "it was adopted by a good many strippers and other exotic performers."

Some early American favorites, often given on the theory that the right name could inspire virtuous behavior, seem destined not to stage comebacks. But then again, if there were a sudden renewed interest in the 18th century or a shift in the moral climate, we could find day-care centers filled with virtuously named tots like Mindwell, Thankful, Hope, Charity, Increase, Waitstill, Sufferanna, and Prudence.

Name expert Professor L. R. N. Ashley has pointed out that names like Clarence, Percival, and Algernon were once considered macho names used by tough Norman soldiers. If these come back, it's doubtful it will be because parents want their kids to be tough.

All of this is fascinating save for one thing. It would appear that some have used name fashions to discriminate. In 1972 a personnel manager told *Dun's* magazine how he could tell a man's age by his name and therefore get around age discrimination laws by just not interviewing men with names from the "wrong" age group. Back in 1972 he could figure that Arthur was 38, Art was 43, Richard was probably 35-40, but you could add five years if he called himself Dick on the application. Marc with a *c* was under 25, but with a *k* was 30-40. Within five years, Walter and Leonard were 40, Victor 46, and Norman 45. There were many more examples, but why make it harder for Harold, Sheldon, and Milton to get jobs because their names date them?

Hurricanes/Himmicanes

Names That Raised a Storm

16

For many decades hurricanes have been given names. In Puerto Rico the custom was to give the storm the name of the saint whose feast day was being celebrated when it hit the island—the second San Felipe, for instance, hit on September 13, 1928, and took 300 lives on the island and nearly 2,000 in Florida.

The modern custom of naming came from a colorful Australian weatherman named Clement "Inclement" Wragge, who gave tropical storms women's names and non-tropical storms men's names (usually politicians he didn't like). The practice was picked up by Pan American Airways as early as 1938, and a fictional storm named Maria was featured in George R. Stewart's popular 1941 novel *Storm*.

At first U.S. government meteorologists shied away from names, but as weather reconnaissance methods improved, it was not uncommon to be tracking two or three storms at a time. Initially letters of the alphabet were used and then the phonetic alphabet. But just after that decision was made in 1952, the old Able, Baker, Charley phonetic alphabet of World War II fame was thrown out in favor of the new international one and things got confusing, so it was decided to adopt girls' names for 1953.

The first list—Alice, Barbara, Carol, Dolly, Edna, Florence, Gilda, Hazel, Irene, Jill,

Katherine, Lucy, Mabel, Norma, Orpha, Patsy, Queen, Rachel, Susie, Tina, Una, Vickie, and Wallis—was well received, and it was decided that it would be used again for 1954.

But in that year of 1954 Carol, Edna, and Hazel came along, creating together over a billion dollars in damage and taking some 176 lives. During that horrific storm season, there were a number of complaints about giving these death-dealing storms women's names, but the furor died out by the end of the season, and the mail to the weather bureau turned in favor of female names. New lists were prepared each year until 1971 when a semi-permanent list of ten sets of names was established.

But then storm clouds gathered in the form of complaints which held that the naming system was not only inherently sexist but also did not take into account the Spanish- and French-speaking victims of hurricanes in the Caribbean. At first the National Weather Service explained that the names were not an insult to women but a compliment to their powerful force in nature. At one point it was officially stated that women's names were easier to pronounce than men's.

"Women," responded the national vice president of the National Organization for Women, "are not disasters, destroying life and communities and leaving a lasting and devastating effect." One feminist, according to a 1972 UPI story, had proposed naming all future hurricanes after congressmen, and a letter to the *Baltimore Sun* suggested that they be given the names of the Joint Chiefs of Staff. Though impractical, such suggestions could have been a headline writer's dream—"Senator Goldwater Slams Into Gulf Coast."

In 1975 the Australians, who started it all, announced that they would alternately name tropical storms with male and female names, and in 1977 the United States went to a meeting of the World Meteorological Organization where it was agreed to alternate male and female names, as well as to take other languages, beginning with French and Hispanic names, into account. The new kind of list went into effect in the Pacific in 1978 and the Atlantic in 1979.

With the help of some of those involved in hurricane naming at the National Oceanic and Atmospheric Administration and the National Hurricane Center in Miami, here are some noteworthy storm names.

Adolph. The first name given to a Pacific storm in 1983. It prompted complaints from people who said it reminded them of Hitler.

Agnes. One of the names which have been "retired," because of the severity of the original 1972 storm. Likewise, there will be no more Alans, Alicias, Davids, Eloises, Frederics, and 33 others with two more (Opel and Marilyn) destined to be retired at the next meeting of the World Meteorological Organization. "Generally speaking," NOAA's Alonzo Smith said some years ago, "if the hurricane is a killer, the name will not be used again." The Hurricane Center's Frank LaPorte adds that any nation affected can retire a name for whatever reason it wants, including historic allusion, economic impact, or insurance claims. As the old names are retired new ones are added to the "semi-permanent" lists. Says LaPorte, "When Hugo was retired, he was replaced by Humberto."

(See the full official list of Atlantic storms retired into hurricane history as offered by the National Oceanic and Atmospheric Administration's National Hurricane Center on the facing page.)

Anita. This name was on the list in 1977 at the same time that a gay rights debate was raging in Florida which had at its center Anita Bryant, whose position was anti-gay. Dr. Neil Frank of the National Hurricane Center in Miami said at the time, "The name was picked five years in advance, but some people thought that it had been created in reference to the fact that Anita Bryant was part of that debate." Frank said that it was the most embarrassing name to be used to this point, but that such coincidences are a constant worry and one of the reasons why alternative systems are still discussed from time to time. In the early 1980s, for instance, it was proposed that the letters of the Greek alphabet be used, but the idea died.

Arlene. Because the names are in quasi-permanent six-year rotation, this was the first Atlantic storm for 1993 and will be the first one in the year 1999. Alberto was the lead storm for 1994 and will lead the pack in the year 2000.

Harry and Bess. In 1949 the news media named two successive Atlantic storms after the president and first lady. It was not long after this that the Weather Bureau took over the naming of storms. There has never been another presidential storm although Walter was listed for 1985, which would have been interesting if Walter Mondale had been elected in 1984.

Hurricane Bob. This was the first Atlantic storm to carry a man's name (Pacific storms had been masculinized the year before), and as it moved into Louisiana in July of 1979, the *Washington Star* observed, "Those storms of the past, which carried the names of women, had a sound of subtle menace. They were women out of James Thurber capable of terrifying mischief. Without an iota of misogyny, we say that Hurricane Bob, in contrast, makes us chuckle."

The chuckling stopped very quickly when David came along to terrorize the Caribbean, followed by Frederic which, according to Dr. Frank, did $2 billion worth of damage, a record amount. The lesson of 1979 was that male-named storms could be just as lethal as their female counterparts. Bob who had given so many chuckles was a killer in 1991, weeks after the *New York Daily News* had asked itself, "Hurricane Bob? Isn't that a little too friendly for a potential killer storm?"

Other male names which have been used since 1979 include Sam, Mitch, Vince, Felix, Isaac, Jerry, Walter, Lester, Virgil, Calvin, Bud, Howard, Olaf, Kevin, Knut, Irwin, and Hector. In the early months of male names, the storms were known as *himmicanes,* but the word is seldom heard anymore.

The fact is that since hurricane David in 1979, the worst U.S. hurricanes in terms of death and destruction have been male: Allen in 1980, Hugo in 1989, and Andrew in 1992. Gilbert in 1988 was the worst Atlantic storm ever recorded.

Peter and Rose. Two names in a row on the 1991 list occasioning many quips on baseball star Pete Rose and his problems with gambling. "Candidates for the Hurricane Hall of Fame?" asked one newspaper, which answered, "Maybe. But don't make book on it."

Retired Hurricane Names

Name	Year	Location(s) Affected
Agnes	1972	Florida, Northeast U.S.
Alicia	1983	North Texas
Allen	1980	Antilles, Mexico, South Texas Andrew
	1992	Bahamas, Southeast Florida, Southeast Louisiana
Anita	1977	Mexico
Audrey	1957	Louisiana, North Texas
Betsy	1965	Texas
Beulah	1967	Antilles, Mexico, South Texas
Bob	1991	North Carolina and Northeast U.S.
Camille	1969	Louisiana, Mississippi, and Alabama
Carla	1961	Texas
Carmen	1974	Mexico, Central Louisiana
Carol[1]	1954	Northeast U.S.
Celia	1970	South Texas
Cleo	1964	Lesser Antilles, Haiti, Cuba, Southeast Florida
Connie	1955	North Carolina
David	1979	Lesser Antilles, Hispañola, Florida and Eastern U.S.
Diana	1990	Mexico
Diane	1955	Mid-Atlantic U.S. & Northeast U.S.
Donna	1960	Bahamas, Florida, and Eastern U.S.
Dora	1964	Northeast Florida
Elena	1985	Mississippi, Alabama
Eloise	1975	Antilles, Northwest Florida, Alabama
Flora	1963	Haiti, Cuba
Frederic	1979	Alabama and Mississippi
Gilbert	1988	Lesser Antilles, Jamaica, Yucatan Peninsula
Gloria	1985	North Carolina, Northeast U.S.
Hattie	1961	Belize, Guatemala
Hazel	1954	Antilles, North and South Carolina
Hilda	1964	Louisiana
Hugo	1989	Antilles, South Carolina
Inez	1966	Lessor Antilles, Hispañola, Cuba, Florida Keys
Ione	1955	North Carolina
Janet	1955	Lessor Antilles, Belize, Mexico
Joan	1988	Curaçao, Venezuela, Colombia, Nicaragua
Klaus	1990	Martinique

[1] The name "Carol" was used again to denote a hurricane in the mid-Atlantic Ocean in 1965. However, because the name does not appear after that time, it is assumed that the name was belatedly retired for the damage caused by the 1954 storm of the same name.

Quentin. Unless the National Oceanic and Atmospheric Administration changes its mind, there will never be a future hurricane with this name. As NOAA has also given up on *U, X, Y,* and *Z* there will never be an Ulrich, Yolande, Xerxes, or Zelda. This policy was adopted, according to the government, because it became too difficult to find names starting with these letters, and they had been forced to settle for such rarities as Udele and Xrae. This decision can be questioned, as there are enough Z's to last for several generations, given the rotation of names and the fact that few names would ever get retired this deep into the alphabet. The Z's: Zabrina, Zada, Zaidee, Zamora, Zilla, Zilpah, Zera, Zenda, Zenia, Zachary, Zadok, Zebulon, Zebadiah, Zack, Zale, Zenith, Zarah, Zenobia, Zoe, Zephora, Zero, Zorabel, Zoril, Zippora, and Zenaida.

Saxby's Gale. One of a number of named 19th-century storms, this one is particularly interesting because it was predicted in 1868, nearly a year in advance, by Lt. Saxby of the British Navy. Other named storms of the last century which appear in Ivan Ray Tannehill's book *The Hurricane Hunters* include "The Long Storm," "The September Gale," "Racer's Storm," and "Antje's Hurricane"—the latter two named after ships which were destroyed in the storms.

Tanya. The name of 1995's 19th-most-active storm. This is the deepest that the storm trackers have had to go into the list since hurricanes and tropical storms were first given names.

John Doe & Company

Symbolic and Generic Naming

17

G.I. JOE

A few names of general interest to John and Mary Q. Public:

Joe Bloggs. Average guy in Great Britain, the British Joe Blow.

Joe Blow. The average American guy. When the *St. Louis Post-Dispatch* interviewed a real Joe Blow, a gent from Festus, Missouri, Joe Blow was defined as "the average American Joe with a wife and 2.3 kids, 1.5 cars, .7 of a dog, a washer with no dryer and 1.8 television sets . . . who always gets a flat tire the day after the warranty runs out on his tires, who can't use the phone because his kids are always on it, who enjoys a few beers now and then and always forgets his wife's birthday." The Blow who was interviewed said, "Yeah, I guess I'm just about as typical as they come. If my name wasn't Joe Blow, I rather doubt you'd be down here writing a story on me."

Having the name has its drawbacks: another Joe Blow from Van, Texas, has been quoted as saying that he has given up trying to write checks out of town, finds that hotel clerks look at him suspiciously, and most strangers he talks to on the phone think he is trying to put something over on them. On one historic day in 1963, Blow was introduced to a real John Doe, at the time a postal employee in Dallas.

Joe College. Less so today than it was once, this is the generic name for the spiffy college man. They are few and far between as a real name. An article in the *Washington Star* in 1973 about a Maryland man with that name noted: "[T]he fact that he's the only Joe College in metropolitan Washington—perhaps in the entire world—pleases him greatly."

Joe Soap. In Britain, a generic stupid person who is used as an object of ridicule; a willing dupe.

John. By itself the closest thing we have to a generic male name in the English-speaking world. There were ten Johns on the Mayflower, six signed the Declaration of Independence, five were president (although John Calvin Coolidge chose to be known by his middle name), and some years ago a jury was empaneled in St. Louis on which all the jurors were Johns except for the lone woman whose name was Johnnie.

Symbolically, we have or have had Johnny-on-the-spot, Johnny Reb, John Bull (Britain personified), John Barleycorn (the personification of liquor), Dear John, Johnny-come-lately, Jack-of-all-trades, and the most famous of all, John Doe. His female counterpart is Mary, and his only real competitor is Joe (as in College, GI, and Blow.)

John Doe. Along with Jane Doe, the most renowned of all generic names. The name was first introduced into British law during the reign of Edward III (1327-1377) in connection with the acts of ejectment. In this legal debate a hypothetical John Doe claimed he had leased land to a Richard Roe who then ejected him. It was decided that if Doe could establish that he was wrongfully ejected then the title to the land was established. The names stuck and still have legal status. In American criminal law, Doe is the first unknown defendant in a proceeding and Roe the second.

In federal courts the order of unknowns is officially John Doe, Richard Roe, John Stiles, and Richard Miles. If the defendant is a woman, she is Mary Major at the federal bench but Jane Doe in most states. In some cases the name is used to protect the name of an innocent, as in the 1980s "right to life" court battle waged to force surgery for a severely handicapped infant identified only as Baby Jane Doe. Since the original Baby Jane Doe case for a baby born in 1983, there have been a number of "Baby Doe cases."

But the Does are also known outside of legal circles. The name shows up on specimen checks and sample airline tickets. Hospitals and psychiatric institutions use the name with a number to name patients who won't or can't give their names when admitted, and it is commonly used by morgues. As for real John and Mary Does, there are very few of them. A note in *Names* magazine in 1972 reported only six John Does in the phone books of the ten largest cities in the United States and no Mary Does.

Kilroy. During World War II the inscription "Kilroy was Here" appeared everywhere there were GIs, along with this little picture.

It even held on for a while after the war. After the first H-bomb test, scientists went in to check the guinea-pig battleships used in the test and found "Kilroy was here" freshly painted on one of the hulls.

Who was he? An ad for the Association of the U.S. Army asked that question of itself and gave this answer: "Some say he was a foreman in a Seattle munitions plant during World War II. Equipment shipped overseas carried his name on the side, showing that it had been inspected and approved. Others insist that he was an unknown infantry soldier who got tired of hearing the Air Force brag that they were always first on the spot. So he began to leave his message wherever his unit saw action....But everyone knows that in a sense Kilroy is no one. No single person, that is. He's every soldier...."

But there is more to this. In 1962 the Associated Press put an obituary on the wire for a James J. Kilroy of Boston who had died at the age of 60. The AP declared that of all the claims to the origin this Kilroy's was "generally credited as the soundest." The obituary went on to say that Kilroy had gone to work as an inspector at the Fore River shipyard in Quincy two days before Pearl Harbor and immediately began writing "Kilroy was here" on the equipment which his gang had checked. As the equipment was shipped around the world the slogan caught on. The AP added that when the war was over the American Transit Association held a contest to see who was the original Kilroy, and this Kilroy, still working at the shipyard, presented his evidence and won. His prize: a 22-ton trolley car.

Mrs. Calabash. For years this was comedian Jimmy Durante's mystery. He would sign off, "Goodnight Mrs. Calabash," and there was much speculation about who she was. In Fred L. Worth's splendid *Complete Unabridged Super Trivia Encyclopedia* the following explanation is given: "Said to be [his] first wife Maude Jean Olson, who died in 1943....For 20 years, Durante kept the identity secret. Calabash was the name of a small town outside of Chicago which Jeannie and Jimmy both fell in love with."

Now the name lives on, having been given to an anonymous woman who keeps donating large sums of money to the food bank in the depressed town of Midland, Pennsylvania.

Podunk. For several generations this has been the name for a hick town filled with boors and suckers. Real Podunks? A number of them exist, including:

• In Massachusetts, Podunk is a sparsely settled rural section of East Brookfield. Founded in 1686, it is the original Podunk, which, according to research conducted by Allen Walker Read, is an Algonquian word meaning "marshy meadow." A 1995 *Boston Globe* article on the town pointed out that the place is divided into two sections: "Upper Dunk" and "Lower Dunk."

• Another is in Tompkins County, New York, and there is still another in Allegany County, New York, which is spelled Podunque. There is still another in Connecticut.

• In 1969 the town of Podunk Center, Iowa, was put up for sale at $7,000. It had no population (although it had once boomed with 21 people) and no zip code and had been expunged from the map. Back in 1964 when a few people remained there and a reporter from the *National Observer* visited he found a sign proclaiming "Podunk Center, Hub of the World."

Homer Smith, who was its mayor and a quarter of its population, told the reporter, "Someone suggested the sign should read 'Axle of the World' instead of hub because everything is moving but it."

Squedunk. The fictional equivalent of Podunk. There are dozens of these places in American lore and literature, including Dogtown, Skunk's Misery, Weazletown, Buzzardsborough, Upper Bugbury, Pigwacket, Hayseed Center, Hog Wallow, Tin Horn Village, Wahoo, Squewdunk, Yokelton, and Pucky-Huddle.

Mr. and Mrs. X. For years the *Bulletin of the American Names Society* has been building a dossier on this couple, who tend to get involved in the damnedest things. One item illustrates this vividly: "In London an unfaithful husband reportedly has been cured of his infidelity by electric shock treatment. The treatment, a 70-volt shock each time the picture of the mistress was flashed on the screen, was administered to Mr. X by two psychiatrists….Mr. X. is now indifferent to his mistress." The reference for the item is the *New York Times*, December 4, 1966.

The X's always seem to have money because they are almost always mentioned in articles about numbered Swiss bank accounts.

Titus and Gaius. These were the names used in Roman law for unknowns and were the antecedents of the Does.

Walter Plinge/Winnie Plinge. In Britain when an actor or actress is filling two roles in a play, the lesser role is listed as Plinge.

Love Handles

Terms of Endearment

18

On the list: Poo, Bubba, Dumpling Head, L'il Mush, Wart Hog, Puddin', Big Looney, Droolbucket, Skunkie Poo, Chipmunk

One of the reasons I look forward to Valentine's Day is that it is the day when people take out classified ads in the newspaper to express their fondness for one another. Some are whimsical while others do nothing less than pledge eternal devotion. "Amy, I will love you 'till the end of time" is typical.

But what I love about them is not the body of the ads but the way people sign them. Most are signed with a special pet name—a love handle if you will—and you seldom encounter a real name like Fred or Mary. Many of these assumed names are predictable ones like "Your Sweetie," "Lover Boy," "Pudding," and the ever-popular "Main Squeeze." There are dozens of Pooh Bears, Bubbas, Bunnies, and whole patches of Pumpkins.

But there are others which are an uncommon treat to find and read. It is not unlike that wonderful moment in the Hepburn-Tracy classic *Adam's Rib,* when they are both in court on opposite sides of a case, and one of them loses control and calls the other Pinkie. The court recorder asks how it is spelled and is told that it is P-i-n-k-i-e for her and P-i-n-k-y for him.

On Valentine's Day morning in 1983, I rushed to my door and grabbed the paper. I knew within moments that it was a great year for pet names because there were ads signed by Smiffer, Woof, Meow, Moopie, Moogie Moogie Moogie, Miss Magic, Boomer,

Duck, Pook-a-Bear, Uncle Rayon, Wabbit, Zoomie, and my favorite, 26811. I also found The Macho Marshmallow, Timbo, Li'l Mush, Pignose, and Beanser. A few were not only signed oddly but addressed oddly as well. "Blockhead," said one ad, "You're the greatest." It was signed Schmeedy.

A few were written in secret codes. Some are ridiculously easy to decipher, such as Ucebray's message to Athykay of Uchmay Ovelay. Others, however, represent high cryptographic art and defy easy deciphering. I'm still working on a one-word message from an early collection: ILYBURPS, spelled I-L-Y-B-U-R-P-S. I think that the ILY stands for "I love you," but I'm lost after that.

A select few contain more than a subtle hint of eroticism, such as those which talk of coming together in the year ahead.

My single regret about 1983 was that I only got one newspaper. I prepared for 1984 and contacted friends across the U.S., Canada, and Great Britain, asking them to grab me a copy of the classifieds for Valentine's Day. The result was a whole box of them from a total of more than 20 newspapers. Others came in over the years from readers of the first edition (*Names*) from as far away as Australia, and in anticipation of the second edition (*What's in a Name?*), another push was made on February 14, 1996. Here then is a series of dated capsule analyses and nickname highlights:

Annapolis Capital (1984).

One from Jello to Puddin', one to Kim ("the greatest little Jiffy Luber in the world"), and one signed by The Fat Devil.

Arizona Republic/Phoenix Gazette (1996).

Buff Puff, Essouffle, Binky (from Binks),

Sweet Cheeks, Pupper-Wuzzle, and many more support the assertion that the desert air is good for goofy love names.

Baltimore Sun (1984).

Angelo: the Love God, Pizzaman, Gumps, Sexy Goods, Nee-Nee, Erohw, My Darling Wart Hog, Big Ragu, Sandy Lambchop, Lady Di, The Wimp, uf244Alan, Stinky, and Goober were all here, along with a number of "Roses are red" takeoffs of which this was typical:

> JANICE
> Roses are red,
> Crabcakes are brown.
> For favorite valentine,
> You win the crown.
> *Ollie and Hardy*

Bloomington (Indiana) (1996).

Fairly cut and dried save for one: "To Honey Bunny Trucker...from Your Dispatcher."

Brunswick Times Record (Maine) (1984).

Some off-the-wall ads including this one:

> DUMPLINGHEAD
> Kisses are nice
> Queefs are mean.
> You're the smelliest little dumpling
> That I've ever seen.
> (Oh brother!)
> Love Ya, *Moose*

California Aggie (1984).

Big, handmade display ads as befits the paper from the University of California at Davis. A few R-rated but for the most part tame, and the names are real and there is nary a Pookems or a Passionpuss in the lot. Most addressed and signed by the likes of Scott and Rebecca.

Coastal Journal **(Maine) (1984).**

A rich and outlandish list of names including Mr. Microphone, Tongue, Poopookinnies, Heather Pooh, Devil Pooh, Urfie, Rubic, Booglie Wooglie (from Kibbles and Bits), The Odd Couple, Thumper, Runt, Hockey Puck, Scoogy-Oogums, Snuggelybumedbear, Little Fruitfly, Mawsquaw, and Punskin. There was also this ad which seemed like it was written for name-lovers:

BABSY, LABSY, POOPLE & DOOPLE,
I love da poops! Zog!
The Omnipotent.

Cleveland Plain Dealer **(1984).**

The Wench, Aunt Smurf, Big Looney, Greaseball, Tenderoni, Cheekies, Chocolate Thunder, Chipmunk Cheeks, Mosquito, Dog Fat, Scruf, Mr. Glove, Droolbucket, Belly, Built But Dumb, Frances the Nutt, Weets, Cavewoman, Chripper, Poogy, Meatball, Mootser (who loves Mookey), Slippery Heel, Possie, Phil the Drill, Petie Pot Belly, Punkinpussy, Ratzo, the White Ape, Lover Goon, Mooshface, Wee Waa, The Void, The Polish Unicorn, and Ya Old Poop make this one of the prime locations to collect love names. One trend here: more than a half-dozen Babycakes.

Courier-Mail **(Queensland, Australia) (1991).**

This section was a first for this newspaper. Lots of bad poetry but some good novel stuff:

No job!
No car!
No money!
Thank God for today!
I love you, *Cameron*

Nubbles, Spunky Bum, Swooz, My English Rose, Haggis, and Snow Pea are among the better handles.

El Paso Times **(Texas) (1996).**

This to Jackie from Romaine: "Eyes of print meet yours as you read, words are lips to kiss you when mouthed, close your eyes and feel a body of sounds embrace you as spoken arms pull you near, and know that as audible echo's fade the words I love you resound forever in my heart."

Findlay Courier **(Ohio) (1984).**

Proves that you don't have to go to the big city to find names like Skunkie Poo, Udder Nose, Rubber Band, and Pupster.

Fort Lauderdale Sun-Sentinel **(1996).**

All sorts of diverse things going on here. Someone named Fat Boy wants Grace to be his wife, someone calling him or herself Insatiable is telling Platonic that it has been a wonderful year, and one from a Chevrolet dealer thanking all the ladies who helped make it the leading dealer in South Florida.

Kansas City Times **(1984).**

Bunny Buns, Fishface, Gock, a Poopoo, and a Doodoo, along with the following which appeared at the bottom of column four:

HIGH,
Buns hard as bricks,
Break a pencil in betwixt.
Love you forever.
Cheeseburgerface

Key West Citizen **(1996).**

Among ads such as one which reads, "Puki! Puki! Snukiughums Love You 50

Times More," is this contained inside a heart:

London Times **(1984).**

Odd Valentine names have been appearing in this newspaper for years, and a number of classics have appeared in Leslie Dunkling's book, *First Names*, including Custard Beasty, Maggot, Ratbag, Ankle Biter, Tiny Tornado, Butter Mountain, Joffa Woofer, One-Tooth Jaws, and Sloppy Sex-Pot Lid. From the 1984 crop: Fuccles Frever, Meeny Poos, Poo Piglet, Ally Gogs, Frogspawn, Wiggle Woggles, Poozal, Poochie Pie, Dotty Twochins, Squidgy Bottom, Skunkette, Fungus, Goobie Booby, Dog Breath, Mrs. Fruitbat, Snortiflugs, Poolie Fuzzee Wackie, Smootchiepie, Diddy Mousee, Pooziwoozie, and Sarah Gorilla Arms.

Here one finds some punky-rotten names like Mangy Bitch, several Rats and Ratbags, and a Smellie, along with an infusion of old-fashioned toilet humor. Some clearly reflect the great British literary tradition, such as:

NOG NOG NIGGINS,
Little Swiss Goblins smoglets shiv bivlits.
Love you, *Poo*

Maine Times **(1984).**

Two memorable ads, including one addressed to a Lance who seemed to have more admirers than any other person in the papers surveyed.

LANCE!!!
Take us to the Aubergine.
You have one more chance
Before June 30th.
We Love you!!!
Your Valentines, *Linda, Cookie, Ginger, Jobie,* and *Schotze*

BIRDLEGS,
You're so tweet
Elizabeth

Miami Herald **(1996).**

Nicknames galore…four in this ad alone:

MOOKIE POOKIE, FUR BUTT,
HONEY BUNNY, FANG,
No matter what you call yourself,
I love you.

Montgomery Journal **(Maryland) (1984).**

Bullit Head, Yip-Yip, Nudie Bee, Chuckwad, Pumpkinhead, the Three Faces, Huzzles Wuzzles, Tuna Boat, Nancy the Goober, and Marionette Chin all appeared.

This was the only newspaper surveyed which went out and asked people where they got the names and wrote an article on the story behind the likes of Little Butt Man—in this case, his being smaller than hers. One intriguing ad not explained was this one:

McCAPTAIN,
Stingy, stingy me,
Guess I'll always be,
Cause I won't agree to pay
your docking fee,
Centimentaly me.
Love, *Iguana*

Nashville Banner (1996).

Rich material here: love from Puppy Toes to Kitten Claws, ditto from Bunny Foo Foo to Thumper, and another from Mushmellow to Moo Moo Honey Dew. The ad from Mooshi-est to Mooshie Thing says, "They forced me to do this." There is also an ad to Phyllis from Satan. The best Nashville feeling may be in this one: "HANK, you ole' wild coyote dog! Come by and see me, and I'll give you something to howl about."

New York Post (1984).

Oddly, this paper with its blatantly sensational headlines attracts Valentine advertisers who write like Victorian pastors. A really wild line in this paper is "How 'bout that Pina Colada?"

Newsday (1984).

It is in this Long Island, New York, newspaper that we learn that Zucchini loves Muffin, Zazzy loves Zammy, Sissy loves Yo-Yo, Stinc loves Porc, The Crazy One loves Puddles, Jelly Belly loves Peanut Butter, BooBoo loves Nimrod, Sweetpea loves Annabelly, Peaches loves Ace, and more.

Ottawa Citizen (1984).

A prime Canadian selection peaking in the P's: Passionpuss, Papooska, Polar Bear, Poodle Woo, Pooger, Pookiepoo, Piglet, Pneu, and, himself, Poupee D'Amour. Also one each of these: Cathy-Boo My Pufferbelly, Earl My Pearl, Elephant Shoes, Euchre Jim, Father Earth, Foin-Foin, Feetie, and Schmoeubs.

Portland Downtowner (Oregon) (1984).

A small downtown paper which appeals to the likes of the Bionic Bunny, Kumquat, Eggtor, Pig's Mother, Coupons, and Weinie Beinie.

Sacramento Bee (1984).

Grisbin, The Amazing Almond, Mr. Potato Head, Woo-Boo Buns, 90% Angel, My Squatty Body, Pooner, Meat, Special K, My NoNo, Boobers, Sweet Baboon, Chubba Bubba, Yinkie, and Bubala Schmubala were all here along with a high percentage of rhymers:

> MOON,
> Roses are Red
> Nachos have cheese
> Would you be mine
> Valentine please?
> *LEG*

> MUFF, MUFF,
> You sweet Cream Puff.
> I love you so much,
> I can't get enuff.
> *Your Secret Admirer*

There were also these love classics:

> To my little DODO bird
> after 10 years in the nest
> *Ooga-Chuck, Ooga-Chuck*

> BOB,
> You are the chocolate chips in
> my cookie. *Eula*

St. Louis Post-Dispatch (1984).

A fertile field for offbeat ads and the leading outlet for "Roses are red," to wit:

> BOBO.
> Roses smell good,
> Your gym bag smells bad.
> But you're the best valentine
> I've ever had.
> *Sonie*

Dear NORMIE,
Roses are red,
Violets are blue.
Please marry me
Before our daughter turns two.
Some Tonight?
Love, *Mikie*

Rosebuds are red.
And sometimes they blossum.
If you send some to me,
Your bill will be awesome.
To MIKE   Love *Rhonda*

San Francisco Chronicle (1984).

Not as crazy as one might expect, but the names reach toward upscale gourmet: Mother Puma, Big Wuss, Cuppy Beans, Tofu, The Big Chill, Garlic, Marathon Man, Meow Mix, Asparagus Legs, Rebecca Pita, Pumpkin Noodles, Windsong, and Zen. Lots of literary references here (Dorothy Parker, Lady Dulcinea), and, perhaps, the best of all the works in the "Roses" genre:

SMITTY IN RENO,
Roses are red,
Violets are green,
Come on down and
we'll be obscene.
Love, *RC*

Seattle Post-Intelligencer (1984).

One ad stands out:

BUNNY MUFFINS
I love you more than ever
Even more than my computer
If I had to do it all again
I'd still pick your toot-tooter
Pooky Lips

Stars and Stripes (1989).

A stunning 32 pages of zesty names:

Seepiefeet, Der Elefant, Love Lee, Jean "Bean Face," Knuddlemaus, Debbie Doo (from Woo), Timmer the Swimmer, Chester the Molester, Poopuma, and this oddity: "To My Waterhorse...Your Lizzard Lips."

Toledo Blade (1984).

Ads from and to the likes of Cooter Coot, RN2B (about to be married?), Petals, Wiggle Worm, Your Sputnik, Cigar, Puff the Magic Dragon, Chooch, Tingles, Chele, Homeny Bunchie, Scratch and Sniff, and Gonzo. Also a good double ad:

JOE and OLD BLUE,
Diamond has the vodka and
Pearl has the juice.
We are coming to your house
and getting real loose.
Don't lock your door and
don't be afraid.
What harm can come from
a couple old maids?

Toronto Daily Mail (1984).

Duckdo, Dumps, Phizz, Mr. Crocus, Pocket Venus, Moo the Mook, Pigbum, Snortiblog, Rubberlips, Yonksy, Plonker, Lawn-Mower, Natopotamus, Passion Waggon, Button Moon, Blobnose, Captain Dang, Bestipoohs, and Knockerflop combine to make this group almost as colorful as the next.

Virginia Pilot (1996).

Lots of ads, mostly conventional names but a few gems like School Bus, Your Ex Poopie, your Shoshone Captor, the Sweeper, Worm, Smoopie, and one signed Pooh #2. A number are dedicated to Heather, including one to "Heather the Princess from the Beach Kingdom."

Westchester Gannett **newspapers (1984).**

Good names like Cheeseball, Little Mush-Mush, Piglet, Princess Boobs, Deer Hoof, Schmoo Bear, Hunskies, Lala, Mr. Liquid, Wanny, Fatty Toes, Honeybubbles, Wawa, Weeble, Peekie-Peekie, and two memorable ads:

ANDY,
539 Roses
Words can't express my love.
All my heart
Only you, *Poo Poo Face*

DEAR PEEB,
Remember, 1984 is the year
of the Booie.
Love, *Peebee*

Are there any conclusions that can be drawn from all of this? Yes.

1. There were a number of names and lines which were obviously coded for the couple involved and meant to tantalize others. A small sampling for codebreakers:

I.L.Y.S.M.I.L.Y

3K

POONER, so, 34 down? Can you handle 720 mo' with your PQS?

TO MY PIG,
Three words sum up how I feel about you—Am U Em.
Love, *Your Pig*

AL ** I love your LOVE ACTION. I lust for your DLD, PLP, SLS and LLL. ILU, *Jill.*

The author suspects that all of these are deeply erotic and does not really want to hear to the contrary. One set of numbers, 143, which appears in ads all over North America, at first seemed to be the secret mark of some strange subculture that did not announce itself. The numbers 143 appeared in all sorts of variations—1.4.3.4.4., 143TT, J143c—making the puzzle all the more interesting.

I asked dozens of knowledgeable people about this and nobody seemed to know. I was even put in touch with a numerologist in Seattle. Then I mentioned it to Faith Eckler of *Word Ways* magazine, who thought for a few seconds and suggested this remarkably simple solution: I (1 letter), love (4 letters), you (3 letters). So much for odd subcultural codes.

Other outstanding mysteries include: XOXHLSFX, A.M.L.A. from your NOJ, and P.T.S.N.F.O.T.T.A.

2. Generally speaking, the further north one goes the better the love names and the stronger the custom of using a newspaper ad to declare your everlasting love. The few southern papers I went through had just a small handful of ads.

3. The custom may be threatened by crass commercialism. In 1984, one spotted ads from radio stations, restaurants, real estate agents, and car dealers slipped in among the personals.

By 1996, ads from massage parlors and escort services were showing up with the ads in several Western papers such as the *Albuquerque Journal*. This should not be tolerated lest the annual love columns turn into just another—sometimes tawdry—classified ad section.

4. Finally, it would appear that people have achieved a mastery of personal sobriquets at a time when everybody else uses your first name. If you are *Bob* and *Mary* to the whole world, why shouldn't you be *Dr. Lovebomb* and *The Blimp* to each other? The trick of course is not to let the rest of the world link your *nom de passion* with your real name, unless, of course, your real name is Poopskanelly or Pumpkinwally—both from the *Boston Herald* of Valentine's Day 1996.

5. The sections are becoming tamer and less provocative. The age of the provocative V-Day newspaper section may be coming to an end. Consider these three sections from the same newspaper:

Washington Post **(1984).**

With 22 tabloid-sized pages, this paper offered what was positively the wildest assortment of names like Moppie-Lady, A. Nony Mouse, Tootipop, Barnsey Doo, Meat, Boobum, Bumbledoo, Bwana Kubwa, Butterduck, Toadface, Chocmool, Clam Chowder, Chica Lica, Dorie Doo, Goomba, Peenhead, Faloosh, Moosh, Bow Toes, Girafee Breath, Gnootz, Googsie, Grofiekius, Puggy Bear, Sugar Bugar, Nerdman, Yodaface, Opusface, Orangutan Arms, Ozer, Pennobutt, Princess Doch Doch, Puftball, Scuzzy, Snooterbalooter, TaTa, Thunda Pie Pie, Wooly Punkeen, Pop 'N' Fresh, Elephant Washer, Tubby, Waumuh, Fluffbug, Meatball, Moonins, Knob, Fishman, Kree, Batto, The Garbanzo Bean, The Weazel, Bean Fluff, and Toozbear.

More than a touch of kinkiness:

ANGEL,
Ropes are nice,
Chains are better.
But I like a Whip w/leather.
Wally

A lot of coded material:

Bill says to Mary: DFJ SHV INH ZCT TRK BUM NCZ VEX KGP

And many examples of fine poetry, such as:

BOB,
Roses are too expensive
Besides they die too quick
But words will last forever
I hope these do the trick.
MEA

BILL,
Micros are sexy
LANs are all right
You're unsurpassed
sharing a bed or a byte.

BUNKY J.,
Roses are red,
Violets are blue.
If you're not my Valentine,
Its meatloaf and okra for you.
Love, *Toots J.*

NANCY,
Roses are red,
Violets are blue.
I am sorry
That I hung up on you.

Washington Post **(1994).**

Same level of zaniness but more that is cryptic. One ad reads simply 3438336, and another is from a romantic named 6 whose love message is totally in coded numbers. A few are in letter codes and variant forms of Pig Latin. There are ads addressed to Joe Studmuffin, Prince Pookie of Waa, Pooh Nugget, Nardi Rudder-cup, and Piggie Pigvert (who is told that the obswine phone calls have got to stop).

Washington Post **(1996).**

A full 18 pages of them: tame, sleep-inducing, pedestrian love handles with little of the zest of earlier years.

The Name is the Game

Great alumni partners

Word games are everywhere, but what of names which seem as if they were meant to be played with? Here is a cluster:

Alums. All you need for this is a college alumni directory which you use to make logical pairings. This game was played not too long ago in the pages of the *Harvard Magazine* when Christopher S. Johnson, '64, used the 1980 *Harvard Alumni Directory* to create these great partnerships: Nippe and Tuck, Boddy and Soule, Hand and Glove, Dire and Strait, Strain and Stretch, Sober and Dry, Boston and Braman, Stix and Stone, Stellar and Celestial, Halfacre and Littlefield, Come and Goforth, Church and Sicular, Bottleman and Casebeer, and Male, Macho, and Stag. His best may be: Darling, Kister, and Breedlove.

This can be played with all sorts of groups. At the 1976 Republican National Convention, James T. Wooten, then of the *New York Times,* came up with a rearranged delegate list with groupings like: Phyllis Barbee and Ken Doll, Eliza Sprinkle and Walter Wrinkle, and Marshall Cain and Peggy Abel.

A further variation on this is to take the Congressional directory to create the names of cosponsored legislation. Randy Alfred played this very game in the *Washingtonian* magazine and came up with these imaginary bills using real names from the 97th Congress: the Dunn-Wright Quality Control Act, the Heinz-Pickle Brand Names Act, the Roe-Hatcher Fishery Act, the Snowe-White Dwarf Labor Act, and the Pickle-Pepper Tongue Twister Act. When the *Wall Street Journal* played the same game in 1983, there was the Little-Man-Staggers Alcoholic-Beverage Control Bill for Minors and the Ketchum-Young Drug Offenders Bill.

All-Stars. The notion is to assemble a baseball team based on a theme. From time to time Red Smith used to devote his *Times* column to such creations. In 1974, with the help of a baseball researcher, he created an all-Watergate team—there were a Nixon, a Mitchell, and a Dean on the 1926 Phillies—and in October 1976, when postseason play moved to Montreal, Smith created a team for wintry nights with players like Icebox Chamberlain and Billy McCool.

The challenge here is to come up with a team half as good as Smith's Culinary All-Stars (in the box below), which he said "would make every mouth in Cooperstown water."

Other categories to play with are the **Anatomical All-Stars** (Rollie Fingers, Tony Armas, Heinie Groh, etc); the **Rainbow Coalition** (Blue Moon Odom, David Green); **Traveling All-Stars** (Todd Cruz, Dan Ford); and **Weathered Players** (Storm Davis, Chili Davis, Tim Raines).

One could try to create a **House Team** (Alan Bannister, Ron LeFlore, Johnny Bench) and a **Time Team** (Rick Monday, Rudy May). Tougher still is a **Palindromic Team** (Toby Harrah is one), but a **Feminine Team** is easy (Nellie Fox, Birdie Tebbetts, Sal Maglie, Lena Styles, etc).

Another baseball game which Joe Falls devoted several columns to in the *Sporting News* had begun in the Detroit Tigers press box. You name a player, and the next person must come up with anoth-

Culinary All-Stars

Pitchers—*Art Herring,* Tigers; *Oyster Burns,* Orioles; *Bob Veale,* Pirates; *John Lamb,* Pirates; *Pete Hamm,* Twins; *Ray Lamb,* Indians; *Bill Currie,* Senators; *Sweetbreads Bailey,* Cubs; *Al McBean,* Pirates; *Lou Tost,* Braves; *Frank Pears,* Cardinals; and *Candy Cummings,* Reds.

Infielders—*Chico Salmon,* Indians; *Spinach Melillo,* Browns; *Pie Traynor,* Pirates; *Cookie Lavagetto,* Dodgers; and *Jack Coffey,* Braves.

Outfielders—*Fred (or Jim) Rice,* Red Sox; *Tony Curry,* Phillies; *Ginger Beaumont,* Pirates; *Goody Rosen,* Dodgers; and *Sherry Magee,* Phillies.

Catchers—*Herman Franks,* Dodgers; *Spud Davis,* Phillies; *Johnny Oates,* Braves; and *Peaches Graham,* Braves.

Umpire—*Beans Reardon.*

Recent additions to Smith's team would have to include *Darryl Strawberry,* Mets; *Chet Lemon,* Tigers; and *Ron Oester,* Reds.

er name using the first or last name of the person you named. One night another writer stumped Falls with Clyde Kluttz. He mentioned this in print, and readers came forth with a number of Clydes and a few variously spelled Kluttzes. The game gets a little easier if you let it drift outside of baseball.

Cast Your Own Show. Author Louis Phillips, in his pamphlet "A Little Bit of Theatre," suggests coming up with logical casts for well-known plays. Several examples from Phillips:

Death of a Salesman. Peter Sellers and Soupy Sales.

K2. With R2D2.

After the Fall. Spring Byington, Elke Sommer, Shelly Winters.

(It should be noted that Phillips has come up with a number of name games and challenges. One which appeared in the "Metropolitan Diary" section of the *New York Times* was his list of films that should be shown at the Metropolitan Museum of Art, including: *The Matisse Falcon, Look Back in Ingres, The Importance of Being Ernst,* and, of course, *Hello, Dali*).

A variation on **Cast Your Own Show** is **Start Your Own Club.** In his book *The Fabulous Adventures of Wilson Mizner,* John Burke tells how in the days before World War I, Mizner would create facetiously named clubs for which he would then make a list of honorary members. His Poultry Club had such real members as "Oscar Egg, the bicycle rider, Judge Swann, Eddie Pigion, Judge Wrenn, Sam Crane, and the famous Chinatown tong warrior Mock Duck."

The Kevin Bacon Game: This one hit the Internet in 1995 and has engaged thousands. One player names an actor or actress, and the other player has to link that person to Kevin Bacon in as few links as possible (usually five or six). Here is how it works:

Challenger: Fred Astaire.
Respondent: Astaire was in *The Towering Inferno* with Dabney Coleman, who was in *The Man With One Red Shoe* with Tom Hanks, who was in *Apollo 13* with Kevin Bacon.

The *Washington Post* reported in late 1995 that there were a number of home pages on the Internet devoted to this fad game. One page is called *Makin' Bacon* and another is called *Six Degrees of Bacon.*

Liff: In their 1983 book *The Deeper Meaning of Liff,* Douglas Adams and John Lloyd came up with ingenious definitions for ordinary place names. For instance:

Glasgow (n.) The feeling of infinite sadness engendered by walking through a place filled with younger people.
Ozark (n.) One who offers to help when all the work has been done.

Since then all sorts of folks have gotten into the act. The *Toronto Globe and Mail,* for instance, has run several Liff contests in which one is to use Canadian place names. Some examples:

Squamish (n.) A feeling of nausea. (v.) To desperately attempt to save face after a strongly stated opinion has been debunked.
Banff (n.) Forced exhalation, as when hit in the abdomen.

Liff is a great game to play in the car as one comes upon a Musquash, Timoneum, Yonkers, or Tullahoma.

Map Stories: This game involves coming up with a sentence or story from a map of the United States by using the names of different towns together. The first two examples in the box first appeared in the January 1958 issue of *Good Housekeeping*. The two other examples—a story and a menu—were created by Charles Knott and appeared originally in the *Bulletin of the American Name Society*.

Map Stories

AUTO	ACCIDENT	REX	CARR	SIREN	WALES
W. Va.	Md.	Ga.	Colo.	Wisc.	Ky.

NORMAL	HEALTH	SOUND	GOWEN	HOME
Ala.	Ark.	N.C.	Mich.	Colo.

LOVELY	MAIDEN	HOOKS	RICH	BATCHELOR	MAN	AZWELL	GIVEN
Ky.	N.C.	Tex.	Miss.	La.	Va.	Wash.	Iowa

HONEYDEW	MELLIN	FRIED	OYSTER	PLATTER	TOMATO
Cal.	W. Va.	N.D.	Va.	Okla.	Ark.

SURPRISE	ROLL	STRAWBERRY	DELIGHT	COFFEE	TEA.
N.Y.	Ind.	Ark.	Ark.	Ga.	S.D.

Marriages. One of the oldest and still most satisfying name games, it asks you to come up with an imaginary wedding in which, say, Lotte Lenya marries Syngman Rhee yielding Lotte Rhee, or if Tai Babilonia married Herb Score she'd be a Tai Score, or if Ella Fitzgerald married Darth Vader she'd be Ella Vader.

Then in the 1980s, the rules changed and, as societal mores shifted, multiple marriages were allowed. An early set of these appeared in a *New York* magazine competition, including these three highly sophisticated examples of the game played with multiple spouses:

If Emma Goldman married Chairman Mao, Joel Crothers, Francis Scott Key, then Raymond Burr . . .

If Lola Falana married Birch Bayh, Paul Anka, then Ted Knight . . .

And the winner of that competition:

If Anna Magnani married Martin Mull, Stepin Fetchit, Walter Abel, Bobby Orr, Ho Chi Minh and Norman Norell . . .

A 1994 *Washington Post* contest yielded the likes of:

crow-Magnon

thought from Herb Caen, who came up with this notion in 1970. The idea was to give animals appropriate names.

Caen and his readers came up with such fine examples as these: "a gopher named *Broke*, a crow named *Magnon*, a rabbit named *Transit,* a sparrow called *Agnew* and an aardvark called *A-million miles-for-one-of-your-smiles.*"

If Judith Light married and divorced, in succession, Terry Waite, Joseph Cotton and Richard Gere…

If Julia Roberts left Lyle Lovett for Bobby Orr and then married Utah Governor Mike Leavitt…

Every so often there is a real marriage which fits the game. This item appeared in Herb Caen's column in the *San Francisco Examiner* in late 1983: "Actor Jack Tate… is marrying Jill Forney March 4, after which they will be known as Jack and Jill Forney-Tate. Dey do?"

Pet Names. Another advance in Western

Saints. The idea here is to take the name of a real saint and pair it with its logical patron. Here are some which were created by three women on the staff of St. Edward High School in Lakewood, Ohio, and reported in the *Catholic Universe Bulletin.*

St. John Bosco—The Patron Saint of chocolate milk drinkers.

St. Francis of Assisi— Wimps.

St. Hedwig—Bald people.

St. Josaphat—Weight Watchers.

St. Colman—Campers.

St. Julie Billiart—Pool players.

St. Martin of Tours—Travel agents.

Postmarks

The idea is to make up or find real town names that fit with apt state abbreviations. These for starters:

Fiven, Tenn.	Houdy, Miss.	Googa, Ga.	Bend, Ore.	Odear, Me.
Carpet, Tex.	Faux, Pa.	Praise, Ala.	Eski, Mo.	Toulouse, Ky.
Shapeless, Mass.	Farmerina, Del.	Acapel, La.	Noaz, Ark	Lowe, Cal.
Proan, Conn.	Seedless, R.I.	Carr, Wash.	Ether, Or.	Sayno, Mo.
Sweetasapls, Ida.	Hoot, Mon.	Reeley, Ill.	Coolidge, Cal.	
Drain, O.	Nohitsnorunsno, Ariz.			

(The bulk of these came from the late Russell J. Dunn, Sr., with others from a list which appeared in the *Bulletin of the American Name Society,* from Dr. Bertram L. Hughes, and from John G. Fuller's *Games for Insomniacs.* Dunn also likes to make up business names like We Fuel You Not (self-service gas station), Chock Full O' Mutts (dog kennel), Delegate-Essen (U.N. restaurant for German diplomats), Shingle Belles (women roofers), and The Yellow Rows of Taxis (cab company parking area).

St. Francis de Sales—Shoppers.

St. Ladislaus—Lost boys.

St. Bernadette—Mortgage payers.

Our Lady of Good Counsel—Lawyers.

This game has also been played in Herb Caen's column in San Francisco, where readers have come up with such pairings as:

St. Martin of Porres—Bartenders.

St. Boniface—Elizabeth Arden.

Sts. Peter and Paul—Bankers.

St. Joan of Arc—Welders.

Titles. Several possibilities here such as coming up with titles based on the writers' names. *Writer's Digest* played this game in a small piece by Dennis E. Hensley, who suggested such works as *The Suitmaker Was a Good Screamer* by Taylor Caldwell and *Lift England's Capitol* by Jack London. Writer Christopher Cerf has taken it to a new level by "discovering" new works by Robert Ludlum (author of such noted works as *The Scarlatti Inheritance, The Osterman Weekend* and *The Bourne Identity*), such as *The Holden Penalty, The Plymouth Fury,* and *The Dolittle Congress.*

VINS (Very Impressive Names). The idea is to come up with a truly impressive name by splicing several together. An item on these conglomerates in the *Bulletin of the American Name Society* said that the original premise may have been to come up with the most impressive name a parent could give a child to prepare it for a college admissions office. For starters:

Harry S. Truman Capote

Norman Rockwell Kent

Joseph Conrad Aiken

James Joyce Kilmer

Matthew Arnold Bennett

Jack Benny Hill

Benjamin Franklin Delano Roosevelt

Thomas Jefferson Davis

Boy George Washington

Robert Sherwood Anderson

Upton Sinclair Lewis Mumford

What Was the Question. Steve Allen pioneered the notion of giving an answer and asking for the question in his book *The Question Man.* For instance,

Answer: 9-W.
Question: Herr Wagner, do you spell your name with a V?

The formula works especially well with names. In *Games for Insomniacs* John Fuller suggests playing with the names of companies in your field of interest. Fuller did it with publishing houses:

Answer: Doubleday.
Question: What wages do you get when you work on a holiday?

Answer: Indiana University Press.
Question: What do they yell in the cheering section at Indiana basketball games?

Another possibility is fictional characters:

Answer: Oliver Twist.
Question: What will you have in your martini?

Trivia

A surprising number of questions which appear in *Trivial Pursuit* and other trivia games have to do with names. Here are a few that don't appear in the games, but should:

1. Her first name and first letter of her last name will spell the name of a U.S. state. Who is this actress? (from Louis Phillips)

2. Altogether there are only six teams in the National Football League, National Hockey League, National Basketball Association, and Major League Baseball whose names do *not* end in the letter *s*. Which teams are they?

3. There is only one radio station in the United States which spells out the name of the city in which it is located. It is?

4. What do the letters B.F. stand for in B. F. Goodrich?

5. Where are the following institutions located: **(a)** Arkansas City Jr. College, **(b)** Ottawa University, **(c)** Miami University, **(d)** Virginia Jr. College, **(e)** New England University, and **(f)** Indiana State College?

6. What is the most populous city in the United States named after a president or a vice president?

7. In the first two pilot episodes of the television show *All in the Family*, Archie Bunker was known as Archie _____?

8. What did the motel in *Psycho* have in common with the high school in *Carrie*?

9. What kind of apple appeared on the Beatles' Apple recording label?

10. A tough question: What was the name of the other driver in the auto accident which killed James Dean?

The answers:

1. UTA Hagen.

2. The six clubs with names not ending in *s* are the NBA's Miami Heat, Orlando Magic, and Utah Jazz; the NHL's Tampa Bay Lightning; and baseball's Chicago White Sox and Boston Red Sox. The late United States Football League had two more in the Chicago Blitz and Denver Gold.

3. WACO. A non-city set of call letters is KERN in Kern County, California.

4. Benjamin Franklin.

5. **(a)** Kansas, **(b)** Kansas, **(c)** Ohio, **(d)** Minnesota, **(e)** New South Wales, Australia, and **(f)** Pennsylvania.

6. Dallas, Texas, which was named for George M. Dallas, who was James K. Polk's vice president.

7. Justice.

8. The name *Bates*—it was the Bates Motel and Bates High School.

9. Granny Smith.

10. Donald Turnipseed. According to *USA Today*, Mike Tormey "astounded the audience" at a national trivia championship when he gave this answer.

Nautical Nomenclature

Names at Sea

20

Names for boats and ships follow all sorts of directions and obey many customs. Years ago, for instance, the *Wall Street Journal* reported on one of the oddest employee perks offered anywhere. The Freeport Sulpher Co. names all its new ships after employees with 30 or more years of service. Among many married owners of pleasure boats there is an odd compulsion to create combo names like *Fredna*, *Micmar*, and *Karenlou* while others try to include the whole family in names like *Kamijoan* (Katherine, Mike, Joe, and Ann). Some have become so common and clichéd that you seem to see at least one every time you get near the water. These include *Mama's Mink*, *The Impossible Dream*, *Deliverance*, *Our Folly*, *Papa's Passion*, and *Sea Horse*.

Some give us great pleasure. "In October 1970," writes name fancier Charles Mintzlaff of Milwaukee, "I was traveling from Bangkok to San Francisco aboard the Pacific Far East Line's freighter S.S. *Oregon Bear*. During the days that we were docked in Hong Kong, the ship was moored at a buoy in the harbor, and going ashore meant about a ten-minute ride by power launch.

"The launch which regularly shuttled us ashore and back aboard was of the type boarded by stepping over the gunwale at the stern, during which it was impossible not to notice the escutcheon proclaiming the boat's name, the *Lee Key*. I saw this name several times and just passed it off as an oriental-sounding name. It was not until I sounded it out to myself that I noticed the several layers of pun compressed into those six letters."

People also take great pleasure in naming boats and ships. My late friend Warren Johnston wrote some years ago from Woolwich, Maine, to tell me about his new boat: "We named [it] *UWASA II*, after our first car, a Model A Ford with rumble seat...12 years old when we got it in 1944, in which we got around the Colorado mountains that summer. We had named the car *UWASA*, the Japanese word for *rumor*—I was a student at the Navy Japanese Language School in Boulder at the time—because it got around."

A raft of boat names and customs:

Adventurer. The name given to a Cunard liner of the early 1970s. It was enough to make Jenkin Lloyd Jones write an editorial in the *Washington Star* calling it a "travel agent's name." It not only violated the old Cunard custom of naming ships with words ending in *-ia* (such as *Britannia*, *Acadia*, *Parthia*, and *Corinthia*) but was also a name that did not connote "noble vessels engaged in the deadly serious business of wrestling with wind and wave to get purposeful voyages from here to there." Jones was also offended by the *Romantica*, *Fantasia*, *Skyward*, *Starward*, and *Oriental Carnival*. This commentary was written in 1971 before there was a *Love Boat*.

Bottoms Up. One of the commonest examples of booze names, which are often given to pleasure boats, although *Scotch Mist, Old Crow, Happy Hour,* and *Cheers* are close behind. In a survey of 1,000 boat names in Florida, John McNamara found that alcoholic names were among the most popular. Commenting on so-named boats in an article in the *Washington Post,*

Lynn F. McGee said of their owners, "They wear blue blazers and sundresses and wave a lot."

Celeste. Could this be the bad luck name to beat all others? Most people have heard the bizarre story of the *Mary-Celeste* which was found without a crew but in perfect order. Even the table was set for dinner. An earlier *Celeste* is described in Horace Beck's *Folklore and the Sea:* "She sailed on a Friday. She nearly sank and had to be repaired. She sailed again and a rabbit was found aboard. Rats left her. Smallpox broke out. Her log was found floating on an empty sea with the last entry only an hour old."

Cirrhosis of the River. One of the many cutesy names for boats, it has been seen moored at more than one port. Others: *Sloop Along Placidly, Sailbad the Sinner, Toy Yot, Myot, Sawsea, Knot Paid IV, Pade IV, Sir Launch-a-Lot, Take V, Escape II, Second Mortgage, In Hoc, Inhocuptohere, Tomato Sloop,* and the ever-popular *Miss Fitz. Capt. Tuna,* one presumes, is owned by a chicken of the sea.

FRED. According to *Sail* magazine this is often an acronym for "Freaking Ridiculous Economic Disaster." *IOMA* is a boat sighted along the Maine coast and stands for "It's Only Money Alice."

HI-DEE-HO. A true reflective name in that it reads the same when reflected in the water as it does on the back of a boat. This was one of a number found by John McNamara in his survey of 1,000 Florida boats. Others included *DIXIE BEE, HOBO, KOO KOO II,* and *BOBBIE O.* Since the only letters that work this way are *B, C, D, E, H, I, K, O* and *X,* there are limits here.

Mayday. Taboo name which cannot be used for a boat name because it is the international distress call.

Obsession. According to the Boat Owners Association of the United States, the ten most popular boat names in 1995 were (in descending order): *Obsession, Odyssey, Osprey, Escape, Liquid Asset, Wet Dream, Serenity, Hakuna Matata* ("No Worries," from a song in the Disney film *The Lion King*), *Fantasea*, and *Therapy*. The fact that the three most popular names began with the letter *O* makes the next entry all the more fascinating.

Oneida. A 19th-century ship out of Searsport, Maine, which was named so despite an old superstition which said that it was unlucky for a ship name to begin with the letter *O*. Nathaniel Bowditch, the navigator, when consulted by underwriters, actually advised against insuring ships whose name commenced with the letter, saying that they were known to be unlucky. This superstition is among a number collected by the staff of the Penobscot Marine Museum in Searsport.

As with most superstitions, one can find a few choice examples where it was borne out—the "unsinkable" battleship *Ostfriesland*, for instance, was taken by the Americans after World War I and sunk off Hampton Roads in an early demonstration of aerial bombing.

Another and seemingly more universal superstition was that one invited the worst sort of luck by changing the name of a ship. One ship launched in 1874 had sailed for ten years as the *Abner J. Benyon*, named for a prominent Boston financier. Back then it was considered prudent to name at least one of the ships for a big money man just in case you ever needed his help. But when Benyon escaped to Canada as a financial scandal was erupting around him, angry ship's owner Sam Watts changed the ship's name to *Alfred Watts*. Everyone told him he was courting disaster, but he maintained that it was a fine ship with ten safe years behind it. It sank on its first voyage under the new name, and her captain and his wife were lost at sea. Other examples of ships that changed names and sank are the H.M.S. *Victoria*, H.M.S. *Cobra*, and *Lusitania*. In his book *Folklore and the Sea*, Horace Beck points out that this superstition is not universal; in Scotland names of hapless ships are changed to improve their luck.

Paradox. Boat reportedly owned by two doctors. Other craft whose owners can be presumed to be in the medical profession: *Freudian Sloop, Panacea*, and *Placebo*. *Forceps* belongs to an obstetrician as, one presumes, does *Upper Birth*. *Housecall* is a doctor's boat's name which one imagines could be useful when the doctor's office says he can't be reached because he is out on a "housecall."

Lawyer's boats: *Loop Hole, Chapter 11, Judge's Chambers*, and *The Lucky Verdict*.

Queen Mary. According to William Safire in his *New York Times* column this great passenger liner was named by an odd mistake. Safire says that the Cunard Line decided in the early 1930s to name its first "Queen" after Queen Elizabeth I. But, writes Safire, "In imparting this good news to King George V, Cunard's chief said, 'We intend to name this vessel after one of England's greatest queens.' Before the shipowner could finish, His Majesty said, 'Her Majesty will be delighted.' The Cunard man gulped, smiled, and the vessel was christened the *Queen Mary*." Before this name was bestowed, all

Cunard ships had names ending in -*ia*: *Columbia, Acadia, Britannia,* and so forth.

Relief. Coast Guard Captain Steve Masse asks, "What's a seafood restaurant without a picture of a lightship with *Relief* written on her side?" He explains, "Of course, lightships have the name of their normal station on their sides and the lightships that went around relieving the normal vessel for overhaul were marked *Relief*."

Tenovus. The boat which his father traded in when Ted Kennedy was born. The new, larger boat, according to an article in *Esquire,* was called *Onemore.*

This is it III. Boat sited near Ocracoke, North Carolina.

Titanic. Horace Beck points out that this is one of the most famous examples of a centuries old belief that you should *never* give a ship an impressive or haughty name. In *Folklore and the Sea* he writes, "A humble name was more likely to pass unnoticed by the elements, and a haughty one was bound to land one in trouble." This belief began being ignored in the 1850s when ships with names like *Sovereign of the Seas* came along, but there were still enough examples of boldly named disasters to keep the suspicion alive.

Turmoil. Ship of Singapore registry spotted in a recent list of ships entering Boston harbor.

USS Buffalo. Unusual in that it is a new name for a U.S. Navy ship. The *Buffalo,* a nuclear attack submarine commissioned in 1983, was named for Buffalo, New York. Time was when the Navy had a rigid code for naming ships, and the

USS Clamp?

The old code which is eroding stated that carriers were to be named for battles, destroyers for dead Navy and Marine Corps heroes, cruisers for cities, and submarines for fish. The code also specified:

Ammunition ships: Named for volcanoes and words suggesting fire or explosives.

Amphibious command ships: Nonvolcanic mountains and mountain ranges.

Cargo ships: Heavenly bodies and American counties.

Destroyer tenders: Locations and areas of the U.S. such as *Dixie.*

Hospital ships: Qualities which suggest their mission such as *Repose* and *Relief.*

Minesweepers: Descriptive words like *Bold, Alert, Aggressive,* and *Caution.* (Apparently the Navy had a real problem coming up with enough words of this type when hundreds of minesweepers were commissioned during World War II. It also had trouble finding names like *Clamp* and *Swivel* for 50 new salvage vessels.)

Oilers: Rivers with Indian names. (A proposal circulating in the Navy would have these ships named for American industrialists, a notion which has cynics referring to them as the "Robber Baron class of oilers.")

Store Ships: Heavenly bodies.

Submarine Rescue Vessels: Birds.

Tugs: Indian tribes and Indian words.

Only battleships are named in accordance with law. They must be named for states.

Buffalo would have been named for a fish. But politics entered the picture, and there is a new Navy truism which says "Fish don't vote" —a line which was attributed to Vice Adm. Hyman Rickover at the keel-laying ceremony for the USS *Memphis* when asked why it was being named after a city and not a fish.

USS Carl Vinson. Another old tradition —never naming a ship for a living person—was put to rest with the naming of the USS *Carl Vinson,* the first ship of the U.S. Navy to be named after a living person in more than 150 years. It was followed by two other monuments to the living: the USS *Arliegh Burke* and the USS *Hyman G. Rickover.* "Imagine the trend this could set," wrote the Navy's Samuel L. Morison in the Naval Institute *Proceedings* in 1982 just after the *Vinson* had been named: "Any member of Congress could hold up a vital government bill as ransom for a ship to be named after him."

Ironically, no amount of lobbying can get other names through. According to the Navy's *All Hands* for June 1968, "It was once suggested that a ship be named for Mom Chung, a Chinese-American plastic surgeon. She was called 'Mom' by many World War II American flyers and submariners—over 2,000 of them, in fact— who all belonged to a sort of club and became her adopted 'sons.'" There was no USS *Mom Chung,* an imposing ship name if there ever was one, because "there was no ship-naming category into which Mom Chung would fit."

USS Corpus Christi. A nuclear-powered attack submarine which was named for the Texas city, but which has offended the National Conference of Catholic Bishops because it is Latin for "the body of Christ." A major campaign by the bishops to get the name changed failed, but the Navy did rechristen it the *City of Corpus Christi.* In 1943, a patrol frigate *Corpus Christi* was launched without objection.

USS Dwight D. Eisenhower. The ship was originally named the USS *Eisenhower,* but President Nixon kept calling it the USS *Dwight D. Eisenhower.* Finally, the White House told the Navy to change the name to conform with Nixonian usage.

Vasa. Famed Swedish ship which capsized and sunk on its initial voyage. The name smacks of such bad luck that Horace Beck and others have never been able to find another ship with the same name.

Wet Dream. One of the ten most popular boat names in 1995. Part of a rich tradition of risqué boat names. Others spotted here and there: *Summer Lei, Sea Duction, Ski-Roo,* and *Sex-Sea.*

Walk-in-the-Water. The first steamboat built for use on the Great Lakes.

Nicknames

Marks of Distinction

21

Fat Tony

Tony the Sheik

Tough Tony   Little Tony   Tony the Geep   Tony Boy   Tony the Bum   Tony Bandnas

Those who have no nicknames have no social existence—they are non-people....
It may be better to be called Sewage than merely John.

—Professor Rom Harre, a lecturer at Oxford University,
writing in the January 1980 *Psychology Today.*

John A. Wilson, an Egyptologist at the University of Chicago, reported in 1952 that nicknames were as common—and often as uncomplimentary—in ancient Egypt as they are in the modern world. Losing seemingly little in translation, common nicknames in the Egypt of yore included Red, Buddy, Tiny, Lazy, Ape, Frog, Donkey, and Big Head—collectively a good set of names for a bowling team.

In Middle English they were known as *eke names*—meaning an "also-name"—which later became *nekenames* and, finally, *nicknames*. They were applied to kings and commoners alike, and in some cases all that is recalled today is the nickname, whether it be Little John or Richard the Lion-hearted.

With the likes of Mad Anthony Wayne and Light Horse Harry Lee, the nickname got a strong foothold in America and grew even stronger, peaking in the first half of the 20th century, when it seemed that groups and subcultures were vying with each other to see which had the most colorful list of nicknames. Colorful nicknames were the norm during the Civil War, especially for the leaders. The irascible, short-tempered George Gordon Meade was "Old Snapping Turtle" to his men. Other names were unflattering comments about the holder of the sobriquet, such as Judson "Kill Cavalry" Kilpatrick or "Beauty" (J.E.B.) Stuart. Then there were "Fighting Joe" Hooker and General Winfield Scott "The Superb" Hancock.

ITEM. In 1936 the FBI announced that it had collected more than 100,000 "criminal nicknames" in a special moniker file. These were nicknames, not aliases. As J. Edgar Hoover later explained, aliases changed all the time but nicknames stuck. Because the nicknames were often based on appearance, mannerism, or attitude, they were considered valuable clues.

The names themselves were enough to awe a law-abiding citizen and, as the old *Boston Traveler* said of these handles in 1938, they "would make the faces of the press agents and movie producers resemble a green light that had the candlepower of a million-watt bulb." There was "Eat Em Up" Jack McManus, "Machine Gun" Jack McGurn, Vincent "Mad Dog" Coll, "Baby Face" Nelson, "Gyp the Blood" Harry Horowitz, Fred "No Nose" DeLucia, "Trigger" Burke, "Kid Dropper" Nathan Kaplan, and so many, many more. Such was the extent of this that by the time Joe Valachi sang to the McClellan Committee in 1963, he had a hard time keeping the Tonys straight—his testimony mentioned Tough Tony, Little Tony, Fat Tony, Tony Boy, Tony the Bum, Tony the Shiek, Tony Cheese, Tony Bananas, and Tony the Geep.

ITEM. Debutante lists were published with real names as well as nicknames. The New York deb roster for 1949-1950 published in the old *Journal-American* contained, among others, a Poo, a Pooh, an Ido, a Poofie, a Gopher, a She, a Bunny, a Dinny, a Daze, a Gini, a Cini, and handfuls of Mimi's and Fifi's.

ITEM. President Franklin D. Roosevelt and his inner circle were so taken with nicknaming that the wire services had to issue periodic reports on which handles were being attached to the cabinet.

Apparently, it was FDR himself who bestowed "Tommy the Cork" on Thomas Corcoran, "Henry the Morgue" on Henry Morgenthau, Jr., "Harry the Hop" on Harry Hopkins, and "Fanny the Perk" for Frances Perkins, the Secretary of Labor and first woman cabinet member.

At the same time the U.S. Congress was filled with men who addressed each other as "Slug," "One Punch," "Ipse Dixit," "The Fountain," "Knitting Hattie," "Puddler Jim," "Cotton Ed," "Louey the Laundryman," and "Dirigible Bill."

The penchant for nicknames that stick for life has been so strong in the U.S. South that public buildings, sports facilities, and highways today have names like "Bones" McKinney Hall at Wake Forest University, the James H. "Sloppy" Floyd Veterans Building in Atlanta, and the Roland "Racehorse" Johnson Parkway in Durham, North Carolina.

The rest of the English-speaking world held up its end of the bargain. Australia became known for certain national nicknaming aptitude, a point that was driven home in a small list contained in a 1991 letter from writer and folklorist W. N. "Bill" Scott of Warwick, Queensland:

The Sitting Shot, Blue Bob From Borralcola, Fol-the-diddle-dido, Jack Without A Shirt, Step-up, Bob the Frog, and the Baking-Powder Cock (all these were cooks).

Dick the Needle, Billy the Whip, Four Ton Jack, Dick the Dog, Billy the Pup, The Jumper, The Maggot, Lovely Les, Pretty Boy, Wednesday Bob, Twenty-foot, Paddy the Fenian, Dick the Devil, The Nip, The Strangler, The Burner Off, and so on. And a husband called The Hurricane Lamp because he never went out.

But then it seemed that in the 1960s or thereabouts nicknames took a nose-dive. Kids with parents with names like Bob, Betsy, Peggy, and Al who had grown up with "Bing," "Bogie," and the "Schnozz" insisted on being called Rebecca, Christopher, and Robert.

Conventioneers' name tags were suddenly stripped of names like Dusty, Buzz, and Bud and it seemed that every Tom, Dick, and Harry was asking, if not insisting, on being called Thomas, Richard, and Harold. One columnist noted that even Chicago bookies were insisting on names like Endicott and Lamar, and in 1975 social critic Benjamin DeMott opined in the pages of the *Atlantic* that "the end of the nickname is the latest symptom of the latest plague—i.e. rampant self-importance, rampant self-love." A defining moment came in 1985 when University of Maryland basketball coach Lefty Driesell let it be known that he was to be known as Charles G. Driesell: "I'm 53 and don't like to be called by a nickname."

To be sure, they were still to be found, but the well-nicknamed seemed to be getting older. By the mid-1980s, we still had Lady Bird Johnson, Scoop Jackson, Broadway Joe Namath, Hollywood Henderson, "Tip" O"Neill and others. Frank Sinatra was Ol' Blue Eyes and the Chairman of the Board, a name given to him by radio personality William B. Williams, who had originally called him "Chairman of the Broads" in tribute to the women who swooned at the sound of his voice.

Other groups kept up their nickname reputation. The followers of American NASCAR racing know that nicknaming lives. This is an area where top drivers are likely to have worn and shed more than a few in a driving career. Dale Earnhardt, for example, has been known as The Intimidator, The Man in Black, and Ironhead. But even here there has been a falloff in the more outrageous brand of nicknaming. "In the formative years of racing, on all the circuits, drivers cultivated their daredevil images," wrote Mark McDonald, staff writer of the *Dallas Morning News* in 1995: "They had nicknames like Buck, Fireball and Speedy, Big Daddy, Snake, and Mongoose. NASCAR drivers, in particular, had reputations as dip-and-spit mountain boys who ran moonshine through the Appalachians just ahead of the revenue agents. These days, because of the corporate demands and the money involved, drivers have to be spokesmen as well as wheelmen."

Modern gangland nicknames collected between 1985 and 1996 from articles with headlines like "'Chin' busted in NYC" (*USA Today*, May 30, 1990) include Cadillac Frank, Skinny, Fat Peter, Raphie Chong, Matty the Horse, The Chin, Three Fingers, Joe Cakes, Wimpy, Gaspipe, Sonny Blue, Benny Eggs, Tash, Skiball, Christy Tick, Tom Mix, and Tony Ducks.

Boxers are another group that have held up to their end of the bargain: Ray "Boom Boom" Mancini, Thomas "Hit Man" Hearns, Hector "Macho" Camacho, James "Hard Rock" Green. Truck drivers proudly held onto their individual "handles," and college students not only name each other but also their professors. A recent wire service story on James M. Dabbs, a psychology professor at Georgia State University, said that his work on hormones in saliva and their effect on personality have earned him the nicknames "Dr. Spit" and "Professor of Spitology."

Then there is music—rap, hip-hop, punk, and jazz are all rife with them. Occasionally one stands out above all others, such as Hootie and the Blowfish, a nickname that collects other nicknames. Singer Darius Rucker has said the moniker stems from the nicknames of two pals at the University of South Carolina. One was called Hootie because of his big eyes. The other's cheeks led to his being nicknamed Blowfish. One night, the odd couple walked into a party together, and Rucker quipped, "Look, there's Hootie and the Blowfish!"

Oddly, at the moment of lowest ebb, senators insisted on the diminutive Bob (Dole, Packwood, etc.) while actors were properly called Robert (DeNiro, Redford, etc.). The president could be Jimmy or Bill but pop singers insisted on the formality of James (Taylor, Brown).

The downward trend may be reversing itself. One barometer of these things is professional sports. Pro football players' names have been getting more rather than less colorful, as evidenced by the likes of "Postbuster" Reece, "Chili" McNorton, "Little Train" James, William Anthony "the Refrigerator" Perry, "Too Hard" Morris, "Spanky" Pankey, etc. The turning point may have come in 1984 when the participants in the National Basketball Association's Slam-Dunk Championship were Julius "Dr. J" Erving, Darrell "Dr. Dunkstein" Griffith, Edgar "the Wild Helicopter" Jones, Clyde "the Glide" Drexler, Dominique "the Human Highlight Film" Wilkins, Michael "Coop-a-Loops" Cooper, Larry "Fancy" Nance, Orlando "Oh! Oh!" Woolridge, and Ralph Sampson—the only player without a nickname.

In order to help put nicknaming back on its proper upward course and inspire nicknamers, here are four small and determinedly diverse collections:

Pool Names.

Writer and pool player John Owen Clark, Jr. of San Francisco has been collecting pool and billiard monikers for some time now and passed these along, most from his own acquaintance. He adds that these tend to change as they get known (Clark used to be Savvy McCue in Ohio) and are often used as aliases in that they serve a real or imagined need for anonymity.

Jersey Red, Boston Shorty, Philippine Gene, Rebel (a woman), Joey (also a woman), Machine Gun Lou Butera (who carries his cue in a violin case), Spider Jack (a.k.a. Spider Man Jones), Rags, The Hat, Dallas West, Cowboy, Portland Don, Pockets Helfert, Styx, Onyx, Fly Boy, Champagne, Cornbred Red, Arizona Lee, Master Stroke Don, Yukon Lou, The Kalderash, Hungry Bob, Inscrutable Joe, Fat Frank, Deadpan Dan, Tory, Sudden Sam Worley, Butch the Horticulturalist,

"Refrigerator" Perry

Eartrumpet Davis, Greasy Thumb Guzik, Johnny Irish, Fat Alice, Bus Stop Whitey, Mister Robinson, Tennessee Tarzan, Weenie Beenie, Bolivar Cotton, Toupee Jay, St. Louie Louie, The Geece, Charlie Tuna, The Spy, Alone Grey (a woman), and Broom-Handle Whitey.

Today it would be hard to think of another realm where such extensive nicknaming takes place, although pro and semi-pro poker players and boxers show considerable strength. In poker, like pool, anonymity figures into the picture, but boxing names tend to be adopted either to give the fighter an extra element of ferocity (as in Dewayne "Chainsaw" Jamison or "Terrible" Tim Witherspoon) or to declare a sweet disposition (as in the two great Sugar Rays). It is also good box office. As Jack Fiske wrote in the *San Francisco Chronicle*, "The 'Manassa Mauler' versus the 'Pottawatomie Giant' sold lots of tickets at Toledo in 1919." There may not be, however, another sport in which the nickname so overwhelms the person's real name as much as it does in pool. How many people know, for example, that the late Minnesota Fats' real name is Ralph Wanderone, Jr?

The Nickname Odyssey of Jay Ames.

Jay Ames of Toronto is a name-collector of the first order. Recently he sent me a very personal collection which in an earlier version was published in the British name journal, *Nomina*. With his permission, here is a slightly abridged version of a recent update of that collection:

"As a lad in western Canada where I was pupped—my family nicknames were Sunny Jim and Rufus. Outside the home, I was as likely to be Red, Redtop, Shorty, Shortstop, and Little Bit. Moving to England while Dad was in the R.A.F. in France, I had to become used to such nicknames as Ginger, (Ginge), Bloodnut, Coppernob, in addition to Titch.

"In my teens and later I got Bricktop, Sorreltop, Stutz, Kuss, Kleiner, Basso, Tazzo, Piccolo, Maleck, Malenko, or Malenki—depending on the ethnic origin of the crew I was working with. In Wales, I was sometimes, though not always, called Cochin-bach (mostly by girls); fellow-dockers, deckhands, or the like renamed me Shunny, Shunny-bach, and Yanto, not being too familiar with a name such as Jay. Irish and Scottish coworkers, and Army comrades at a later date, altered Jay to John, Jake, Joe, or Shawn, Jamie, even Jummie and wee Will, or wee Ahmess—a neat, near play on Hamish and on my complete signature.

"Among Germans—both before the war and since, and no better able to cope with the name Jay—they've opted for dubbing me Hans, Hansi, Yan, and Janni, even Joe. Slavic-speaking mates, etc. have done almost the same, save that their use of Joe or John is as apt to emerge as Yishko and Yanko. Italians and some of my French-Canadian buddies and neighbors have elected over the years, to dub me Pepi and Pepino, or again, plain John. Oddly, they've never seen me as a Jean or even a P'ti-jean, as I might have expected.

"Cockneys I've worked with overseas, disbelieving or doubtful about my Canadian origins, have variously dubbed me Yank, Scottie, or Jock, Irish, Paddy, and Taff or Taffy.

"One current Greek neighbor and his family call me Stavrides—after a teacher the man had as a boy in Greece. Another neighbor, also Greek, gave me the name Colonel from a fancied resemblance to the

continued on page 163

Presidential Nicknames

What better way is there to map the changing fortunes of nicknames in America than to see how the president was addressed informally? In almost all of these cases the names did not come from the president himself but from friends and enemies.

George Washington: "The Father of His Country,""American Fabius," "The Farmer President," "The Old Fox," "Sage of Mount Vernon," "Savior of His Country," "Surveyor President," "Sword of the Revolution," and "Stepfather of His Country."

The Father of His Country

John Adams: "His Rotundity," "Atlas of Independence," "Duke of Braintree," and "Colossus of American Independence."

Thomas Jefferson: "The Sage of Monticello," "Long Tom," "Father of the Declaration of Independence," "Pen of the Revolution," and "Philosopher of Democracy."

James Madison: No nickname survives; however, his name was so linked with the War of 1812 that it was called "Mr. Madison's War."

James Monroe: "Lost Cocked Hat" and "The Era of Good Feelings President."

John Quincy Adams: "The Accidental President"—the first of five given an "accidental" nickname—and "Old Man Eloquent."

Andrew Jackson: "Old Hickory," "King Andrew the First," "Hero of New Orleans," "Mischie-Andy," "The Pointed Arrow," "Sage of the Hermitage," and "The Sharp Knife."

Martin Van Buren: "The Enchanter," "The Fox." "The American Tallyrand," "Kinderhook Fox," "King Martin the First," "Little Magician," "Little Van," "Red Fox," "Machiavellian Belshazzar," "Mistletoe Politician," "Petticoat Pet," "Sage of Lindenwald," "Albany Regency," and "Whiskey Van"—the last because of his ability to hold his liquor.

William Henry Harrison: "Tippecanoe," "Farmer President," "Log Cabin Candidate," "Old Granny," and "Washington of the West."

John Tyler: "His Accidency" or "The Accidental President," so called because he succeeded Harrison, the first president to die in office.

James Knox Polk: "The Napoleon of the Stump," "Young Hickory," and "The First Dark Horse."

Zachary Taylor: "Zach" and "Old Rough and Ready."

Millard Fillmore: "His Accidency" and "The American Louis Philippe."

Franklin Pierce: No nickname survives.

James Buchanan: "The Sage of Wheatland," "Ten-Cent Jimmy" (because he was an advocate of low tariffs), "Bachelor President," "Old Buck," and "Old Public Functionary."

Abraham Lincoln: "Honest Abe," "The Illinois Baboon" (by his enemies), "The Ancient," "The Emancipation President," "Father Abraham," "The Great Emancipator," "Greatheart," "Old Abe," "The Railsplitter," "Sage of Springfield," "Massa Linkum," and "The Sectional President." (Lincoln, like FDR, was a great lover of nicknames. Back in 1937 the Library of Congress discovered that Lincoln "loved" to find nicknames for his friends and cabinet officers. Secretary of the Navy Gideon Wells, for instance, was "Ichabod" or "Neptune," and Secretary of War Edwin M. Stanton was "Mars."

Andrew Johnson: "His Accidency," "Daddy of the Baby," "King Andy," "Sir Veto," and "Father of the Homestead."

Ulysses S. Grant: "Unconditional Surrender," "United States," "Useless," "The Butcher from Galena," "The Great Hammerer," "Hero of Appomattox," "Hug Grant," "Lyss," "Old Three Stars," "The Man on Horseback," "Uncle Sam," "Texas," and "Uniformed Soldier."

Rutherford B. Hayes: "His Fraudulency," "Dark Horse," "Granny Hayes," "Old Eight-to-Seven," and "President De Facto."

James A. Garfield: "The Canal Boy," "Martyr President," "The Preacher," and "The Teacher President."

Chester Alan Arthur: "His Accidency," "Prince Arthur," "Our Chet," "First Gentleman of the Land," "The Dude," and "Arthur the Gentleman."

Grover Cleveland: "Big Beefhead," "Uncle Jumbo," "Buffalo Hangman" (because he was responsible for hanging a man as a New York state sheriff), "The Claimant," "Dumb Prophet," "His Accidency," "Man of Destiny," "Old Grover," "Old Veto," "People's President," "Perpetual Candidate," "Pretender," "Sage of Princeton," and "Stuffed Prophet."

Benjamin Harrison: "Baby McKee's Grandfather," "Chinese Harrison" (because of his immigration policy), "Grandfather's Hat," "Kid Gloves" (because of his less than aggressive campaign style), and "Little Ben."

William McKinley: "Wobbly Willie," "Idol of Ohio," "Napoleon of Protection," "Prosperity's Advance Agent," and "Stocking-Foot Orator."

Theodore Roosevelt: "Old Rough and Ready," "The Hero of San Juan Hill," "TR," "The Roughrider," "The Bull Moose," "The Driving Force," "The Dynamo of Power," "Four Eyes," "The Great White Chief," "The Happy Warrior," "Haroun-al-Roosevelt," "The Man on Horseback," "The Old Lion," "Telescope Teddy," "Theodore the Meddler," "Wielder of the Big Stick," "The Trust-Buster," and "The Typical American." Roosevelt seems to have attracted more nicknames than any other president.

William Howard Taft: "Big Bill" (because he weighed more than 300 pounds).

Woodrow Wilson: "Big One of the Peace Conference," "The Phrasemaker," and "The Schoolmaster." ("Woody" is listed in *The American Thesaurus of Slang* but it somehow seems wildly inappropriate.)

Warren G. Harding: "The Shadow of Blooming Grove."

Calvin Coolidge: "Silent Cal."

Herbert Hoover: "The Chief."

Franklin D. Roosevelt: "The Squire of Hyde Park," "The New Dealer," "FDR," "Mr. Big," "Boss," "Houdini in the White House," "Sphinx," "The Roosocrat," "The Gallant Leader," "The Raw Dealocrat," "Kangaroosevelt," "Deficit," "The Featherduster of Dutchess County," and "That Man in the White House" by those who could not bear to say his name. Those people sometimes branded him "A Traitor to His Class."

(His vice president John Nance Garner had a whole pile of them, including "Texas Jack," "Cactus Jack," "Sage of the Uvalde," "Poker Face," "Uvalde Jack," "The Owl," "The Favorite Son of Texas," and "Mohair Jack." The last name came from the fact that he advocated tariffs favoring the interests of Texas goat breeders.)

Harry S. Truman: "The Haberdasher," "High Tax Harry," and "Give 'Em Hell Harry." As he was born with the Harry, it was not a nickname.

Dwight D. Eisenhower: "Ike."

John Fitzgerald Kennedy: "JFK. " Soon after he was elected in 1960, he let it be known that he did not want to be known publicly as Jack, a request that the press honored to the extent that a *New York Times* Sunday magazine article on nicknames referred to him as "J—k."

Lyndon B. Johnson: "LBJ" and "Big Daddy." The nickname that he did not like was "Landslide Lyndon" which was bestowed on him because of the narrow (and, some add, questionable) margin that elected him to Congress in 1936.

Richard M. Nixon: "Tricky Dick," a name he acquired early in his career which prompted one commentator to recall the old proverb which states that "A nickname is the heaviest stone that the devil can throw at a man." At one point in his career, his followers tried to get the "New Nixon" to stick. It didn't.

In *More Super Trivia*, Fred L. Worth reports that Nixon was called "The Iron Butt" in college and "Gloomy Gus" at Duke University Law School.

Gerald R. Ford: "Jerry."

James Carter: "Jimmy," who insisted that the diminutive form of his name be used at all times. Many people put a spin on it, and Jimmy came out as the mock-Georgian "Gym-ma." William Safire points out in his *Political Dictionary* that he was the first president to insist on the diminutive.

Ronald Reagan: "Dutch," "The Gipper," "The Great Communicator," "The Oldest and the Wisest" (sometimes shortened to O&W), and "The Defender." The name "Dutch" was given to him when he was a baby, and his father said he looked like a "fat Dutchman." (During his first term at least, Reagan was surrounded by nicknamed individuals, including Casper "Cap the Knife" Weinberger; James Brady, widely known as "The Bear"; and David Stockman, who won the "Grim Reaper" sobriquet.)

George Bush: Although a few old friends called him "Poppie," a childhood nickname, he took an anti-nickname stance as president. In July 1988, a Bush spokesman told the *Washington Post*: "George Bush has no nicknames. He's just George."

William Clinton: "Bill," "Bubba," and, to his detractors, "Slick Willie," a parallel to Nixon's "Tricky Dick."

late Harlan B. Sanders, America's once-famed Chicken King. I fail to see it because I'm handsomer, smoother, funnier, and still living—though he was undoubtedly far better dressed and wealthier than I'll ever be (if that counts for anything). The same goes (or went) for the name Beverbrook I acquired for a short spell during WWII in Malta, given me by a C.O. we had at the time, also over-pretentious for a damn roughneck, farmhand, miner, log swamper, who'd also been a fence-rider, railroader, mule-skinner, bridge-painter, deckhand, stevedore.

"Perhaps the oddest nickname ever was Stuka, bestowed on me by German nurses and ward orderlies when in field hospitals in Athens and Salonika in 1943-44. Happily, it 'dive-bombed' by the time I was moved to similar quarters in Germany proper. It was based, of course, on my POW dog-tags, number 88. But why they'd bother nicknaming one of the 'enemy' puzzled me, and still does, years after the event.

"Beachball was another nickname I neither liked nor was proud of owning— even on a short-term basis. Happily, I lost both, when I became no longer 'too short for my weight' as we quaintly put it; the once ugly 'beergut' or 'bay-window' or what we dub a 'Molson muscle' and the uglier moniker, have disappeared—long may they keep their distance.

"The shipping-room crew of a firm I worked in and out of for eight years changed Jay to Jay-jay; through a handful of stages—Jay-bird, Blue-jay, Blue-bird— it was ultimately reduced to plain Blue....

"Oddly and only since I came to Toronto in 1947 and worked as a night-foreman/freight checker for two large transport companies—both of which had multi-ethnic truckers/dock workers, I got

Tee-Zhawn from a few of the 'Pea-Soupers' who spoke as much English as I spoke 'le joaul' of Quebec. Thankfully, I never got Runt, Squirt, Shrimp, or Wimp though...such epithets fitted."

An American CB Atlas.

For a very short time, at about the time the United States was celebrating its bicentennial, the CB craze hit, and all sorts of ordinary drivers were trying to sound like truck drivers from Alabama as they memorized lines like "A big ten-four to that, good buddy" so that they could impress other ordinary drivers. As quickly as it had hit, it was gone, and the garage sale market was glutted with CB radio equipment.

As the fad passed so did the lingo—at least for the general population. Living within CB range of an interstate and possessing a multiband radio with a CB band, I can report that the trucker's lingo is still ten-two (coming in well, in case you have already forgotten). If anything, the language is more arcane, determinedly saltier, and everybody goes by a handle (Tennessee Stud, Missing Link, etc.) rather than a real name.

One of the things that truckers talk about on the radio is destinations, which are seldom if ever referred to properly, making it fun for the casual listener who has to figure them out. With the aid of several of those guides to CB which came out in 1976, and the help of several name collectors, here then is my ever-growing collection of past and present names for places.

A

Akron = Rubber City
Alaska = Eskimo Pie Land
Amarillo = Big A

B

Baltimore = Bag City, Ballmer
Belchertown, Mass. = Burp
Boise = Spud City, the Big Potato
Boston = Bean Town
Breezewood, Pa. = Motel City

C

California = Shakyside
Charleston, W. Va. = Pothole City
Chattanooga, Tenn. = Choo Choo,
    Choo Choo Town
Chicago = Chi Town
Cincinnati = Queen City
Covington, Ky. = Sin City

D

Dallas = Big D
Denver = Mile High City
Detroit = MoTown, Diesel City
Disneyland (Cal.) = Cinderella City
Disneyworld (Fla.) = The Real World

E

Elizabeth, N.J. = Big E

F

Flagler, Ariz. = Flag Town
Florence, S.C. = Tooth Town (because of
    a large "dentures-in-a-day" dental
    clinic there)
Florida = Alligator Alley, the Bikini State,
    St. Peter's Waiting Room
Fort Worth, Tex. = Cow Town

G

Gary, Ind. = Soot City, Smokestack City
Graham, Tex. = Cracker Town

H

Harrisburg, Pa. = H-Town
Hershey, Pa. = Chocolate City
Hollywood = Tinseltown
Hot Springs, Ark. = Hot Water City
Houston = Astrodome City
Huntsville. Ala. = Spaceship City

I

Idaho = I-Down
Indianapolis = Circle City
Iowa = I-Up
Irvine, Cal. = Bung Hole City

J

Jackson, Miss. = Capital J
Jacksonville, Fla. = J-Ville

K

Kansas City, Mo. = Kay Cee City
Kentucky = Finger Lickin' Country

L

Las Vegas = Dice City
Little Rock, Ark. = Rock City
Los Angeles = Shakytown
Louisiana = Lucy Anna
Louisville, Ky. = Derbytown

M

Maryland = Piggybank State
Memphis = Big M, River City
Milwaukee = Beer City, Brown Bottle City
Mississippi = Magnolia State
Missouri = Tell-Me State
Montauk, N.Y. = Shark City
Montgomery, Ala. = Monkey Town

N

Nashville = Nastyville, Music City, Guitar Town
Newark, N.J. = Dirtyside City
New Orleans = Superdome City
New York City = the Apple, the Big Apple, Fun City, Dirty City
New York State = The Rock's Park

O

Ohio = Buckeye State
Oklahoma City = O-City
Omaha = O-Town
Oregon = God's Country

P

Palestine, Tex. = the Holy City
Phoenix = Cactus Patch
Pittsburgh = Power City
Portland, Me. = Shy Town
Portland, Ore. = Rose City

R

Reno, Nev. = Divorce City
Rhode Island = Mini State

S

San Clemente, Cal. = Tricky Dick's
San Diego = Dago
Sandusky, Ohio = Sharp City
San Francisco = Hill City, the Gay Bay
Shreveport, La. = Sport City

T

Tampa = Cigar City
Topeka = Twister City
Tucson = Big T

W

Washington, D.C. = Watergate City
Washington State = George's Country
Wheeling, W. Va. = the Hole in the Wall
Wisconsin = Land of Milk and Honey

That's a ten-ten.

City nicknames should be used with caution as your idea of a good name may actually offend those who live there. A case in point is "Frisco" for San Francisco. In September 1996, according to newspaper accounts, two escapees from a Utah prison blew their cover by breaking an unwritten local law on acceptable nicknames for San Francisco. Anthony Scott Bailey and Eric Neil Fischbeck said they were from "Frisco" when questioned by University of California officers who found them sleeping on campus. The use of the name—loved by tourists but loathed by residents—set off the alarm bells that their prison break didn't. "No one from here ever says that," campus police sergeant David Eubanks said.

Other Names

Without any ado, some name species and subspecies:

Censored Names. When the U.S. Board on Geographic Names changed Oregon's Whorehouse Meadow to Naughty Girl Meadow, locals protested but the federal body refused to budge. The field got its name from the fact that four Ontario, Oregon, prostitutes used to set up a tent each spring to service shepherds coming down from the mountains. Other "cleaned-up" names include the one for an Arizona mountain once known as Nellie's Nipple but now called College Peak.

Exonyms. An exonym is a place name given by a foreigner which does not correspond to the native name. Livorno, Italy, is *Leghorn* in the English-speaking world, and Wien became *Vienna*. For years there has been talk of ironing out these inconsistencies, but they remain. All of this was underscored in 1967 when the United Nations held a meeting on name standardization in Geneva, which to the various delegates was variously Genève, Genf, Ginevra, Geneva, and Ginebra.

Fictional Names. Bestowing fictional names is a rarely acknowledged art, which we tend to be reminded of only when reading the right author. For many, the right author is Charles Dickens. Addressing this issue in *Westways* magazine, Norman Corwin concludes, "Of course the greatest gallery of names is that of Dickens. Never mind the most familiar ones—Pickwick, Copperfield, Scrooge, Rudge, Nickleby, Pecksniff, Micawber, Chuzzlewit, Uriah Heep. Think of the luxuriance of the lesser population: Pumblechook, Dolge, Crummies, Miss Snevellicci, Gamp, Squeers, Buzfuz, Gargery, Piripp, Teppertit, Perrybingle, Boffin, Gradgrind, Veneering, Twemlow, and Stiltstalking."

The late P. G. Wodehouse gave us Gussie Fink-Nottle, Sir Roderick Glossop, Boko Bickerton, Psmith, Galahad Threepwood, Stiffy Byng, and many others. And then there is that newcomer Mark Helprin who in *Winter's Tale* introduced The Reverend Mootfowl, Daythril Moobcot, Rupert Binky, and Pearly Soames.

An honorable mention in all of this should go to Chester Gould (1900-1985) of Dick Tracy fame. He named his characters after their looks, traits, or vices. His legendary "Grotesques" included Mrs. Pruneface, Flattop, The Blank, The Rodent, Itchy, Measles, The Brow, The Midget, Flyface, Mumbles, B-B Eyes, and the Mole. B. O. Plenty, the smelly ne'er-do-well hillbilly, and his wife Gravel Gertie were honest, good-hearted folk, who, in May 1947, gave birth to beautiful Sparkle. This event drew national press attention and resulted in the sale of millions of Sparkle Plenty dolls. The name Sparkle Plenty is in use today as the name of a cleaning agent for metal, crystal chandeliers, and lampshades.

The great names went to Gould's rogues' gallery of more than 200 fiends, which included Itchy Oliver; Pouch, a slimmed-down circus fat man whose excess skin provided snap compartments for contraband; Pucker Puss, who fired bullets from his bridgework; Blowtop, Flattop's explosive brother; and Gargles,

an underworld figure who made big money selling phony mouthwash. Gould sometimes spelled names backwards for effect: midget man Jerome Trohs; Ankle Redrum, a.k.a. The Blank; and ex-baseball hero Nuremoh.

Norman Corwin, one of America's most versatile writers, has strongly suggested in a letter to the author of this collection of name lore that no book on names could hope to be complete without acknowledging the fictional names of S. J. Perelman, a man Corwin regards as a "writer's writer." Corwin, despite his love for names Dickensian, writes, "Nobody, including Dickens, ever had as much sport with character names. In their variety and range of associations, they go well beyond anything to be found in the pages of what we loosely call humor, and they make a roster worth emblazoning on a wall of some comic hall of fame."

Here is some of the evidence submitted by Corwin from his own list of Perelman names:

Vernon Equinox, artist.

Gerlad Suppositorsky, Reuters correspondent.

Harry Hubris, film producer.

Irving Stonehenge, biographer.

Yale Lox Associates, an alert outfit which delivers salmon to one's door.

Monroe Sweetmeat, agent.

Sigmund Rhomboid, owner of Jampolski Arms.

Candide Yam, Chinese secretary.

Claude Nasal-Passages, French author.

Thimblerigg & Bilk, furniture sellers.

Arpad Fustian, rug chandler.

John Greenblatt Whittier, author of *Snowbloom.*

Derek Inveigleman, of Her Majesty's Secret Service.

Dr. Prognose, Dr. Peritonides, and Dr. Myron Vulpein, physicians.

Seamus Mandamus and Otis Vivendi, lawyers.

Pierre Flatulin, public-relations man for All-Gaul Airlines.

Urban Sprawl, architect.

Montague Pauncefoot, English market checker, somehow elevated to the title of Lord Grubstone.

Lois de Fee, lady bouncer.

Vyvyan Figgis, white hunter in Africa.

Noel Desuetude, English sculptor.

Mr. Forepaugh of South Dakota, founder of a new religion predicated on a massive intake of figs.

Pellagra & Wormser, biggest chain store in Richmond.

Gastlich's, a store in London.

The El Poltroon Tux Rental Shop.

Basil Scrymgeour, British publicist.

Diego Satchel, Mexican muralist.

Joyce and Waldo Muscatine, a couple enslaved by six poodles.

Stephen Surreptici, billionaire.

Mucho Dinero, Newport mansion of **Wolfram and Bonanza Frontispiece.**

Wheatena Frontispiece, their daughter.

Daniel Mariana Trench, tycoon.

Waldemar Knobnose, author of a best-seller.

The Royal Weevil Hotel, Sidmouth, Devonshire.

Prof. Henri Manatee-Dugong, staff clinician, Hospital Laiboisiere.

Singleton, Doubleday & Tripler, advertising agency.

Lothar Perfidiasch, noted Hungarian playwright.

Fern Replevin, an utterly lovely creature of 24 whose mouth wanders at will over her features.

Lafcadio Replevin, her father. (Lafcadio asks Fern, "Why are you staring at those clouds so pensively?" Fern: "Perhaps I'm more cirrus-minded than other girls.")

Tony Morninghoff, decorator (his second in command is Eveninghoff).

Perfidio's, a restaurant.

Peculators' & Predators' National, a little family bank in Sphagnum, New Jersey.

Neurotica, a magazine.

S.G. Pefelman, an 11-year-old sleuth who effortlessly solves cases that stump Scotland Yard.

The list goes on and on: Polly Entrail, Sandra Vermifuge, Marty Torment, Rolf and Capricia Trubshaw, Curt Broomhead, Simeon and Drusilla Quagmeyer, Rex Beeswanger, Bedraglia Thimig, Charlotte Russo, Manuel Dexterides, and Valuta Imbrie.

Case made.

Folk Etymologies. Some names have wonderful histories that just don't happen to be true. A good example is Azusa, California, because so many people know how it was named, but they are almost always wrong. In truth the name comes from the Gabrielino Indian word for skunk, but most people have heard the version which appeared in a 1948 issue of the *American Magazine:* The early town fathers of Azusa had an awful time naming the place. They thought of and suggested every possible name, but none seemed quite suited either to the village or the people vitally interested. So, after considerable delay, one bright person said, "Well, we've suggested every name from A to Z in the United States of America, so why not take the first letter of each word and call it Azusa."

Hoax Names. On rare occasions one of these slips into being. Two examples:

Goblu, Michigan. One of two towns which appeared on the 1979-1980 Michigan State Highway Commission map but were wiped off the 1980-1981 map. Both Goblu (for Go Blue!) and Beatosu (for Beat OSU) were created as rallying cries for the football game with Ohio State and were taken out by the Commission's new chairman. With any luck this explanation will be lost over time, and a hundred years from now, doctoral theses will be written on the sudden disappearance of two small Michigan towns.

The Levys of New Orleans. Myth has it that Levy is one of the most common last names in New Orleans. H. L. Mencken in *The American Language* asserted that it was second only to Smith. This has been disproven, and the assumption is that Mencken and others were taken in by a hoax based on an old vaudeville gag:

Pat: *Mike, I hear you've been in New Orleans. What did you think of the levees?*

Mike: *They were out of town and so were the Cohens.*

A 1964 article in *Names* pins the hoax on a "serious onomastician" named Harold F. Baker who trapped Mencken among others. Mencken was twice burned because he repeated the error in *Supplement Two* of *The American Language*. It's an ironic mistake because Mencken was a hoaxer of the first order.

Middle Names. So rare before 1750 that Charlie Rice wrote in his column in *This Week* magazine that you could do this:

1. Have a friend choose any noted American patriot born before 1770. (He can consult a book.)

2. Tell him that if he will give you the first initial of his middle name, you can name the man.

Although it sounds impossible, you only have to remember eight initials:

C = Charles Cotesworth Pickney

H = Richard Henry Lee

L = Francis Lightfoot Lee

P = John Paul Jones

Q = John Quincy Adams

S = William Samuel Johnson

T = Robert Treat Paine

Rice adds, "From there on, you're in the clear, because strange as it may seem, no other noted patriot born before 1770 possessed a middle name! Or at least I couldn't find any other."

In the United States, middle names began to become fashionable about 1780 and eventually became almost universal, and by the time of the Civil War, many used middle initials as integral parts of their names (Robert E. Lee and Ulysses S. Grant are the most notable examples). As *Woman's Day* magazine noted in an article on naming babies, it is "poor economy" not to give a child a middle name because it adds prestige, aids identification, and gives an out to people who dislike their first name (William Somerset Maugham, John Calvin Coolidge, etc.).

Today if you don't have one and go into the armed forces, you will be assigned *NMI* (for no middle initial) for a middle name, and if you go into politics and don't have one—or only have an initial—newspapers will write articles about your name. Such was the case with Harry S. (for *S* only) Truman, and later with Nixon aide Murray M (for absolutely nothing) Chotiner.

When parents give a middle name, care must be taken that the initials of the names do not complete a negative three-letter word like RAT (Robert A. Taft), CAD (Charles André de Gaulle), or GAS (George A. Smathers). Spelling out a word, however, may have a bright side. An article in *Midwest Folklore* reported that kids in Indiana used to believe that such a set of initials would bring material success.

Then there is the complicating issue of having two middle names and the resulting two middle initials. Listen to the plight of a New Jersey woman Margaret R. S. Ellis as outlined in a letter to the author: "I have two middle initials. I came by them honestly and for family reasons refuse to give them up. Nowadays no one is allowed [to have multiple middle initials]. One middle initial or NMI and that's it. So I apply for everything as Margaret R. S. Ellis, and credit cards, licenses, etc. come back with the middle initial of their choice—either R or S, rarely both."

In 1983, when First Lady Hillary Clinton let it be known that she wanted to be called Hillary Rodham Clinton, the press turned it into a controversy. There was even a *Wall Street Journal*/NBC News Poll which breathlessly told the world that 62 percent of all Americans preferred the simpler name.

Mnemonics (ni-MON-iks). Devices for recalling names. Some of the best are the lusty ones created by medical students to recall lesser body parts. *Never Lower Tillie's Pants, Mama Might Come Home* yields the carpal bones: Navicular, Lunate, Triquetum, Pisiform, greater Multangular, lesser Multangular, Capitate, and Hamate. Here are some which have been in use for years because they work:

Do Men Ever Visit Boston? for the ranking order of the British peerage: duke, marquis, earl, viscount, baron.

HOMES for the Great Lakes (Huron, Ontario, Michigan, Erie, and Superior).

King Paul Came Over From Germany Seeking Fortune for the Linnaean system of classification: kingdom, phylum, class, order, family, genus, species, form.

My Very Earnest Mother Just Served Us Nine Pickles for the planets in order going away from the sun—Mercury, Venus, Earth, Mars, Jupiter, Saturn, Uranus, Neptune, and Pluto.

Roy G. Biv for the colors of the rainbow in order: Red, Orange, Yellow, Green, Blue, Indigo, and Violet.

SALT for learning to remember people's names: *Say* the name aloud; *Ask* a question using the name; *Learn* it by repeating the name in conversation; and *Terminate* the conversation using the name.

Numerical Names. A teacher named Michael Herbert Dengler petitioned the North Dakota courts to let him change his

Ill-Pronounced Names

In his *An Almanac of Words at Play,* Willard Espy reports that some people believed that John F. Kennedy failed to carry the state of Washington in 1960 because he called the city of Spokane *Spokayne* rather than the native *Spoke-ann*. If this is so, it would not be the first time pronunciation has led to problems.

When, for instance, Calvin Trillin insisted that it was *Missoura* not *Missouree* in an op-ed piece in the *Washington Post*, the paper was forced to publish a number of letters from native-born Missourians on either side of the issue, including one from a man who insisted that "MissouREE loves CompaNEE." Everybody wanted to get into the act. Ann Landers told her readers that it was *Missoura*. Governor Christopher Bond declared himself a *ra* man but Don Lance, a University of Missouri linguist, told *USA Today* that natives preferred *ree* 3 to 1 over *ra*.

Back in the 1950s, the town board of Greenwich, Connecticut, became mired in the issue of whether it was *Gren-ich* or *Green-witch*, with the town split 50-50 on the matter. The English call their Greenwich *Grinidge*.

For Americans and others, Britain is a veritable minefield of names waiting to be mispronounced: Leicester is pronounced *Lester,* Harwich rhymes with *carriage,* Majoribanks is *Marchbanks,* Magdalen is *Maudlin,* Cholmondeley is *Chumley,* and so forth. In consolation, a letter from J. R. Jump of Essex on this phenomenon points out that residents themselves find it odd that Cirencester comes out as *Sissister* and that Featherstonehough is pronounced *Fanshaw.*

But the United States is also mined to the extent that the locals can identify out-landers by their inability to handle Stanislas, California (rhymes with *cole slaw*), say Silver Spring, Maryland without pluralizing *Spring,* or say the *h* in Amherst, Massachusetts. Foreigners find it a sign of American eccentricity that, despite spelling, Arkansas and Kansas don't rhyme and that in Baltimore, Maryland, the people sound as if they are calling the place *Balamer, Murlin.* Lead, South Dakota, home of the famous Homestead Mine, is pronounced *leed* as in *need,* not *led* as in *bed.*

Even people's names come into play here. In 1961, members of the historic Pepys family, that of diarist Samuel Pepys, told the world that it was not *Peeps,* as the *Encyclopædia Britannica* says is correct, but *Pepp-iss.* Yeats called himself *Yates,* and Synge was *Sing.* Then there is the great matter of *stine* vs. *steen* with Albert Einstein and Mayor Diane Feinstein in the *stine* corner, and Leonard and Carl Bernstein in the *steen* corner.

A few helpful hints are in order at this point: It is *Ark-an-saw,* not *sas; I-oh-wuh,* not *I-o-way; Ill-in-oy,* without an *s;* ditto for Des Moines; and *Or-ig-un* or *Arr-ig-un,* not *Arr-ee-gahn. Lee-ma* is in Ohio, not *Ly-ma; Kay-ro* is in Illinois, but *Ki-Row* is in Egypt; and Athens, Georgia, is *Ath-ins,* but Athens, Illinois, is *Ay-thens. Loo-i-vul* works best for Louisville, and San Franciscans are about as impressed with people who say *Frisco* as St. Louisans are with those who say *St. Louie.* In South Dakota, the state capital is known as *Pier,* despite the fact that millions say *Pee-aire.*

name to *1069*. The petition was denied first by a lower court and then by the state supreme court. (North Dakota said *One Zero Six Nine* might be acceptable but not the numbers.) This drove him to Minnesota, where he tried again, only to have a judge rule against him with this opinion: "Dehumanization is widespread and affects our culture like a disease. . . . To allow the use of a number instead of a name would only provide additional nourishment on which the illness of the dehumanization is able to feed and grow to the point where it is totally incurable."

Finally the Minnesota Supreme Court told him in 1975 what the North Dakota court had told him: he could use the numbers spelled out, but not the numerals, which had special significance to Dengler, who did not want them spelled out. Many editorialists commented on the *1069* case, with most appalled by the notion that a human would choose to be numbered. In 1980, the U.S. Supreme Court turned him down as well. He did get the name listed in the phone book as a number, and he got his friends and employer to call him by his number.

It appears to be a strong, late-20th-century taboo which has applied in other incidents, as when Canadian Eskimos succeeded in getting their government to stop referring to them by number.

One of the numerical names that did make it was that of 5/8 Smith, who was mayor of Pearson, Georgia in the 1950s and said his father gave him the name to distinguish him from other Smiths.

In 1986, I got a letter from *Love 22*, a gent from Rhode Island, who had changed his name in 1976. He pointed out, "It's on my driver's license, Social Security card, and passport. I gave a judge 22 reasons to change it. My fraternity house was 22 Campus Avenue, my foot-ball # was 22 at U.R.I. (University of Rhode Island), and my mother was born on the 22nd."

Titles. Without an aristocracy, people in the United States are not faced with the problems of recalling—let alone pronouncing—titled names that have appeared in *Debrett's Guide to the Peerage*. Sir Robert Algernon Forbes-Leith-of-Fyvie is simple compared to, say, Sir Charles Michael Delwyn-Venable-Llewelyn of Penllergaer, Lang-felach, and Yvis-y-Gerwyn, Cadoxton Juxta Neath.

But this is not to say we are not without titles and such burning issues as this: Why is Henry Kissinger referred to as Dr. while other Ph.D.'s—Arthur Burns, James Schlesinger, George Schultz, among others—seldom are? One solution to this modern dilemma was suggested in the *Washington Post* by English professor Burling Lowrey, who said that this ruling principle should apply: "Doctor" should only be used for active scholars and teachers, not for Ph.D.'s in other walks of life.

Unique Names. *Unique* is a word that is misapplied more often than almost any other word in the language, but each of the following has its own element of uniqueness and is therefore the rarest of collector's items:

Ab C. Defghi. According to an undated and yellowing newspaper clipping, a farmer who once lived in Villa Park, Illinois, was called Abner C. Defghi or Ab C. Defghi for short, which works out to the first nine letters of the alphabet.

Baer. The Social Security Administration has pegged this as the surname with the largest number of spellings—36 variations. Snyder is second with 29, and Bailey has 22. There are only three versions of Smith.

Bambi Tascarella. Her name appeared on the list of credits for the *NBC Nightly News* where she timed scripts. A Sioux City, Iowa, man was so taken with the name that he started a Bambi Tascarella Fan Club in her honor. Soon there were BTFCs in other cities—David Brinkley headed the Washington chapter, and John Chancellor was president of the New York unit—and on April 1, 1978, Sioux City held a "Bambi Tascarella Day." *TV Guide* called it "one of 1978's oddest success stories."

Derrick Bang! A Californian legally made the "!" part of his name. In 1982 Bang! gained notoriety by creating what may be the world's largest Monopoly board from a parking lot. There is a comic book artist named Scott Shaw!; a village in England named Westward Ho!, after the novel by Charles Kingsley; and back in the 1980s, the city of Hamilton, Ohio, changed its name to Hamilton!

Edsel Ford Fung. The late waiter at Sam Wo's in San Francisco, whose fame was greatly magnified by his name and his hints that he was related to the automotive family. John Clark of San Francisco recalls that Fung's first appearance in print went something like this:

Who are you named after, Edsel?
My sister.
And what's her name?
Mary.

Fernand J. St Germain. Through many terms in the House of Representatives, this Rhode Island Democrat made sure that all of his colleagues knew that he did not use a period after the first two letters of his last name, therefore implicitly avoiding any claims of sainthood.

Geo. R. Ge. A farmer living in Chapin, Louisiana, who was able to execute his full signature by writing his first name.

Hell. Town in Norway. Train buffs go there to say they've been to hell and back. There are other hells on earth, including Cow Hell in Laurens County, Georgia, which was so-named because of treacherous bogs in which cattle got trapped—a "bovine Hades" according to *Georgia Place Names.*

Izaak Walton. This may be the most often misspelled name in history. In 1971, A. J. McClane, the fishing editor of *Field and Stream* magazine, investigated the odd spelling of Walton's first name and found that his christening and marriage certificates carried him as Isaac, as did his tombstone at Winchester Cathedral. Nobody, not even the Izaak Walton League, could explain the discrepancy.

Mario. The only name with its own day and postmark which is MAR 10. A few years back, a group of men named Mario held a party for themselves in Chicago on March 10th.

Martha's Vineyard. The government has decreed this the only place name in the country with a possessive apostrophe.

Ole Lee. Not an odd name, until you find out that this man from Cashton, Wisconsin, was given the auto registration number 337-370, which is his name spelled upside down and backwards.

Pakistan. According to a 1972 *New York Times* article, the name was coined by a young philosophy student at Cambridge who combined *P* for *Punjab*, *A* for the frontier provinces bordering on *Afghanistan*, *K* for *Kashmir*, *S* for *Sind*, and *TAN* for *Baluchistan*.

Underwood. A name particularly well suited to rebuses. An old story tells of a letter addressed:

Wood

John

Mass

It was promptly delivered to John Underwood, Andover, Massachusetts, by wily postal employees.

Ura Hogg. Perhaps the fictitious person most often regarded as real. The old story is that Gov. James Stephen Hogg of Texas had two daughters whom he named Ima and Ura. Ima Hogg was a real person active in the arts and philanthropy until her death in 1975, but there never was a Ura nor, for that matter, were there brothers named Hesa and Bea. In his *Names* article, "The Alleged 'Hogg Sisters' or Simple Ground Rules for Collectors of 'Odd' Names," R. M. Rennick suggests that Ura was

probably either created by a journalist trying to make a good story or by one of the governor's political enemies. Rennick quotes a Texas newspaperman on the subject: "I have always felt that the pun names created by the good governor's political detractors served him right for his utter thoughtlessness in imposing such a ridiculous name upon his daughter."

Vlk. Richard Vlk of Pittsburgh didn't think there was anything special about his vowelless last name until Pepsi-Cola ran a contest in 1983 in which the company would pay cash for people who could spell out their last names from letters found on flip tops from Pepsi cans. Vowels were hard to find but *v*'s, *l*'s, and *k*'s were common. He rounded up 1,393 sets spelling out *Vlk* and—at $5 a letter—collected over $20,000.

IMA HOGG, URA NOT!

Psychonomics

What's in a Name?
Theories.

23

There was a time when people were named by intuition and tradition. The system worked well. A baby girl became Bertha because the name had a nice, solid ring to it, and it would honor her grandmother whose name was also Bertha.

Things have changed. There has been a virtual explosion of name studies in the last forty or so years as psychologists and others have tried to tell us what influences—often dreadful—our names have on us. These are the kinds of studies which determine, as several have, that Bertha is an abomination among names but Karen is not.

A 1984 study by Edward Callary, an associate professor of English at Northern Illinois University, showed that first-graders would much rather have a substitute teacher named Stephanie than one named Bertha. Among other things, it was felt that Bertha would make the kids work harder.

But we shouldn't waste all our pity on Bertha, because we have a body of studies that tell us that 26% of college men don't like their last names, and 33% of women don't like theirs. First names? Most Alberts, Hazels, Mildreds, Henrys, and Franks don't like their names, and researchers have come up with lists of male names that females don't like (Isadore, Aldo, Rollo, and Archibald), and women's names that men don't like (Claire, Shelly, Lauren, and Valentine). Other studies have concluded that names like Edith, Cameron, Sterling, and Bernice are widely disliked. Studies tell us that women like unique names more than men do.

There have even been studies on how you sign your name. Psychologists tell us that if your name is John Edward Harris, much can be told by how you choose to be called. John Harris is a hail-fellow-well-met type; J. E. Harris tends to be self-contained and conservative; John E. Harris is a middle-of-the-roader; J. Edward Harris has a pretty high opinion of himself; J. Harris is extremely controlled (and may harbor grandiose ideas of self-importance); and John Edward Harris is an assertive chap.

These tidbits are just a sampling of all the studies and analyses that have been applied to personal names. (What we are finding above all is how important our names are and how early they become part of our world. A 1994 study presented at a meeting of the Acoustical Society of America showed that infants as young as 4½ months can recognize their names, much earlier than previously thought. This may have been a brilliant piece of research, but it came as no surprise to millions of parents.)

For years I have been fascinated with all these different theories and studies and decided that it would be a public service to collect, distill, and lay them all out under one roof. So here is a whole pile of them—serious and not-altogether-serious, scientific and seat-of-the pants—to check your name against. Needless to say, not all the theories and findings agree with each other.

Bowen's Executive Theory. In the 1970s, Stephen N. Bowen of TRW Inc. examined the rosters of 1,000 large corporations and came to the conclusion that less common first names tend to rise higher than common ones, and that an initial instead of a first name is effective. An ideal name for the corporate climb according to Bowen: T. Armstrong Ashburton.

The Casler/Slovenko Effect. Two papers published in psychological literature argue that a person's surname is frequently related to his or her occupation (Lawrence Casler, *Psychological Reports*, 1975) and that our names are, in large measure, our destiny (Ralph Slovenko, *The Journal of Psychiatry and the Law*, 1984). Casler was able to identify, among others, contraception researchers named Gamble and Zipper, and Slovenko tells us of gastroenterologists named Belcher and Rumble.

Gaffney's First Law of Nomenclature. Authored by Wilbur G. Gaffney of the University of Nebraska, this law states that your career is determined by your character, and your character is determined perhaps unalterably by the name under which you grew to adulthood. He based his research on 40 years of analysis of Army rosters and university faculty lists, concluding that military officers tended to have short, he-man names, while professors had names like his own, Wilbur. The theory was presented at the American Name Society meeting in 1959.

Garwood's Desirable Name Theory. S. Gray Garwood, a Tulane psychologist, created a list of boys' names that teachers considered desirable (Craig, Gregory, James, Jeffrey, John, Jonathan, Patrick, Richard, and Thomas) and a list they felt to be undesirable (Bernard, Curtis, Daryl, Arnold, Horace, Jerome, Maurice, Roderick, and Samuel). He found that boys with the more desirable names thought of themselves in a more positive way than the others and had higher aspirations. Garwood concluded, "If we perceive a person in a certain way, we act a certain way toward that person, and he, in turn, acts a certain way back. It's the old self-fulfilling prophecy."

Hall's Law of Social Standing. After studying thousands of British names, Ron Hall published an article in 1960 in which he announced the discovery of a law which stated, "For any sufficiently large number of people, the average number of initials possessed by members of that group is a direct measure of the social class of that group." Hall found that upper-class groups had an "initiant" of 3.30 upwards, upper-middle-class 3.00 to 3.30, lower-middle-class 2.60 to 3.00, and working-class 2.60 downwards. Dukes, at the top of the list, averaged 4.0 initials. Hall also discovered the Law of Diminishing Initiants, which holds that in any administrative hierarchy there is a point where the initials begin to decrease. This he attributed to the fact that there is a point where ability counts more than name and "the old school tie."

The Harari-McDavid Loser Theory. Psychologists Herbert Harari of San Diego State University and John McDavid of Georgia State University conducted oft-quoted tests which point to the conclusion that certain first names like Hubert and Elmer are more likely to attract lower grades than names like David and Michael. The results were not quite as clear for girls' names—Bertha gets lower grades, but Adelle, another unpopular name, tends to get higher grades than Karen and Lisa. All of this was demonstrated by giving teachers essays from hypothetical children. They were graded consistently lower when they bore unpopular names.

Harari sees all of this as a problem of stereotyping and has pointed out that many Americans have suffered from "loser" names. Disputing this is Thomas V. Busse, educational psychologist of Temple University, who says in his *Professor's Book of First Names*, "Louisa Seraydarian and I did a similar study using undergraduate teacher education students. However, we found that grades assigned to children's essays were unaffected by the children's first names."

The Linville Sexy Name Theory. A study conducted by Deborah Linville, a graduate student at Rensselaer Polytechnic Institute, concluded that women with sexy first names have less chance of being selected for managerial jobs than those with non-sexy first names. The sexiest names in the study included Dawn, Jennifer, Cheryl, and Michelle, and the least sexy were Ethel, Mildred, and Esther. Whether a name was sexy or non-sexy was determined by student vote, and a number of names fell in between, including Anne, Barbara, Catherine, Elaine, Jill, Joyce, Linda, Marcia, Ruth, Virginia, and Yolanda.

The Loyola Criminal Name Discovery. It was once concluded that criminal acts were four times more frequent among men with unusual names. This finding was published in 1968 after three researchers from Chicago's Loyola University—Robert C. Nicolay, A. Arthur Hartman, and Jesse Hurley—studied the cases of 10,000 white, delinquent men and boys. Names that were considered odd were, for example, Lethal, Oder, and Vere.

The Loyola study may be the most dramatic of those showing that odd names are a heavy burden. Back in the 1940s, B. M. Savage and F. L. Wells looked at the records of 3,000 Harvard students and found that those with odd names were more likely to flunk out of school and be neurotic. A study conducted by two British psychologists at the University of Sussex in the early 1970s further established the link between names like Stutter, Pansey, and Fidget (all real names in the study) and unpopularity and mental illness.

On the plus side, women with unusual names are not especially neurotic or troubled, and an informal study by another researcher found that West Point graduates and college professors tend to have unusual first names.

The Newman Two-Last-Name Theory. In *Strictly Speaking*, Edwin Newman advanced the notion that college presidents and the heads of foundations are men with interchangeable first and last names. He goes on to list five pages of names like Kingman Brewster, Atlee Kepler, Landrum Bolling, McGeorge Bundy, and Mayo Bruce. Although he stops short of saying it, it is clearly implied that giving a child two last names will help that child become a college president.

Rice's Comment on Common Names. Charlie Rice, who devoted many of his "Punchbowl" columns in *This Week* magazine to names, wrote one in 1966 in which he tried to fathom the essence of giving a child a "successful" name. His theory: "If your last name is a very common one, do not give your child a very common first name." In other words, there has never been a famous William Smith, and one has to go all the way back to Pocahontas's boyfriend to find a notable John Smith, who is remembered as Captain John Smith. In his book *The Book of Smith*, attorney and name expert Elsdon C. Smith devotes a chapter to famous Smiths in which there is a huge cast of Smiths, but very few Williams and no Johns save for the Captain.

The Sorensen Sure-Shot System. Back in 1964, Ted Sorensen discovered that

Republican candidates for president had names more likely to end with *-on* than *-er* (to that point *-on*'s had served a total of 48 years while *-er*'s had been in office a mere 12). That year the theory led him to bet on William Scranton and Richard Nixon, but Barry Goldwater got the nomination, and Johnson won.

Another fascinating presidential name theory that has been kicking around for years is that the voters favor the candidate with the longer name. For the first 17 elections of the 20th century, this held with only one tie (Woodrow Wilson vs. Charles Hughes), but then the trend turned around, starting with Johnson over Goldwater, favoring the shorter name until Carter came along. Carter beat Ford, with the shorter name, and was beaten by Reagan with the longer name. The shorter-name trend resumed when Reagan beat Mondale and continued with Bush over Dukakis, but Clinton's victory over Bush in 1992 turned the trend back to the longer names.

The Price-Stern Theory of Names. In their long-popular book *What Not to Name the Baby*, Roger Price and Leonard Stern stated the theory this way: "All babies, when they are first born, are just about the same. Until a baby is given a Name, it has no personality. . . . But once you give the baby a Name, society begins to treat it as if it had the type of personality the name implies, and the child, being sensitive, responds consciously and unconsciously and grows up to fit the name."

All of this was rendered with tongue in cheek, especially clear when you get to the definitions—Alvin, for instance, has fat, hairy legs and wears garters. But the notion of name fitting shows up in more subtle terms in psychological studies.

The Weston Alphabetic Neurosis Theory. In 1967, Trevor Weston, M.D. created quite a stir when he presented a paper at the British Medical Association convention in which he maintained that people whose last names began with the letters *S* through *Z* were twice as likely to get ulcers, twice as likely to be neurotic, and three times more likely to get a heart attack than those named with *A* through *R*. He based his findings on ten years of statistics taken from London hospitals and said that the reason for S-Z ills was the strain of waiting for your name to be called, of always being last. The total effect of "alphabetic neurosis," according to Weston, was to shorten the lives in the S-Z group by 12 years.

This finding was tested by journalist Christopher P. Anderson in his book *The Name Game*. He reviewed a roll of prominent people who had died between the end of 1973 and the end of 1974 and found that the A-R's averaged 76 years and 4 months, and the S-Z's 68 years—a difference of 8 years and four months.

Be this as it may, others have tested the S-Z neurosis theory, including newspaper columnist Charlie Rice who in 1967 took all sorts of lists of names to see how they fared when broken into last-name groups. He first took the 200 most common last names in America and found they broke into four neat quarters: A-D, E-J, K-Q, R-Z. He then compared the R-Z's to the A-D's who, according to Weston, should be least troubled. Rice's findings:

	A-D	R-Z
Presidents	6	13
Chief Justices	1	8
Who's Who	658 pages	716 pages
Governors	13	15
Noted present-day Americans	43	67

In an overall tabulation of 1,098 notables the R-Z's won (308), followed by the K-Q's (298), the A-D's (258), and the E-J's (236).

There have been other letter theories, including one which appeared in the the the *New York Times* in 1968: the head of the Glasgow, Scotland, Council on Alcoholism announced that you are more likely to be an alcoholic if your last name begins with *M*. The *Bulletin of the American Name Society* asked, "Don't surnames of all Scots begin with M?"

The Winsome Image Theory. Baby-naming books list names and give the etymological meaning of the name, but as we all know, people in the modern world seldom think of these historic meanings. Psychologist Ralph Winsome questioned some 1,100 people to see what kind of person they expected to meet when they heard a given first name. Definite patterns emerged which did not jibe with the traditional definition of the name. Here are Winsome's findings, followed in parentheses by the meaning most often given in the baby-naming books.

Boys' Names.

Allan = serious, sincere, sensitive. (fierce one)

Andrew = sincere but immature. (strong, manly)

Anthony = tall, wiry, and elegant. (priceless one)

Benjamin = dishonest. (son of the right hand)

Daniel = manly. (judged of God)

Dennis = clumsy. (belonging to Dionysus)

Donald = smooth and charming. (dark or brown-haired stranger)

Edward = thoughtful. (rich guardian)

George = aggressive. (an earth worker or farmer)

Harold = coarse. (powerful warrior)

Hugh = mediocre. (spirit)

Joseph = intelligent, earnest, but a little dull. (he shall add)

Keith = hard, self-reliant, ambitious. (wood-dweller)

Mark = spoiled. (a warrior)

Paul = cheery, honest, and proud. (little)

Richard = very good-looking. (stern king)

Robert = diffident. (bright fame)

Simon = introverted and mean. (the hearing one)

Thomas = large, soft, and cuddly. (a twin)

Girls' Names.

Barbara = fat but sexy. (stranger, foreigner)

Emma = pretty but silly. (nurse)

Florence = masculine. (flourishing)

Gillian = temperamental but likable. (youthful)

Louise = pretty. (famous warrior)

Maureen = sultry and surly. (bitter)

Nancy = spiteful. (grace)

Pamela = hard, ambitious, and domineering. (entirely of honey)

Patricia = plain. (of nobility)

Sally = childish. (princess)

Sarah = sensual and selfish. (princess)

After going through all of these 20th-century name theories one can only conclude that names are terribly important to the individuals who carry them and that a really odd name is more likely to be a burden than an asset—that is, unless you want to become the president of a university or Fortune 500 company.

One result of all the aforementioned studies, which say that an odd or outdated name is a handicap, may be to make names blander and blander. William Tammeus has devoted one of his *Kansas City Star* columns to this problem and predicts that eventually "we're going to be down to maybe 20 names." He points out, "Parents today seem to want to make their offspring as invisible as the next kid. If you are named Jason or Michelle, you're no doubt going to be noticed a lot less in places like school than if you were named, say, Augustus or Ernestine."

If all of this seems too confusing, one can always test a name against the old rigors of numerology. There are many systems, but this one, according to Evelyn Wells in her *Treasury of Names*, was originally worked out by Pythagoras about 500 B.C. First, all letters have a numerical value:

1	2	3	4	5	6	7	8	9
A	B	C	D	E	F	G	H	I

1	2	3	4	5	6	7	8	9
J	K	L	M	N	O	P	Q	R

1	2	3	4	5	6	7	8
S	T	U	V	W	X	Y	Z

Now, you write down the entire name—first, middle, and last—and give each letter its value. Add up the numbers, which will give you a two-digit number, and then add those two digits until you get a single digit, which is the key number. It is then matched with the corresponding destiny.

1—Creative. Many world leaders have come from this group.

2—The friendly mixer, a follower rather than a leader. Always has friends.

3—Inspired and artistic.

4—Honest, trustworthy lovers of home and country.

5—Good companions with many friends, who tend not to be tied down.

6—Deep, sincere, scholarly people with a social conscience.

7—Intelligent people who use that intelligence well.

8—Organizers, executives, and planners.

9—The number of justice and righteousness, the ultimate number according to Pythagoras, saved for those who will fight for what they believe is right.

The author (a 1) finds this fascinating and eagerly awaits his fate as a world leader.

Analysis by the numbers and by the individual letters of a person's name is faddish. In the 1920s, there was a rash of this activity, and there were all sorts of books you could buy for advice. One numerologist, who called herself a name psychologist, was even able to use the theory to tell you what were good and bad places to live in. The best place was Spokane (optimistic and inspiring) and the worst was Tacoma (terrible vibrations—a depressing place).

Punstores

Some Hairy Propositions

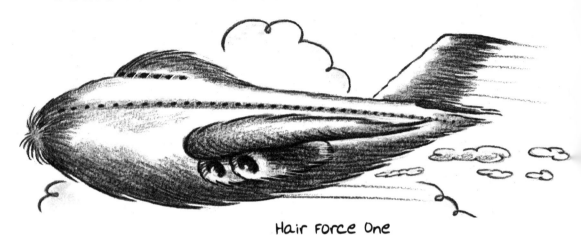

24

Hair Force One

Once they were few and far between but now they are everywhere and still proliferating. They are stores and businesses that use cute or atrocious puns to announce themselves. One theory is that it all started in San Francisco, where there were oddly named places like the Hungry i (a nightclub), The Glass Crutch (a bar), and Minimum Daily Requirements (a coffeehouse), while the rest of the country was still naming places the old-fashioned way. Today, you can travel around the country and find places like:

Florinstance—Florist.

Pen Station—Writing instruments.

Frame-Ups, Prints Charming, Harvey Wallhanger—Frames.

The Glasses Menagerie, The Glass House—Opticians.

Heir Apparent, Great Expectations—Maternity stores.

Lickety Split —Ice cream.

Sufficient Grounds—Coffee.

Beau Thai—Thai restaurant in Chicago.

Embraceable Zoo—Toy animals.

Yesterday's Tree—Antiques.

Another One Bites the Crust—Pizza.

Buenas Noches Roaches—Exterminator.

Hernia Movers—Movers with the slogan "The Potentate of Totin' Freight."

Shoplefters—Stores for left-handed people.

The Tulle Shed, A Material World or Sew It Seams—Dress material.

The Summer of Our Discount Tent—Camping gear.

The Bottom Half, Top Drawers—Pants stores.

Simply Beastly, Fish and Cheeps —Pets.

Mother Tongue, Squid Row—Restaurants.

The Hangar Club—A place featuring male exotic dancers.

Your Clothes Friends—Dry cleaner.

Bug Parts—Automobile parts.

Brick Shirt House—Shirts.

Hats in the Belfry—Hats.

O, The Booby Trap—Lingerie.

Hum Aditti—Rainwear.

Moby Discs—Records.

Disguise the Limit—Costume rentals.

Cecile B. DeMeal—Catering.

The Way We Wore, Suit Yourself, Seconds to Go—Used clothing.

Second Hand Prose, Yellow Pages—Used books.

Wok Around the Clock, Dragon Out, Food Man Chew, and **Genghis Cohen Carry-Out**— Chinese food carryout.

But the greatest inroads have been at places where they cut, set, or otherwise deal with hair. Suddenly it seemed that the old names which ran to the quasi-French (Salon d'Charm, Maison de Beauté) and Mr.'s (Mr. Tyrone, Mr. Philip) were out, in favor of punny, unisex names like *Bushwhacker* and *The Hair Shack*.

These were collected in Baltimore, Boston, Chicago, Cleveland, Denver, Detroit, Kansas City, Los Angeles, San Francisco, Toronto, Washington, and several smaller cities. Russell Ash contributed his "Forty Punning London Hairdressers' Names" to take the list to the other side of the Atlantic.

Hair goes:

Hair Today, Gone Tomorrow

A

About Faces
Ace of Blades
Alias Quiff & Combs
Ali Barber
Atomic Beauty Lounge

B

Bangs
The Beauty and the Beast
The Beauty Hut
Beneath Your Hat

Best Little Hairhouse in Town
Beyond the Fringe
Blow-Inn
Blow-Up Hair Designers
Bushwhacker
Buzz-Bees

C

The Clip Joint
Cliptomania
The Coliseum of Hair
Cookie's Cuttery

Crowning Glory
Curl Harbor
Curl Up 'n Dye (founded in 1979, this was the 1994 winner of the *Independent Business* magazine Name Game contest)
Cut Above
Cut Loose
Cutting Loose in Boulder

D

Deb 'n' Hair

Do Inn
Do Yer Nut

E

The Electric Chair
Electric Hair
Every Hair in Place

F

Fresh Hair
Fringe Benefits

G

The Gold Slug
The Grand Strand
Great Lengths

H

Hair
Hairacy
Hair Apparent
Hairazors
Hair Brothers
The Hair Cartel
Hair Castle
The Hair Closet
The Hair Conspiracy
Haircutect
The Hair Dynasty
The Hair-Em
The Hairess
The Hair Fare
Hair Fever
Hair 1st
Hair Force One
The Hair Garage
Hair Gate
The Hair Hut

The Hair Inn
Hair is Us
Hairitage
Hairizona
The Hair Lab
The Hair Lair
Hair Landing
The Hair Loom
Hair Mechanics
Hair Movement
Hair 'n' Now
Hair-o-Bics
Hair on Earth
Hair on Wheels
The Hair-O-Scope
The Hair People
Hair Personnel
Hair Plus
The Hair Port
The Hair Raid
Hairsay
The Hair Shaft
The Hair Shortage
Hair's to You!
The Hair Study Group Inc.
Hair's What's Happening
Hair Today
Hair to Eternity
Hair Tree Beauty Salon
The Hair Tunnel
Hair 2000
Hair Uporium
Hair Village
Hair We Are!
Hair We Go
Hank Of Hair
Hats Off
Hazel Nutz

Head First Hairdoers
Head Honchos
Head Hunters
Headlines
Headmasters
A Head of Our Time
The Head Shed
Head Start
Head's Up
Heads We Do
Heads You Win
Headway
Heatwave
His and Hairs
House of Hairs
How the West Was Cut
Human Head Renovations

I

It'll Grow on You
It's a Jungle in Hair
It's Only Hair

J

Julius Scissors
Just Hair

K

Kiss My Act

L

The Lady's Room
Lockworks
Loose Ends
Lunatic Fringe

M

Makin' Waves

The Mane Attraction
The Mane Concern
The March Hair
Moving-A-Head
My Braids Are You

N

Nar-Scissors
New Wave
Norm's Head Shop

O

Off the Top
O'Hair

P

Pat Your Hairdresser
The Permanent Solution

R

The Rape of the Lock
Rapunzel's
Rollickin' Follicle

S

Salon Muffie
Salon Salon
San Francisco Hairport
Seven Hair Itch
Shear Artistry
Shear Genius
Shear Heaven
The Shear
   Joy
Shear Madness
Shear Paradise
Shear Pleasure

Shear Power
The Shearing Station
Shearlocks
The Short Cut
Shylocks
Sis-Sir For-Tress
Sonny and Shears
Split Ends
Stark Raving Hair
A Step Ahead
Streaks Ahead
Styles A Head
The Subject is Hair
Sweeney Todd's

T

Tarzan and Jane
Tomorrow's Headlines
Tortoise & the Hair
Total Eclipse

U

Untangles
Uppercuts

V

The Vain Mane

W

Wavelength
The Wild Hair
The Witch's Hut

Y

The Yankee Clipper
Your Basic Haircut

Z

Zen Hair Styles

A Hairy Proposition

Robots

Woids for Droids

25

Rhino XR

In June of 1984, I was able to get a glimpse of the future by attending a major show of industrial robots in Detroit. It was called Robots 8 and was billed as the "world's largest robots event."

The robots—and what they could do—were fascinating, but as a person who is mesmerized by words and names, I came to see if I could get a bead on how these new steel-collar workers were being named.

To a large degree these new robots look alike—one big arm and a body that supports the arm—and are named alike. The vast majority are given a few letters and a couple of numbers, yielding us such unmemorable names as S-108, IRB 60-2, HR-63, AKR 3000, FR-400, NM-6200, ASEA IRb6, EPR-400, Prab G-36, V15, T-3 776, H80E, and PRI-1000.

Some had real names that you could get your teeth into, but even these lacked character; none could be described as memorable or distinctive. Among these the best I could find were Pathfinder, Troikabot, Nascomatic 2001, the P&H Robot's Robot, and, perhaps the best of the lot, the Rhino XR. (A later Rhino has been announced and is called the Rhino Scorpion, one of the few products ever named after a mammal and an insect at the same time.)

All of this was disappointing to me. I mentioned to a man who was exhibiting at the show that his robot and most of the rest of the robots in the convention hall were poorly named.

"You're missing the whole point," he said: "These things end up in factories, and that's where they get named. We just give them model names, but in the factory they get nicknames like 'Fat Alice' and 'Knucklehead.'"

I think the man has a point because a few days later a friend, who had heard me comment on the poor names of robots, sent me an article from *American Machinist* reporting on robots at a Volvo automotive plant in Sweden. Underlined was this sentence: "Operators have personified each robot by inking names across their 'backs'; a robot named Speedy Gonzales tends this cell." Later in the article, we hear about another robot called Napoleon.

So there's still hope for robot names, especially with Speedy Gonzales at work deep in the heart of Sweden. Here are some other names and nicknames for robots and other automatons, past and present, real and fictional. A great deal of help was given in compiling this list by Lane Jennings, formerly of the World Future Society, who was able to find at least one robot name for each letter of the alphabet, although he had to fudge a little when it came to the letter *N* (see below). The collection keeps growing as robots find more and more uses and so does this who's who of automatons.

A

Alpha. A chromium-plated pioneer performing robot shown at the London Radio Exhibition in 1932. It could tell time in several languages and read newspapers.

B

B.O.B. A personal robot. B.O.B. stands for Brains on Board. Tim Knight, an editor at *Personal Robotics Magazine*, supplied these other personal robot names: Amazing Avoider, Androbot, ComroTOT, Dingbot, Hubot, Marvin, Showbot, Turtle Tot, and Zylatron. A number of these domestics are like a new robot described in *Robotics Today:* "The nameless robot serves drinks, sweeps the carpet, tells jokes, plays obstacle games, and lifts and transports loads weighing up to 5 pounds."

Bob and Hank. First robots to have been the target of a lawsuit for being too much like their human counterparts. These are robots which sit on barstools in bars, based on the theme of the television show *Cheers,* and chat in the manner of the characters Norm and Cliff on that long-running show. The actors who played the two barflies, George Wendt and John Ratzenberger, have sued, claiming the automatons resemble them too closely.

C

Crow and Tom Servo. The first comic star robots, they are two of the three stars —the third is human—of the cable television hit *Mystery Science Theatre 3000.* The robots make wisecracks, as they sit and watch the world's cheesiest science fiction movies.

D

Dante II. A 1994 spider-like robot used to explore the inside of an Alaskan volcano, Mount Spurr, considered too hazardous for human exploration. Dante I was lost in

1993 after its cable broke during a mission to explore Mount Erebus in Antarctica.

D.C.-1. A personal robot. The D.C. stands for Drink Caddy.

Diktor. The metallic lover of space sex-heroine Barbarella in the comic strip epic by Jean-Claude Forest.

E

Electro. Cigarette-smoking robot created by Westinghouse for its exhibit at the 1939-1940 World's Fair.

F

F.R.E.D. Friendly Robotic Educational Device, an educator. (See also **Rover**.)

G

Golden Goat. Nickname for a popular automaton which devours cans and pays recyclers the going price for scrap aluminum.

Gunslinger. The amusement park robot which runs amok in Michael Crichton's novel *Westworld*.

H

Harry. Swedish robot that accepts returned library books and puts them in order for reshelving.

Helpmate. A service robot which found one of its first uses as a hospital robot serving meals and bringing sterile material to night nurses.

Henry David Therobot. A HERO robot (see below) running with the "Poet" program from Arctec Systems of Columbia, Maryland; it has a vocabulary of 120 words and with it composes "poetry" on the order of Japanese haiku.

Herman. A robot used by the U.S. government which is sent out on especially ticklish jobs like cleaning up radioactive messes at nuclear power plants.

HERO. Very popular robot from the Heath Company. (When I began my research in the mid-1980s, there were more HERO-1's in the world than any other type of robot.) Douglas M. Bonham, Heath's Director of Educational Marketing and Development, explains how it got its name and how well the name has worked: "We realized from the start that choosing the right name for the robot was vitally important to our marketing efforts. So, a year before we introduced our product, we held a company-wide 'Name the Robot' contest and received well over one hundred entries. As you might expect, we received some duplicates. Surprisingly, six different people all working independently came up with the name HERO. And, all for the same reason: HERO is an acronym for Heath Educational RObot.

"Needless to say, we were all very impressed with this great coincidence. Furthermore the name was short and easy to remember. It conveyed a very strong positive image, and yet it was warm and cute and friendly when applied to our little robot. Because of the short name, a very bold, striking logo was possible. Finally, a trademark search revealed that the name HERO was permissible."

The extreme aptness of the name was revealed to Bonham a month after the first HERO had been introduced: "We were in the ABC studio in New York doing a late night talk show called *The Last Word*. One of the research people for the show made the off-hand comment, 'I'm glad you named him after Hero: he doesn't get nearly the recognition he deserves.'

"When I asked what she was talking about, she explained 'Surely you knew that Hero of Alexandria (also called Heron) wrote the first book on robotics in the third century AD.' As it turns out, I didn't know that and neither did any of the six people who had independently and unknowingly named the world's first personal robot after the first man to write a book on the subject."

I

ITSABOX. Described by *Popular Science* as a computer-carrying "turtle" that manipulates objects on a tabletop. Built by Micro Systems Inc.

J

Jock-bot. A custom-built robot, ordered by a racehorse owner, who uses it to exercise horses by remote control. It is a plastic box mounted on a saddle which is able to manipulate reins, apply pressure to the sides of the horse, and give verbal commands like a human rider. Featured in Phil Berger's *State of the Art Robot Catalog*.

K

King Grey. A nine-foot-tall "Electric Titan" invented by an Alton, Illinois, inventor named Vern Pieper and displayed in 1916. It caused quite a stir, and *Illustrated World* magazine featured a fighting Grey on its cover and an article which said, "There is a possibility that before the close of the present conflict

[World War I], we will see his fearsome bulk adapted to the grim business of war."

Klaatu. The robot-master of the movie *The Day the Earth Stood Still*. A later robot **Klatu,** which was invented by Anthony Reichelt of Hackensack, New Jersey, was reportedly so named because of an error in its voice recognition system. According to the story, the first words addressed to it were "You talk," and the robot repeated it backwards, which comes out as "klatu."

L

Locoman. A British industrial robot.

M

Maria. One of the first diabolical robots. She was featured in Fritz Lang's classic film *Metropolis* in 1921 as the evil counterpart of a human named Maria. A later example of evil electronics was the computer HAL, alleged to be the letters *IBM* rolled back one letter, which appeared in Stanley Kubrick's *2001*.

Meldog. An experimental Japanese robot that functions as a Seeing Eye dog. The *Washington Post* has said that it has an "unlovable name."

Moose. One of the first "muscle" robots, it boasted six wheels and a scabber, a device using compressed-air-driven pistons to deliver 1,200 hammer blows per minute with seven carbide tipped bits. It was used to remove contaminated paint and concrete at the Three Mile Island nuclear power plant after the near-disaster there in 1979.

N

Nando. A Japanese toy robot from the 1950s, shown at the American Craft Museum's 1984 Robot Exhibit. It, along with the industrial NM-6200, eliminates the necessity of having to include in this chapter the name **Nobot**—which was invented by Lane Jennings "in sheer frustration at being unable to locate any robot, real or fictional, whose name begins with the letter 'N.'"

O

Olivaw R. Daneel. The *R.* stands for "Robot" and is about the only way a reader would know that this companion of space detective Lije Baley is not human. Olivaw and Baley are creations of Isaac Asimov, first introduced in his 1953 story "The Caves of Steel," and were still going strong in the author's 1983 novel *Robots of Dawn*.

P

Dr. Prepper. The respectful way to address a Dallas robot named Prepper, Ph.D. It gets its name from its job—preparing, or "prepping," DNA for the Human Genome Project. The project's aim is to determine the makeup of the DNA in every human gene. Prepper is one of several robots working at the new human genome lab at the University of Texas Southwestern Medical Center at Dallas.

Prowler. A military robot from Robot Defense Systems of Denver. It is an acronym for Programmable Robot Observer With Logical Enemy Response, which is a fancy way of saying that it will be able to kill.

Punk'N Time. Robot created to play punk.

Q

QT. One of many robots named by Isaac Asimov in his stories about them. QT appeared in the 1941 story "Reason" as the first robot to exhibit curiosity about its own existence.

R

Radius. Key figure in Karel Capek's 1921 play *R.U.R* in which the word *robot* was first introduced. In Capek's native Czech it is related to the word for slave. Radius starts a revolt among the artificial workers created to replace human factory hands and ends up killing off the entire human race.

RB5X. One of the more popular personal robots. Sharon D. Smith, the RB Robot Corporation's manager of corporate communications, explains how it got its name: "When we were naming both the product and the company, we looked for initials that sounded good together—ET and JR were both popular fictional characters at the time. 'RB Robot Corporation' had a nice ring to it. Some people have wondered if the 'RB' stands for Robbie Bosworth—Robbie being the name of one of science-fiction writer Isaac Asimov's first robotic heros, and Bosworth being the last name of the president and founder of our company. Clever, but alas, not true."

The *5* in the name indicates the series, with RB4, RB3, etc. to follow (RB1 would be the ultimate home robot), and the X designates "experimenter's model."

Robix. Educational robot kit which debuted in 1993. Students assemble parts to create a robotic entity that can deal cards, throw a ball, and more.

Robot Redford. Believed to be the first robot ever to give a commencement address, it discussed the impact of technology at Anne Arundel Community College in Maryland in 1983.

Robug. A series of climbing robots from the University of Portsmouth in England that can scale walls without the aid of external ropes or frames. Robug III has eight feet with vacuum-driven suckers that enable it to crawl up glass and metal.

Rover. Name of the two robots—Rover 1 and Rover 2—used to clean up sediment in the basement of the Three Mile Island nuclear power plant near Harrisburg, Pennsylvania, after the near-disaster. Rover 2 was a training robot. Other robots used in the historic cleanup of America's worst nuclear mishap were Fred, Louie 1, Louie 2, and the aforementioned Moose.

S

Snail. A firefighting robot created by the Scottsdale, Arizona, Rural-Metro Fire Department. It can carry a hose into places where humans can't go.

Sweetheart. A female robot complete with aluminum breasts that was banished from a University of California robot exhibit in 1983 when several people complained. The creation of sculptor Clayton Bailey, Sweetheart can make coffee (her body is a coffee urn) and has breasts which the *Oakland Tribune* said "compare favorably with the bumper bullets of a '52 Caddy."

Here, directly from Bailey, are the names of some of his other robots:

> **On/Off.** A menacing, wisecracking robot.

> **Marilyn Monrobot.** Female robot sex symbol.
> **Rube Goldbird.** A wind-powered bird contraption.

T

Tommy Atomic. One of many named toy robots that walk, flash lights, and spin away from objects. Other toy names have included Mr. Sandman, Mego Man, Robert the Robot, and Go Bot.

Topo. Short for *topographic* because of the versatility in its patented motion system. It is made by Androbot Inc., which also makes B.O.B. and F.R.E.D.

U

Unimate. Patented in 1954, it was the first industrial robot. Today the name refers to any of several robots manufactured by Unimation, now a Westinghouse subsidiary.

V

Viking I Lander. NASA's remote controlled exploration vehicle that landed on Mars in 1976. It collected soil, sent back images, and conducted experiments. Viking I Lander and Viking II Lander are regarded as the most complex robots ever built.

W

William Teller. Name for an automated teller machine in Williamsport, Pennsylvania. Banking machines generally have good names, as demonstrated by: Ginny the Green Machine, Marianne (as in "all day, all night Marianne"), MAC (Money Access Center), MAX, Miss X, Personal

Feller, Tellerific, Jeanie, The Owl, BOB (at the Bank of Bethesda in Maryland), Sam, Tillie the Teller, 24-Hour Jack, Harvey Wallbanker, and MOM (for Money Operating Machine; it is found at branches of the First Woman's Bank of Maryland).

Then, according to Herb Caen in the *San Francisco Chronicle*, there are two units at a Bank of America branch in Berkeley known as ATM and EVE. The only difference between the two is that EVE accepts deposits while ATM is a dispenser only. Caen has noted that the machine outside the Bechtel building is called Bechteller.

Xanthippus. Male robot in Sheila MacLeod's 1977 novel *Xanthe and the Robots*, which includes one of the few examples in science fiction of affection between a robot and a woman (here, the programmer Xanthe).

Y-12 Plant Mobile Manipulator. Herman's official name (see above).

Z

Zymate. A chemical laboratory robot, which is able to prepare samples, transfer test tubes, and perform other delicate tasks.

Recordbreaking Names

The Short and Long of It

26

The Shortest.

On July 20, 1931, the Associated Press reported the death of H. P. Re of Coldwater, Michigan, who had claimed to have the world's shortest name. This report set off a chorus of new claims, led by a J. Ur of Torrington, Connecticut, who felt he was unbeatable because he had no middle initial. The AP reported:

> C. Ek and J. Ek, brothers from Duluth, promptly entered the lists as cochampions. Mrs. V. Ek, not to be outdone, claimed not only the woman's title, but the mixed doubles championship. A former Duluth policeman said his name was C. Sy.
>
> Then Fairmount, Minnesota, entered E. Py, farmer; Clinton, Iowa, put forward C. Au, J. Au, and W. Au, triple threats; Indiana offered Ed Py, inmate of Newcastle Jail; and Indianapolis made a poor try with Fix Ax.

Then at the last minute, just before the AP's announced deadline for entries, a Mr. A. A of Chicago stepped forward and claimed the title. His full name was Aaron A, but he went by A. A.

You can't get shorter than A. A, but there are doubtless a number of people in the U.S. who could tie the record. In 1974, the Social Security Administration analyzed the names of people with Social Security numbers. There were 221 people with single-letter surnames ranging from a high of 24 A's to only two each of N's, Q's, and X's. In his *Book of Names*, J. N. Hook suggests that maybe the I's (of whom there were 12 in 1974) should win because it is the skinniest letter.

Having a single letter for a last name presents problems in a cybernetic age. In 1991 the *New York Times* reported the plight of a man named Stephen O who was, among other things, twice turned down for credit cards because the banks' computers did not recognize a single-letter last name. He finally went to court and changed his name to Oh.

There were, incidentally, 3,693 people with two letters and a whopping 10,782 with three-letter surnames.

If one counts changed names, there is the case of Barry John Thomas of Canberra, Australia, who in 1971 had his name legally changed to the single letter Z.

The shortest place names in the world are Y, France; U in the Caroline Islands in the Pacific Ocean; and three A's—one each in Denmark, Sweden, and Norway. There was once a town in West Virginia named 6. Second place is shared by Oo in the Pyrenees; Au, Gy, Lu, and Ob in Switzerland; Au and Oy in Germany; Al, Bo, and Ed in Norway; Li in Finland; Ur in Iraq; and Ai in Fulton County, Ohio, among others. In fact, there are so many two-letter names that a record of sorts can be established from a finding reported in *Word Ways* magazine to the effect that the Commonwealth of Kentucky has no less than eight of them (Ed, two Eps, Ex, O.K., Oz, Uz, and Vi).

The United States has all sorts of three-letter towns. A list of these shortly named places from the Zip Code Directory reads well: Ace, Ajo, Amo, Arp, Art, Bee, Bim, Bow, Coy, Day, Ely, Fox, Fry, Gap, Gas, Gay, Guy, Hye, Joy, Jud, Kim, Odd, Ona, Opp, Ord, Pep, Rex, Rig, Roe, Rye, Sod, Sun, Tad, Tow, Tye, Usk, Ute, Why, Win, Yoe, and Zap.

The Longest.

Moving from the short to the long of it, we have the following entrants. People first, then places.

Some crazy things have been happening since parents with an eye on the *Guinness Book of World Records* started giving their children absurdly long names. In September 1984, a Beaumont, Texas couple gave their daughter a 948-letter name, which was 337 letters longer than the 611-letter name of a girl born in 1980 to Missoula, Montana parents who say they did it to throw a monkey wrench into computers and who got into the *Guinness Book of World Records* in the process. Two months later, the Beaumont couple filed an amendment that gave their daughter a first name with 1,019 letters and a middle name with 36 letters. That name includes the names of several cars and several movie titles and still holds the record according to the 1996 version of the *Guinness Book of World Records*.

These "Guinness names" are not to be confused with naturally long names like:

Admiral, the Honorable Sir Reginald Aylmer Ranfurly Plunkett-Ernie-Erle-Drax. Britons have long admired this noble name as the longest titled name, but it's short when compared to the full name of the Sultan of Brunei, which is **Kebawah Duli Yang Maha Mulia Paduka Seri Baginda Sultan Dan Yang Dipertuan Sir Muda Hassanal Bolkiah Muizzaddin Waddaulah Ibni Duli Yang**

Teramat Mulia Paduka Seri Begawan Sultan Sir Muda Omar Ali Saifuddin Sa'adul Khairi Waddin. When the Sultan was host to Prime Minister Pierre Trudeau of Canada in the 1980s, it was learned that he insisted that the local press use his full name when writing about him.

Samuel Kauionaleinaniokauakukala-hale Kupihea For Lleiusszuieusszss. He displaced **Hurrizzissteizzii Ileiuss** as the longest name in the VA files according to the *Veterans Administration News* of June 7, 1970.

The longest natural names in the world would appear to come from Fiji, where it is the custom to connect the names of relatives and natives to come up with real names like **Talebulamaineiili-kenamainavaleniveivakabulaimaku-lalakeba**—the name of a Fijan who played cricket in New Zealand. In 1967, a man living on the island of Vanua Levu was found with a 120-letter name, which I will try to write: **Tuimidrenicagitokalauena-tobakonatewaenanonaskoktamanakiso-mosomomelakivolaikouaenaivo-lanikawabulasokomailesutalesigadua.** Basque surnames are also long, and in Spain there is a popular expression *tan largo como un apellido vasco*—"as long as a Basque name": **Garnorreguinicorrigarri-choegarregaga,** for example.

Places? For starters we have:

Chargoggagoggmanchauggauggagogg-chaubunagungamaugg. A lake in Webster, Massachusetts, it has the longest place name in America. Known locally as Lake Chargog—or The Lake—it means "fishing place at the boundaries; neutral meeting ground," but it has been rendered more colorfully as "You fish at your side, I'll fish at my side, and no one fishes in the middle." Some maps cut the name short, but back in 1927, the Commonwealth of Massachusetts set up a commission to give it the authorized spelling which appears above. Locals who can pronounce it do it like this: *Char-gogg-a-gogg-*(pause)-*man-chaugg-a-gogg-*(pause)-*chau-bun-a-gung-a-maugg.*

Llanfairpwllgwyngyllgogerychwyrn-drobwllllandysiliogogogoch. A town in Wales which is widely credited as having the longest place name in the English world. It means "St. Mary's Church in a hollow by the white hazel close to the rapid whirlpool by the red cave of St. Tysilio." The sign at the railway station has become a tourist draw as people like to have their pictures taken standing next to it. The station was recently put up for sale for 180,000 pounds as a tourist attraction.

Taumatawhakatangihangakoauauo-tamateaturipukakapikimaunga-horonukupokaiwhenuakitanatahu. Martin Glassner, a geographer at Southern Connecticut State College, used the *Bulletin of the American Name Society* to nominate this as the world's longest place name. It is a Maori village in New Zealand and was given to Glassner by a New Zealand geographer. It gets the nod from the *Guinness Book of World Records,* along with Bangkok, which has an official 167-letter name which is seldom used.

First and Last, Alphabetically.

Back in 1957, when the Social Security Administration still made the names on its rolls public, it announced that the names in the system ran from Aaaaa to

Zyzya. It would seem hard to best Aaaaa except with six *a*'s. However, a number of names have bettered Zyzya. In 1978 the *New York Times,* for instance, carried a story about Hero Zzyzzx (pronounced Zizzicks) who is the last listing in the Madison, Wisconsin, phone book. In September 1970, the *Washington Post* carried an AP story reporting that Zero Zzyzz was knocked out of last place in the Miami phone book by Vladimir Zzzyd. The San Francisco phone book used to carry a Vladimir Zzzzzzzabakov but he was replaced by a Zachary Zzzzra—who made it into the *Guinness Book of World Records* before changing his name to Zachary Zzzzzzzzzzra. Now *Guinness* lists him under the title of "Most contrived name."

It is important to realize that some of these last and first names in the phone book are bogus. For example, George A. Heinemann recounts, "Years ago, I lived in the Boston area with a group of other young men, and we had our communal telephone listed under the name *Zzyzzer,* so all we had to do was tell people to look for the last number in the book."

Geographically, Dimitri Borgman noted in an article in *Word Ways* that, using ordinary standards of alphabetization, the first and last names in the United States are Aabye, Minnesota, and Zyrza, Georgia. Borgman adds that if we broaden our notion of a community, we can go further down the list to Zzyzx Springs, California, which is both a hydrologic feature and a privately owned spa.

Most Common.

Chang is the most common name in the world. A full 20 percent of South Korea's 41 million residents are named Kim.

Smith is the most common in the English-speaking world with an estimated 2,382,509 of them in the United States alone. Using Social Security Administration tabulations from 1974, when such information was still public, the 50 commonest American last names—based on the first six letters—were: Smith, Johnson, Williams(on), Brown, Jones, Miller, Davis, Martin(ez/son), Anderson, Wilson, Harris(on), Taylor, Moore, Thomas, White, Thompson, Jackson, Clark, Roberts(on), Lewis, Walker, Robins(on), Peters(on), Hall, Allen, Young, Morris(on), King, Wright(son), Nelson, Rodriguez, Hill, Baker, Richard(s/son), Lee, Scott, Green, Adams, Mitchell, Phillips, Campbell, Gonzalez/s, Carter, Garcia, Evans, Turner, Stewart, Collins, Parker, and Edward.

To give some idea of relative commonness, 200th on the charts was Chapman, Swanson was 300th, 400th was Hines, McFarland was 500th in the ranking, Waldron was 1000th, Loomis 2000th, and Hopson 3000th. Only names with more than 10,000 people by that name were listed, and the 10,001 listed Thatches of America just made it under the wire in 3169th place. Chang, the world's most popular surname, ranked 2,292nd. Reagan ranked 1970th, Nixon 806th, Ford 113th, and Kennedy 115th.

The most common surname initial was *S* (at 9.7%) while *X* (at .056%) was the least common.

Using this same guide, it is impossible to come up with a least common name since there were 448,663 people with a surname that was unique on the Social Security rolls. All told there are more than 1.1 million different surnames in the United States.

As for geographic names, there are

various ways of looking at it. When he compiled *Simons' List Book*, Howard Simons charted town names in the United States and found 515 names which appeared in no less than eight states. Of these, the clear leader was Franklin, a town in 28 states, followed by Madison (27), and Washington (26, including the District of Columbia). In fourth place there was a three-way tie between Chester, Clinton, and Greenville (25 each). Simon also found 22 Lincolns, eleven Brooklyns, a dozen Eurekas, ten Moscows, and nine Climaxes.

However, if you count all municipalities and subdivisions, as the U.S. Geological Survey has done, you come up with these top ten names:

Fairview = 104

Midway = 90

Centerville = 72

Oak Grove = 68

Riverside = 67

Five Points = 65

Mount Pleasant = 56

Oakland = 54

Pleasant Hill = 54

Georgetown = 49

This all gets confusing. In 1988, *Business Week* reported that a major company was opening a large new plant in Decatur, Illinois. The mayor of Decatur said in a letter to the magazine that when he called the company, he was told the plant was to be built in Decatur, Indiana. The Illinois Decatur with 94,000 residents is the largest of more than 20 Decaturs in the U.S.

When it comes to county names, Washington—in 31 of the nation's 50 states—is the clear winner. The most common street name is Second Street.

In 1989, *USA Today* did a ranking of presidential city names and concluded that Jefferson with 28 led the pack. Lincoln and Washington tied for second with 27 apiece, followed by Monroe (25), a Jackson-Madison tie (24), Cleveland (23), and Wilson (19).

Stage Names, Pen Names, Changed Names

Also a Few Who Stood Pat

27

John wayne

It would seem that the dual customs of assuming pen and stage names are not what they once were. Increasingly, public figures change their names only for good reason—David Cornwell, for instance, began writing as John Le Carré because he was still in the diplomatic corps and needed anonymity—and most writers, except in the field of romantic fiction, and a great number of actors, keep the names they were born with.

Yet, even as the customs change, it can still be said that celebritydom is divided into two camps—those who changed their names and those who stuck with what they were born with. A sampling from each camp.

A Roll Call of Changes

Just about everybody knows that John Wayne was originally Marion Morrison and Judy Garland was Frances Gumm, but here are some that are not household name changes:

A

Eddie Albert = Eddie Albert Heimberger, who dropped his last name when he broke into show business and was referred to as "Eddie Hamberger."

Robert Alda, father of Alan Alda = Alphonso D'Abruzzo.

Woody Allen = Allen Konigsberg.

Julie Andrews = Julia Wells.

Eve Arden = Eunice Quedens, who created the name as a blend of "Evening in Paris" and Elizabeth Arden (whose given name was Florence Graham).

Beatrice Arthur = Bernice Frankel.

Jean Arthur = Gladys Greene.

Fred Astaire = Frederick Austerlitz.

Charles Atlas = Angelo Siciliano.

Alan Autry = Carlos Brown.

Gene Autry = Orvon Gene Autry.

B

Lauren Bacall = Betty Joan Perske.

Lucille Ball = Dianne Belmont.

Anne Bancroft = Anna Maria Italiano.

Brigitte Bardot = Camille Javal.

Orson Bean = Dallas Burrows, who tried Roger Duck and Hornsby Shirtwaist before settling on Bean.

Pat Benatar = Patricia Andrejewski.

David Ben-Gurion = David Green.

Tony Bennett = Anthony Benedetto.

Jack Benny = Benjamin Kubelsky.

Robbie Benson = Robert Segal.

Joey Bishop = Joseph Gottlieb.

Janet Blair = Martha Janet Lafferty, who was born in Blair, Pennsylvania.

Dirk Bogarde = Derek Jules Gaspard Ulric Niven Van Den Bogaerde.

Victor Borge = Borge Rosenbaum.

David Bowie = David Robert Jones.

Boy George = George Alan O'Dowd.

Fanny Brice = Fanny Borach.

Charles Bronson = Charles Buchinski; he was Buchinski in his first 11 movies.

Albert Brooks = Albert Einstein.

Mel Brooks = Melvin Kaminsky.

Anthony Burgess = John Burgess Wilson.

George Burns = Nathan Birnbaum.

Ellen Burstyn = Edna Gilhooley.

Richard Burton = Richard Walter Jenkins, Jr.

Red Buttons = Aaron Chwatt, the red-haired comedian who got the name as a nickname when he worked as a bellboy, wearing a jacket with 48 buttons.

C

Nicolas Cage = Nicholas Coppola.

Michael Caine = Maurice Micklewhite, who has said that his last name came from *The Caine Mutiny.*

Vikki Carr = Florencia Casillas.

Diahann Carroll = Carol Diahann Johnson.

Cyd Charisse = Tula Ellice Finklea.

Ray Charles = Ray Charles Robinson.

Cher = Cherilyn LaPiere.

Patsy Cline = Virginia Patterson Hensley.

Lee J. Cobb = Leo Jacoby.

Claudette Colbert = Lily Chauchoin.

Michael Connors = Kreker Ohanian.

Robert Conrad = Conrad Robert Falk.

Alice Cooper = Vincent Furnier.

David Copperfield = David Kotkin.

Howard Cosell = Howard Cohen.

Elvis Costello = Declan Patrick McManus.

Lou Costello = Louis Cristillo.

Joan Crawford = Lucille Le Sueur.

Tom Cruise = Thomas Mapother.

Tony Curtis = Bernard Schwartz.

D

Vic Damone = Vito Farinola.

Rodney Dangerfield = Jacob Cohen.

Bobby Darin = Walden Robert Cassotto.

Doris Day = Doris von Kappelhoff.

Jimmy Dean = Seth Ward.

Yvonne De Carlo = Peggy Middleton.

Sandra Dee = Alexandra Zuck.

John Denver = Henry John Deutschendorf, Jr.

Bo Derek = Cathleen Collins.

John Derek = Derek Harris.

Danny DeVito = Daniel Michaeli.

Susan Dey = Susan Smith.

Angie Dickinson = Angeline Brown.

Bo Diddley = Elias McDaniel.

Phyllis Diller = Phyllis Driver.

Doctor John = Malcolm Rebennack.

Diana Dors = Diana Fluck.

Kirk Douglas = Issur Danielovitch.

Melvyn Douglas = Melvyn Hesselberg.

Joanne Dru = Joanne LaCock.

Bob Dylan = Robert Zimmerman.

E

Sheena Easton = Sheena Shirley Orr.

Barbara Eden = Barbara Huffman.

Duke Ellington = Edward Kennedy Ellington.

Ron Ely = Ronald Pierce.

Chad Everett = Raymond Cramton.

Tom Ewell = S. Yewell Tompkins.

F

Douglas Fairbanks = Douglas Ullman.

Morgan Fairchild = Patsy McClenny.

Alice Faye = Ann Leppert.

Stepin Fetchit = Lincoln Theodore Monroe Andrew Perry.

Sally Field = Sally Mahoney.

W.C. Fields = William Claude Dukenfield, who once told an interviewer that he took the name "from an empty peach crate, which he broke over his father's head upon leaving home at the age of 15." It bore the trademark "Pick the Fields."

Peter Finch = William Mitchell.

Barry Fitzgerald = William Joseph Shields.

Rhonda Fleming = Marilyn Lovis.

Joan Fontaine = Joan de Havilland.

Dame Margot Fonteyn = Margaret Hookham.

John Ford = Sean O'Feeney.

John Forsythe = John Freund.

Red Foxx = John Sanford, who was the star of "Sanford and Son."

Anthony Franciosa = Anthony Papaleo.

Arlene Francis = Arlene Kazanjian.

Connie Francis = Concetta Franconero.

Kay Francis = Katherine Gibbs.

World B. Free = Lloyd Free.

G

Greta Garbo = Greta Gustafsson.

Vincent Gardenia = Vincent Scognamiglio.

Ava Gardner = Lucy Johnson.

John Garfield = Julius Garfinkle.

Crystal Gayle = Brenda Gayle Webb.

Paulette Goddard = Marion Levy.

Whoopi Goldberg = Caryn Johnson.

Eydie Gorme = Edith Gormezano.

Stewart Granger = James Stewart.

Cary Grant = Archibald Leach. In his 1940 film *His Girl Friday* he spoke this line: "The last person to say that to me was Archie Leach, just before he cut his throat."

Lee Grant = Lyova Rosenthal.

Peter Graves = Peter Aurness, whose brother is James Arness (nee Aurness).

Joel Grey = Joe Katz.

Robert Guillaume = Robert Williams.

H

Buddy Hackett = Leonard Hacker.

Halston = Roy Frowick.

Hammer = Stanley Kirk Burrell.

Jean Harlow = Harlean Carpenter.

Rex Harrison = Reginald Carey.

Laurence Harvey = Larushka Skikne.

Helen Hayes = Helen Brown, who doubtless suffered from the old line "You look like Helen Brown?" (Reply: "I don't look that good in yellow either.")

Susan Hayward = Edythe Marriner.

Rita Hayworth = Margarita Cansino.

Buck Henry = Henry Zuckerman.

Pee-Wee Herman = Paul Rubenfeld.

Barbara Hershey = Barbara Herzstine.

Anne Heywood = Violet Pretty.

Jack Higgins = Harry Patterson, writer of thrillers, who took the name of an uncle. He has used a number of other names including James Graham and Hugh Marlowe.

William Holden = William Beedle.

Judy Holiday = Judith Tuvim (*tuvim* means "holiday" in Hebrew).

Victoria Holt = Eleanor Burford Hibbert. Hibbert uses three pen names depending on what she is writing about. For romantic suspense she is Victoria Holt, for historical novels she becomes Jean Plaidy, and she is Philippa Carr for romantic novels with historic settings.

Harry Houdini = Ehrich Weiss.

Leslie Howard = Leslie Stainer.

Moe Howard = Moses Horowitz.

Rock Hudson = Roy Scherer, Jr., who was Wallace Fitzgerald for a while.

Engelbert Humperdink = Gerry Dorsey, whose name was changed by his manager Gordon Mills, who also turned Thomas Woodward into Tom Jones. Mills gave Dorsey the name of a German composer best known for his children's opera *Hansel and Gretel*. The protests from the composer's family were such that when the singer performs in Germany he only uses his first name.

Kim Hunter = Janet Cole.

Betty Hutton = Betty Thornberg.

I

Robert Indiana = Robert Clarke.

Grizel Inge = Grizel Thomson. The name of this British woman may not ring a bell, but she was the person with the greatest known incentive to change a name. By changing to Inge back in 1954, she was able to inherit $3,640,000 from a cousin who stipulated that his inheritance must remain in the ownership of another Inge. The will also stipulated that if she married, her husband could share in the estate but only if he took the Inge name. There have been other cases like it—in 1963 Anthony Duckworth became Anthony Duckworth-Chad for $781,000—but none in which the new name was worth close to a million dollars a letter.

J

David Janssen = David Meyer.

Robert Joffrey = Abdullah Jaffa Anver Bey Khan.

Elton John = Reginald Dwight.

Don Johnson = Donald Wayne.

Jennifer Jones = Phyllis Isley.

Tom Jones = Thomas Woodward.

Louis Jourdan = Louis Gendre.

K

Boris Karloff = William Henry Pratt. He changed it to play Frankenstein because he felt a menacing name was needed.

Danny Kaye = David Kaminsky.

Diane Keaton = Diane Hall.

Boris Karloff

Michael Keaton = Michael Douglas.

Howard Keel = Howard Leek.

Carole King = Carole Klein.

Larry King = Larry Zeigler.

Ben Kingsley = Krishna Banji.

Nastassja Kinski = Nastassja Nakszynski.

Ted Knight = Tadeus Wladyslaw Konopka.

L

Patti LaBelle = Patricia Louise Holte.

Cheryl Ladd = Cheryl Stoppelmoor.

Veronica Lake = Constance Ockleman.

Dorothy Lamour = Mary Kaumeyer.

Michael Landon = Eugene Orowitz.

Mario Lanza = Alfredo Cocozza.

Stan Laurel = Arthur Jefferson.

Steve Lawrence = Sidney Leibowitz.

Brenda Lee = Brenda Mae Tarpley.

Bruce Lee = Lee Yuen Kam.

Gypsy Rose Lee = Rose Louise Hovick.

Michelle Lee = Michelle Dusiak.

Peggy Lee = Norma Egstrom.

Pinky Lee = Pinkus Leff.

Janet Leigh = Jeanette Morrison.

Vivien Leigh = Vivien Hartley.

Huey Lewis = Hugh Cregg.

Jerry Lewis = Joseph Levitch.

Hal Linden = Harold Lipshitz.

Carole Lombard = Jane Peters.

Jack Lord = John Joseph Ryan.

Sophia Loren = Sophia Scicoloni.

Peter Lorre = Laszio Lowenstein.

Joe Louis = Joe L. Barrow.

Myrna Loy = Myrna Williams.

Paul Lucas = Lucas Paul.

Bela Lugosi = Bela Ferenc Blasko.

M

Moms Mabley = Loretta Mary Aitken.

Shirley MacLaine = Shirley Beaty.

Madonna = Madonna Louise Ciccone.

Lee Majors = Harvey Lee Yeary 2d.

Karl Malden = Malden Sekulovich.

Jayne Mansfield = Vera Jane Palmer.

Fredric March = Frederick Bickel.

Alicia Markova, the ballerina = Alice Marks. Neither the first nor the last to Russianize a name.

Peter Marshall = Pierre LaCock.

Dean Martin = Dino Crocetti.

Walter Matthau = Walter Matuschanskayasky.

Ethel Merman = Ethel Zimmerman.

George Michael = Georgios Panayiotou.

Vera Miles = Vera May Ralston, who changed her real name when she got to Hollywood and found that it was "taken" by Vera Hruba Ralston.

Ray Milland = Reginald Truscott-Jones.

Ann Miller = Lucille Collier.

Joni Mitchell = Roberta Joan Anderson.

Marilyn Monroe = Norma Jean Mortenson, (later) Baker.

Yves Montand = Ivo Levi.

Ron Moody = Ronald Moodnick.

Demi Moore = Demi Guynes.

Garry Moore = Thomas Garrison Morfit, who had already become a radio personality when he decided to change his name.

According to Joseph F. Clarke in his book *Pseudonyms*, "A contest was held to select a new name, and a Pittsburgh woman won $50 and a trip to Chicago for suggesting Garry Moore."

Rita Moreno = Rosita Alverio.

Harry Morgan = Harry Bratsburg.

Jelly Roll Morton = Ferdinand Joseph La Menthe.

Paul Muni = Muni Weisenfreund.

N

Pola Negri = Appolania Chalupee.

Mike Nichols = Michael Igor Peschowsky.

Chuck Norris = Carlos Ray.

Sheree North = Dawn Bethel.

O

Hugh O'Brian = Hugh Krampke.

Maureen O'Hara = Maureen Fitzsimmons.

George Orwell = Eric Arthur Blair.

P

Patti Page = Clara Ann Fowler.

Jack Palance = Walter Palanuik.

Bert Parks = Bert Jacobson.

Minnie Pearl = Sarah Ophelia Colley Cannon.

Pele = Edson Arontes do Nascimento.

Bernadette Peters = Bernadette Lazzaro.

Edith Piaf = Edith Gassion.

Slim Pickens = Louis Lindley.

Mary Pickford = Gladys Smith.

Stephanie Powers = Stefania Zophia Federkiewicz.

Paula Prentiss = Paula Ragusa.

Robert Preston = Robert Preston Meservey.

Prince = Prince Rogers Nelson, now known as the Artist Formerly Known as Prince.

R

Ayn Rand = Alice Rosenbaum.

Sally Rand = Helen Beck, who took her stage name from a Rand McNally map.

Tony Randall = Leonard Rosenberg.

Man Ray = Emmanuel Rudnitsky.

Martha Raye = Margaret O'Reed.

Donna Reed = Donna Belle Mullenger.

Della Reese = Delloreese Patricia Early.

Joan Rivers = Joan Sandra Molinsky.

Edward G. Robinson = Emmanuel Goldenberg.

Sugar Ray Robinson = Walker Smith.

Ginger Rogers = Virginia McMath.

Roy Rogers = Leonard Slye.

Mickey Rooney = Joe Yule, Jr.

Lillian Russell = Helen Leonard.

Therese Russell = Theresa Paup.

Winona Ryder = Winona Horowitz.

S

Susan St. James = Susan Miller.

Soupy Sales = Milton Hines.

Susan Sarandon = Susan Tomaling.

Lizabeth Scott = Emma Matzo.

Randolph Scott = George Randolph Crane.

John Sedges = Pearl Buck, who used this name for books with an American setting. Pearl Buck, her real name, was, she once explained, linked to books with Asian settings.

Jane Seymour = Joyce Frankenberg.

Omar Sharif = Michael Shalhoub.

Martin Sheen = Ramon Estevez.

Talia Shire = Talia Coppola.

Beverly Sills = Belle Silverman.

Phil Silvers = Philip Silversmith.

Nina Simone = Eunice Waymon.

Adam Smith = George J. W. Goodman, the financial writer, who was given the name by *New York* magazine for his first column.

Jane Somers = Doris Lessing. Doris Lessing created a great stir when she announced that she had written two books under the name of Jane Somers. She did this to demonstrate the plight of unknown writers. Her Somers books sold poorly and were not promoted.

Suzanne Somers = Suzanne Mahoney.

Ann Sothern = Harriette Lake.

Mickey Spillane = Frank Morrison.

Robert Stack = Robert Modini.

Kim Stanley = Patricia Reid.

Barbara Stanwick = Ruby Stevens.

Jean Stapleton = Jeanne Murray.

Ringo Starr = Richard Starkey.

Connie Stevens = Concetta Ingolia.

Sting = Gordon Sumner.

Gale Storm = Josephine Cottle, who later insisted that she missed the pun for a long time after she had been given the name in Hollywood.

Donna Summer = La Donna Gaines.

T

Rip Taylor = Charles Elmer, Jr.

Robert Taylor = Spangler Arlington Brugh.

Danny Thomas = Muzyad Yakhoob, Amos Jacobs

Terry-Thomas = Thomas Terry Hoar-Stevens, who said of his name, "The hyphen's the gap between my teeth."

Tiny Tim = Herbert Khaury.

Kwame Toure = Stokely Carmichael.

Randy Travis = Randy Traywick.

Sophie Tucker = Sophia Kalish.

Tina Turner = Annie Mae Bullock.

Conway Twitty = Harold Lloyd Jenkins.

V

Rudolph Valentino = Rudolpho D'Antonguolla.

Frankie Valli = Frank Castelluccio.

W

Jersey Joe Walcott = Arnold Cream.

Muddy Waters = McKinley Morganfield.

David Wayne = Wayne McMeekan.

Clifton Webb = Webb Parmalee Hollenbeck.

Raquel Welch = Raquel Tejada.

Tuesday Weld = Susan Ker Weld, who has given interviewers all sorts of explanations for the Tuesday, including that it is (a) a mispronunciation of "two days," which is how long her mother was in labor with her, and (b) based on a childhood corruption ("Tu-tu") of her given name of Susan.

Gene Wilder = Jerome Silberman.

Arthur M. Winfield = Edward Stratemeyer. Stratemeyer used more than 60 pseudonyms for the hundreds of series books for boys and girls that he wrote or had written for him from 1894 to 1960. He and his syndicate were Franklin W. Dixon for the Hardy Boys, Victor Appleton for Tom Swift, Carolyn Keene for Nancy Drew, and Laura Lee Hope for the Bobbsey Twins, to name just a few. He wrote the Rover Boys under the name Arthur M. Winfield, and later explained that the Arthur was for author, the M. for the hope that it would sell thousands of copies, and Winfield for "win the field."

Shelley Winters = Shirley Schrift.

Stevie Wonder = Steveland Morris.

Natalie Wood = Natasha Gurdin.

Jane Wyman = Sarah Jane Fulks, whose original name appeared on the marriage license when she married Ronald Reagan.

Tammy Wynette = Wynette Pugh.

Gig Young = Byron Barr.

Loretta Young = Gretchen Jung.

A Roll Call of Non-Changes

(Folks who did or could not change their names or only changed them a little)

Bradford Dillman. Dillman was quoted by J. F. Clarke in the book *Pseudonyms:* "Bradford Dillman sounded like a distinguished, phoney, theatrical name so I kept it."

Chevy Chase.

Clark Gable.

Eddie Rabbitt.

Ellen Donna Cooperman. Ms. Cooperman, a Long Island woman who owns a feminist film company, attempted to have her name changed to Cooperperson in 1978 because it would "more properly reflect her sense of human equality than does the name of Cooperman." It was turned down by the New York State Supreme Court, which thought that it would lead to a rash of such changes (Carmen to Carpersons, Manson to Peoplechild, etc.). A lower court had held that the change would serve to hold the women's movement up to ridicule.

George Raft. He removed the *n* from George Ranft.

Humphrey Bogart.

Jack Lemmon. He refused to change it because he had suffered for years as Jack U. Lemmon and had gotten used to it.

Jimmy Stewart. He did not change his name when he became an actor. When a second actor whose real name was Jimmy Stewart came along, the first insisted that the second man change his. The second Jimmy Stewart became Stewart Granger.

Jo Ann Pflug. When this actress was asked if it was her real name, she said, "Of course, Pflug is a name you change from, not to." One evening on *The Tonight Show* with Johnny Carson she listed stage names she had considered: Hope Chest, Kitty Litter, Sara Endipity, and Gilda Lilly.

John Hodiak. One of the first to refuse a name change, this World War II era star told Louis B. Mayer that he would not accept a new name, adding, "I look like a Hodiak."

Jon Voight.

Katherine Hepburn.

Leonard Bernstein. In 1980, Bernstein

revealed in a *60 Minutes* interview that his idol, conductor Serge Koussevitzky, had told him to change his name to assure success in America because *Bernstein* would stand in his way. "He proposed to me the 'nom' that I should change it to, which was Leonard S. Berns," said Bernstein in the interview; "I lost a night's sleep over it and came back and told him I had decided to make it as Leonard Bernstein or not at all."

Lorne Greene. He added an *e* to Green.

Meryl Streep. Commenting on this name in his column in the *San Francisco Chronicle,* Gerald Nachman wrote, "At a time when studios created names and images to go with them, 'Meryl Streep' wouldn't have lasted 10 minutes."

Paul Newman.

Robert Goulet.

Ronald Reagan. His real name, which was unusual for actors of his generation in Hollywood.

Sigourney Weaver.

Spencer Tracy.

Swoozie Kurtz. She was quoted in the September 1984, *Esquire* on her name: "I'm named after 'The Swoose,' a B-15 bomber, which my father—Colonel Frank Kurtz, the most decorated pilot in World War II—flew."

Tom Mix.

Warren Beatty. He added a *t* to Beaty. His sister Shirley MacLean Beaty became **Shirley MacLaine.**

Street Talk

I'll Meet You at the Corner of Nixon and Bluett

28

Few things express changing name fashions as well as the names of streets. Each year, according to one estimate, there are some 8,000 streets which come into being and have to be named. With that in mind, consider this rough division of three periods in American street naming.

1682 – 1945

In 1682, William Penn laid out the plan for the city of Philadelphia and gave the streets names. Moving from east to west he numbered them, and he gave the other streets names which tended to honor botany rather than his cronies or the British crown. You can still walk from Chestnut to Walnut to Spruce and to Pine. In laying out and numbering the city, says George R. Stewart in *Names on the Land*, he "established the basis of the most far-reaching and typical habit of American naming."

Because of the Penn "plan," most American towns are numbered along one axis and named along the other. Many adopted the tree idea, and Stewart notes that there are towns in the Southwest with streets called Chestnut and Spruce, where such trees never grew. There was considerable variation, as some cities and towns opted for the names of the Great Lakes or rivers, or for some other natural set of names.

Since the bulk of the nation's streets were named following Penn's plan, it should come as no shock that the number one street name in the United States is *Second*. The R. L. Polk Co., which keeps track of addresses on motor vehicle registrations, has tabulated the most common names. Following 4,308 streets named *Second*, were *Park* (close at 4,265), *Third* (in third place), *Fourth, Fifth, First, Sixth, Seventh, Washington, Maple, Oak*,

Eighth, Elm, Lincoln, Ninth, Pine, Walnut, Tenth, and *Cedar.*

Other streets and avenues were named for what went on there, who lived there, or where the road went. Occasionally a byway was named to honor a person, ranging from a hero of the Revolution like Washington or Lafayette to a local mill owner. Changing functions and politics saw some names change. If markets cropped up along First Street, the odds favored a change to *Market Street,* and after the Revolution, many overtly British names were scrubbed in favor of more democratic ones. Queen Street in Portland, Maine, for instance, was renamed Congress Street after the war.

It also seemed that there was room for a hero. World War I, for instance, brought us names like *Pershing Drive* and *York Drive* (after Sgt. Alvin York), and the custom is still observed in places like Neil Armstrong Circle in Fort Wayne, Indiana, and Alan Shepard Street in Las Vegas. Nor did the heroes have to be of the moment. Howard Channing, who has done considerable street name research, which he kindly shared with the author, has discovered a remarkably common occurrence of names relating to the Robin Hood legend, especially in the Southeast. Besides *Robin Hood* himself, he found *Friar Tuck, Sherwood Forest, Nottingham,* and the like.

1945 – 1960

As postwar developers warmed up their bulldozers, they found that a lot of the old names were taken, and local fire and police departments, planning boards, and postal authorities were not going to allow a second *Oak* or *Walnut* in their jurisdiction. Some opted for variations like *Oak Forest* and *Walnut Grove,* and others went for the safety in a mix of bird, flower, and

presidential names. Some broke with democratic tradition and picked regal names like *King* and *Queen Anne* streets. Many grabbed names from their own families, and a few even used the names of World War II leaders and battles.

What was beginning to happen for the first time in history was that names were, for the most part, being given by people whose primary purpose was selling houses and were being ratified by planning boards whose interest was in growth. Names were penciled in before people lived on the street, and the name was part of the appeal along with the rec room and the two-car garage. This is not to say that there were no developments before that, but it was not until the postwar period that it became so common.

These names were bestowed because they sounded nice, and many bucolic but totally misleading names were put on street maps.

Spring Valley Lanes were laid out where there had never been a spring or a valley. Words like *Glen, Haven, Ridge, Stream, Brook, Grove, Woods,* and *Crest* appeared everywhere and in all sorts of combinations with little regard for geographical reality. In 1995, the *Arizona Republic* ran a short piece entitled "Greenery Gone; Names Remain" which talked about two new developments—one is called The Orchard, the other The Vineyards. The paper explained: "Before the ground was leveled for those homes a few months ago, crews with chain saws chopped down all the fruit trees except two and bulldozed every vine, shrub, or patch of grass. Two trees do not an orchard make—and where's the vineyard?"

The result of all this bucolic naming was so dull that reading a list of new street names was a cure for insomnia—soft marketable names like *Pinecrest Terrace, Glenhaven Road, Thornapple Terrace, Sweetgrass Street, Weeping Willow Way, Cedarcrest Lane, Oakview Drive.*

Satirist Vic Sussman has come up with the master generator for these names, which he revealed in 1988:

Now it can be told: They use the Master List of Country Image Names, a closely guarded secret in the realty world. Using it is easy and enormously profitable. Merely choose one word from each column, starting from the left:

Red	Ridge	Acres
Silver	Mountain	Estates
Blue	Falls	Landing
Harvest	Creek	Glen
Hunt	Hills	Farm
Summer	Spring	Retreat
Colonial	Pond	Valley
Olde	Quail	Highlands
Heritage	Lake	Vista
Rustic	Fox	Village
Rocky	Skyline	Manor
Hidden	Haven	Chase

As more roads are built and more developments rise, the names become more and more alike. Occasionally, someone takes a stand against the Spring Dale Places and Holly Hill Lanes. In 1987, the planning board on the island of Nantucket, facing the fact that there was a lot of development going on, preapproved a list of names for new roads. The names had been taken from historic documents and were related to the island's Indians, early European settlers, whaling ships, and traditional nicknames. According to the Nantucket *Inquirer and Mirror*, the names included *Sousoaco, Pleeya, Pile, Nanahuma, Quaap, Spotso, Nopque, Pacummohquah, Treat, Unique, Mamuck, Coggeshall, Jernegan,* and *Whippey.*

Others are beginning to object to the numbing sameness of newer street names. Down in Rowlett, Texas, the town council in 1995 changed the name of state Highway 66 to *Lakeview Parkway*, in spite of the objections of a businessman, who said Rowlett was already awash in street names that begin with *lake: Lakeshore, Lakewood,* and so on. "For God's sake, if you're going to change it, change it to Genesis or something," said Adam Welch, who owns a video store on the state highway, to the *Dallas Morning News.*

1960 – 1995

Developers started playing with theme areas. Some were startling departures—a Jacksonville, Florida, development was given nursery-rhyme names such as *Peter Pan Place, Tom Thumb Drive,* and *Tinker Bell Lane,* and in Fairfax, Virginia, a Camelot subdivision went up complete with a battlement entrance and streets like King Arthur Road and Round Table Court. The random mix of birds, flowers, groves, and developers' daughters' names was out as developments were thought of as a coherent whole, and one could live in a neighborhood where *all* the streets were named after racehorses, wines, musical instruments, French ports, famous artists, poets, Civil War generals, precious stones, Indian tribes, explorers, British names, or any number of others.

A letter from Edgar C. Chamberlin of Potomac, Maryland, tells of his own theme area:

"Our neighborhood, located near the intersection of Falls Road and Tuckerman Lane in Potomac, was laid out by an antique car buff who proceeded to immortalize a few of the antique cars as well as a few of the world-famous automobile racing sites.

"He started by naming the neighborhood Oldfield, after the one and only Barney. We live on Daimler Court, at the intersection with Maxwell Drive. Around the corner is Duryea Drive. Up the other direction is Toulone Drive and Cord Circle. A few others, like Cherbourg Drive, complete the neighborhood.

"Unfortunately, he broke the pattern with Karen and Judy, which I understand were the names of his two daughters."

In a few places the themes verge on overwhelming. Joseph Badger, formerly of Santa Claus, Indiana—where the Holiday World theme park is the major business—wrote to the author about names in his community when he still lived there:

"The name of our subdivision is Christmas Lake Village . . . . The shopping center, albeit small, has a 'super market'. . . . The center is Holly Plaza, and the store is Holiday Foods. The only restaurant is 'The Snowflake.' The Village itself has three main roads: Balthazar, Melchior, and Kasper . . . all other streets have names that have something to do with Christmas or the winter season. There are streets named for all the reindeer, plus such roads as Chestnuts by the Fire, Blue Spruce, Ornament Lane, Chimes Drive, and subdivisions like: Polar Shores, Evergreen Addition and Carol Hills . . . . (I live in Noel Shores.) I'm on the volunteer fire department, and the firemen monitor channel 1 on CB radio. You know the CB handle for the fire truck: Rudolph! It leads the way, and yes, there is a special extra red light mounted in the center of the hood."

As explained in the introduction to this book, Badger has since moved, in part because of the burden of living in a place called Santa Claus.

As a retired developer told the

Washington Post, a theme can give a neighborhood "a little bit of class." That developer, Harold Wolkind, said that he had had the most fun naming a Hamlet subdivision with names like *Romeo Court* and *Elsinore Avenue.* But if there was a number one theme, it had to be "antique Americana," giving us scores of names like *Quail Runn, Flintlock Drive,* and *Cider Press Run.* The 18th century was alive and well in the Betsy Ross Subdivision, and superfluous *e's*—as in Olde Towne Road —became a sure sign that a road had come into being since the invention of the microwave oven.

In his 1978 article in *Names,* entitled "From Classic to Classy: Changing Fashions in Street Names," John Algeo studied the street names in Athens, Georgia, contrasting the old names to the new ones which were created in the 1960s as the small city went through a period of "rapid growth." He found three changes:

1. The old names were appropriate to the area, honoring residents, telling where streets led (Foundry Street, for example) or otherwise reflecting the local scene, while the new ones generally had nothing to do with the area but were, in fact, "decorative" and picked for their "pleasant associations and hence for their commercial value."

2. The aforementioned internal patterning or themes of the new names as opposed to the random naming of the old. Algeo wrote that the themes themselves seemed particularly ill-suited to the community. (It would seem that there have been a few locally relevant themes elsewhere, but they are extremely rare. There is, for instance, a development near Dulles International Airport in Virginia where airline names are the theme.)

3. *Street* and *avenue* went into decline as the generic portion of new names. In

Athens, Algeo found the new names favored *drive, court, circle, place, road, run, way, lane,* and *trail,* preferred in that order.

The University of Georgia professor concluded that, "Whereas once a street name was an integral part of the history and life of the community, today it is often an artificial appliqué, a mere decoration of doubtful taste."

Some went beyond a single theme to the full range of decorative names. Few places better exemplified this than the "new town" of Columbia, Maryland, which began in the 1960s but really got rolling in the 1970s. Howard Channing, who has studied the 759 streets of Columbia, has deemed it the most "provocatively and imaginatively" named town of the many he has studied. Channing was amused by a number of streets termed *garth* (as in *Gray Owl Garth*), which is "a small yard or enclosure," according to *Merriam-Webster's Collegiate® Dictionary, Tenth Edition.*

These were just a few of Channing's favorites: Airybrink Lane, April Day Garth, Attic Window Way, Banjo Court, Barefoot Boy Street, Better Hours Court, Black Velvet Street, Browsing Deer Street, Celestial Way, Cloudburst Hill, Crow Flock Court, Deep Calm Street, Dragon Claw Street, Drowsy Day Street, Elfstone Way, Encounter Row, Feathered Head Street, Flapjack Lane, Forty Winks Way, Frostwork Row, Fruitgift Place, Gray Mouse Way, Great News Lane, Half Dollar Court, Hat Brim Lane, Hawkeye Run, Hermit Path, High Beam Court, Honey Salt Row, Hundred Drums Row, Ivoryhand Place, Jacob's Ladder Street, Kind Rain Street, Latchkey Row, Lifequest Lane, Little Boots Street, Mad River Lane, Matador Road, Melting Shadows Lane, Mystic Court, Old Man Court, Oven Bird Green, Paul Revere Ride, Prophecy Place,

Pushcart Way, Quiet Hours Street, Quilting Way, Rawhide Ridge, Resting Sea Street, Roll Right Court, Rustling Leaf Street, Saddlebag Row, Satan Wood Drive, Scarecrow Court, Sealed Message Street, Sharp Antler Street, Silver Sod Street, Sinbad Place, Sleeping Dog Lane, Snuffbox Terrace, Spelling Bee Street, Straw Turkey Court, Tufted Moss Street, Tunemaker Terrace, Wineglass Court, and Youngheart Lane.

One attribute of names like *Stone Boat Row* and *Woven Moonbeam* is that, unlike so many development names, they are hard to forget. On the other hand, some take a while to write, and one imagines that a Columbian writing return addresses on a pile of Christmas cards gets tired of writing *Sealed Message Road* or *Wedding Ring Way* over and over. And some are misfits in a town which is 15 miles west of Chesapeake Bay (*Offshore Green, Sea Change,* etc.). But one must generally agree with Channing that Columbia's names are a far cry from the flat and listless ones of most new developments. Of course, few have any real relationship to the place itself or the people who live there and are the ultimate in what Algeo termed "decorative" names.

(A minor fantasy of the author's would be to name a suburban development. He would wait until the people bought the houses, and if there were a lot of lawyers on a street it would become Tort Trail; a street with a lot of preschoolers would be Big Wheels Way [after that group's preferred method of transportation], and there would have to be a Crab Grass Court. He would also have a Noisy Mower Lane, a Burning Barbecue Garth, a Surly Teen Terrace, and a Screaming Infant Mews.)

One other trend of this decade was to erase any old names which might reduce property values. In Westchester County, New York, Incinerator Road, which led to an incinerator, was renamed Burnam Drive. In Fairfield County, Connecticut, Skunk Land Road was scrubbed for the upscale *Buckingham Ridge Lane*. This trend continues, as indicated by a recent news item about the people living on Tobacco Road in Hutchinson, Kansas, petitioning to have that name, synonymous with rural squalor, changed, while residents of Hopewell, Virginia, have petitioned to have Hooker Street (named for Gen. Joseph Hooker of the Union Army) renamed.

Trends notwithstanding, there is an amazing diversity in street names which is good for name collectors who may have noted some of these oddities in their travels.

A

AAA Drive. A Wilmington, Delaware, byway found by the indefatigable Howard Channing in his city-by-city examination of street names. Others from a list of Channing favorites: Polled Hereford Drive (Birmingham, Alabama), Bootlegger Cove Drive (Anchorage), Elephant Way (Fort Myers, Florida), The Uncommons (Fort Wayne, Indiana), Bordello Street (Lexington, Kentucky, which also has both a Backhand Court and a Forehand Court, but no Tennis Court), Hoo Shoo Too Road (Baton Rouge), Circus Time Road (Portland, Maine), Milk Shake Lane (Annapolis, Maryland), Krum Strasse Street (Battle Creek, Michigan), Snaffle Circle (Lincoln, Nebraska), Kingdom Come Street (Manchester, New Hampshire), Bunny-friend Road (Charlotte, North Carolina), Memory Lane (Eugene, Oregon), Chubba Kula Road (Charlestown, West Virginia).

Atteentee Road. Developer's name in Springfield, Virginia, so called because AT&T had a cable there before there was a road. It is a good example of a new name that is functional rather than decorative.

B

Brown Material Road. An unfortunate Los Angeles County name. Another, according to an article in the *Los Angeles Times*, is *South Exa Court*, which sounds fine until it is abbreviated on maps as S.Exa Ct. The article also pointed out that every zodiacal name has been used in the county except *Cancer*.

C

Cass Place. A street in a Manassas, Virginia, subdivision named for pop singers and musicians. It is named for Cass Elliot of the Mamas and Papas. There is also Croce Court for Jim Croce, and a Mangione Court for trumpet player Chuck Mangione.

It is uncommon for theme areas to be this current. (If you can have this, how many years before there is a theme development devoted to the early names of punk rock?) Route 78 in Mississippi is officially known as the Elvis Aaron Presley Highway.

Christmas Seal Drive. Street in Rochester, New York.

Colusa Street. Butte, Montana, has two of these—one that runs east and west, and one that runs north and south. It also has a Pine Street, a Pine Avenue, a Center Street, and a Center Avenue. Because of possible confusion, in many jurisdictions fire departments can veto duplicate names as well as those which might sound alike over the phone. (In one real example, *Shadow* was vetoed, because it sounded too much like an existing *Chateau*.) Perhaps the most confusing situation of all exists in Salisbury, Massachusetts, where one street goes by three names: *Water Works Road* (what the street's residents voted to call it), *Lena Mae Way* (what the town planning board named it), and *Toll Road Extension* (what it has been called traditionally). *USA Today* reports that it has three street signs.

F

Forkover Place. When the city of Greensboro, North Carolina, needed a name for the street on which the local IRS office was located, the planning board recommended this apt name. The government objected to the "demeaning" name, and in 1972 it was named Federal Place.

G

German Street. One of those street names that were changed in cities across America at the beginning of World War I. In 1995, the city of Cincinnati added back the original street names that were changed during the Great War. The old names will supplement the new names. The current names of Cincinnati streets renamed during World War I, followed by their former German names:

Beredith Place – Schumann Street
Connecticut Avenue – Frankfort Avenue
English Street – German Street
Merrimac Street – Hapsburg Street
Orion Avenue – Wilhelm Street
Panama Street – Vienna Street
Republic Street – Bremen Street
Stonewall Street – Hamburg Street
Taft Road – Humboldt Avenue

Woodrow Street – Berlin Street
Yukon Street – Hanover Street

Goethe St. A well-known Chicago street which is pronounced *goth-ee* locally, even though it is named for the German poet, whose name is pronounced *ger-tuh*. There's an old joke about a guy going to a Goethe Street address, but he can't pronounce it, so he takes a cab to the next street over and walks a block.

H

Haig Road. Street in Valley Stream, New York, which is one of a group in that suburb named for brands of liquor: Gordon, Road, Carstairs Road, Wilson's Road, etc. This was pointed out in a letter from Mrs. Mary Santner, who also reports: "I live in Valley Stream, New York. There is no valley—the land is flat as a pancake—and there is no stream."

J

J Street. A Washington, D.C., street famous for the fact that it was left out of the lettered streets downtown; one moves a block from I Street to K Street. Local legend has it that it was left out because of John Jay's unpopularity in the post-Revolutionary period. Not so, according to the experts at the Columbia Historical Society, who say that it was omitted because in the script of the 18th century the letters *I* and *J* looked almost identical, and it was skipped to prevent confusion. There is, in fact, a Jay Street, named for John Jay, in the northeast section of the city. As a play on this idiosyncracy, the Sunday *Washington Post Magazine* carries a section of oddments called "J Street," which in 1991 took note of the fact that Anchorage, Alaska, lacked a J Street as well.

Washington lacks X, Y, and Z streets, and the B streets in the south and north sides of the district, which long ago became Independence and Constitution avenues respectively.

L

Labor-in-Vain Road. Spotted in Ipswich, Massachusetts, by Jon B. Jolly, who found that it was so called because workers "labored in vain" to fill its swampy areas with rocks to make a road bed. Jolly, who once worked a prospect list as a salesman, was taken with two other names: *Skunk's Misery Lane* in Syosset, New York, and *Hoof Print Trail* in Woodstock, Vermont.

N

Nixon and Bluett. In 1984, National Public Radio's "All Things Considered" held a contest to find the best intersection in America, and this Ann Arbor, Michigan, location won handily. A Beaver and Cherry intersection has been reported in Santa Rosa, California; Lee and Grant intersect in Manassas, Virginia; and Fort Holabird in Baltimore boasts a corner where Counter and Intelligence intersect. During the great Nancy-Tanya ice skating flap of 1993-1994, the Associated Press photographed the signs at the intersection of Kerrigan and Harding roads in Long Island.

No Name St. There are a number of these in the United States, including one in Millersburg, Ohio.

P

Pig Lane. Street on which the police station is located in St. Ives, England. The police tried to have it changed in the 1970s, when such a name was particularly loathsome to them, but a judge ruled that it could not be changed. (It was also pointed out that the station was technically on a side street called Cemetery Road.)

Preserved Arnold Court. Howard Channing was so taken with this name in Lincoln, Rhode Island, that he wrote to the local postmaster to find out how it was named. He had imagined that it was named for a local inebriate or an early citizen who had been mummified in the Egyptian style. Not so. Preserved Arnold was the name of an early mill owner. It is still a fine name.

R

Rue de Vallee. For years, according to a 1972 item in *Time,* crooner Rudy Vallee worked to have the Hollywood street that ran by his home renamed in his honor. But the other residents of Pyramid Place got the idea tabled. Taking pity, the town of Lake Forest, California, created a Rue de Vallee (which runs through a trailer park). A few other stars have streets named in their honor, like Debbie Reynolds Drive in Burbank.

Ruthelma St. A street in Palo Alto, California, which is the combined names of the wives of two real estate developers. A survey by the local historical society, reported in the *Palo Alto Times,* found that streets named after women in that town outnumber those named after men by 5 to 1. The explanation given was that the names were given by developers and real estate agents, who named the streets for "wives, sweethearts, daughters, grand-daughters, secretaries and, in a few cases, for dear old Mom."

S

Sesame Street. A case of a street name which was vetoed by local authorities in Montgomery County, Maryland, for the simple reason that it would invite sign theft. It was to be part of a spice theme area along with the likes of *Red Pepper Court* and *Tumerick Court,* which were permitted. In a nearby Virginia subdivision, signs for a Yellow Brick Road have been stolen more than 30 times.

Street Blvd. This apparent Joplin, Missouri, redundancy is named in honor of St. Louis Cardinals great Gabby Street, who lived there. In Lincoln, Rhode Island, there is a Boulevard Avenue, a true redundancy.

Supreme Court. Not far from where the author lives in Maryland, there is this fine and rare example of a pun name. Mike Webb reports that there is a Lois Lane in rural Skagit County, Washington. There is also an Easy Street in Woodbridge, Virginia, and another in Camp Springs, Maryland. He hopes to turn a corner someday and find a Bowling Alley, a See Ya In Court, or, better yet, a Sex Drive.

T

Tenbrook Road. In Montgomery County, Maryland, where there are more than 73,000 named roads, this name was axed by officials because it would confuse emergency personnel to whom it would sound like 10 Brook Road. This county also has taboos on new streets which sound like existing names and names with a high ROF (Rip-Off Factor) like *Lisa Way* and *Kevin Drive.* The problem of street sign theft is immense. Places named High Street or Easy Street are targets. In Howard County, Maryland, there is a Greek Boy Place, signs for which are often stolen by fraternity pledges. There is an intersection in Woodbridge, Virginia, of Jenny Lane and Christopher Court where the signs are stolen on the average of every two months.

Thaddeus Kosciuszko The American Revolutionary hero's name has become anathema to frugal municipal street czars, who find it too long for signs. Some years back the Los Angeles city council voted 12 to 0 against using the name because of its length. Local Polish-Americans protested, and the city reversed itself. Anna Higgins, a librarian from Sharon, Pennsylvania, wrote in 1987 to tell an even better Kosciuszko Street story:

When I was a little girl, growing up in Brooklyn, New York, my father told me about another Kosciuszko Street. (Your story concerned such a street including Kosciuszko's first name, Thaddeus, which was too long for a street sign in Los Angeles.) My dad said that a policeman found a dead horse on Kosciuszko Street, and since he couldn't spell the name, he dragged the horse around the corner, and so was able to write his report without a mistake.

Well the story was probably a joke. I was only a child when my father told it, more than 50 years ago, when horses were still pulling the wagons of peddlers, and children believed everything. But just in case you might be inclined to take it seriously, I looked up Kosciuszko Street on a map of Brooklyn at the library, and one of the intersections is Reid Avenue, which is certainly easier to spell.

Some places on this earth actually suffer from a lack of named streets. In a 1995 report by Kevin Sullivan and Mary Jordan in the *Washington Post*, we learn that Japan has a nearly impenetrable address system. Handed down through centuries and modified by 1960s urban planners, few streets have names, and most places are described by a landmark, like "near the big dog statue" or "behind the Honda showroom."

In many areas, houses are numbered not consecutively but in the order in which they were built. Where several houses were built on property once owned by a single landlord, they all have the same number. Many Japanese don't put a number on their house.

Team Tags

29

Terrible Swedes, River Rats, and Lady Friars

F ew things are quite as exciting to a name collector as a list of teams. For starters, there are the marvelous incongruities and odd nuances which show up in such listings of names. A city softball league ranking, which appeared in the *St. Petersburg Independent*, redefines the word *motley* with an assortment of team names including *Mudlarks, Ace Pawn Shop, Central Christ, Bay Area Bombers, Red Shack Snack, Local 747, Maximo Presbyterian*, and *George's Pools*. A ranking of top women's slow-pitch softball teams is a rich dessert for someone who appreciates names like *Zandarettes, Lady Comets, Gremlins, Stompers*, and *Famous Recipe*. As for women's fast-pitch, there are the perennial world beaters known as the Raybestos Brakettes, arguably one of the better team names ever emblazoned across a jersey.

Now, an all-star team of team nicknames:

A

Anteaters. Since 1965, the mascot of the University of California at Irvine, and inspired by the anteater in Johnny Hart's "B.C." comic strip. The idea was put across by a student named Schuyler Hadley Bassett III, who skillfully bested factions plumping for the unicorn, eagle, and roadrunner. Bassett helped his cause considerably when he showed up at the new school's first intercollegiate event—a waterpolo game—and led this cheer, "Give 'em the tongue. Give me a Z, give me an O, give me a T—what have you got? ZOT."

Artichokes. Name for the teams of Scottsdale (Arizona) Community College, deemed by the *Christian Science Monitor* to be the "most outlandish" from a list of the most unusual college nicknames compiled by sports writer Mike Welds, whose other nine were *Spiders, Blue Hens, Presidents, Fighting Engineers, Student Princes, Vulcans, Poets, Flying Nanooks,* and *Fighting Kangaroos.*

Not bad, but he overlooked the Gorillas of Kansas State Teachers College, the Akron University Zippers, the Terrible Swedes of Bethany College in Kansas, the Fighting Saints of Montana's Carroll College, and the Skibos of the Carnegie Institute of Technology. Then you've got the Illinois College Blueboys, the Pamona-Pitzer College Sagehens, and the Campbell (North Carolina) Fighting Camels. For those who recoil from snarling, clawing mascots, it is hard to beat the Glassboro (New Jersey) Profs, the New Hampshire Penmen, or the Centenary College (Louisiana) Gentlemen.

Incidentally, the Artichokes (actually the Fighting Artichokes) got their name, according to information supplied by Al Fisher of Scottsdale C.C.'s information office, in a long struggle between students and administrators and jocks and anti-jock factions. The name was originally picked by students in a protest against the overemphasis on athletics and the lack of academic facilities. After three years of resistance, administrators (who favored the *Drovers* as a nickname) gave in. The *Scottsdale Progress* noted that this gave the mascot "more meaning than most such symbols."

B

Battle Creek Golden Kazoos. One of a growing number of non-conformist minor-league baseball club names, along with *Winston-Salem Warthogs, Brevard County Manatees, Butte Copper Kings, Clinton Lumber Kings, Frederick Keys, Salt Lake Buzz,* and *Hardware City Rock Cats.*

The reason for the trend is, as a writer for the Knight-Ridder newspapers put it in 1995, "money, money, and more money," adding: "People like to wear caps and T-shirts and sweat shirts with unusual logos and exotic team names on them. They may have never seen the Rancho Cucamonga Quakes play, but they like wearing clothing with that name on it." This modern trend was helped by the Mud Hens, a Toledo minor-league club which was given a boost when M*A*S*H's Cpl. Max Klinger let it be known he was a Mud Hen man.

There used to be many good names in the minors. Go back to 1936 and find the Atlanta Crackers, Des Moines Demons, Durham Bulls, Longview Cannibals, Marshall Orphans, McKeesport Tubers, and the Eau Claire Bears. In 1968, the *Sporting News* bemoaned the trend by parent teams to name the farm team in their image as a means of product identification—as in, "he's a Red Sox farmhand"—and to save money by using hand-me-down uniforms. The editorial pointed to some fine names from 1948 which had been lost: "Canaries, Egyptians, Canners, Drillers, Planters, Johnnies, Bathers, Foresters, Slaters, Peps, Coal Barons, Rugmakers, Luckies, Soos, Cayugas, Cloverleafs, Cherokees, Goldbugs, Loboes, Brahman, Bulls, Berries, Gasers, Flashers, Boll Weevils, and many others." It has been suggested that the most appropriate minor-league moniker was the old *Hollywood Stars*.

Bees. Adopted in 1936 as the new name for the Boston Braves baseball team, it lasted about as long as two of the team's earlier names—*Doves* and the *Beaneaters*. The name *Bees* was selected by sportswriters from 1,327 entries from fans. The runner-up names were *Beacons, Blue Birds, Bulldogs, Colonials*, and *Blues*. The Bees became the Braves again and moved to Milwaukee in 1953 and Atlanta in 1966. The original *Braves* name was applied in 1912 by Jim Gaffney, a Tammany Hall chieftain who had first called them the Gaffers.

Billikens. The mascot of St. Louis University since 1910, when someone (there are various versions of the story) noted that the school's football coach, Charlie "Moonface" Bender, looked like the popular little carved doll of the era known as the Billiken and identified as "The God of Things as They Ought to Be." For several years, the bullet-headed imp was everywhere and in every form (belt buckles, salt and pepper shakers, pickle forks, hood ornaments) but the fad died

out in 1912. Female Billikens are called Millikens.

Blue Hens. Long-established University of Delaware name which has been given a more ferocious incarnation in recent years as the *Fightin' Blue Hens*.

Blue Jays. The name of the American League baseball team from Toronto. It was also the name of the Philadelphia Phillies for a short period. In 1944, team owners, tired of hearing the team called "the futile Phillies," held a "pick a new name" contest. The prizewinning "Bluejays" was hooted down by sports writers and fans alike, and it just wouldn't stick.

Bridegrooms. Before moving to the National League, the Brooklyn AA baseball champs of 1884 were known as the Bridegrooms because of the number of newlyweds on the team. The following year, they were renamed the Trolley Dodgers because of the hazardous maze of streetcar tracks in the borough.

Burning Sensations. Softball team fielded by the San Francisco City VD Clinic. Softball teams tend more to punning than other athletic organizations. Among the teams in the Environmental Protection Agency's softball league are the Reg Sox, Air Heads, and Effluent Society.

Consistently, however, the most outlandish names tend to come from intramural sports and tend to get raunchier and wilder the further one travels west. (For a list of outlandish California intramural team names, see the box on the opposite page.)

Outlandish California Intramurals

One would be hard-pressed to come up with wilder team names than these, which were collected at the University of California at Davis by Tom Gill. Gill gathered hundreds from the period 1978-1988 as they appeared in the *California Aggie.* Here are a few of the names which can appear in a book intended for the family trade. Many names omitted from the full Gill collection are about as off-color and/or offensive as can be imagined.

Football. Mars Needs Women, Dog Drool, Tree Dwellers, Lizard Muck, Bongo Palms, Joy of Six, We Have the Runs, Babies on Fire, Hump that Ball, Just Out For a Tan, Team Shasta, the Scoring Libidos, Ray Has Roids, New York Life, Skin Tacos, Painful Death, Kamakazee Smurfs, Tupperware (a woman's team), We Bad, the Mutants, Gets Traded to Seattle, Cheesy Sebaceous Matter, Stupid Football Tricks, We Love Big TDs, I'll Pass, Herpes Goes to College, Hybrid Vigor, Get a Job, Poignant Yet Tasteful Social Commitment, and the Split Ends.

Baseball/Softball. Moist Pits, the New York Hankies, Puking Peking Pygmies With Sticks, Doomed to Win, Roman Polanski's Day Care, Dr. Strangeglove, Glove Me Tender, Penguins in Bondage, Send in the Clones, Bats Out of Hell, Dull People of the Future, Mildew, Sit on my Base, Charles Darwin and the Beagles, Spam and the Weenie Arms, and Oh God It's Alive.

Water Polo. Eureka Eunodat?; Peter, Polo and Mary; the Titanics; Wet and Willing; the Squid; and We Lost Our Moose.

Basketball. Dribbling Idiots, I Knew This Was a Bad Idea, Attilla the Ton, the Basket Cases, Lord of the Thighs, Poster Children, Chairmen of the Boards, Human Speed Bumps, the Human Tripods, and No Blood No Fowl.

Soccer. Nell Carter's Phlegm, Win or Lose We Booze, Skidmarks, Road Apples, Mangled Baby Ducks, Staff Infection, The Iron-on Transfers, Scorgasms, Balls to the Wall, No Bozos, Return of the Housewives, Look Ma No Hands, Chateaux Le Feet, and Soccertease.

Volleyball. Big Fat Clams from Outer Space, Leach Babies, the Wall, Revenge of the Nerds, Existential Blues, Cockroach That Ate Davis, Are We Having Fun Yet, Oxymoron, the Airheads, Pubes and Cubes, Club Web, Tuna Patrol, CCCP, the Flaming Squids, Homicidal Tendencies, Spiked Drinks, Psychedelic M&M's, He's Dead Jim, the Lumpen Proletariats, Murphy's Law School, Human Zoo, Spike Jones, Sprouts With Clout, Volley of the Balls, Biohazards, Severe Tire Damage, Acute Death, and Block, Spike One for Zippy and Go Naked.

C

Cardinals. Just before the turn of the century the baseball team came out on the field in new red uniforms. Legend has it that a woman seated near the press box declared, "What a lovely shade of cardinal!" and the name stuck.

Colt 45's. Franchised in 1960, this Houston baseball team's name misfired, and when it moved to the new Astrodome in 1965, the name was changed to the *Astros*. The team that is now the Chicago Cubs was called the Colts in 1896 after their manager Cap Anson appeared in the play *A Runaway Colt*, especially written for him.

E

Eagles. Ray Franks, author of *What's in a Nickname? Exploring the Jungle of College Athletic Mascots*, surveyed 2,000 colleges and junior colleges in the United States and Canada and found *Eagles* in the lead with 72, followed by *Tigers, Cougars, Bulldogs, Warriors, Lions, Panthers, Indians, Wildcats*, and *Bears*.

F

Fearsome Foursome. An early example of a unit within a team with its own nickname, the "Fearsome Foursome" played for the Los Angeles Rams. Then came the "Purple People Eaters" (Minnesota), "Doomsday Defense" (Dallas), and "Wild Bunch" (University of Southern California). Unit nicknaming had developed to such a point that when the Washington Redskins went to the Super Bowl in 1984, the team had "The Hogs," "The Smurfs," "The Fun Bunch," "The Blue Collar Crew," and "The Pearl Harbor Crew."

G

Giants. Once called the Green Stockings and then the Mutuals, this New York baseball team became the Giants in 1885, when manager Jim Mutrie began referring to his team of particularly large strapping fellows as giants. A better story, but one with the ring of the apocryphal to it, had the team traipsing into the White House and President Benjamin Harrison looking up and exclaiming, "Why, they're all giants."

H

Hall of Famers. It only exists on paper, but it is real: the Scholastic Sports America Nickname Hall of Fame. A few of the inductees: the Belfry (Montana) Bats, the Hoopeston (Illinois) Cornjerkers, the Teutopolis (Illinois) Wooden Shoes, the Hickman High Kewpies of Columbia, Missouri, and the Freeport (Illinois) Pretzels.

Hoyas. Nickname for Georgetown University teams which were originally called the Stonewalls. Somewhere along the way students started using the Latin *hoia saxa* or "what rocks" for their teams. In other words, the "Whats" have become a college basketball powerhouse. It is also true that when people say, "What's a Hoya?" they are giving the answer, and a conversation on the matter can sound like the Abbott and Costello "Who's on first?" routine.

J

Jaspers. Manhattan College in New York uses this name, which is in memory of the school's Brother Jasper, who was deeply

Indians

Formerly the Blues, Naps (in honor of Napoleon Lajoie), Mollie McGuires, Bluebirds, Bronchos, Forest Cities, and Spiders (because of the number of skinny players on the team), the Cleveland Indians baseball team received its name in 1915, when a fan came up with the name in a newspaper contest. According to the team's official scorebook, the fan "said he was doing it in honor of an Indian player named Luis Francis Sockalexis, who was known as the Chief—the first American Indian to play in the Major Leagues." He was born in Old Town, Maine in 1873 and died in 1913.

In the early 1970s, the Indians—along with the Redskins, Warriors, Chiefs, and Braves—came under attack by Russell Means and others in the Indian rights movement for being insulting and demeaning. While the professional teams weathered this storm, a number of colleges with Indian mascots and nicknames dropped them, including Dartmouth (now Big Green), Stanford (today a less than ferocious Sequoia), and Syracuse (Orange). At one point the student body at Stanford voted to name its teams after its founder Leland Stanford and call them the Robber Barons. University officials decided against it.

There is a price to be paid for not changing. The University of Iowa Hawkeyes, the University of Wisconsin Badgers, and the University of Minnesota Gophers will not play nonconference games against teams using Indians as mascots or symbols.

While some universities have stopped using Indian-related nicknames and/or mascots, others have not. Despite the lawsuits, protests, legislation, and even a boycott of an Atlanta radio station that carries Braves games, no pro team has changed an Indian name. The outcry has gotten louder in the 1990s:

- The Atlanta Braves' "tomahawk chop," an arm motion made increasingly popular during the 1991 World Series, was the last straw, said Rachel Joseph, executive director of the National Congress of American Indians. It also was the beginning of an increased cultural awareness movement that has included protests, proposed legislation, and lawsuits against several professional sports teams.
- U.S. Sen. Ben Nighthorse Campbell (R-Colorado), the only American Indian in Congress, introduced a 1991 bill that would have forced the Washington Redskins to change their nickname because of its offensive nature.
- In March 1992, American Indians, blacks, and Hispanics launched an aggressive campaign to persuade the owner of the Washington Redskins to change the team's name. Jack Kent Cooke, owner of the Redskins, replied that he would not consider changing the name because it is neither offensive nor derogatory. A statement released by Cooke stated, "The Washington Redskins were renamed in 1933 to differentiate between the Boston Braves of the National [Baseball] League and the Boston Braves of the National Football League. The name was never intended to offend anyone. Over the long history of the Washington Redskins, the name has reflected the positive attributes of American Indians such as dedication, courage, and pride."
- In 1993 an Ohio state lawmaker asked the legislature to force the Cleveland Indians to drop their nickname.

Such efforts will doubtless continue until the names change, in the meantime fueling a great number of letters to editors, editorials, and protests.

involved in athletics and is credited with inventing the seventh-inning stretch.

Jazz. Once the New Orleans Jazz, the Utah Jazz ranks with the Los Angeles Lakers (once the Minneapolis Lakers) as one of the most incongruous teams in all of sports. Ah, those southern California lakes and that hot Salt Lake City music!

Other teams are more aptly named. The *Pittsburgh Steelers, Minnesota Vikings, Boston Celtics,* and *Baltimore Orioles* are a few that defy improvement.

Jumbos. Name attached to Tufts University because P. T. Barnum used to be on the board, and when his monstrous elephant Jumbo was killed in 1885 by a train, he had its skin (which weighed 1,538 pounds) sent to the college as a gift. Jumbo was stuffed and displayed but was destroyed in a 1975 fire. "However," says a press release from Tufts, "a resourceful administrator in Tufts' athletic department, Phyllis Byrne, went to the fire scene and scraped the elephant ashes into a peanut butter jar (what else?) and returned it to her department, where it is kept in a vault. It has become recent tradition that Tufts athletes who rub the jar before entering a competition are usually successful."

L

Lady Friars. One of a growing number of women's teams with less than logical nicknames, the Lady Friars hail from Providence College in Rhode Island. In an article on team names in the *Smithsonian* magazine, W. Patrick Resen pointed to other examples, including the Lady Knights of Central Florida and the Rams (not Ewes) of Cornell College in Iowa. The Lady Bulls of the State University of New

York at Buffalo have, however, become the Royals. The Lady Cavaliers of the University of Virginia suggest the last thing a lady would want to be, even if she could be, which she cannot, because as one critic of the name puts it, "a cavalier is a gentleman by definition, one especially gallant and much given to escorting ladies past the rough spots of life." Female athletes at the University of Texas are known as the Lady Longhorns. A lady longhorn is as difficult to imagine as an Arkansas Lady Razorback, but the females of the animals in question are cows and sows.

N

Nordiques. National Hockey League team from Quebec, whose name was chosen, in part, because it was uniquely French and would not easily translate into English. The name, however, was easily changed when the team moved and became the Colorado Avalanche.

P

Pirates. Once known as the Alleghenies, this baseball team got its new name in 1891, when it signed a Phillie who had been accidentally released. One of the Phillies lawyers termed the act "piratical," and the team seized on the nickname.

R

Red Devils. A number of high schools and colleges use this or a similarly diabolic nickname, and from time to time a stir arises concerning the religious symbolism expressed. A recent case involved the Red Devils of Springville (Utah) High School, which hung onto the nickname after a student referendum (704-22 in favor). The Utah school adopted the name years ago, when it was built with a foundation of Red Devil brand cement.

Reds. The Cincinnati Red Stockings, the first professional team in baseball in 1869, got the name because of their hose. Quickly the name was shortened to *Reds*, and much later, a movement began to go back to *Red Stockings* to forestall any association with communism. In the early 1960s, a justice of the Pennsylvania Supreme Court even got into the act by publicly admonishing the club for its unpatriotic name. "Let the Russians change," was the altogether proper response of *Cincinnati Enquirer* sports editor Lou Smith: "We had it first."

It is the oldest surviving nickname in organized baseball. The oldest nickname of all, however, is *Knickerbocker*. Inspired perhaps by Washington Irving's fictional *Knickerbocker's History of New York* or by the subsequent practice of attaching the name *Knickerbocker* to anything related to New York, Alexander Cartwright, who put forth the rules of baseball in 1845, used the name for the baseball team he founded in the same year. The name lives today in the National Basketball Association as the New York *Knicks*.

Rejected Stems. One of a number of competitive chili-cooking teams whose exploits are covered in *The Goat Gap Gazette* ("a newspaper mainly for chiliheads and their ilk"). Other teams mentioned in the *GGG:* Homeless Hillbillies, Texas Swindle, Slap Happy, Ta-Kill-Ya-Chili, Gutter Sluts, The Lost Dutchman Chili Team, Ike's Chili Inferno, Kid Cuisinart, Buzzard Breath, Aztec Cafe, Pure Purgatory, Miss Guadalupe Vander Buehl's House of Chili and Other Delights, Boy George Chili Team, Death Row, Mother Murphy's Celtic Thunder, Side Effects, and Dead on the Road.

River Rats. One of the few teams ever named for a rat, this was

Evansville, Indiana's professional baseball team in 1908, according to that year's edition of *Lajoie's Official Base Ball Guide*. A few other names from that guide: the *Oakland Commuters, Wheeling Stogies, Canton Chinamen, Leavenworth Woodpeckers*, and the *Los Angeles Seraphs*. There were two professional teams named the Coal Barons, one from Wilkes-Barre and another from Birmingham.

S

Siwash. Many years ago a writer named George Fitch created a fictional college for a series of novels. Fitch went to Knox College of Galesburg, Illinois, and even though Siwash was supposed to be a composite, his alma mater adopted it as its nickname. But what is a Siwash? Rich Lorenz of the *Chicago Tribune* researched it and concluded, "It is a word in Chinook jargon, a mixture of Russian, French Canadian, and northwest American Indian. Its root is the French word *sauvage,* which means savage. It is not the most flattering term, often having the connotation of something done in a sloppy manner. It has also come to represent any inland college that is provincial in outlook."

Student Prince. The mascot of Heidelberg College in Tiffin, Ohio. It was inspired by a title on a theatre marquee, *The Student Prince of Heidelberg.* Unfortunately, there is no student prince logo. Al Kath, director of the school's news services, points out, "We have wanted to develop a Student Prince logo but all attempts have fallen short of the mark. Should a Prince be on a charging horse? And, indeed, what does a Prince look like?"

T

Tigers. In 1932, Bert Walker of the *Detroit Times* noted that the team had been called the Wolverines. "However," he wrote, "when the wolverine became extinct and even the oldest inhabitant didn't know whether a wolverine was a fish or a squirrel, the name lost its significance. . . . Then one season the team blossomed out in its brown stockings with yellow stripes running horizontally. This inspired the fan to dub the team either the Tigers or the Zebras and soon the Tigers chased the Zebras off the landscape and the Tigers they became."

Tip Tops. According to Bert Randolph Sugar's *Who Was Harry Steinfeldt & Other Baseball Trivia Questions,* this Brooklyn squad was the only major league team to be associated with a commercial product. It advertised bread for its two years in existence from 1914 to 1916.

U

The Unique Baseball Club. A team which emerged in 1890 in Chicago which was composed entirely of brothers of the Karpen family. Another family team, the Lennon Family of Joliet, beat the Karpens in September of that year. The Lennon team was composed of eleven brothers (12 if you count a very young boy who was the mascot) and also called itself "unique." Meanwhile, another team composed of Eugene McEntee and his eight sons made itself known in Rochester, New York. Despite the challengers, the Karpens held onto the *Unique* title because they were the first to claim it.

W

Whippers. Hampshire High in Illinois has combined its colors—white and purple—to get this one-of-a-kind nickname.

White Sox. The Chicago Cubs, the oldest baseball franchise in continuous operation, were first called the White Stockings but they dropped the name, and it was picked up and shortened by the American League team in 1901.

Wombats. Until 1982, this was the name for the Skidmore College teams, which are now called the Thoroughbreds. A school spokeswoman told *USA Today* that it was changed to prevent further embarrassment to the school's athletes. The University of Wisconsin at Sheboygan proudly displays the Wombat mascot.

Y

Yankees. Originally known as the New York Highlanders (because of their location on high ground), they became the Yankees through the constant repetition of sportswriter Mark Roth of the *New York Globe* and other writers, who felt *Yanks* fit headlines better. The fans, who had never liked *Highlanders*—or the alternative *Hilltoppers*—quickly accepted *Yanks* and *Yankees*.

Trade Names

Genericide Prevention

30

Aunt Jemima Meets Betty Crocker

These days virtually every product imaginable is given a trade name, including pet contraceptives, canned wine, and earwax remover. One earwax remover is aptly named Hear Hear, and a hospital-strength vomit deodorant is called Oh Dear!

Companies spend great amounts of time and energy protecting their names, lest they fall into common use and are deemed to be in the public domain. Despite these efforts, however, product names are sometimes swept away by the tide of common usage and join the long list of trade names which are now generic. The list includes *aspirin, kerosene, mineral oil, pilsner beer, celluloid, trampoline, cube steak, windbreaker, raisin bran, yo-yo, mimeograph, milk of magnesia, lanolin, thermos, nylon, calico, dry ice, shredded wheat, zipper, hansom, cellophane,* and *escalator*. The director of the U.S. Trademark Association has termed this process "genericide."

Here is a sampling of trade names with their diverse origins.

A

Alpo. This dog food was first called All-Pro, but that name ran into trademark complications, and so the *l* and *r* were jettisoned.

Atra and **Trac II.** Both of these Gillette products are acronyms. *Atra* = automatic tracking razor action. *Trac* = tandem razor and cartridge. The "II" is added for emphasis.

Aunt Jemima. When Chris L. Rutt created the first pancake mix in 1889, he took the name Aunt Jemima from a popular vaudeville song of the period. After the Davis Milling Co. took over the product, famous black cook Nancy Green was hired to pose as Aunt Jemima. She has become as famous as Betty Crocker.

B

Betty Crocker. A mix of several different ideas, Betty was the most popular name in America at the time she was created in 1921. Crocker was the name of a General Mills director as well as the name of the first flour mill in Minneapolis, where the company is headquartered. Her portrait has been made over seven times—most recently in 1995—and her image appears on only a handful of the products which carry her name.

Ann Page, of A&P fame, was a pseudonym for a home economist who wrote for the company in the 1920s, and Sara Lee is named for the daughter of Charles Lubin, who started that company. Uncle Ben was a made-up name, but the face was that of a Chicago hotel dining room maitre'd named Frank Jones. The model for the "Sun Maid" on the raisin box was Lorraine C. Patterson, who passed away

in 1983 at the age of 90. She had posed for the picture in 1915. The chubby Campbell Soup kids were created by artist Grace Drayton in 1904—although they have been slimmed down in recent years.

Birdseye. Named for the late Clarence Birdseye, who once explained the name to a newspaper reporter this way: "One of my ancestors was a page boy to some queen or other and used to go hunting with her. Well, one day a hawk or some other big bird, started to swoop down towards the queen. And this page boy ancestor of mine, according to the records, took out his trusty arrow and shot that bird right in the eye. The queen was so tickled she gave him that name right on the spot, and now I'm stuck with it."

B.V.D. Many insist that these initials stand for "Best Ventilated Drawers" or some such, but they really stand for Bradley, Voorhees and Day.

Corfam. One of the computer-generated names that actually made it to market. According to the *Wall Street Journal*, the name for Du Pont's synthetic leather was picked from 153,000 offered by a machine. Du Pont also got *Nordel*, the name for a synthetic rubber, from the computer.

Cupid's Quiver. The name of a scented douche.

G

Greyhound. The name and the trademark are among the few animal trademarks that remain in what was once a large menagerie, which included the Kool penguin, the Sinclair dinosaur, and the NBC peacock. Elsie is still the Borden cow, but she is much less important than in the days when she came in second only to the president in a public recognition test, and her husband Elmer's picture is not on the glue that bears his name. In 1969, RCA dropped its dog Nipper (listening for "His Master's Voice") but then reconsidered and began bringing him back in the late 1970s, in part because the public missed the famous fox terrier. The Quantas koala was bumped and replaced with a kanga-roo.

Those that remain include the Playboy bunny, Mack Truck bulldog, Hartford Insurance Company elk, MGM lion, and the Bon Ami chick, who was about to be bounced for an abstract sym-bol in the 1960s when market researchers found that people vastly preferred the chick. Although she has been reduced to a black and white silhouette, Chessie the cat is now both the name and the symbol for the Chessie System, which combines four railroads (the C&O, B&O, Western Maryland, and Seaboard).

Another area where animals are hav-ing troubles is as clothing trademarks. The trend started with the Izod Lacoste alliga-tor and produced a zoo full of imitators, including dogs, foxes, pigs, bears, uni-corns, turtles, frogs, armadillos, and drag-ons. However, led by the Sears horse and the J.C. Penney fox, the animals are begin-ning to disappear from clothing.

Such animal desertions aside, General Mills, which owns the American rights to the alligator, and the parent Lacoste SA of Switzerland defend the trademark with zeal, having gone after dragons, dead alli-gators (the Croc O'Shirt), and other rep-tiles. One case that Lacoste lost was its attempt to get the Everlast company to take a dragon emblem off its judo and karate uniforms. The administrative judge who ruled in the case decided that alliga-tors and dragons were not similar and

that "St. George did not become the patron saint of England because he slew an alligator."

H

Hotpoint freezer. Proof that a brand name need not be rational to be success-ful. Chock Full O'Nuts Coffee is another.

I

Irish Mist. A liqueur with a different name in Germany, where *mist* means "manure."

Ivory. After discarding dozens of names for his new soap, Harley Procter was sit-ting in church in 1878 when he heard a passage from the Bible about "ivory palaces." Almost 100 years later, Procter's (and Gamble's) company had to change the Ivory Snow soap box when the woman nuzzling her baby on the box illustration, Marilyn Chambers, gained notoriety as a porn star.

K

Kodak. The result of George Eastman's quest for a short vigorous name that would mean nothing, resist misspelling, and totally belong to his cameras. Although the company has had good luck with names, one recent name bombed. In 1983, a few days after Kodak had named its domestic camera-making group the U.S. Equipment Division, it was realized that the acronym was USED. Kodak hasti-ly changed the name of the unit to the U.S. Apparatus Division.

L

Lane Bryant. An immigrant girl named Lena Himmelstein married David Bryant, who died shortly after they were married. Lena began sewing to support herself and an infant son, and soon got the backing of her brother-in-law, who gave her $300 to expand the business. According to Tom Mahoney in his book *The Great Merchants*, she became so flustered when she deposited this money in a Wall Street bank that she transposed the letters of her first name on the deposit slip and became Lane Bryant.

Leica. It is a blend of *Leitz*, the company which makes it, and *camera*. A number of other camera companies have taken the *ca* from *camera* since Leica started the trend (Konica, Fujica, etc.). The camera got an unexpected bit of publicity when film critic C. A. Lejeune summarized *I am a Camera* in three words: "Me no Leica."

Log Cabin. Named by P. J. Towle, the St. Paul grocer who created the blend of maple and sugarcane syrup in 1887. It was named in honor of Towle's boyhood hero, Abraham Lincoln.

M

Maxwell House. This coffee is named after a hotel in Nashville which is no longer there. It was at the Maxwell House Hotel that President Theodore Roosevelt sampled the coffee and coined the slogan "good to the last drop."

Mr. Peanut. This highly successful personification was created in 1916 by a Suffolk, Virginia, schoolchild who won $5 in a design contest sponsored by Planters Peanuts.

N

N. The *N* logo developed for NBC at a cost of $600,000 got the company in a jam when a Nebraska station sued because it was using a similar N-logo, which it had developed for less than $100. The red *N* may be the most expensive letter in the history of trademarks and trade names.

No Deer–Not Tonight. A deer repellent.

Noxzema. "Could knock out eczema" was what an early user of this product wrote to its inventor, who immediately changed its name.

Nuclear Freeze. A frozen dessert from Garden of Eatin', a California health food manufacturer.

O

Odo-Ro-No. How could one list trade names without at least mentioning this Colgate-Palmolive deodorant which, says Adrian Room in his *Dictionary of Trade Name Origins*, "is both a fairly playful pun (odor? oh no!), and at the same time suggestive of the nature of the product (a deodorant)."

P

Psyche. The topless goddess of purity who appears on the White Rock bottle. In 1975, the *New York Times* charted her body changes since 1894 when she first appeared and found that she had grown taller (from 5'4" to 5'8") and thinner (from 140 pounds to 118 pounds). She has been banned in Saudi Arabia.

Pupperoni. A trademarked name for dog treats. Puns are very popular in product naming, as in a makeup brush named Sweeping Beauty, a skin moisturizer called Self Defense, and a cleanser called

Tyrone Scour. Traditionally, the girdle and foundation trade has done well with puns. This is where such names as *Line Tamer, Anchors-A-Waist, Sweet Add-a-Line, Anything But the Truth,* and *Waist-a-way* have abounded.

R

Red Zinger. One of a number of wild names used by the people who make Celestial Seasonings tea. Others include *Almond Sunset, Grandma's Tummy Mint, Morning Thunder,* and *Sleepytime.*

S

Sanka. A play on "sans caffeine." To help protect the name, it is referred to as "Sanka Brand" decaffeinated coffee in ads. Others which are protected with zeal include *Styrofoam, Ping-Pong, Kleenex, Q-Tip, Caterpillar, Coca-Cola, Xerox, Scrabble, Frigidaire, Vaseline, Kodak, Polaroid,* and *Band-Aid.* Xerox, for instance, has long urged writers and editors to "*copy* things, don't Xerox them."

7 Up. Great name for the soft drink invented by C. L. Grigg in 1929. The original name was *Bib-Label Lithiated Lemon-Lime Soda.* Double Bubble Gum was first sold as Blibber Bubbler.

Sköl. A vodka. Bob Skole, an American living in Sweden with more than passing interest in the name, writes that "there is no such thing as *Sköl.* It is *Skål.* To a Scandinavian, the name *Sköl* is as funny as a whiskey named *Chirs* or *Chears* would be to an American."

Smokey. The Agriculture Department's symbolic bear, who is by a 1950 act of Congress the property of the U.S. government, and as much a "property" as the Greyhound dog. If, for instance, you wish to make a Smokey keychain, you must pay the government a royalty. Named for Smokey Joe Martin, a famous turn-of-the-century firefighter, he became a living symbol when rangers found a badly burned cub in the embers of a New Mexico forest fire. Smokey is probably the best government symbol ever and is in a different league from that of Mr. Zip, Woodsy Owl ("Give a hoot, don't pollute!"), McGruff (the crime-fighting dog), and Johnny Horizon. Maybe the worst of all was the IRS "eagle" which went on tax forms in the 1960s but was pulled in 1973, when the new IRS Commissioner, Donald Alexander, looked at a version of the eagle on his wall and decided that the scowling, vulture-like eagle scared him.

Smurf. A four-fingered blue character with the magic marketing appeal of a name like *Mickey Mouse* or *Snoopy.* Created by a Belgian artist named Peyo, they are called Schtroumpfs in their native land and France, and Puffos, Pitufos, and Schlumpfs elsewhere.

Sn- An old dictum in the trade name business is that one should never name a product with a word beginning with these two letters, which suggest *snake, snore, sneeze, snare,* etc. It is, however, not that hard to find products which have done well in spite of their first two letters— Snickers, Snow Crop, Snacktime Pretzels, Snack Pack, Snugli (the infant carrier), and Snap-on Tools, to name a few.

Sweet'n Low. Trivia buffs will want to know that this trademark was the 1,000,000th awarded by the Patent Office.

T

Teflon. Du Pont name for nonstick coating which became political metaphor when in 1983 Rep. Patricia Schroeder (D-Colorado) called Ronald Reagan the "Teflon president" because of her belief that Reagan's political image remained strong in spite of negative events. Du Pont, which lost its rights to the word *cellophane* many years earlier, has had to remind people that the use of Teflon as metaphor is an infringement.

Touch of Yogurt. Clairol tried this shampoo in 1979 and quickly abandoned it. Wonder why?

Trade and Mark. The name people associate with the Smith Brothers of cough drop fame. Their real names were William and Andrew, but they have been known as Trade and Mark ever since a printer put those words under their pictures on the box. They are no relation to the Mrs. Smith of pie fame. She was Amanda W. Smith, a widow who supported her family by cooking pies. Her company was bought out by the Kellogg Co. in 1976.

Trim Pecker. A Japanese brand of trousers given this odd English name. It is one of a number of products given American-sounding names which, intended for the Japanese market, have strange connotations for Americans. *Advertising Age* singled out some others, including Green Piles, a lawn fertilizer; Creap, a non-dairy creamer; and Calpis, a soft drink. The *Washington Post,* on the other hand, recently reported a candy called Carap, a drink called Pocari Sweat, and chocolates in a Band-Aid style box called Hand-Maid Queer Aids. Oddest of all is Nail Re-mover, a fingernail cleaner. A recent book called *Japanese Jive* featured Armpit, an electric razor; Babe Soda, a candy; Blue Jeans, a pork sausage; and Mouth Pet, a breath freshener.

W

White Stag. This clothing name began as Hirsch-Weis in the 1880s, but when looking for a brand name, the two immigrant German founders translated their names into English and reversed their order.

Y

Yuban. A contraction of "Yuletide banquet." It was first created by a coffee merchant for his business friends at Christmas.

Ywuvite. One of many thousands of computer-generated drug names that will never see the light of the marketplace because they just don't sound right. With thousands of drugs on the market, getting just the right name for a medication has become an art in itself. A soothing name like *Valium* works for a tranquilizer, and it is hard to imagine a more effective name for a vitamin than *One-A-Day*. A gold-based drug for treating arthritis has been named Ridaura by its manufacturer SmithKline Beecham Corp. It breaks down nicely: *Rid* (obvious) *au* (symbol for gold) *ra* (rheumatoid arthritis).

Many drug names are suggestive of what they are intended to do. Joe Turner of Vista, California, has collected a number of these. A few examples:

Preludin as in "prelude to a big meal." This is an appetite suppressant.
Tenuate as in "at ten you ate." Again a diet pill.

Presate as in "pre-satiated."
Ditto.
Voranil as in "no voracious appetite."
Ditto.
Sinequan as in "sine qua non."
An antidepressant.

Ultimately, one of the problems with these creations is that occasionally two are so similar that when written by doctors in their notorious poor handwriting, one can get confused with another. Such was the case with Levoxine (a heart drug) and Lanoxin (a synthetic hormone), which were causing problems because the handwritten *ev* of *Levoxine* could be confused with the *an* of *Lanoxin.* In 1993, Levoxine became Levoxyl.

B.V.D's: Best Ventilated Drawers?

Unfortunate Names

Some Names Don't Wear as Well as Others

31

Mr. Donald Duck—Alabama School Teacher

All names are not created equal. Some have definite overtones and drawbacks. Consider, for example, a list put together by Alex Fraser, head of Washington's Open University, when he was an airline clerk in his 20s. An admitted "adolescent interest" compelled him to record such names given to him by travelers as Pimp, Hoar, Fruit, Tart, Crapsey, Groundwater, Girlie, Titt, Crapp, Philpot, Titty, Lust, Outhouse, Braziere, Klapp, Combest, Dong, Pistoff, Fartz, Holjammer, Pecker, Teets, Whorer, and Krack.

Open any large metropolitan telephone directory—as Jay Ames did with the Toronto white pages—and you will find names like Arson, Bastardi, Booze, Bozo, Bubbass, Crapper, Dodo, Freake, Groper, Hardstaff, Hustler, Kaka, Maggott, Moron, Mummy, Pork, Putz, Rump, Shagass, Spittle, Tugnutt, Wart, and Worm.

Here are some other names which are—um—less than fortunate, concluding with a finale of first names which defy the imagination.

B

Beaglehole. A man named George Beaglehole used the *Times* of London to declare his name "the most uncommon in the land." Other Beagleholes stepped forward to prove that it was probably not the most uncommon, but it did show that there is a certain pride in a name that others might find odd.

Bupb. B. Bupb, an Ohio man, found that an odd name can have its drawbacks. According to a 1951 UPI story, Bupb was fishing in Florida and broke his glass eye and wanted to send a telegram to his wife to send him his "spare." Quoting from the original story, here is what transpired:

> "I want to send a telegram," he told the Western Union operator by telephone.
>
> "Your name?" asked the operator.
>
> "B. Bupb."
>
> The disbelieving operator asked him to repeat. Bupb did.
>
> "Don't you be-bop me," she said, starting to hang up the receiver.
>
> Bupb finally convinced the operator that was his real name.
>
> "All right," she said, "Where do you want the telegram sent?"
>
> "Wapakoneta, Ohio."
>
> "Wapako-who?" demanded the operator. "Now, that's enough. Goodby, sir."
>
> "No, wait!" cried Bupb. "That's the real name of a real town in Ohio. I live there. Honest. My wife is there, believe me.
>
> "All right, sir," said the skeptical operator.

> "Your name is B. Bupb. And you want to send a telegram to Wapakoneta. Now what is the message."
>
> "Please send other eye immediately...."
>
> "Oh, no you don't!" shouted the operator as she hung up the receiver.

C

Claghorn. Ever since Fred Allen brought the pompous Senator Claghorn on his radio show, the name has been used for bombastic, tinhorn politicians—usually from the South. For instance, in 1963, Florida Governor Leroy Collins was referring to unnamed Southern politicians when he asked: "How long are the majority of Southerners going to allow themselves to be caricatured before the nation by these Claghorns?" People named Claghorn objected.

Crummy. When the word "crummy" was used to describe an inferior product on the BBC consumer show *Watchdog*, a Mrs. Crummy wrote to protest its negative overtone, which no one disputed. According to the *Times* of London the show apologized: "Before our next programme, we should first like to spend five minutes apologizing unreservedly to people with the following names (in order of appearance), which may be thought to have a negative overtone: Nazi, Putrid, Shoddy, Ugly...."

D

Donald Duck. The name of an Alabama high school principal, who told an interviewer that his father named him Donald because he knew that he would be called Donald, no matter what he was named.

F

Fink. What do you do if your name happens to be the same as the slang word for a labor scab, a stool pigeon, and a generally undesirable person? Answer: You proudly celebrate National Fink Day in Fink, Texas, with other members of the International Order of Finks.

According to one story, *fink* entered the language after Pinkerton detectives broke up an 1890 strike with violence, and immigrant steel workers corrupted the word *Pink*, short for *Pinkerton*.

H

Hicksville/Hicks. Terms of derogation for a backward town or rural buffoon. When used in this manner by a newspaper, it will almost always yield an angry letter from a reader named Hicks. When the *Washington Post* referred to a Virginia town as Hicksville in 1989, a reader named Norman L. Hicks reminded the paper: "The Hicks family has a long and noble tradition and includes such people as Robert Hicks, who came to Massachusetts in 1621; Elias Hicks, the famous Quaker preacher; Edward Hicks, an early American artist; and John R. Hicks, Nobel laureate in economics."

Hitler. An article in *Names* by Robert M. Rennick entitled "Hitlers and Others Who Changed their Names and a Few Who Did Not" says it all in the first two sentences: "Before Adolf Hitler became chancellor of Germany in 1933, there were some 22 families named *Hitler* or *Hittler* listed in the New York telephone directories. By the end of the war there were none." The cruel irony which Rennick reported was that most of the Hitlers in America were Jews from Galicia.

The name Hitler may be dying out completely because of its associations, just as Judas is virtually a dead name because of the biblical Judas Iscariot who betrayed Christ. (There were three other Judases in the Bible—all good men—but this is forgotten.)

Hooker. A proud last name that has become synonymous with "prostitute." A family which signed itself "Respectable Hookers" recently wrote to Ann Landers with the plea that people stop using the name when referring to harlots. Ann's sad reply: "I hate to be pessimistic, but I see no hope for your crusade."

Hooligan. This once proud name ran into trouble late in the last century when a London family by that name kept running afoul of the law. The patriarch Patrick Hooligan ended his career in prison after killing a constable. The name became synoynmous with rowdy ruffians and was used in a book (*The Hooligans*, about London low life), a song about a riotous clan ("The Hooligans"), and a comic strip about a simpleminded hobo (*Happy Hooligan*). For this reason, the name was declared extinct in the early 1970s when one writer was unable to find a Hooligan in Ireland or the United States. Many had become Holohans, Nolans, and Hollands—to get away from wild Hooligan.

L

Lockerbie butter. A product name that can take on a disturbing association because of the 1988 explosion of a Pan Am plane over Lockerbie, Scotland, by a terrorist bomb. Lockerbie butter existed before the disaster and is still sold in Great Britain.

M

Monster. One of those last names which are changed for obvious reasons. Others who have made the news with such changes include Pigg, Bugg, Smellie, and Bozo. One clever change, reported in the *Bulletin of the American Name Society*, is a Peter Twatt becoming Peter T. Watt. The Long Island newspaper *Newsday* reported in 1986 about a Brooklyn judge named Peter Schmuck, who made it difficult for people to come into his courtroom for a name change.

Mudd. A letter to the editor of *The Economist* tells it all: "Sir—The advertisement for gas, on page 23 of your issue of July 29th, used the expression 'our name was mud.' There are nearly 300 heirs of Dr. Mudd (the physician who was imprisoned for life for setting the broken leg of Lincoln's assassin), and they are unhappy about this sort of thing." Actually, there probably is no connection between Dr. Mudd and the phrase "one's name is mud."

N

Noma. One of those not-unpleasant-sounding first names with a ghastly meaning which was probably not known to the parents who assigned it. In her *Dictionary of Given Names*, Flora H. Loughead explains Noma: "In the list of students enumerated in the annual catalog of a great western university, there is a young lady bearing the name of Noma, which in medical nomenclature is a gangrenous ulceration of the mouth in children." She also mentions Nedre, which is the name of a poisonous adder.

O

Outlaw. When Archie Outlaw was charged with selling heroin in 1981, he petitioned a New York court for a name change because he felt he could not get a fair jury trial with that last name. He was allowed to change his name—to Simmons—and then pleaded guilty. In opposing his motion, an assistant district attorney pointed out that such cases as *People v. Bruce Bimbo, People v. Anthony Oddman, People v. Bernard J. Outlaw,* and *People v. Anthony Savage* had "passed through the criminal justice system without apparent prejudice."

P

Part. Good name as long as you are not drafted. Richard Boston wrote in the *Guardian,* "A friend of a friend of mine is called Part, and when he was in the army during the war, like everyone else he started off as a Private, but rose from the ranks to become a Major Part of the British army."

Peculiar. A town in Missouri, which could be the most unfortunately named place to be from if you are sensitive to lines like "Here comes a peculiar person." The town got its name when the postal authorities in Washington told the local postmaster to pick a name for the town. After suggesting dozens which were rejected, he was told that he should pick a peculiar name, which he did. (In a similar development, the Missouri town of Enough was named by postal authorities who, after 200 names were rejected, presumably threw up their hands and said "Enough.")

In the realm of unfortunate American place names there is also Bad Axe, Michigan; Belcher, New York; Eek, Alaska; Hell, Michigan (which made the news in the very cold winter of 1995-1996, when it froze over); Horseheads, New York; Muck City, Alabama; Panic, Pennsylvania; Pitts, Georgia; Radium, Minnesota; Roach, Missouri; and War, West Virginia.

S

Sexauer. A perfectly fine last name, but one that is forever encumbered with this probably fictitious story, which over the years was repeated with some regularity about an executive for the Sunbeam Corp. named Loren Sexauer:

> *Caller to switchboard: "Do you have a Sexauer there?"*
>
> *Switchboard operator to caller: "Sexauer! We don't even have a coffee break!"*

(This version from a *Chicago Daily News* article of January 1970.)

Spenkelink. Maybe the bad luck name to beat all. When John Spenkilink was executed in the Florida electric chair in 1979, the state insisted on spelling his name wrong right to the end—even his drab prison uniform had it spelled Spinkellink.

T

Theopholis. A no-doubt apocryphal but oft-quoted story has someone asking a professor why he named his child Theopholis. "I took one look at him and decided that he was Theopholis looking baby I had ever seen," is the alleged reply.

The story has done little to increase the popularity of the name.

Twins. A 1974 article in the *Chicago Tribune* quoted Everett Williams of the Florida Bureau of Vital Statistics, who has seen the following names officially recorded for twins in his state: Pete and Repeat, Early and Curly, AC and DC, and Bigamy and Larceny.

W

Water. If you consider Waterloo, Watergate, and Whitewater, you can only conclude that water has a great ability to dilute one's reputation.

Wettfahrt. German name for a race on which bets are placed. With the unification of Europe the British press has had fun with terms like *wettfahrt* and *fahrtwind*, which signifies the pleasant rush of wind one experiences when traveling at a high speed.

Z

Zilphia. Just one of a number of clearly uncommon first names collected by Leland Hilligoss and now a part of the aforementioned Raspberry Collection.

Reading through that collection, one gets the feeling that there are few combinations of letters which have not been used to name a baby somewhere in the United States.

Some rare and unusual real names from that collection, with additions made by the author and his name-spotting friends over a decade, include:

Hostina, Oveeda, Eppmethus, Luecrecer, Mannervia, Offencries, Celestial, Samella, Larnela, Lavette, Sofus, Curlura, Patch, Exzear, Rotcher, Dwarwod, Benolen, Palasteen, Reversie, Hyphil, Uldene, Margarine, Teelfatha, Tennis, Blewmer, Chicawan, Loverstine, Duester, Ivlar, Carder, Gattis, Elibella, Wilco, Uzzle, Walena, Clarinett, Irenner, Dust, Idorice, Plevna, Glidewell, Ruble, Eratta, Versie, Odeal, Wordia, Ivo, Gaudie, Amplias, Bottis, Letcher, Boitnott, Dahdee, Sirviter, Texal, Coatree, Raydene, Molar, Snora, Floisell, Marvelene, 3-in-1, Parizada, Ettarhea, Monyerdill, Cleader, Erdeal, Icyphine, Detroy, Almateen, Mossalene, Lather, Ondrewal, Degena, Carmage, Mayanice, LaVora, Exzonia, Rubidick, Warrenzetta, Dionioush, Zaltha, LaVilla, Costromia, Weedia, Errieabelle, Curnel, Idiat, Lassie, Yuletide, Dilemma, Exmeater, Dusner, Colbertine, Neathel, Sompoon, Mancle, Condromel, Amyet, Arstralia, Voneita, Woolfolk, Gairoid, Glennietta, Epluribus, Nature, Earth, Floryburtus, Clevious, Sylzetta, Bethene, Aldurie, Aftion, and Cefus.

Uncommon first names start seeming not all that uncommon when you consider the likes of Alduris, Crese, Cube, Efel, Elector, Gurthur, Oather, LaKay, Celius, Derl, Theester, Theople, Vanora, Cala, Pantelis, Doisia, Hylden, Youlon, Creme, Orion, Novelite, Baisber, Cordis, Delissa, Dorty, Heard, Lupton, Oena, Shed, Safronia, Sequoia, Sattoria, Crumly, Autice, Cola, Marbeline, Odis, Prew, Valleylord, Baz, Boss, Ecton, Valmont, Azoline, Antoon, Etura, Ortheldo,

Orgia, Osco, Oakfred, Loumisha, Flake, Vermel, Beausee, Mygleetus, Domingle, Barbanel, Plomer, Whirlee, Fairy, Lionginas, Square, Budge, Dimple, Earslean, Flavel, Jetty, Leadith, Lorce, Neotris, Nozilion, Petroleum, Nudie, Idus, Omerzell, Burlie, Truvan, Vyrilla, Walterbelle, Luster, Beadie, Bluncie, Eldorado, Dull, Drone, Bugg, Bumm, Burden, Izula, Peanut, Louder, Grisgbeth, Velva, Mebane, Grasper, Congress, Fructuoso, Collus, Aluscious, Sulvylyty, Ostrich, Ozelma, Quetta, Blizzard, Ambrizella, Newborn, Yourene, Especulia, and Dink.

To repeat, these are all real first names, as are these: Noba, Literee, Uuno, Vanilla, Lavatrice, Ottar, Lugertha, Tulio, Pando, Given, Welcome, Calvester, Orrige, Risker, Bullock, Laughter, Ether, Ophalandus, Guffie, Laychester, Iduma, MaGirl, Sebaldus, Vesta, Ferrel, Norment, Banana, Oquinee, Elephair, Flenell, Dortch, Cage, Stick, Corpus, Bunch, Diddle, Memoree, Chess, Chlorine, Xzin, Bondola, Stid, Zerhona, Zula, Ozro, Brain, Ermal, Pirttrue, Parreadier, Puella, Frizzell, Frizette, Mirtnia, Rudenia, Reboykin, Dermes, Fedlise, Boost, Boot, Binge, Suck, Spjut, Lockytee, Social, Hurtless, Orloph, Rayvon, Canary, Desselonger, Fonisha, Litrid, Moton, Quince, Weeter, Hugger, Jelley, Monador, Chastine, Ortrue, Hival, Utley, Sledge, Skink, Eureka, Grizell, Onan, Tarward, Emerine, Thelbert, Toxie, Birdia, Atari, Kook, Toiletta, Strophair, Brie, Lurty, and Lemonella

The point is made by now, but it would be a shame to leave out Skurdy, Blottie, Permel-ley, Jobyna, Hudeter, Kolon, Layfonza, Swarnery, Pecola, Thousand, Tschopp, Walkup, Whitehair, Weepie, Wedlock, Volgan, Valex, Nedator, Kenolin, Bessola, Dauffus, Exabelle, Zephame, Zorable, Oversia, Loss, Tute, Okla, Nylon, and Rearis.

Reading this list helps one understand why a recent survey which asked students about their first names yielded a whopping 46% who said they were unhappy with the names their parents had given them.

Well-Named!

A Train of Thought 32

When it was announced in 1984 that a train was about to start a run between New York and Washington, I was thrilled to hear that it would be called the American Zephyr. It was an appropriate name for a luxury train with cars from the 1940s which have been restored to their original art deco elegance. In some small degree, this offset the news of a year earlier that the Rio Grande Zephyr had made its last pass through the Rockies as Amtrak took over the last of the old private passenger trains.

This announcement created an immediate craving for more train names. To be sure, there are still a small handful of impressive "name" trains in the Amtrak system, among them the Coast Starlight, the Southwest Limited, and the Desert Wind. But I needed old, evocative names—names that stood by themselves as intense, undiluted nostalgia.

If *American Zephyr* has the unmistakable ring of the 1940s or early 1950s, it is because that was when the nation had hundreds of named trains. A list of 700-odd named trains, published by the Association of American Railroads in 1952, offers a rich sampling of adventurous naming with the Afternoon Steeler, the Aroostook Flyer, the Atlantic Express, the Broadway Limited, the California Zephyr, the Choctaw Rocket, the City of New Orleans, the Connecticut Yankee, the Dixie Flyer, El Capitan, El Dorado, the Fast Flying Virginian (F.F.V., for short), the Eskimo, the Hawkeye, the King Coal, the Nellie Bly, the Night Owl, the Powhatan Arrow, the Silver Comet, the Super Chief, the Tuxedo, and the Twentieth Century Limited.

One needs more, though, and next I found myself in the library of the Association of American Railroads flipping through the 1937 list, where I found hundreds of names that were new to me—the Egyptian Zipper, the 11 O'Clock Katy, the Green Diamond, the Maple Leaf, the Scranton Flyer, the Tippecanoe, the Azalean, and the Anthracite

Express, to name a few. I found that the naming of the whole train is a relatively recent development, but that locomotives have been named since 1831.

I was hooked. I learned that the C&O once named its new passenger diesels after famous race horses—Dan Patch, Seabiscuit, Twenty Grand—and that freight trains had names, and I savored a new list with names like *Hobo, Naked Lady, Blue Streak, Long Suffering, Mad Run,* and *Bethlehem Star.* Next I find in an old issue of *Names* a collection of 19th-century names for locomotives of the Central Pacific. These were great steel machines with befitting names: *Rattler, Apollo, Clipper, Jupiter, Vesuvius,* and, for a monster freight locomotive, *El Gobedor.*

El Gobedor is a wonderful name rendered doubly wonderful when you realize that many bridges and trestles had to be reinforced to take its weight. So too is *Phoebe Snow,* which graced the cars of the Lackawanna R.R. It is a beautiful, haunting name which loses none of its allure when you learn that she was a fiction—a name plucked out of the air by an advertising man who needed a name for a woman in a white dress, who could ride the line all day without getting dirty. She was there to show that the Lackawanna locomotives burned anthracite coal and not soft coal. So the line became "the Route of Phoebe Snow."

I was not finished until I ended up, on a Sunday afternoon when I should have been weeding or walking around in a museum, inside a building where railroad collectors and buffs assembled to buy, sell, and trade rail memorabilia. I came to collect names, and they were everywhere, not just as names, but as logos on dining car china, timetables, and posters. *Silver Meteor* is written in blue and silver; the name *Golden State* encircles a cluster of oranges, and I find stationery which says "En Route: The Grand Canyon Limited."

Driving home from this event with a pad full of names and a few yellowing sheets of stationery from the parlor cars of these trains, I tried to analyze the odd craving which has come on me and is only just now being satisfied after hundreds of these names have been whispered and inhaled. (Name collecting involves lip movement—you cannot fully savor a name by just reading it, any more than you can enjoy a good wine by just looking at it.)

I think that it has to do with poetry, but not poetry in the normal sense of structured verse. It is the poetry of names themselves—one, a few, hundreds—and is celebrated in a few lines by Stephen Vincent Benet, which kept running through my mind as I stalked train names at a show for railroad buffs:

> *I have fallen in love with American names:*
> *The sharp, gaunt names that never get fat;*
> *The snakeskin-titles of mining-claims;*
> *The plumed war-bonnet of Medicine Hat,*
> *Tucson and Deadwood and Lost Mule Flat.*

Benet's point about "the snakeskin-titles of mining-claims" led to a hunt for some of these, and the result was the list in the box on the opposite page, based in large part on names appearing in *A Treasury of American Folklore.*

Benet was writing of place names, but it applies to train names as well. It does not apply to commercial aviation. Part of the romance of railroading is the names—not just the trains, but the lines. On the other hand, this romance is lacking when we ride in numbered things like Flight 457 that have no names. Could there have been romance associated with the Orient Express or the Empire Builder if their names had been three-digit numbers? Of course not.

While planes have succumbed to numbering, it was not always so. Lindbergh named his plane the Spirit of St. Louis, and Wiley Post had his Winnie Mae, and during World War II, B-29 bombers had nicknames illustrated on the side of the plane. Fine nicknames they were too: consider *Mad Russian, Arkansas Traveler, Banshee, Royal Flush, Impatient Virgin, First Nighter, Sexy Texan, Never Satisfied, Bugs, El Diablo,* and *Spare Parts.*

I have an unprovable theory that plane names ceased being amusing and usable when the Enola Gay, named for the pilot's mother, dropped an atomic bomb named Little Boy on Hiroshima, and a plane named Bock's Car (after one of its pilots Capt. Fred Bock) dropped one named Fat Man on Nagasaki. Later Dave's Dream dropped Gilda on Bikini. This kind of gross incongruity has not stopped. To this day nuclear tests have disarming names; over the years the names have come from golf (Backswing), mixed drinks (Daiquiri), boat parts (Rudder), games (Backgammon), and cheeses (Edam, followed by Stilton, Camembert, and Muenster). In 1983, the folks at the Los Alamos nuclear laboratory told reporter Harry Jaffe of Network News Service that future tests would be named for kinds of pasta, Spanish names for birds, and New Mexico localities.

One old railroad tradition which has been transferred to planes is giving them derogatory nicknames that are close to the real names. In the old days, the Toledo, Peoria and Western had so many nicknames that it published a booklet of them, ranging from "Tired, Poor and Weary" to "Tried, Proven and Worthy." In addition, there were: Leavenworth, Kansas and Western as "Leave Kansas and Walk"; the

Mining Claims

American Hollow.

Barefoot Diggings, Bloomer Hill, Blue-Belly Ravine, Bob Ridley Flat, Bogus Thunder, Brandy Flat, Brandy Gulch.

Cayote Hill, Centipede Hollow, Chicken-Thief Flat, Christian Flat, Chucklehead Diggings, Coon Hollow.

Dead Man's Bar, Dead Mule Cañon, Dead Wood, Devil's Basin.

Gas Hill, Git-up-and-git, Gold Hill, Gopher Flat, Gospel Gulch, Gouge Eye, Graveyard Cañon, Greasers' Camp, Greenhorn Cañon, Gridiron Bar, Grizzly Flat, Ground Hog's Glory, Guano Hill.

Happy Valley, Hell's Delight, Hen-Roost Camp, Humbug Cañon, Humpback Slide, Hungry Camp, Hog's Diggings, Horsetown.

Jackass Gulch, Jim Crow Cañon.

Ladies' Cañon, Ladies' Valley, Last Chance, Lazy Man's Cañon, Liberty Hill, Loafer Hill, Loafer's Retreat, Logtown, Lousy Ravine, Love-Letter Camp.

Man Cañon, Miller's Defeat, Mount Zion, Mud Springs, Murderer's Bar.

Nary Red, Nutcake Camp.

One Eye.

Paint-Pot Hill, Pancake Ravine, Paradise, Pepper-Box Flat, Petticoat Slide, Piety Hill, Pike Hill, Plug-Head Gulch, Poker Flat, Poodletown, Poor Man's Creek, Port Wine, Poverty Hill, Puke Ravine, Puppytown, Push-Coach Hill.

Quack Hill.

Ragtown, Rat Trap Slide, Rattlesnake Bar, Red Dog, Rough and Ready.

Seven-by-nine Valley, Seven-up Ravine, Seventy-Six, Shanghai Hill, Shinbone Peak, Shirt-tail Cañon, Skinflint, Skunk Gulch, Slap Jack Bar, Sluice Fork, Snow Point, Stud-Horse Cañon, Sugar-Loaf Hill, Swellhead Diggings.

Whiskey Bar, Wild Cat Bar, Wild Goose Flat.

Yankee Doodle.

Lancashire and Yorkshire as "Languid and Yawning"; and the Midland and Great Northern as "Muddle and Get No-where." This process is not over for trains. Long-suffering London commuters call the new railway line from Bedford to St. Pancras "the Bedpan Line."

Today we have United as "Untied"; TWA as "Try Walking Away"; Air France as "Air Chance"; Misrair (Egypt) as "Misery Air"; and El Al as "Every Landing Always Late". But this is hardly compensation for the loss of named trains.

When I grieve for the loss of train names and the lack of plane names, I seek comfort elsewhere, for example, in the comfort station. Working within a very confined field, those who name portable toilets have demonstrated ability in naming: Comfort Castles, Porta-John, Sani-Hut, Trail Can, Honey Pots, Head House, Johnny on the Spot, and Rosepot.

Collecting odd lists of names is an old and cherished tradition which has engaged some of our finest minds. Some collectors are private people, who make little of this hobby, but others show off their work. A classic example was the poet W. H. Auden, who published some of his findings in his book *A Certain World*. Auden's tastes ran from "Names of Veins in the Lead-Mining District of Tideswell, Derbyshire" to those for genitalia.

Examples from the former:

> Barbara Load
> Dirtland Rake
> Pyenest
> Old Nestor's Pipe
> Horse-Buttock

And from the latter:

Male	Female
Stargazer	Fumbler's Hall
Bald-headed Hermit	Growler
Jack-in-the-Cellar	Millner's Shop
Impudence	Penwiper

If one reads back through the *Bulletin of the American Name Society* and the journal *Names*, one finds that members have collected in such diverse realms as shrine temples, cigars, engagement rings, pencils, massage parlors, bowl games, prescription drugs, street gangs, and San Francisco taverns (although that collector missed my favorite, a bar called He's Not Here). One man actually came up with 32 names for sea floor habitats, while another has found 65 children's nicknames for fingers and toes from old nursery rhymes, including these for the third toe: *grimthistle, Tommy Tistle, Tommy Tissle, Harry Whible,* and *Minnie Wilkin*.

Here are some lists put together by the author as well as friends and associates. They are not meant to be comprehensive but rather a finale to show the unlimited possibilities of name collecting.

Comfort Castle

A

Associations and societies. Londoner Denys Parsons has long collected association names, and he has provided his all-time favorites for use here, some of which appear in his book *What's Where in London*. His all-star list:

The Large Black Pig Society, the Midland Area Netherland Dwarf Club, the National Federation of Master Steeplejacks and Lightning Conductor Engineers, the American Cockroach and Blackbeetle Solvent Company, the National Association of Boot & Shoe Toe Puff Manufacturers, the National Feather Purifiers Association, the Shot and Grit Association, the Association of Animal Gut Cleaners, the Shoddy and Mungo Manufacturers' Association, the Committee on Slipperiness of the Permanent International Association of Road Congresses, the Potato Synonyms Committee, and the Self-Opening Box Company, which is his favorite. "What's the point of buying one?" he asks. "How on earth would I keep it shut?"

Awards.

Arkies (arcade games).
Bennies (printing, after Ben Franklin).
Bessies (dancing, after dance teacher Bessie Schonberg).
Bloopies (radio and TV bloopers).
Clios (TV commercials).
Daphnes (furniture design).
Edgars (mystery novels and books).
Emmys (TV, a personalizing of Immy, for image orthicon, the television picture tube).
Hugos (science fiction writing).
Oscars (movies).
Tonys (theater).

C

College humor magazines. A few of many names from S. Percy Dean, who has an amazing collection of the actual magazines. Only a handful are still being published.

Alabama *Rammer Jammer*, Arkansas *Hogwash*, Bates *Buffoon*, Bowdoin *Bear Skin*, Brigham Young *Y's Guy*, Colorado *Dodo*, Denison *Flamingo*, Florida *Orange Peel*, Georgia *Cracker*, Hobart *Pot*, Illinois *Shaft*, Indiana *Bored Walk*, Johns Hopkins *Black & Blue Jay*, Kansas *Sour Owl*, Kentucky *Sour Mash*, Maine *Mainiac*, Massachusetts *Yahoo*, Middlebury *Blue Baboon*, Minnesota *Ski-u-mah*, Montclair *Gallumph*, North Carolina *Tar & Feathers*, Northwestern *Purple Parrot*, Oberlin *Interabang*, Occidental *Fang*, Oregon State *Orange Owl*, Purdue *Rivit*, Rider *Roughrider*, Rutgers *Rut*, St. Lawrence *Scarlet Saint*, San Francisco *State Fog*, South Dakota *Wet Hen*, Toronto *Goblin*, UCLA *Satyr*, USC *Wampus*, VMI *Sniper*, Wabash *Caveman*, Western Reserve *Red Cat*, West Virginia *Shampain*, and Williams *Purple Cow*.

F

Flies for fishing. All of these were collected in the fishing department at L.L. Bean in Freeport, Maine. They possess a remarkable diversity: Rusty Rat, Gray Ghost, Royal Coachman, Woolly Leech, Senator Muskie, Blue Dun Midge, Cinnamon Fur Ant, Libby's Smelt, The Horror, Mouse Rat Bug, Blue Spent Damsel Dragon, Matuke Sculpin, Harold's Tiger, Callibaetis, Black Nose Dace, Bolshevik, Magog Smelt, Mickey Finn, Mary Pickford, Warden's Worry, Pink Lady, Olive Latex, and Rat Face.

G

Grams. In 1975, Western Union signed off on its singing telegram. The void was filled by hundreds of independent companies, who have been offering outlandish services for the last 20 years:

Act-A-Grams

A&H Sizzlegram (features, among other things, a stripping bag lady who turns into a sexy lady)

Bagelgram

Basket-gram

Belly Telegram

Buddha-Gram

Cuddlegram

Give-A-Gram

Gorillagram

Impression-Gram

Melodeegram

Monkeygram

Pizza Gram

Preppygram

Salami-A-Gram

Sleepygrams, and, of course, the

Strip-A-Gram, which in turn leads us to stripper stage names.

Over the years, I have collected these fine examples: Candy Barr, Norma Vincent Peel, Sybil Rights, Rachel Prejudice, Celestial Body, the Gaza Stripper, Thoroughly Naked Millie, Sakatumi (who is Japanese), and Luna Walker (her motto: "A Celestial Body. . . . Step Out for All Mankind").

H

Hong Kong businesses. Partially because the Chinese custom is to name businesses with good fortune in mind, lists of Hong Kong businesses are a delight to read. Here is a small selection of past and present enterprises, with a few other eastern institutions with English names thrown in for good measure.

Those marked with an asterisk were listed by the *China Morning Post* of Hong Kong in 1983 as companies which have been created and registered as ready-made entities waiting for a buyer. Some may still be for sale.

Amazing Grace Elephant Co.

Angel Visiting Massage.

Brightest Optical Co.

Cheerful Consolidated Enterprises Ltd.

Cheerful Development Corp.

Chinese Permanent Cemeteries

Cunning Investments Co. Ltd.*

Darling Hand Glove Factory

Earth Fat Investments Co. Ltd.*

Eternal Life Co.

Everlasting Incombustible Celluloid Works.

Excelling Other Trading Co. Ltd.*

Fever Summer Co. Ltd.*

Fulminate Co. Ltd.*

Garble Gardens (an apartment complex).

God Given Development Co. Ltd.*

Happy Marriage Curtain Co.

Happy VD Clinic (Taiwan).

Honey Moon Factory.

Hung Fat Brassiere Co. I wrote to Ursula Roberts, who does a weekly column on words for the *Hong Kong Post*, and who added many names to this list, to check this entry. She replied that there was such a company and that there were three columns of Hung Fats in the business telephone directory, adding "But I don't think you should include these in your book, because funny though they sound in English, Hung Fat in Cantonese means Prosperity, so it's a good name for an enterprise." The point is well taken, but I had to include just one, and I omitted Hang Ons, of which there are many.

Lucky Horse Cake Factory. According to a 1982 *Wall Street Journal* item on Hong Kong business names, there were 201 businesses whose names began with the word *Lucky*.

Marvelous Investment Co.

Morally Excellent Trading Ltd.*

More Profit Enterprises Ltd.*

Plastic Bacon Factory.

Porn Beauty Shop (Thailand).

Sincere Underwear Co.

Until Rich Enterprises Co.*

Venice Mechanical Macaroni Factory.

Walking Medicine Co.

Wider Garments Ltd.

Win Hand Full Co. Ltd.*

House and farm names.

After Math. Home of a retired professor of mathematics.

Bedside Manor. A doctor's house.

Chez When. Residence of a journalist who loved his toddy.

Dunrovin. One of the ever-popular Duns along with *Dunrentin* and *Dunmovin*. People who use Dun names tend to go to out to dinner at places called the Dew Drop Inn and the Elbow Room.

Drop Anchor. Home of someone formerly at sea in the Navy or merchant marine.

Fallen Arches. Cottage with structural decay.

Gross House. No. 144.

Lake Inferior. A small body of water on poet Louis Untermeyer's estate.

Lost Horizons. House on the south coast of Britain whose view was blocked by a new building.

No Trespassing. Cole Porter's summer place, which is reminiscent of an old Maryland plantation "The Knave Keep Out."

Oshim. Acronym for "Our Summer Home in Maine."

Wit's End. Alexander Wollcott's apartment, named by Dorothy Parker.

Writer's Cramp. Home of writer Jerome Beatty.

M

Mc's. These are all real and come from telephone directories. The collection was inspired by the McChicken and McMuffin.

McCargo	McBroom
McJunkin	McCoo
McGull	McCave
McGlumphy	McCrank
McBorrows	McSwords
McPoland	McCommon
McQuestion	McClam
Mc-Million	McHerald
McLuckie	Mc-Cluggage
McClay	McGuinea
McNail	McAvinue
McProud	McBath
McCrystal	McDerby
McCruel	McClew
McCrone	McColour
McCluster	McNatt
McBrin	McHorse
McZeal	McGlory
McGirl	McQuality
McWeeny	McOstrich
McBroom	McZinc
McThirsty	McClean
McClear	

MX missile schemes. When President Reagan's plan to deploy the MX missile ran into trouble in 1982, he renamed it Peacemaker. This made an already confusing picture even more confusing because of the many schemes for basing the missile that have been advanced since 1976. Senator Ted Kennedy was able to find 34 separate plans which he inserted in the *Congressional Record* on May 20, 1983. Kennedy's list vividly displays how hard it is to keep track of the ever-changing names for weapons projects.

The list:

1. Launch Under Attack.
2. Orbital Based.
3. Shallow Underwater Missile.
4. Hydra.
5. ORCA.
6. Ship-Inland.
7. Ship-Ocean.
8. Sea Sitter.
9. Wide Body Jet.
10. Short Takeoff and Landing.
11. Vertical Takeoff and Landing.
12. Dirigible.
13. Midgetman.
14. Hard Rock Silo.
15. Hard Tunnel.
16. South Side Basing.
17. Sandy Silo.
18. Commercial Rail.
19. Dedicated Rail.
20. Off-Road Mobile.
21. Ground Effect Machine.
22. Road Mobile—Minuteman.
23. Road Mobile—New Missile.
24. Covered Trench.
25. Hybrid Trench.
26. Dash to Shelter.
27. Mobile Front End.
28. POOL.
29. Minuteman/MPS.
30. MX/MPS.
31. Continuous Airborne Aircraft.
32. Deep Underground Basing.
33. Ballistic Missile Defense.
34. Dense Pack.

N

Nuclear power plants. These are fascinating because they sound more like names you might expect to find on jars and spray cans in the personal products section of the drug store. Whisper them:

San Onofre	Zimmer	Seabrook
Summer	St. Lucie	McGuire
LaSalle	Bellefonte	Catawba
Ginna	Kewaunee	Oconee
Peach Bottom	Salem	Sequoia
Surry	Susquehanna	

About the only reactor names that sound like reactors are *Diablo Canyon* and *Vogtle*, which is pronounced *vo-gel*.

R

Roller coasters. Texas Cyclone, Texas Giant, Screamin' Eagle, Great American Scream Machine, Rebel Yell, Python, Screamin' Demon, King Kobra, Turn of the Century, Berserker, Big Bad Wolf, Thunderbolt, Fury of the Nile, Hydro-Force Rampage, Edge, Mind Bender, Big Dipper, Sky Rocket, Montezooma's Revenge, Z-Force, Viper, Chaos, Steel Phantom, Mean Streak, Kumba, Raptor, Demon, Mister Twister, Beast, Comet, Wildcat, and Batman: The Ride.

S

Shaving colognes. Royal Saddle, Green Moss, Live Oak, Panache, Aromatic Tabac, Manzanilla, Scoundrel, and Careful How You Use It.

Soda fountain apparatus. Gordon

Dean, the great collector of soda fountain apparatus, helped put this list together. Most of these regal names came from the period 1875-1890 and were produced by the Lippincott and Tufts companies.

Mayflower, Siberian Arctic, Tudor, Norman, Chimborazo, Clarendon, Ursuline, Alaska Spray, Polar Wave, Minneapolitan, Minnehaha, Magnolia, Emperor, Crusader, Cyprus, Manitoba, Polaris, Nanon, Naxos, and L'Orient.

T

Tests and other educational materials. Many of these are from Robert S. Shaver, a speech pathologist whose mailbox is constantly filled with catalogs offering such things as:

GIFT: Group Inventory for Finding Creative Talent.
PIAT: Peabody Individual Achievement Test.
SICCS: Social Interaction and Creativity in Communication System.
SIT: Slossen Intelligence Test.
TIME: Training in Marriage Enrichment.
TOLD: Test of Language Development.
TOWL: Test of Written Language.
WRAT: Wide Range Achievement Test.

Towns and Villages in England and Scotland which I would like to visit because of their names. This list was created for this chapter by two English gentlemen, Jimmy Jump of Essex and Ross Reader of Hampshire, proving that English village names are not odd-sounding only to people outside of the British Isles.

A

Affpuddle, Aird of Sleat, Allhallows, Alsop-en-le-Dale, Amble, Aquhythie, Artentinny.

Punk Rock Groups

No gourmet set of name lists would be complete without at least a handful of punk/new wave names which already have a certain quaintness about them.

Billy Clone and the Same, Bad Brains, Jody Foster's Army, Meat Puppets, Platinum Slugs, Soylent Greene, The Irving Thunderbutt Project, Sweaty Tools, Suicidal Tendencies, The Hump, Voidoids, The Last Words of Dutch Schultz, Cheap Perfume, Plummet Airlines, Johnny and the Self-Abusers, Buzzcocks, Tim Buk 3, X, Curse of the Atomic Greasers, Intestines from Space, Insurance Salesmen from Saturn, Tongues on Fire, Impaler, Jack Rubys, Yuppies Suck, Teenage Jesus and the Jerks, Immaculate Consumptive, KGB Secret, Single Bullet Theory, 10,000 Maniacs, Violent Fems, Penetrators, Fad Gadget, Siouxsie and the Banshees, Discharge, The Stains, 17 Pygmies, Cardboard Brains, Zero Option, Chronic Submission, Dick Duck and the Dorks, Ant in Yer Pants, Rubber Rodeo, DOA, Sub-Mensas, Cramps, and The The.

Correspondent Scott A. Beskow of De Kalb, Illinois, creates punk/alternative band names as a hobby. Some of the groups that have played in his mind: Burlap Panties, Liverwurst, Grampa's Libido, Napalm Whisper, Newt, The Ombudsmen, Headless Torso, Zoo Parents, Limping Sisters, Fruity Toes, Rubber Baby Buggy Bumpers, Brick Windows, Bladderwort, No Eraser, and Lint.

B

Bag Enderby, Bandoddle, Beer, Boot, Booth, Bowling, Bride, Buckler's Hard, Bugthorpe, Bulldoo, Bunny, Burpham.

C

Canton, Cargo, Chalk, Chewton Mendip, Chimney, Chipping Sodbury, Clatter, Coat, Cotton, Creed.

D

Druid, Duddo.

E

Edith Weston, Egypt, Enterkinfoot, Eye.

F

Flag, Forest, Foxholes, Freefolk, Friday Bridge, Friendly, Frog End, Fugglestone St. Peter.

G

Gallowstree Elm, Gedney Drove End, Gibralter, Good Easter, Great Snoring.

H

Heyop, Hinton-in-the-Hedges, Hook, Hope, Hope Bowdler, Horsey, Hose, Huish Champflower, Huish Episcopi, Harbottle, Hartburn, Hutton Le Hole.

I

Idle, Inch, Inkpen, Intake, Iron Cross.

J

Jump.

K

Knotting.

L

Landewednack, Laysters Pole, Leek, Libanus, Lickey End, Loose, Lower Peover, Lower Upham.

M

Martin Hassingtree, Maypole, Melbury Abbas, Melbury Bubb, Merlin's Bridge, Moneydie, Mousehole, Mucking.

N

Nasty, Nap End, Nempnett Thrubwell, Nocktorum, Nomansland.

O

Oare, Oath, Ogle, Over Wallop.

P

Piddletrenthide, Pig Street, Pill, Plush, Polyphant, Potto, Puddletown.

R

Rails, Rake, Rassa, Ripe, Rotton Row.

S

Sail, Salt, St. Just-in-Roseland, St. Michaels-on-Wyre, Sebastopol, Seething, Selling, Shelf, Shut End, Shutta, Sliddery, Snig's End, Snitter, Spittle, Steeple Bumstead, Stobo, Stow-cum-Quy, Stragglethorpe, Strata Florida, Swine.

T

Toller Fratrum, Toller Porcorum, Tongue, Triangle, Troy, Tumble, Twenty.

U

Ugley, Up Hill, Upper Slaughter.

W

Warmley, Welcome, Whale, Wildboarclough, Wincle, Wool, Wormhill, Worthy, Wrangle.

Y

Yelling.

Z

Zeal Monachorum.

Mr. Jump adds: "In England there are places named Hoo, How, Wye, Ware and Wyche, but I can't find any place called When." Ross Reader adds that she is also infatuated with these English names: the *Church of St. Petrock*, *Christmas Pie* (an area near Puttenham Surrey), and *Dunkery Beacon* (a hill in Somerset).

Towns and villages in Australia which I would like to visit because of their names.

B

Badgebup (Western Australia), Banana (Queensland), Basin Pocket (Queensland), Blanket Flat (New South Wales), Blowhard (Victoria), Bob's Farm (New South Wales), Boinka (Victoria), Botany (New South Wales), Bow Bowing (New South Wales), Bowelling (Western Australia), Brit Brit (Victoria), Broad Arrow (Western Australia), Brungle (New South Wales), Buckleboo (South Australia), Bumbaldry (New South Wales), Bunyip (Victoria), Burpengary (Queensland) Burrumbuttock (New South Wales), Byaduk (Victoria).

C

Carapooee (Victoria), Cement Mills (Queensland), Charleyong (New South Wales), Cheepie (Queensland), Chinkapook (Victoria), Chittering (Western Australia), Chorkerup (Western Australia), Colly Blue (New South Wales), Come-By-Chance (New South Wales), Coolongalook (New South Wales), Crooble (New South Wales).

D

Dandongadale (Victoria), Devils Gate (Tasmania), Diddleum Plains (Tasmania), Drik Drik (Victoria), Dumbleyung (Western Australia), Dunbible (New South Wales).

E

Egg and Bacon Bay (Tasmania), Elong Elong (New South Wales).

F

Fairy Dell (Victoria), Fannie Bay (Tasmania), Fiddle Town (New South Wales), Fine Flower Creek (New South Wales), Flowerpot (Tasmania).

G

Galore (New South Wales), Geranium (South Australia), Gnotuk (Victoria), Gol Gol (New South Wales), Goodnight (New South Wales), Goshen (Tasmania), Grabben Gullen (New South Wales), Gringegalgona (Victoria), Grong Grong (New South Wales), Gumly Gumly (New South Wales), Gunpowder (Queensland).

H

Hat Head (New South Wales), Hicksborough (Victoria), Hollow Tree (Tasmania), Howlong (New South Wales), Humpty Doo (Tasmania).

J

Jaspers Brush (New South Wales), Jeetho (Victoria), Jingalup (Western Australia).

K

Katamatite (Victoria), Keepit Dam (New South Wales), Ki Ki (South Australia), Killcare (New South Wales), Kindred (Tasmania), Knorrit Flat (New South Wales).

L

Launching Place (Victoria), Lottah (Tasmania).

M

Ma Ma Creek (Queensland), Marble Bar (Western Australia), Meander (Tasmania),

Merrigoen (New South Wales), Merrijig (Victoria), Merrywinebone (New South Wales), Miners Rest (Victoria), Missabotti (New South Wales), Mohomets Flat (Western Australia), Mooball (New South Wales), Mossiface (Victoria), Mumballup (Western Australia).

N

Naringaningalook East (Victoria), Nar Nar Goon (Victoria), Nevertire (New South Wales), Nildottie (Western Australia), Number One (New South Wales).

O

Ozenkadnook (Victoria).

P

Patchewollock (Victoria), Pearshape (Tasmania), Perisher Valley (New South Wales), Putty (New South Wales).

R

Retreat (Victoria), Rollingstone (Queensland).

S

Salmon Gums (Western Australia), Salt Ash (New South Wales), Seventeen Mile Rocks (Queensland), Smiggin Holes (New South Wales), Snug (Tasmania), Sodwalls (New South Wales), Spit Junction (New South Wales).

T

Tabberabbera (Victoria), Tallygaroopna (Victoria), Taylors Arm (New South Wales), Terry Hie Hie (New South Wales), The Risk (New South Wales), The Spectacles (Western Australia), Thredbo (New South Wales), Tin Can Bay (Queensland), Toodyay (Western Australia), Tumbi Umbi (New South Wales), Tumbulgum (New South Wales).

U

Ubobo (Queensland), Underbool (Victoria).

W

Waaia (Victoria), Wagga Wagga (New South Wales), Wandering (Western Australia), Warrumbungle (New South Wales), Wee Jasper (New South Wales), Wee Waa (New South Wales), Wickepin (Western Australia), Woohlpooer (Victoria), Wyalkatchem (Western Australia).

Y

Yackandandah (Victoria), Yass (New South Wales), Yea (Victoria), Yorkeys Knob (Queensland), Yunderup (Western Australia).

Yellows. Colors represent one of the greatest opportunities for the name collector. I am partial to names that describe a color without naming the color (*emerald* for a green, rather than, say, *deep green*). The National Bureau of Standards keeps tabs on color names from a number of fields (paints, textiles, biology, etc.) and periodically publishes vast lists of them. Here are just a few yellows which don't use the word *yellow* to get the idea across:

Old Gold, Popcorn, Orpin, Lemon, Oxgall, Veiled Sun, Maize, Cockatoo, Cornsilk, Indian Saffron, Honeysweet, Mustard, Sunlight, Apricot Sherbet, Jonquil, Sauterne, Cuban Sand, Bamboo, Chamois, Buttercup, Dandelion, Flavus, Pond Lily, Turmeric, Snapdragon, Ceres, Luteolus, Wheat, Ecru-Olive, Murmur, Milwaukee Brick, Spanish Flesh, Canary-bird Green, Melleus, Fall Bronze, Curcuma, and Mimosa.

The national listing, published as *Color: Universal Language and Dictionary of*

Names, is a delightful directory for those who like names like *Cold Morn*, *Vamp*, *French Nude*, *Pearly Gates*, *Wafted Feather*, *Paris Mud*, *Kitten's Ear*, *Teen Age Pink*, and *Folly*, or find it intriguing that African Green is a blue or that there are more than 50 names for black (including *Iron Mask*, *Raven*, *Bayou*, *Lava*, and *Nubian*) and several hundred grays (such as *Gargoyle*, *Mole*, *Pigeon's Neck*, *Slag*, and *Rodent*).

Jan Kusko of the National Bureau of Standards Public Information office, who found a copy of *Color* for me some years ago, noted in a cover letter, "I'm particularly fond of Deep Dull Violaceous Blue and Livid Violet."

An Apt Name for an Association

Naming Names

An Acknowledgment

Mainly because of an earlier book I wrote on words, I got a lot of letters from people whom I was able to tell about my plans for this book. They, and a number of old friends, helped with this book. Here is a list of helpmates who together possess more than half the collective generosity of the Western Hemisphere and at least a quarter of its IQ. I thank them here in the most important list of names in the book.

A

Mabel Adams
Reinhold Aman
Suzie Radus Ament
Jay Ames
W. R. Anderson
Russell Ash
Jack Van Auken

B

Joseph E. Badger
Dr. Robert Baker
Kathy Bankhead
J. T. Battersby
Scott A. Beskow
Ray Boltha
Elizabeth Brooks
David Broome
M. M. Bruce
Caroline Bryan
Charlie Bryant
Wendell E. Bulger
Judy Burr

C

Chris Carlisle
Lawrence Casler
Martha Cornog
Frank Celentano
Edgar C. Chamberlin
Howard Channing
Phillip Chaplin

Pete Christianson
John Clark
Gerald Conrad
Kate Contos
Norman Corwin
Raymond G. A. Cote
Dan Crawford
Don Crinklaw

D

Gordon B. Dean
S. Percy Dean
L. Sprague de Camp
Gene Deitch
Al deQuoy
Andrew Dickson
Nancy Dickson
Brian Doyle
Stephen B. Dudley
John Duffie
the late Russ Dunn, Sr.
Frederick C. Dyer

E

Gerald M. Eisenhower
Margaret R. S. Ellis
George Englebretsen
Willard Espy
Cleveland Kent Evans

F

James E. Farmer
Felix Fellhaur

Wayne H. Finke
the late Barbara Rainbow
    Fletcher
Joe Foote
Ray Foster
Alex Fraser
Ira Freedman
Lewis Burke Frumkes
Monika Fuchs

G

Martin Gardner
Walt Gianchini
Tim Gibson
Dorethea Gildar
Robert B. Giles
Ray Gill
Thomas E. Gill
E. S. Goldman
Joel Goodman
Joseph C. Goulden
Anne Graham

H

Stephen Haase
the late Irving Hale
Don Hall
Kelsie Harder
Raymond Harris
Bonnie Hartwig
Edwin A. Haselbauer
John Hazlitt
George A. Heinemann

the late Bob Snider
Ron Stall
Warren E. Steffen
Norman D. Stevens
J. O. Stevenson
Dick Stewart
Carol N. Stix

T

Bill Tammeus
Laurie Taylor
the late James Thorpe III
Robert J. Throckmorton
Dan Tilque
William Tilton
Joe M. Turner

U

Laurence Urdang

V

Scott L. Vanatter
Elaine Viets

W

David Walsh
Roger D. Way
Mike Webb
Martin Weiss
Bob and Mary West
Roy West

J. van de Weyer
Robert D. Wheeler
Joe White
Rick Winston
Margaret Whitesides
Neal Wilgus
Austin Tack Wilkie
Ben Willis
Robert J. Wilson
Mrs. Kenneth Worthing

Y

Philip A. Young

Z

Robert J. Zani

Thanks once again.

A large part of the research for this book was done with the aid of hundreds of newspaper articles found in clipping morgues including the old *Washington Star* files now at the Martin Luther King Library in Washington, the National Geographic Library, the *Boston Globe*, the *Chicago Tribune*, the *St. Louis Post-Dispatch*, and the *Detroit Free Press*. Most newspapers have files on the topic of names and are great troves of name lore. In searching for particular sources of names, I used the archives of the National Aeronautics and Space Administration in Washington and the Baseball Hall of Fame in Cooperstown, New York.

I also used the good offices of the American Name Society to go through back issues of the journal *Names* and the *Bulletin of the American Name Society*. Many individual members of the Society were most helpful in sharing their files and collections of names. Anyone at all interested in names should consider joining the Society, not only for its publications but for the network of name scholars and collectors. One can join for a mere $15.00 which should be sent to Professor Wayne H. Finke, Romance Languages, Box 340, Baruch College, 17 Lexington Ave., New York, New York 10010.

Besides the ANS periodicals, name lovers will find much of interest in *Word Ways: The Journal of Recreational Linguistics* (Spring Valley Rd., Morristown, NJ 07960).

As for the specific books and articles which I consulted, the following were most helpful:

Adamic, Louis. *What's Your Name*. New York: Harper and Bros., 1942.

Adams, J. Donald. *The Magic and Mystery of Words*. New York: Holt, Rinehart and Winston, 1963.

American Craft Museum. *Robot Exhibit*. New York: Author, 1984.

Anderson, Christopher P. *The Name Game*. New York: Simon and Schuster, 1977.

Auden, W. H. *A Certain World*. New York: Viking, 1970.

Bachner, John Paul. "Naming New Streets is No Primrose Path." *Washington Star*, 14 Sept. 1979.

Bailey, L. H. *How Plants Get Their Names*. New York: Dover, 1963.

Bardsley, Charles Wareing. *English Surnames: Their Sources and Significance*. London: Chatto and Windus, 1906.

Bauer, Andrew. *The Hawthorne Dictionary of Pseudonyms*. New York: Hawthorne, 1971.

Beadle, Muriel. "The Game of the Name." *New York Times Magazine*, 21 Oct. 1973.

Beeching, Cyril Leslie. *A Dictionary of Eponyms*. London: Clive Bingley, 1983.

Blumberg, Dorothy Rose. *Whose What?* New York: Holt, Rinehart and Winston, 1969.

Borgmann, Dmitri A. *Beyond Language*. New York: Scribners, 1967.

Bowman, William Dodgson. *The Story of Surnames*. London: George Routledge, 1931.

Boycott, Rosie. *Batty, Bloomers and Boycott*. New York: Peter Bedrick, 1982.

Brandreth, Gyles. *More Joy of Lex*. New York: Morrow, 1982.

———. *Pears Book of Words*. London, Pelham Books, 1979.

Brooke, Maxey. "Everybody Comes from Somewhere." *Word Ways,* Aug. 1983.

Busse, Thomas V. *The Professor's Book of Names.* Elkins Park, Penn.: Green Ball Press, 1984.

Campbell, Hannah. *Why Did They Name It?* New York: Bell, 1964.

Carton, Barbara. "Living it Up at Tuba and Trombone." *Washington Post,* 19 Oct. 1984.

Cheasley, Clifford W. *What's In Your Name.* New York: Edward J. Clode, 1916.

Clarke, Joseph F. *Pseudonyms: The Names Behind the Names.* Nashville: Nelson, 1977.

Collocott, T. C., and Thorne, J. O. *The Macmillan World Gazetteer and Geographical Dictionary.* New York: Macmillan, 1955.

Cushing, William. *Initials and Pseudonyms.* New York: Crowell, 1885.

Davies, C. Stella, and John Levitt. *What's in a Name?* London: Routledge and Kegan Paul, 1970.

Dawson, J. Frank. *Place Names in Colorado.* Denver: Golden Bell Press, 1954.

Dennett, Daniel, and Karel Lambert. *The Philosophical Lexicon.* Privately published and available from Prof. Dennett, Tufts University, Medford, Mass. 02155.

Dixon, B. Homer. *Surnames.* Boston: Wilson and Son, 1855.

Dolan, J. R. *English Ancestral Names.* New York: Potter, 1972.

Dunkling, Leslie Alan. *First Names First.* New York: Universe Books, 1977.

———. *Our Secret Names.* London: Sidgwick and Jackson, 1982.

———. *What's in a Name.* London: Ventura, 1979.

Dunkling, Leslie Alan, and William Gosling. *The Facts on File Dictionary of First Names.* New York: Facts on File, 1983.

Eckler, A. Ross. *Word Recreations.* New York: Dover, 1979.

Espy, Willard R. *An Almanac of Words at Play.* New York: Clarkson Potter, 1975.

———. *Another Almanac of Words at Play.* New York: Clarkson Potter, 1980.

———. *Thou Improper, Thou Uncommon Noun.* New York: Clarkson Potter, 1978.

Fireman, Judy. *The Cat Catalog.* New York: Workman, 1976.

Flaste, Richard, "When That Baby Comes, What's in a Name?" *New York Times,* 4 Feb. 1977.

Fletcher, Barbara. "Rainbow." *Don't Blame the Stork.* Seattle: Rainbow Publications, 1981.

Flexner, Stuart Berg. *I Hear America Talking.* New York: Van Nostrand, 1976.

———. *Listening to America.* New York: Simon and Schuster, 1982.

Friend, John Newton. *Words: Tricks and Traditions.* New York: Scribners, 1957.

Fuller, John G. *Games for Insomniacs.* Garden City, N.Y.: Doubleday, 1966.

Funk, Charles Earle. *Thereby Hangs a Tale.* New York: Harper and Bros., 1950.

Gannett, Henry. *The Origin of Certain Place Names in the United States.* Washington, D.C.: U.S. Geological Survey, 1905.

Gard, Robert E., and L. G. Sorden. *Romance of Wisconsin Place Names.* New York: October House, 1968.

Gephart, Joseph Curtin. "Nicknames of Baseball Clubs." *American Speech*, April 1941.

Gibson, John E. "How Important is Your Name?" *This Week*, 22 Nov. 1953.

Hanson, Rau McDill. *Virginia Place Names*. Verona, Va.: McClure Press, 1969.

Harder, Kelsie B. *Illustrated Dictionary of Place Names*. New York: Van Nostrand, 1976.

Hendrickson, Robert. *Human Words*. Philadelphia: Chilton, 1972.

Hook, J. N. *The Book of Names*. New York: Franklin Watts, 1983.

Jacobs, Noah J. *Naming Day in Eden*. New York: Macmillan, 1969.

Kane, Joseph Nathan. *The American Counties*. Metuchen, N.J.: Scarecrow Press, 1972.

Laffoon, Polk. "Playing the name game: A 'Crispy' by another name would be a 'Crunchy." *Detroit Free Press*, 11 June 1978.

Lake, Antony B. *A Pleasury of Witticisms and Word Play*. New York: Bramhall, 1975.

Lambert, Eloise, and Mario Pei. *The Book of Place Names*. New York: Lothrop, Lee and Shepard, 1961.

———. *Our Names: Where They Came From and What They Mean*. New York: Lothrop, Lee and Shepard, 1961.

Lederer, Richard M., Jr. *The Place Names of Westchester County*. Harrison, N.Y.: Harbor Hill, 1978.

Lewis, Flora. "What's in a Name? Lots." *New York Times Magazine*, 28 Aug. 1955.

Lieb, Frederick G. "How the Big League Clubs Got their Nick Names." *Baseball*, February 1922.

Lindsay, T. S. *Plant Names*. London: Sheldon Press, 1923.

Loughhead, Flora Haines. *Dictionary of Given Names*. Glendale, Cal.: Arthur H. Clark, 1958.

Manguel, Alberto, and Gianni Guadalupi. *The Dictionary of Imaginary Places*. New York: Macmillan, 1980.

Martin, Judith. "Tamara is Tops, Oscar is Out." *Washington Post*, 16 Sept. 1977.

Matthews, C. M. *English Surnames*. New York: Scribners, 1966.

———. *Place Names of the English-Speaking World*. New York: Scribners, 1972.

Mawson, C. O. Sylvester. *International Book of Names*. New York: Crowell, 1934.

McDonough, Susan. *The Cat Doctor's Book of Cat Names*. New York: Dell, 1983.

Megargee, Edwin. *The Dog Dictionary*. Cleveland: World, 1954.

Mencken, H. L. *The American Language*. New York: Knopf, 1919.

———. *Supplement One to the American Language*. New York: Knopf, 1945.

Michaels, Leonard, and Christopher Ricks. *The State of the Language*. Berkeley, Cal.: University of California Press, 1980.

Mitchell, Edwin Valentine. *It's an Old New England Custom*. New York: Vanguard, 1946.

Moore, W. G. *A Dictionary of Geography*. New York: Praeger, 1969.

Morgan, Jane, Christopher O'Neill, and Rom Harre. *Nicknames.* London: Routledge and Kegan Paul, 1979.

Morgan, Ted. *On Becoming American.* Boston: Houghton Mifflin, 1978.

Morison, Samuel L. "Pride in Her Name." Naval Institute *Proceedings,* June 1982.

Morris, William, and Mary Morris. *The Word Game Book.* New York: Harper and Bros., 1959.

Mouat, Lucia. "What's in a name? Kirstin's in, Henry's out." *Christian Science Monitor,* 22 Aug. 1983.

Nakahara, Liz. "You: The Name of the Game." *Washington Post,* 12 Oct. 1981.

National Bureau of Standards. *Color: Universal Language and Dictionary of Names.* Washington, D.C.: GPO, 1976.

Newman, Edwin. *Strictly Speaking.* New York: Warner, 1975.

Noble, Vernon. *Nick Names.* London: Hamish Hamilton, 1976.

Noel, John V., Jr., and Edward L. Beach. *Naval Terms Dictionary.* Annapolis, Md.: Naval Institute Press, 1973.

Partridge, Eric. *Name into Word.* New York: Macmillan, 1950.

Payton, Geoffrey. *Payton's Proper Names.* London: Frederick Warne, 1969.

Pizer, Vernon. *Ink, Ark., and All That: How American Places Got Their Names.* New York: Putnam's, 1976.

Price, Roger, and Leonard Stern. *What Not to Name the Baby.* Los Angeles: Price/Stern/Sloan, 1960.

Radford, Edwin. *To Coin a Phrase.* London: Hutchinson, 1973.

Reps, Paul. *Exploring Our Name.* Montrose, Cal.: Preview Publishers, 1938.

Rice, Charles. "Don't Be Common." *This Week,* 28 Aug. 1966.

———. "Fireman, Name My Street!" *This Week,* 27 Jan. 1963.

———. "What's Your Initial?" *This Week,* 26 Nov. 1967.

Room, Adrian. *Dictionary of Trade Name Origins.* London: Routledge and Kegan Paul, 1982.

Rorback, Abraham. *A Dictionary of International Slurs.* Waukesha, Wis.: Maledicta Press, 1979.

Rule, La Reina, and William K. Hammond. *What's in a Name?* New York: Pyramid Books, 1973.

Severn, Bill. *Place Words.* New York: Ives Washburn, 1969.

Shipley, Joseph T. *Playing with Words.* Englewood Cliffs, N.J.: Prentice-Hall, 1960.

Smith, Benjamin E. *The Century Cyclopedia of Names.* 4 vols. New York: Century, 1895.

Smith, Elsdon C. *The Book of Smith.* New York: Paragon, 1978.

————. *Naming Your Baby.* New York: Greenburgh, 1943.

————. *The New Dictionary of American Family Names.* New York: Harper & Row, 1973.

Smith, H. Allen. *People Named Smith.* Garden City, N.Y.: Doubleday, 1950.

Social Security Administration. *Report of Distribution of Surnames in the Social Security Number File.* Washington, D.C.: GPO, 1974.

Spaull, Hebe. *New Place Names of the World.* London: Ward Locke, 1970.

Steel, William Gladstone. *Steel Points: Place Names.* Vol. 1, No. 4. Eugene, Ore., n.d.

Stewart, George R. *American Given Names.* New York: Oxford University Press, 1979.

————. *Names on the Globe.* New York: Oxford University Press, 1975.

————. *Names on the Land,* New York: Random House, New York, 1945.

Taggert, Jean E. *Pet Names.* New York: Scarecrow Press, 1962.

Tarpley, Fred. *Ethnic Names.* Commerce, Tex.: Names Institute Press, 1978.

Tarpley, Fred, and Ann Moseley. *Of Edsels and Marauders.* Commerce, Tex.: Names Institute Press, 1971.

Teague, Jim. "Christening a Navy Ship: What's in a Name?" *All Hands,* June 1968.

Train, John. *Even More Remarkable Names.* New York: Clarkson Potter, 1979.

————. *Remarkable Names of Real People.* New York: Clarkson Potter, 1977.

Wagner, Rudolph F., and Marney H. Wagner. *Stories About Family Names.* Portland, Maine: Weston Walch, 1961.

Weekley, Ernest. *Jack and Jill: A Study of Our Christian Names.* Ann Arbor, Mich.: Gryphon Books, 1971.

————. *The Romance of Words.* London: John Murray, 1913.

Wells, Evelyn. *Treasury of Names.* New York: Duell, Sloan and Pearce, 1946.

Wells, Helen T., Susan H. Whiteley and Carrie Karegeannes. *Origins of NASA Names.* Washington, D.C.: GPO, 1976.

Wilen, Joan, and Lydia Wilen. *Name Me, I'm Yours!* New York: Fawcett Columbine, 1982.

Wolk, Allen. *Everyday Words From Names of People and Places.* New York: Elsevier/ Nelson, 1980.

————. *The Naming of America.* Nashville: Nelson, 1977.

Worth, Fred L. *Incredible Super Trivia.* New York: Greenwich House, 1984.

————. *More Super Trivia.* New York: Greenwich House, 1981.

————. *Super Trivia Encyclopedia.* New York: Brooke House, 1977.

Worthing, Ruth Shaw. *The History of Fond du Lac County as Told by Its Place Names.* Oshkosh, Wis.: Globe, 1976.

Youmans, Charles L. *What's in a Name?* Lancaster, N.H.: Brisbee Press, 1955.

Index

About the Author

Paul (the name means small, which he is not, and it is the 27th most popular male name in a recent survey) **Dickson** ("son of Richard" and the 822nd most popular last name in the United States) is a writer who lives in Garrett Park (where all the street names come from places in Sir Walter Scott's Waverley novels), which is in Montgomery County (named for Major General Richard Montgomery, the early patriot who never saw the county), Maryland. He was born in Yonkers (from the Dutch word for gentlemen, *jonkeer*), New York, attended Wesleyan (after John Wesley) University and has been a freelance writer since 1967. He and his wife Nancy (grace) have two sons, Alexander (helper of mankind) and Andrew (manly). They have a cat named Moxie (from the character trait and the soft drink).

He will continue to collect names and would love to hear from other collectors (Box 80, Garrett Park, MD 20896).

About the Illustrator

Rick Meyerowitz's work will probably look familiar to many readers, as his drawings often appear in ads, magazines, books, and on TV. Rick became an illustrator after studying fine arts at Boston University, and now he creates illustrations that evoke a smile from all but the most malcontent. Perhaps his most recognizable work comes from his long association with the *National Lampoon*. During this period, Rick created the *Mona Gorilla*, a parody of the *Mona Lisa* that became the signature work of the *Lampoon*, and he produced the poster for the movie *Animal House*.

His books include *Nosemasks* (silly little masks you can wear on your nose), and *Dodosaurs – The Dinosaurs That Didn't Make It*. He has also adapted and illustrated *Rabbit Ears* videos for children: *Paul Bunyan*, narrated by Jonathan Winters; and *Rip Van Winkle*, narrated by Anjelica Huston with music by Jay Ungar and Molly Mason. His newest book for children is *Elvis the Bulldozer*.

Rick lives in New York's Greenwich Village with his wife and children.